Eco-Sonic Media

The publisher gratefully acknowledges the generous support
of the Humanities Endowment Fund of the University of
California Press Foundation.

Eco-Sonic Media

JACOB SMITH

University of California Press

University of California Press, one of the most distinguished university presses in the United States, enriches lives around the world by advancing scholarship in the humanities, social sciences, and natural sciences. Its activities are supported by the UC Press Foundation and by philanthropic contributions from individuals and institutions. For more information, visit www.ucpress.edu.

University of California Press
Oakland, California

© 2015 by The Regents of the University of California

Library of Congress Cataloging-in-Publication Data

Smith, Jacob, 1970- author.
 Eco-sonic media / Jacob Smith. — First edition.
  pages cm
 Includes bibliographical references and index.
 ISBN 978-0-520-28613-9 (cloth : alk. paper) — ISBN 0-520-28613-8 (cloth : alk. paper) — ISBN 978-0-520-28614-6 (pbk. : alk. paper) — ISBN 0-520-28614-6 (pbk. : alk. paper) — ISBN 978-0-520-96149-4 (ebook) — ISBN 0-520-96149-8 (ebook)
 1. Sound recordings—Environmental aspects. 2. Sound—Recording and reproducing—Equipment and supplies—Environmental aspects. 3. Audio equipment industry—Environmental aspects. 4. Sound—Recording and reproducing—Equipment and supplies—History. 5. Sound in mass media—History. I. Title.
 P96.S66S64 2015
 384—dc23

2014043916

24 23 22 21 20 19 18 17 16 15
10 9 8 7 6 5 4 3 2 1

Contents

Acknowledgments   vi

INTRODUCTION   1

1. GREEN DISCS   13
2. BIRDLAND MELODIES   42
3. SUBTERRANEAN SIGNALS   80
4. RADIO'S DARK ECOLOGY   110

THE RUN-OUT GROOVE   142

Index   249

Acknowledgments

Collaborative relationships made this book possible. It has been a joy for me to feel part of an emerging sound studies community as embodied by something like the *Sounding Out* blog. My thanks go to Jennifer Stoever for asking me to contribute to the blog, where a section of chapter 4 appeared under the title, "Devil's Symphony: Orson Welles's 'Hell on Ice' as Eco-Sonic Critique." Neil Verma read a draft of that material and helped me to sharpen the prose and clarify the argument.

Eco-Sonic Media relies on historical research and so has involved collaboration with many people at archives, libraries, and a range of other institutions. I wish to thank Karen Fishman at the Library of Congress; Laura LaPlaca, Robert Wild, Linda Hogan, Phil Scepanski, Sascha Förster, Jochen Klähn, Hans-Gunter Scharf, Ramani Ranganathan and the staff at the Indian Institute of Natural Resins and Gums in Ranchi; Gauri Nori and Chris Higgins at Annapurna Studios in Hyderabad; Robert Shuster at the Billy Graham Center; Laura Kissel at the Byrd Polar Research Center Archive at Ohio State University; and Ron Shore at Windy City Detectors.

The University of California Press continues to make the publication process pleasant and efficient. Bradley Depew was extremely conscientious and helpful as I compiled the manuscript. I am very grateful to Tang Yau Hoong for allowing me to use his remarkable image *Songbird* on the cover of the book. Thanks are due as well to the designers at the press.

Colleagues and friends have provided much inspiration and encouragement, among them Frauke Behrendt, Nadia Bozak, Lisa Parks, Jonathan Sterne, Robert Ray, Dale Lawrence, Greg Waller, Haidee Wasson, Charles Acland, Barbara Klinger, and James Naremore. David Haberman planted the seeds of eco-awareness in my mind and has long been a role model for what an environmentally engaged scholarship might look like. I owe a special thanks to Patrick Feaster for his continued friendship, support, and invaluable advice. At Northwestern, I wish to thank Barbara O'Keefe, Heather Trulock, Michelle Yamada, Shatoria Lunsford, Laura Brueck, Bryan Pardo, Nina Kraus, Tracy Davis, David Tolchinsky, Debra Tolchinsky, Bill Bleich, Jeff Sconce, Hamid Naficy, Ariel Rogers, Miriam Petty, Scott Curtis, Lynn Spigel, Mimi White, and Neil Verma.

As with all of my work, this book would not have been possible without the love and support of my family, especially Freda, Jonah, Henry, and Bing.

The most significant collaborator in the life of this book, however, was Mary Francis. More than simply editing a manuscript, she saved the project from several false starts and dead ends and steered it with great agility toward its present form. I am enormously indebted to her patience, faith, and sonic imagination.

Introduction

In 2001 the conceptual artist Katie Paterson created an art installation titled "As the World Turns," in which a phonograph record was made to rotate "in time with the earth." Paterson's work gave new meaning to the phrase "long-playing record" because her adjusted turntable revolved at the rate of one revolution every twenty-four hours. At that rate it would take four years to play Vivaldi's "Summer Concerto." Paterson's primary goal was not to reproduce music, however, as indicated by the fact that the disc rotated so slowly that its movement was invisible to the eye and produced no sound. In other words, "As the World Turns" aligned sound technology with planetary rhythms, but did so at the price of making the apparatus fall silent. Paterson's installation seems to ask us to choose between enjoying mediated sounds and fostering ecological awareness, with her motionless turntable as a silent emblem of a media culture out of sync with the natural world. Understood in this manner, Paterson's work poses provocative questions: Can an ecological critique be brought to sound media in a way that still allows us to hear them? Can we have a *sound media* that is *ecologically sound?* In this book I seek out affirmative answers to those questions and offer ways in which mediated sounds can be modulated to a greener key. When they are, the result is what I call "eco-sonic media."

I am one of a growing number of media scholars who feel the need to address the ways in which media culture is implicated in the ecological crisis.[1] Film production depends on the expenditure of large amounts of energy and natural resources, resulting in what Nadia Bozak calls the "cinematic footprint."[2] The cathode ray tubes, liquid crystal displays, and plasma screens in televisions, computers, and handheld devices contain neurotoxins like lead and mercury and take part in a culture of obsolescence that sends increasing amounts of "high tech trash" to the landfill.[3] Despite marketing rhetoric that characterizes digital technologies as weightless, virtual, and environmentally clean, we learn more every day about the energy, resource, and labor costs that undergird the Internet and our digital devices. Allison Carruth writes that Google's data center operations require 260 million watts of energy continuously, "the equivalent of the annual energy consumption of two hundred thousand US homes." "In stark contrast to visualizations of the cloud as ethereal, magical, and organic," she writes, a new image is taking shape of the digital cloud as "akin to heavy manufacturing like the automotive sector."[4]

Environmental issues such as these have been peripheral to the study of film and television, but in recent years a growing body of publications have addressed the role of filmmaking in raising environmental consciousness, the history of the wildlife documentary, the ethics of nonhuman animals as media performers, and the ways in which various genres of media entertainment depict the natural landscape.[5] Scholarship in the emerging subfield of eco-media studies has been almost entirely concerned with mediated images, with little attention paid to mediated sounds or the material culture of sound technologies. In a recent collection of essays on "eco-cinema," for example, Sean Cubitt observes that the field has developed a close affinity with photographic and animated images. Cubitt urges scholars to broaden the scope of their analysis to include "all the visual media," but he leaves sonic media off the agenda.[6]

Sound media can do more than simply fill a gap in eco-media literature since they represent an important alternative to screen-based media in terms of technological infrastructure and cultural practice. Let me provide an example. A 2005 report by the National Resources Defense Council (NRDC) estimated that televisions in the United States consumed about 4 percent of the nation's residential electricity use and caused about thirty-one million tons of CO_2 to be emitted from coal-burning power plants. The NRDC claimed that a 25 percent reduction in TV power usage would prevent the emission of about seven million tons of CO_2.[7] The television sets analyzed in the NRDC study typically consumed between 100 and 400 kilowatts per hour (kWh) of electricity per year (although some home theater models consumed more than 650 kWh per year). A 2011 study found that the average television had a unit electricity consumption of 183 kWh.[8] The NRDC's solution was to call for the industry to promote more energy-efficient TVs, but it might have pointed out that a large percentage of a television set's energy expenditure is directed toward illuminating the screen.[9]

Note that an average radio has an average unit electricity consumption of only 15.7 kWh.[10] In other words, shifting an hour or two of the average

American's five hours of television per day to radio listening would achieve the same results as the sale of more energy-efficient TVs. The commercial radios in these studies use less power than laptops and televisions but, as we shall see, other forms of sound media production and playback require *no electricity at all*. Media critics Richard Maxwell and Toby Miller ask, "how much communication and entertainment media is enough to attain a system that serves everyone on the planet fairly without contributing to 'ecological suicide?'"[11] One answer to that question involves a shift in the diet of media consumption toward comparatively eco-friendly forms of sound media.

The fact that sound media can be an energy-efficient alternative to screens is the beginning, not the end of the discussion. Media technologies are not the same as toasters; they are material components in a complex web of social communication and sites of struggle over social power and cultural meaning. Moreover, media consumption makes up a small percentage of the national carbon footprint when compared to travel and housing, and the added value that media content provide in terms of education, activism, and global awareness are significant. We need to strive for energy-efficient media infrastructures and practices, but an assessment of comparative energy costs can be only one criteria in a broader cultural and historical analysis, one that integrates the insights of eco-criticism, environmental history and cultural studies. What we need is what Maxwell and Miller call an "up, down, and sideways" study of the conditions under which the media are "made, circulated, received, interpreted, criticized, and disposed of."[12] In *Eco-Sonic Media* I bring an "up, down, and sideways" methodology to twentieth-century sound media to examine biological ecosystems and industrial infrastructures that enable sound reproduction and to assess the eco-cosmopolitan potential of various modes of sound-media communication.[13]

Sound technologies broaden the scope of the green-media agenda, and, conversely, eco-media scholarship is enriched by a strong ecological orientation within sound studies.[14] R. Murray Schafer's influential work on "acoustic ecology" encompassed both natural and human soundscapes and drew inspiration from the environmental movement of the 1970s. Schafer's study of environmental sound has inspired work on historical soundscapes, the history of noise control, and acoustic design in architecture, and his legacy is perhaps the most significant zone of contact between sound studies and ecological critique. Schafer is not alone, however, and we should also note Hildegard Westerkamp's pioneering work on sound walks, Pauline Oliveros's notion of the "sonosphere," Douglas Kahn's investigation of "natural radio" (the sounds produced by the earth's ionosphere and magnetosphere), and

Jonathan Sterne's pioneering research on both sound technology and media infrastructure.[15] I add my voice to this chorus in the hope that *Eco-Sonic Media* will amplify the ecological component of sound studies and turn up the audio in discussions of greening the media.

Some of the most influential work in sound studies has been grounded in a historical analysis of sound technologies, and I share that commitment to historical research. My argument is built on a scaffolding of case studies taken from the nineteenth and early twentieth centuries. That emphasis on the past might surprise readers who are primarily interested in addressing the dire environmental situation of the present. Historians in the field of environmental history have argued persuasively that history has an important role to play in environmental awareness.[16] Knowledge of the past serves as a counterweight to the common tendency to look for solutions to complex social problems in new technologies. The threat of ecological collapse compels us to question powerful cultural myths about technological progress and reconsider alternatives that can be found in the past.[17] In this context, the technological networks of previous eras gain new relevance as models for more eco-friendly systems of media communication.

It is time to reopen the books on the failed experiments, outmoded techniques, and "also-rans" of media history, not out of a fascination with the quirky marginalia of the past, but because the media culture that became dominant—the "winners" of technological history—are complicit in a material culture that has caused so much environmental damage. "We've gotten it wrong so far," Timothy Morton writes, "that's the truth of climate disruption and mass extinction."[18] Environmental historian Donald Worster suggests that we approach the record of the past with respect, in the knowledge that "most of the innovations we have recently made are not likely to survive, that what is old is by that very fact worthy of study and mimicry, and that what is *very* old is likely to be wise."[19] Many environmentalists look for inspiration to the sustainable lifestyles of native or first peoples. In a similar way, eco-media scholars might look to the practices of the "first users" of early modern media technologies.[20]

Reengaging with old media in this spirit can be understood as a form of "media ecology," which Regis Debray describes as the reengagement with extinct or residual media practices. Debray writes, "Consider a letterpress printer's workshop using lead type in its distinctiveness as the locality of a culture, or a film editing room with its technicians. Are not such places as precious, and precarious, as a patch of green in a suburban district of concrete?"[21] Debray's media ecology can be put into practice through a media archaeology that studies the media assemblages of the past. "Media archaeology" is the term that has been used to designate a number of historical approaches to media technology that investigate "new media cultures through insights from past new media, often with an emphasis on the forgotten, the quirky, the non-obvious apparatuses, practices and inventions." Media archaeology offers a method for discovering alternative histories and questions dominant narratives of technological progress, but even its proponents acknowledge that it can become a "curiosity-cabinet" for "quirky devices and pre-cinematic toys."[22] One way to address that problem is to implement a "green-media archaeology," in which forgotten or quirky media technologies from the past are excavated, not for their own sake, but as part of a search for more sustainable media cultures of the future.

Green-media archaeology offers the potential to complicate conventional narratives about the media. For example, scholars in the field of film studies tend to situate cinema in the context of turn-of-the-century modernity, but they rarely direct their attention to the ecological consequences of that historical era: to species extinction, for example; or the rapid acceleration of non-renewable fossil fuel use; or the development and mass marketing of toxic chemicals and synthetic plastics. Media history that is guided by an eco-critical agenda is drawn to those components of modernity, as well as to periods of economic and political crisis when consumers and producers of media are compelled to "make do with less." Where previously those moments might have appeared as exceptions to the norm of limitless economic growth and abundant consumer culture, I now see them as important lessons for a post-carbon era in which the "new normal" includes extreme weather events, shrinking natural resources, and long-term financial instability.

There are strong arguments then, for taking a historical approach to greening the media: media history gets a new set of priorities and a strong sociopolitical valence, and eco-media criticism gains access to the "great museum of the past" as a resource in the practical search for alternatives at a time when "the end of the world has already happened."[23] In sum, this book uses a green-media archaeology to make sound studies vibrate at an ecological frequency and to open the ears of eco-criticism. I do not want to suggest that sound is the only path to an ecologically responsible media, nor that sound media are always a greener option than screens. It can never be that simple. Sustainability is complex and systematic, and decisions about ecological practices always have to account for "numerous secondary factors and unintended consequences."[24] Instead of making sweeping claims about the ecological status of all sound-based media, this book is guided by a few central questions: How can we evaluate sound-media technologies and practices from an eco-critical perspective? What might a sustainable sound-media culture look and sound like? How can sound media be mobilized to increase environmental awareness? In short, how can sound media become eco-sonic media? The four chapters that follow advance four different answers to that question: sound media become eco-sonic media when they manifest a low-impact, sustainable infrastructure; when they foster an appreciation of, or facilitate communication with, nonhuman nature; when they provide both a sense of place and a sense of planet; and when they represent environmental crisis.

ECO-SONIC MEDIA MANIFEST A LOW-IMPACT, SUSTAINABLE INFRASTRUCTURE

Katie Paterson, the artist responsible for the slow-motion turntable described earlier, created a 2008 work titled "Langjökull, Snæfellsjökull, Solheimajökull." Paterson made sound recordings of three melting glaciers and pressed those sounds onto phonograph records made from frozen water taken from the same glaciers. The ice records were then played on a turntable, reproducing the audible traces of climate change until they melted.[25] In an era when recorded music is marketed as immaterial bits of information existing in a digital "cloud," Paterson's work is a vivid reminder that mediated sounds always depend on finite material resources. Her transparent ice discs also make a material connection between the consumption of media texts in the West and natural events taking place on the other side of the planet, but the same might be said of the opaque black discs that played in American homes a century earlier. The main ingredient in pre-1950s disc records was shellac, a natural bioplastic produced by insects in the forests of India, Burma, and Thailand.[26] The fact that the modern record industry relied on the labor of the lac insect is one of the reasons why, in chapter 1, "Green Discs," I argue that early twentieth-century phonography can be understood as an eco-sonic medium.

Maxwell and Miller write that the search for ecological media practices requires us to direct our attention to "low-wattage culture and nonhuman nature."[27] Between the 1890s and the mid-1920s, many facets of the phonograph industry were low- or even *no-wattage*. That period of phonography is often referred to as the "acoustic" era, as distinct from an "electric" era after the introduction of radio microphones, loudspeakers, and amplifiers. Historians also distinguish between an era when discs were made out of shellac and spun at the rate of 78 rotations per minute (rpm) and the era when long-playing records (LPs) were made of the synthetic plastic polyvinyl chloride (popularly known as PVC or vinyl) and rotated at either

33⅓ or 45 rpm. The period when phonography was acoustic and when discs were made with shellac is what I call the "Green Disc" era, green to the extent that its media infrastructure was "unplugged," incorporated human and nonhuman industry, and facilitated a culture of resource conservation.

Chapter 1 pivots on the record industry's shift from using a biodegradable, nontoxic bioplastic (shellac) to one of the most toxic, difficult to recycle, and environmentally harmful synthetic plastics (vinyl). Plasticity is a recurring theme of the chapter, encountered in the lac insect's translation of sap into resin, the industrial transformation of raw materials, the transduction of sound waves into the grooves on a phonograph disc, and even the plasmatic quality of sound itself. The technological assemblage of the phonograph might be conceptualized in terms of energy cycles and the malleability of form, and to that end I mobilize theories of technological networks, industrial ecology, and sound reproduction to reassess the era of early phonography. The Green Disc era should be appreciated not as a form of antiquated material culture or an archive of outdated performance styles, I argue, but as an alternative model for new, eco-ethical modes of producing and consuming sound.

ECO-SONIC MEDIA FOSTER AN APPRECIATION OF, OR FACILITATE COMMUNICATION WITH, NONHUMAN NATURE

Vinyl is notoriously difficult to recycle, with the result being that vinyl records are "hyperobjects": a term Timothy Morton uses to describe substances such as Styrofoam and plutonium that exist on an "almost unthinkable" timescale.[28] When discs were eclipsed by subsequent audio formats, many of the record industry's nonbiodegradable hyperobjects were destined to join the mountains of discarded plastic consumer goods in the world's landfills. A small number of vinyl records have been redeemed from this fate by the New Zealand artist Aimee Gruar, who uses old LPs as the raw material for a remarkable series of sculptures. Gruar takes discarded vinyl LPs and cuts them into silhouettes of the Huia bird, which was driven to extinction by reckless human hunting and habitat destruction during the same decades that saw the birth of the record industry. Gruar's sculptures link birds and LPs through the theme of extinction and force us to acknowledge the troubling irony that, although the Huia and the LP are both "extinct," the vinyl artifact will last forever, while the bird is irrevocably lost.[29]

Like Gruar, I am interested in harmonizing birds and audio technologies, and in chapter 2, "Birdland Melodies," I explore the history of birds *in*

FIGURE 1. A sculpture by the New Zealand artist Aimee Gruar, who cuts vinyl LPs into silhouettes of the extinct Huia bird. Author's collection. Photograph by Henry Smith.

sound media and the history of birds *as* sound media. Trained cage birds were biotechnologies designed to provide sonic entertainment in the home during the decades before and during the invention and proliferation of domestic media technologies, and birdsong provided content for those industries. The history of nineteenth- and early twentieth-century "bird media" reveals the role of nonhuman animals in the culture of sound recording, as well as sound media's potential as a site of cross-species communication.

The last living Huia bird was seen in 1907, seven years before the last American passenger pigeon died in the Cincinnati Zoo.[30] During the same decades that native birds like the passenger pigeon and Carolina parakeet were disappearing from North American fields, marshes, and meadows, millions of foreign songbirds were imported into American homes as pets, most prominent among them, the canary bird. Canaries were cherished domestic pets during the nineteenth and early twentieth century, but the canary cage was more than a fashionable knickknack for middle-class American parlors. Canaries were prized for their exceptional vocal ability and were trained to produce sounds deemed beautiful to humans. They were, in other words, the living components of a technological network of prephonographic sound recording. Bird media biotechnologies developed a symbiotic relationship with the twentieth-century sound-media industries, with birds serving as performers on radio programs like *Hartz Radio Canaries* and the *American Radio Warblers*, as well as on phonograph records meant to teach canaries to sing, which were addressed to both human and avian listeners.

Chapter 2 explores a contact zone that existed between domestic pets and domestic media and adds a sonic component to Donna Haraway's investigation of "cross-species sociality."[31] Sound provided the primary means for the cross-species sociality between birds and humans, with human trainers whistling to their songbirds to teach them melodies, and turn-of-the-century stage performers building careers out of their ability to imitate birdcalls. Whistlers and bird mimics were popular performers in the early phonograph industry, and recording artists such as Joseph Belmont, Alice Shaw, Margaret McKee, Edward Avis, Charles Gorst, and Charles Kellogg developed their whistling and animal mimicry through the careful observation of the natural world. The whistle is a zoosemiotic mode of communication shared by humans and birds, and it was a prominent part of turn-of-the-century sound culture.[32] Chapter 2 investigates how sound media could become eco-sonic through participating in a multispecies knot among humans, birds, and media technologies and in the process providing a platform for a polyphonic chorus of human and nonhuman communication. That chorus has become vitally important to hear and amplify as we live through the largest mass extinction of nonhuman species since the disappearance of the dinosaurs.[33]

ECO-SONIC MEDIA PROVIDE BOTH A SENSE OF PLACE AND A SENSE OF PLANET

German sound artist Christina Kubisch is known for her "Electrical Walks," during which participants wear special headphones that convert the electromagnetic signals that permeate the urban environment into sound. When listeners equipped with one of Kubisch's headphones move through the spaces of a city, they discover an invisible electromagnetic infrastructure emanating from florescent lights, automatic banking machines, security systems, surveillance cameras, and cash registers. Kubisch's "Electrical Walks" provide a sonic map of an invisible urban soundscape at the same time that they allow for a visual and tactile engagement with a particular place. In other words, they provide a multisensory media experience in which participants are connected to a local place while being made aware of how it is shot through with flows of information and energy that extend far beyond it, including, in some instances, to the sounds of natural events such as distant lightning strikes.[34] We might say that Kubisch's work mobilizes sound media's potential for synthesizing a sense of place and planet.[35] Note that portability is key to the blending of spatial scales found here, and the fact that sound media are unencumbered by an electronic display makes them eminently portable.[36] In chapter 3, "Subterranean Signals," I examine a family of devices that have provided a sense of place and planet since long before the invention of fluorescent lights or cash machines: divining rods and their modern electronic descendants, Geiger counters and metal detectors.

Divination devices such as these are not usually included in scholarly discussions of portable sound media, which tend to focus on the Sony Walkman and the Apple iPod.[37] Such devices broaden the definition of what counts as portable sound media and direct our attention to a set of practices that have the eco-cosmopolitan potential to engage users with the lived environment as well as the unseen depths of the earth. Twentieth-century metal detectors indicate unseen materials by producing sonic signals in the user's earphones, and they emerged from the same technological lineage as radio and the telephone. In other words, they are portable sound-media devices, and they became the centerpiece of a vibrant hobbyist culture that emerged during the postwar era but has experienced a significant reemergence in recent years.

Practices of popular divination are eco-sonic when they align the user's personal space with the social spaces of collective memory and a planetary space experienced through sonic signals thought to emanate from the subterranean world. Metal detecting hobbyists developed vernacular practices that calibrated place and planet, and, at the same time, they were amateur archaeologists who recovered discarded artifacts and recharged them with social meaning. Scavenging has become the subject of considerable interest for environmental activists because it recycles scarce materials, conserves natural resources, and extends the life of landfills. Metal detecting can be appreciated along similar lines, and I argue that this technological hobby be reconceptualized as an alternative to unsustainable practices of reckless overconsumption and planned obsolescence.[38]

ECO-SONIC MEDIA REPRESENT ENVIRONMENTAL CRISIS

In 2005 the digital media artist Andrea Polli, working in collaboration with sound artist Joe Gilmore, created *N.*, an installation that depicts conditions at the North Pole. The piece combines time-lapse images from an immobile camera at the pole with signals from a radio receiver at NASA's Marshall Space Flight Center and eerie sonifications of data relating to the polar climate. Despite its rather abstract and statistical content, Polli and Gilmore's work could produce surprisingly strong emotional responses in audiences. A reviewer in *Art Monthly* wrote that *N.* was "as melancholy as a whale song" and wondered at the fact that a work primarily constructed from empirical scientific data managed to produce "such a palpable and emotive sense of loss."[39] Another critic noted that the title *N.* had an onomatopoeic resemblance to the word "end." In fact, the work's emotional charge is inseparable from the apocalyptic resonance that the polar regions have acquired in an era of anthropogenic global warming, and Polli and Gilmore intended the project to address the alarming acceleration of climate change by tracking conditions at the North Pole and asking, "how much warming is too much?"[40]

Polli and Gilmore's radio transmissions from the frozen north are an appropriate preview of chapter 4, "Radio's Dark Ecology," in which I analyze radio plays that represent both spatial and temporal "ends of the earth." Radio should be high on the green-media agenda because it provides media communication to large numbers of people at relatively low costs to the planet's resources. The central concern of chapter 4 is the eco-sonic poetics of radio theater, and my goal is to identify formal techniques and narrative themes that can serve as expressive resources for ecological critique. Inspired by eco-theorist Timothy Morton's notion of "dark ecology" and M.M. Bakhtin's work on literary chronotopes, I describe a dark ecological radio aesthetic that can be heard in radio plays that take place at the polar regions and oceanic islands and that feature themes of environmental crisis, the collapse of human society, planetary destruction, and species extinction.[41]

The chapter begins with a comparison of two productions of Orson Welles's *Mercury Theater of the Air*: the legendary "War of the Worlds" broadcast and a show that aired three weeks earlier and depicted a failed attempt by an American expedition to reach the North Pole, titled "Hell on Ice." Moving from the far north to the far south, we next attend to radio's central role in Adm. Richard E. Byrd's Antarctic expeditions of the late 1920s and early 1930s. From there we move to a nightmarish reimagining of the Byrd expedition in a radio adaptation of H. P. Lovecraft's novel *At the Mountains of Madness* (1936). The chapter concludes with two radio series by the British writer Douglas Adams that depict the end of life on Earth: *The Hitchhikers' Guide to the Galaxy* (1978) and *Last Chance to See* (1989), the latter a documentary series in which Adams and zoologist Mark Carwardine of the World Wildlife Fund travel the globe in search of species on the brink of extinction. The radio texts in this chapter are linked by themes of crisis, collapse, and catastrophe, and when they are held under the black light of Morton's dark ecology and placed in dialogue with classic works of American environmental literature, they emit the low hum of an eco-sonic poetics.

The four chapters of *Eco-Sonic Media* bring an environmental critique to the domain of sound media to forge interdisciplinary connections, open new avenues of historical research, and pose fresh theoretical questions. To use a sonic metaphor, the four chapters take historical case studies as a rhythm track over which are layered the overlapping melodies of environmental history, eco-criticism, and sound studies. The result is a chorus of interdisciplinary harmonies and unexpected theoretical overtones, but there are more practical results as well. In the concluding chapter, I describe my experience putting some of the ideas from the book into practice, in the form of phenomenological and collaborative experiments in eco-sonic media.

The concluding chapter is meant to begin a discussion, not end one, and to enact a mode of environmental reform that offers hope for a better future instead of the petrifying fear of a "looming apocalypse."[42] At the 1992 Earth Summit in Rio de Janeiro, President George H. W. Bush famously declared that the "American way of life is not up for negotiation."[43] The Western consumer lifestyle is neither ecologically sustainable nor socially ethical and therefore must be up for negotiation.[44] Our contemporary media culture is intricately bound up with that way of life and so must be "up for negotiation" as well. You might think of this book as an attempt to start the negotiation about sound media. We need not approach that project in the spirit of an elitist rejection of popular culture or a chimerical search for a pretechnological utopia that never existed or a retreat from the global dimensions of the crisis into enclaves of privilege that are devoid of social and cultural difference. *Eco-Sonic Media* aims to make sound media negotiable in a way that hears a future in the sustainable media practices of the past, that listens to more of the world with less environmentally harmful technology, and that orchestrates an ecologically sound media that is also a feast for the ears.

1. Green Discs

"It doesn't sound very much like an insect, does it," asked the author of a 1928 article in *Nature*, "this great, soaring tone of [opera singer Enrico] Caruso's matchless tenor?" Aware that many readers were probably scratching their heads at this odd question, the author quickly revealed his motivation for asking it. Caruso's phonograph records were, in fact, the work of an "unassuming, short-lived, tiny, reddish-colored" insect and, not too long before, had been "gum-like lumps on the twigs of a far-off forest." The *Nature* author marveled at the strange agencies of modern invention and industry that had allowed this "humble child of Nature, hidden away on the other side of the world," to catch and hold the sounds that human listeners found delightful.[1] That humble child of Nature was the Indian lac insect, and the "gum-like lumps" were composed of a material secreted by the lac insect called shellac, a nontoxic bioplastic that was the key ingredient in most of the phonograph discs manufactured before the mid-1940s.

The phonograph industry's reliance on the lac insect may appear at first to be a trivial subject best passed over on the way to more serious topics such as the human scientists and inventors who developed sound-recording technologies, the record industry's corporate organization and marketing strategies, or the aesthetics of recorded sound. If our goal is an eco-centric criticism that engages with the materiality of the media, however, then the relationship between Caruso's matchless tenor and the labor of an unassuming reddish insect becomes a means to explore the strange agencies of the nonhuman world in modern media.[2] The lac insect played an essential role in the technological assemblage of recorded sound, and over the course of this chapter, the "up, down, and sideways" mode of eco-critical analysis will reveal the eco-sonic dimension of the early phonograph industry's infrastructure.

My study of the material infrastructure of phonography heeds Jonathan Sterne's recent call for media scholars to shift their attention to "the stuff beneath, beyond, and behind the boxes our media come in."[3] I am interested in the ways in which the early record industry circulated both material and sonic goods through infrastructural systems and the ways in which those human-made systems depended on natural systems to provide raw materials like shellac.[4] When an ecological dimension is added to the study of media infrastructure, the result is what Robert B. Gordon calls "industrial ecology," the study of the ways in which a modern industry consumes natural resources, releases wastes, and attends to the afterlife of its products. The guiding principle of industrial ecology is sustainability, which Gordon defines as "the concept that each generation should leave to the next undiminished opportunities for fulfillment of material needs."[5] I am guided by a similar goal and utilize green-media archaeology to explore the history of media technology of the past as a resource for alternative designs of the future.[6]

With the goal of sustainability guiding my research, I want to tell a new story about the American record industry between the 1890s and the 1940s, a story in which lac insects and Indian workers are just as important as Western inventors, industrialists, and recording stars and in which ecological models are just as relevant as technological ones. Historians have tended to subdivide the first half century of the phonograph business in two ways. First, a historical demarcation is made based on the various disc formats that were on the market: consumers bought shellac discs that spun at 78 rotations per minute (rpm), and then they bought long-playing vinyl records that spun at either 33⅓ or 45 rpm. A second historical division is based on the type of studio technology used in the recording and playback of sound: there was an "acoustic" era of spring-wound motors and recording horns, and then there was an "electric" era of electric motors and electric amplification through the use of microphones and loudspeakers. Given these common historical divisions, we might visualize two fields, the first representing the period of the 78 rpm shellac disc and the second the period of acoustic recording and playback. Aligned as a Venn diagram, the overlapping area in the center is the domain that I call the era of "Green Discs." The discs of this era were green because they were produced through the labor of both human and nonhuman actors, required little electricity and so left a minimal carbon footprint, and were made from a reusable, nontoxic, biodegradable bioplastic taken from a potentially sustainable source.

My understanding of the phonograph industry as a technological network has been shaped by Bruno Latour's notion of an actor network. One of

Latour's key insights is that agency in a network extends beyond human actors to include nonhuman, nonindividual entities, which he calls "actants."[7] Latour is one of several influential scholars who have conceived of technology as an assemblage of articulations (or "dynamic interminglings") among such actants.[8] Jennifer Daryl Slack and J. Macgregor Wise write that a technological assemblage draws together a "territory" that includes "the bodies of machines and structures" as well as a range of "other kinds of bodies: human bodies, governmental bodies, economic bodies, geographical bodies, bodies of knowledge and so on."[9] To understand the territory drawn together by the Green Disc network, we must take vegetable and insect bodies into account as well. The fact that Latour's actor-network theory has sometimes been abbreviated as "ANT" serves as a subtle prompt to consider the bugs in the sound system.[10] Media theorist Jussi Parikka has embarked on a related project, fusing entomology and cultural theory in the pursuit of a "joint history of media and nature" that encompasses the ways in which nonhuman forces express themselves as part of the "media assemblage of modernity."[11] My examination of the natural history of lac insects and the plants cultivated by record enthusiasts for their needles aims for a similar joint history of media and nature.

Nonhuman actors play an important role in my analysis of the phonographic assemblage, but I do not want to undervalue the human actors in the Green Disc network. Latour writes that the various local sites of a network should not be understood as a hierarchy, but, instead, all the various links and connections in the system should be given equal weight: the landscape of the network should be kept "flat."[12] To flatten the topography of the phonographic network, I give equal time to performers in Western acoustic-era phonograph studios and the workers in India's shellac industry. Both made the network possible, and both embodied traditional knowledge that has new significance in the era of the eco-crisis.

In his discussion of eco-centric education, Patrick Curry describes the importance of learning from "surviving local indigenous traditions" because they embody models of "non-modern sustainability." Curry uses the phrase "traditional ecological knowledge," or TEK, to refer to a "fluid but tightly-knit mixture of local or bioregional scientifically ecological wisdom, spiritual values," and "socio-political ethics." TEK developed out of hundreds, and even thousands, of years of "direct contact with the natural world," he argues, and so where such knowledge survives, "it is extremely important to protect and encourage it."[13] There is clearly a danger in romanticizing cultural traditions deemed "non-modern." Anna Lowenhaupt Tsing warns that categories like "indigenous people and wild nature" exist only in opposition to modernist programs, and so "any generalizations we make about them are likely to be wrong." Nonetheless, she concludes that we cannot give up such "fantastical categories," in part because the "alternative fantasy" of a "falsely uniform modernism" is much worse. Moreover, the "regularizing modern imagination has had *such* a destructive effect on species diversity that almost any other human lifeway is likely to be better at maintaining it."[14]

When Curry writes about traditional knowledge, he is thinking primarily of land use, but the concept can be adapted to media culture. Early media practices were hybrids of modern and traditional knowledge, making them useful sources of alternative models as we contemplate a "postcarbon world" marked by diminishing fossil fuels, economic insecurity, and climate disruption. Indian lac workers, performers in early recording studios, and home consumers who operated spring-driven phonographs all embodied what we might call "traditional technological knowledge," or TTK, and eco-minded media scholars should strive to understand these practices as they existed in the past and encourage them where they still exist in the present.

Nadia Bozak is one such eco-minded media scholar, and I have drawn inspiration from her analysis of early cinema's "pre-industrial use of sunlight." Bozak refers to early film producers as exemplars of a "proto-solar cinema" because their glass-roofed studios did not rely on electrical lighting. Films made in this manner are, for Bozak, "textbooks for an 'unplugged' cinema, filmmaking off the grid."[15] Early phonography was similarly "off the grid," with recording studios powered by weight and pulley systems, home record players driven by hand-wound springs, and recorded vocal performances reliant on the "wind power" of the human breath. All that said, I do not want to exaggerate the early phonograph industry's eco-credentials. Jonathan Sterne reminds us that "if you can call something a medium, then it has a physical infrastructure," and any mass media infrastructure will leave behind an ecological footprint.[16] Readers will be quick to notice that I am not discussing *every* articulation in the Green Disc assemblage: not the coal-burning ships that carried shellac from India to the United States, for example, or the electricity used in pressing discs or the gas-burning vehicles used to transport shellac discs from manufacturers to retail outlets. Nonetheless, I believe that I cover enough of the Green Disc network's territory to demonstrate that it is worth remembering and might even serve as a blueprint for an alternative model for recorded sound in an era of MP3 files, iPods, and digital clouds.

By exploring the materiality of early phonography, I hope to counter a rhetoric of virtuality and dematerialization that has long been encouraged by the technology industries and that often functions to conceal the ecological costs of the media.[17] My ultimate goal in mapping the Green Disc network, then, is not to chart a nostalgic return to the past but to sketch the possible future of a more convivial phonography—convivial in Ivan Illich's sense of recognizing "natural scales and limits." Gordon writes that industrial ecology must begin with a consideration of natural resources, and so our first stop in mapping the Green Disc network takes us, not to the grooves of the record, but to the groves of the Indian trees that served as hosts to that "humble child of Nature," the lac insect.[18]

A HUNDRED THOUSAND LAC INSECTS CAN'T BE WRONG

Laccifer lacca is a scale insect of the Coccidae family that lives in the forests of India, Thailand, and Burma. The life history of the lac insect begins when two hundred to five hundred larvae emerge from their mother and swarm over the branches of a host tree, usually a kusum, palas, ber, or peepal tree.[19] The larvae typically appear in the early morning hours of a sunny day, and, according to a 1921 report, the "great swarm of tiny slow-moving light crimson or mauve specks" on the trees make for a "remarkable sight."[20] The mass emergence of the larvae is the source of the insect's name: the term lac derives from the Sanskrit numeral *lakh,* which means one hundred thousand and refers to the large numbers of swarming larvae. The lac's name is thus a vivid example of a prevalent tendency to see insects as an undifferentiated swarm that is radically nonhuman.[21]

After several days of wandering about, the young insects select a suitable location on one of the tender shoots of the tree and settle close together. Each insect pierces the bark of the tree with a long proboscis and proceeds to suck the plant's sap. The sap provides nutrition to the growing insect, but some of it is exuded from glands on the lac's body as a golden secretion that forms a coating around the creature and protects it from predators and weather. The insects spend most of their lives under this "amber shield," and because they are crowded closely together, the hardened resin forms a continuous layer that covers the branch.[22] According to one observer, the host tree appears to be coated with "a multitude of little flat gummy domes," each one a "living tomb for a member of the lac tribe."[23]

The insects stay alive by maintaining three openings in their "gummy domes": two for breathing and one for the removal of excrement. These pores are kept open by waxy white filaments secreted by the insects, which give the encrustations on the branch a "snowy or frosted" appearance. After eight to fourteen weeks, the lac attain maturity, and the males, who constitute only

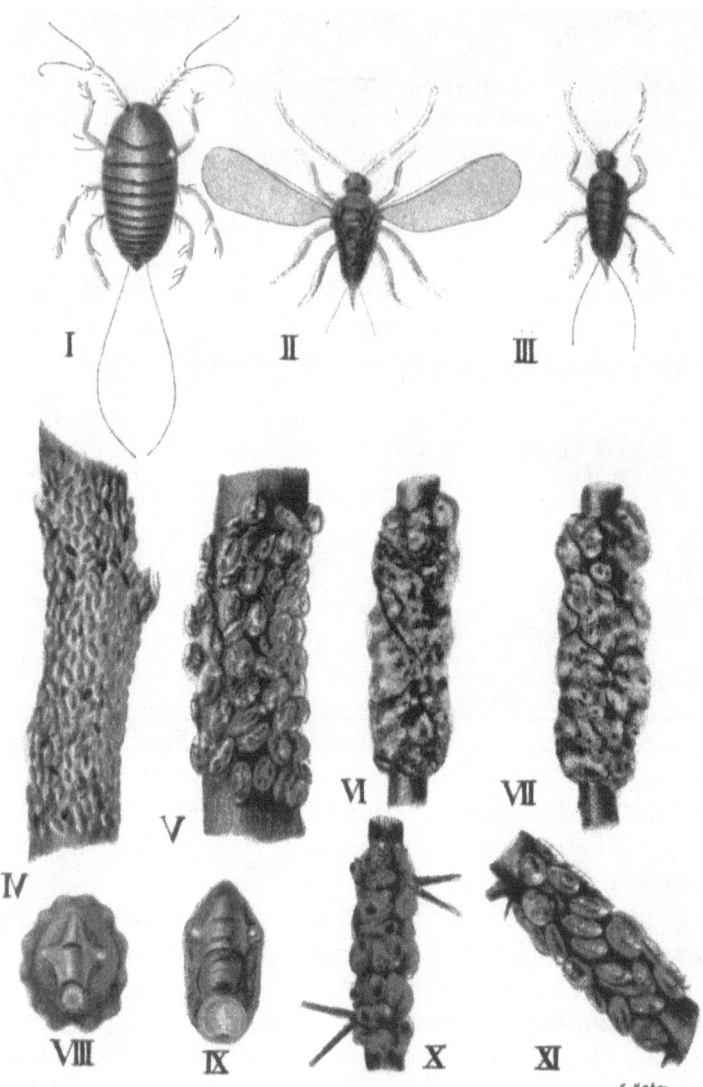

FIGURE 2. *Laccifer lacca,* a scale insect that lives in the forests of India, Thailand, and Burma. Frontispiece from Ernest J. Parry, *Shellac: Its Production, Manufacture, Chemistry, Analysis, Commerce and Uses* (London: Pitman and Sons, 1935).

20 to 40 percent of the population, back out of a trapdoor in their cubicle and proceed to fertilize the females through the pores in their resinous chambers. The males die soon thereafter, but the females continue to grow, secreting large quantities of resin until their eggs hatch, at which time they cast off their eyes and legs and die. The process begins again as the larvae swarm out to find a new spot on the host tree. Lac insects typically go through two generations in this fashion every year.[24]

The resinous encrustations left behind by the lac life cycle become the raw material for the shellac industry, making lac insects "actants" in a biotechnological network. Bruno Latour uses the term "translation" to refer to the process by which an actant alters its environment to bring it into alignment with a network.[25] Lac insects translate tree sap to resin and do so in a manner that is still not completely understood. A 1937 article in the popular press declared that the sap was transformed "by some mysterious chemical action within the body of the strange lac insects."[26] The lac's act of chemical translation was sometimes explained through an analogy to modern industry. A 1921 report explained that the lac insect "manufactures" the resin in its body from the "raw materials" it gets from the tree.[27] The author of a *Popular Mechanics* article called the lac "an insect in industry, a bug whose product has become a big business." "Mr. and Mrs. Lacca," the author continued, "retain the world monopoly on the shellac business."[28] Comments such as these are symptomatic of a long-standing tendency to anthropomorphize insect activity: we tend to see "busy bees" and "industrious ants." That tendency was strong during the nineteenth century, when insects were often described as builders, architects, and industrialists: social roles idealized by the Victorians.[29]

Where the Western observers compared the lac's act of translation to industrial manufacturing, I want to describe it using the language of ecology, in which energy is defined as "the ability to do work" or "the capacity to move or change matter." The prime source of energy on the earth is the sun. Plants like the Indian kusum or palas tree are "producers" that draw energy directly from the sun and nutrients from the soil and then convert those resources into sap. Animals such as the lac insect are "consumers" that digest compounds produced through plant-based photosynthesis and generate waste (like the lac's resin).[30] The lac insect's "manufacture" of resin is thus a stage in an energy cycle that is only two steps removed from the solar source. Latour writes that a network is "not a thing, but the recorded movement of a thing" and suggests that scholars attend to "*what moves through* a network and how this movement is recorded."[31] The network drawn into being by the labor of the lac insect records the movement of solar energy through various states of matter and, given a stable forest ecology, remains sustainable. The maintenance of that ecology was one of the principal duties of the human actants drawn into the shellac network.[32]

TRADITIONAL TECHNOLOGICAL KNOWLEDGE

The Indian shellac industry was concentrated in the northern states of Bihar and Jharkhand. During the early nineteenth century, the lac insect's resin was most valuable to humans as a source of red dye. European demand for dyes like cochineal had driven the early exploitation of lac, which was controlled by the British East India Company. The colonial dynamics of the early industry are difficult to miss. The first Western lac factory in Calcutta was established in 1855 by Martin Kenneth Angelo and Elliott Angelo, two grandsons of a soldier who served as bodyguard for the first governor-general of India. The Angelo brothers supplied red dye for the scarlet dress uniform of the British troops.[33] The market in lac dye went into rapid decline in the 1880s as the result of competition from synthetic alternatives, and it had practically disappeared by 1900.[34] At around the same time, the demand for the lac insect's resin began to rise.

The Angelo brothers held a monopoly on machine-made shellac, but the majority of manufacturing took the form of traditional, small-scale operations that had existed for centuries. In the early twentieth century, traditional shellac manufacturing provided income for somewhere between one and four million poor *adivasi*, or indigenous people, in northern India.[35] The industry was based on the ownership of lac-bearing trees, which were rented to cultivators, called *raiyats*.[36] An important function of the shellac laborers was to maintain the health of the trees: the successful cultivator of lac, a 1935 text explained, pruned and fertilized the trees to ensure the healthy flow of rising sap and the growth of tender young twigs. In addition to forest husbandry, shellac workers were breeders of "tiny livestock" and carefully observed the female lac insects for indications that they were due to give birth. Lac-encrusted branches (or "brood lac") were then transported to the branches of other trees. In this manner, the *raiyats* could monitor the extent of lac infestation on a given tree: an important task given that host trees had poor growth, few leaves, and often lacked flowers and fruit.[37]

Raiyats were thus required to be stewards of the forest eco-system to ensure a sustainable production of resin: a 1921 report states that one of the main aims of lac cultivation was to "maintain an equilibrium between the lac and the tree and not to over-infect or too frequently infect the same host-tree."[38] We might say that shellac production was an "ecological economy" that yielded both ecosystem goods (in the form of raw materials used in human industry) and ecosystem services (in the form of forests that regulated the climate, controlled atmospheric gases, provided habitat for a variety of species including the lac insect, and served as a space for human recreation and spiritual enrichment).[39]

Shellac workers collected the branches that had become coated with resin, known as "stick lac," and sold them to traveling peddlers, or *baiparis*, who then sold the stick lac to a broker *(arhatiya)*, who in turn sold the merchandise to a manufacturer.[40] The majority of manufacturing before the 1930s was done in small village operations that utilized traditional tools to transform stick lac into a marketable commodity.[41] The first step was to scrape the resin from the sticks to produce what was called "seed lac." Seed lac was then taken to washers *(ghasandars)* who stood in a stone vessel and washed it with their feet. Washed seed lac was given to workers *(karigars)*, who placed it in a long tubular bag and twisted it over a charcoal oven called a *bhatta*. A melted mass oozed out of the bag and onto a stone slab, and workers *(bhilwayas)* stretched the hot mass into thin four-foot-square sheets by holding it with their toes, hands, and sometimes teeth. An 1876 report claims that it was not uncommon to see workers "lift the hot sheet to their mouths and bite out any foreign substance, such as dirt or sand, that may appear in the semi-transparent yellow surface."[42] These large sheets were dried and cooled and then cut into shell-like shapes, hence the designation of the finished product as "shellac."

Western accounts of Indian shellac manufacturing from the first half of the twentieth century often described the various stages by which workers transformed raw materials into a finished product. As such, they resembled films of this era that depicted processes of industrial manufacturing. A staple of filmgoing by the late 1920s, "industrial films" used editing techniques to provide a comprehensive view of the stages by which modern companies turned raw materials into marketable goods.[43] Often featuring an image of the *bhilwaya* stretching a sheet of hot shellac, Western depictions of shellac production combined the desire to see the details of industrial transformation with an Orientalist fascination with the bodies engaged in modes of labor that seemed to be compellingly "pre-modern."[44] Indian shellac manufacturing was not simply premodern, however, but simultaneously traditional and modern.

The shellac industry was traditional to the extent that it was small-scale, lacked precise standardization, and resisted modes of scientific efficiency. In

1920 a writer for the phonograph-industry trade journal *Talking Machine World* complained that Indian shellac production was not reaching its full potential because "the native of India has no ambition to make money": "He goes out and makes a few baskets of shellac and sells these for enough money to satisfy his simple wants. To go out and gather twice the number of baskets and earn twice as much money never even occurs to him. There are here and there a few enterprising natives with some business sense, but the great majority are supremely indifferent."[45] Ten years later Max Weber described this phenomenon in his influential book, *The Protestant Ethic and the Spirit of Capitalism*. Weber argued that, for "pre-capitalistic" laborers, the opportunity to earn more money was less attractive than the opportunity to work less: the worker did not ask "how much can I earn in a day if I do as much work as possible?" but instead, "how much must I work in order to earn the wage … which I earned before and which takes care of my traditional needs?" Weber claimed that this attitude offered stubborn resistance whenever modern capitalism began its work of "increasing the productivity of human labor by increasing its intensity."[46]

Indian shellac manufacture was precapitalistic in this regard, and, moreover, it relied on traditional knowledge related to the life cycles of trees and insects. Nonetheless, it resulted in a quintessentially modern material: one of the first mass-marketed plastics. The push and pull between modern and nonmodern modes of production is captured in Ben Singer's notion of the "ambimodern." Singer writes that modernity is best understood as "a heterogeneous area of modern and counter-modern impulses" that yields cultural expressions on both ends of the spectrum as well as "ambivalent or ambiguous positions in between." Shellac production certainly falls in the "ambiguous" category, but it is less "counter-modern" than "extramodern," Singer's term for those cultural traditions and practices that continued into the modern era and coexisted alongside "modern currents and countercurrents."[47] The situation becomes even more complex when we consider that shellac is a *bioplastic* that is biodegradable, nontoxic, reusable, and sustainable. The development of bioplastics is now a burgeoning area of cutting-edge research, making the Indian industry appear not so much premodern as a century ahead of its time. Timothy Morton makes a similar claim when he counters Western notions of a timeless, premodern Tibetan culture with the argument that, due to the fact that Tibetans live at remarkably high altitudes and have long included notions of outer space in their culture, they "would make the best space pilots." Morton concludes that traditional Tibetan culture does not belong in the past or in a museum but rather in the future.[48] Similarly, the *baiparis*, *karigars*, and *bhilwayas* of the

Indian shellac industry do not belong in a museum but rather at a green manufacturing expo.

Regardless of how we classify the shellac industry in relation to the currents of Western modernity, it produced a special kind of commodity: plastic. In a well-known essay Roland Barthes writes that plastic is less a substance than "the very idea of its infinite transformation," less a "thing" than "the trace of a movement."[49] In one regard, Barthes is certainly wrong. Landfills overflowing with product packaging, urban landscapes littered with discarded carrier bags, and the troubling phenomenon known as the Great Pacific Garbage Patch: all of these make clear that plastic is very definitely a "thing."[50] We will return to the environmental costs of plastic at the end of the chapter, but Barthes's discussion of plastic prompts us to return to Latour's suggestion that a network is less a thing than the recorded movement of a thing.

Lac insects were part of an energy cycle in which sunlight was translated into tree sap, and tree sap into resin. Human actants continued that process of translation, transforming brood lac to stick lac, then to seed lac, then to shellac. In these regions of the Green Disc topography, what circulates is a form of matter that "remembers" its previous existence as energy by maintaining the plasticity of that earlier state. In that regard, we might note that one of shellac's first industrial uses was in the European hat industry, where it stiffened the felt in formal hats like the bowler but, at the same time, gave them a certain malleability, so a hat could adapt its shape to the contours of the wearer's head.[51] In India, shellac had been used primarily for wood finishing, coloring, and the production of jewelry. Recall that the demand for shellac resin had grown during the decades around the turn of the century, just as the demand for lac dye was shrinking. The increase in demand for shellac at that time was largely the result of the nascent industry of recorded sound.[52]

Thomas Edison's earliest cylinder phonograph inscribed sound waves onto fragile tin foil sheets, but cylinders were made of wax by the 1880s.[53] Emile Berliner's first gramophone discs were composed of hard rubber, but his employee Fred Gaisberg made sample records from shellac after he learned that the Newark Durminoid Company was making buttons with the material. After these discs were judged to be superior to rubber, Berliner switched to a shellac mixture in 1896.[54] Shellac had a number of properties that made it congenial to record production: it required only moderate temperatures and pressures to shape it; it held a stable and accurate molding; it combined well with various fillers and pigments; and manufacturers could rework the scrap into the production process.[55] Due to these qualities, shellac became the key resinous ingredient in most phonograph records made between the 1890s and 1940s, although the particular recipe used by each company was a closely guarded trade secret.[56] In 1906 the newly launched trade journal *Talking Machine World* claimed that more than six thousand of the thirteen thousand tons of shellac that had been exported from India the previous year had come to the United States—a significant increase from previous years and one due directly to the manufacture of records. Four years later shellac exports from India had quadrupled. By the end of the 1940s the United States was the world's largest importer of shellac, acquiring between half to two-thirds of the total quantity sent abroad, most of which was used to make phonograph records.[57]

The next phase of my analysis of the Green Disc network follows the trail of shellac exports, moving from work done in the forests of India to that done in American recording studios. These two nodes in the network mirror each other as sites of material transformation and traditional technological knowledge. Thus far, I have been exploring the area on the Venn diagram that includes Green Discs and the shellac era. In the next section my focus shifts to the area formed by Green Discs and the acoustic era of phonography. Acoustic practices of record production and consumption demonstrate another way in which phonography of this era can be understood as eco-sonic.

UNPLUGGED PHONOGRAPHY

Acoustic-era studio production, like Indian shellac manufacturing, was both modern and traditional at the same time. Recording did not require electricity during this period and so was a form of low- or no-wattage media production. An 1890 instruction manual for recording operators assumed that "all recording apparatuses are constructed with manual operation" and advised workers to practice rotating the machine's hand crank while watching a clock to assure the proper rate.[58] Manually powered devices were succeeded by gravity or weight-driven motors. Several industrial handbooks of the early 1900s discuss the merits of mechanical weight motors. One author noted that the "obvious superiority" of the weight motor was due to the fact that the source of its power was "even and constant" and that its simple construction meant that it was not likely to get out of order.[59] The Gennett Records studio in Richmond, Indiana, was still using a cable-and-pulley system "much like a grandfather clock" in the early 1920s. According to historian Rick Kennedy, Gennett's recording machine was attached to a cable with a large weight on the other end, and the turntable spun when the weight was lowered into a shaft.[60] Acoustic studios were reliant on gravity, human muscle power, and mechanical knowledge, and so fall into the category of ambimodern TTK, as much as do Indian *karigars* and *bhilwayas*.

Muscle power was required not only of the operators who turned the crank on the apparatus but also of the performers who stood before the recording horn. Sound was funneled through a horn to a flexible diaphragm that transferred vibrations to a stylus that engraved grooves onto a wax disc. No electronic amplification was involved in this process, and so performances had to be quite loud to produce a viable recording.[61] Vocalists needed stamina as well as sheer volume, since they were frequently required to perform their material multiple times. In her study of American recording studios, Susan Schmidt Horning writes that before methods of mass duplication were perfected, "the work of recording studios was truly labor-intensive. Recordists and performers simply made multiple copies, one after the other, to fill demand."[62] Dynamics of the acoustic-era studio thus favored those performers who had developed techniques to address audiences in large spaces, such as opera singers, political orators, variety show performers, auctioneers, and street performers.[63] Jonathan Sterne has argued that early phonograph exhibitors "helped the machine" by using well-known rhymes, quotations, and other forms of conventionalized language to make sound recordings more immediately understandable. Vocalists of the acoustic era "helped the machine" in another way by lending it the power of their breath in a wind-powered phonography that distributed the energy costs of recording between human exertion and the apparatus.[64]

We have thus far encountered two kinds of transformation achieved by the Green Disc network: the lac insect's translation of energy and the shellac worker's transformation of raw materials. Recording studios were the site of another kind of transformation that Sterne has defined as "transduction"—the process by which audible vibrations are changed into another form, in this case, the grooves on a phonograph disc.[65] These various registers of material transformation were interlinked when sound waves were pressed into a shellac disc. The undulating waves of air that entered the acoustic horn draw our attention to yet another dimension of transformation in this network: the plasmatic quality of sound itself.

The Soviet film director Sergei Eisenstein famously describes the "plasmatic" quality of the characters seen in animated cartoons, by which he means their "ability to dynamically assume any form." Eisenstein also finds the quality of protean changeability in folktales, "spineless circus performers," the movements of fire, and music, which he considers remarkable because "the images created by it flow continuously, like flame itself, eternally changeable, like the play of its tongues, mobile and endlessly diverse."[66] Not just music, but all sound is characterized by that plasmatic quality. Michel Chion makes a similar point when he writes that the voice is "the mother of all special effects": "imagine someone who in a matter of seconds could double in height, expand like a balloon and retract into a string bean, or change their face from sweet and harmonious to horribly disfigured—that's what the voice can do with no external props or tricks, just through the natural means of phonation."[67]

The record industry used plastic to make sound into a marketable commodity, and at the same time it made a commodity out of the plasmatic quality of sound. The avatar of Green Disc plasticity was Gilbert Girard, the early phonograph industry's premiere animal mimic. A French Canadian born in San Francisco, Girard was said to be fond of imitating animals as a boy. He became a stage performer as a young man, working as a circus clown and a musical comedian before finding success as part of the first theatrical troupe to visit Alaska.[68] Girard began recording in the mid-1890s and often worked in collaboration with pioneer recording artist Len Spencer, who took the lead speaking parts while Girard populated the aural scene with a host of stunning animal characterizations.[69] Several records cast Spencer in the role of an auctioneer, with Girard voicing the various creatures on sale. In *Auction Sale of a Bird and Animal Store* (1902), Girard is a cat, a monkey, and a parrot; in *Auction Sale of Household Goods* (1902), he is a crying baby and a cuckoo clock; and in *Auction Sale of a Stranded Circus* (1908), he is a dog, a hyena, a goat, and an elephant. In the 1902 barnyard farce, *Daybreak at Calamity Farm*, Girard voices a rooster, a chicken, a cow, a dog, a horse, and a crow. That same year he collaborated with Spencer on *Passing of a Circus Parade*, where he is an elephant, a donkey, a lion, a dog, and a pony. Girard made a number of children's records on his own, such as *Mother Goose and Other Rhymes* (1901), in which he animates Mother Hubbard's dog, the little pigs going to market, and Bo Peep's sheep.[70]

Girard created a plasmatic phonography in which a single performer uses the natural means of phonation to transform from species to species. We might pause for a moment to recognize that Girard was producing some of the same effects as the much-heralded digital morphing or computer-generated imagery of our own era, but at a tiny fraction of the energy and labor costs. Girard's records are eco-sonic because they were made during the low-wattage Green Disc era, but also because they make audible the plasmatic quality of sound and so subtly acknowledge the phonograph network's reliance on plastic materials and the natural and social support systems required to produce them.

I have been focusing on weight motors, recording horns, and the performance techniques found in early studios, but the first decades of the twentieth century are also known as the "acoustic era" because of the hand-cranked playback machines in American homes. Edison's earliest cylinder machines were given their motive power through a variety of means: hand cranks, water power, treadles similar to those on sewing machines, springs, and, in some cases, primitive electric batteries.[71] Berliner's first disc gramophone machines of the mid-1890s relied on hand cranks to propel the turntable.[72] This was a time when the majority of American homes were not wired for electricity, and battery-operated machines were messy and impractical for home use.[73] Berliner's spring-wound motor was developed by a young mechanic from Camden, New Jersey, named Eldridge R. Johnson, who also adjusted the machine's sound box and vertical crank, resulting in the "improved gramophone" of 1897.[74] The fact that Johnson rose to the top of the industry as the cofounder of the Victor Talking Machine Company is emblematic of the industry's ambimodernity: he was both the head of a modern media corporation known for its cutting-edge marketing strategies and a machinist skilled in forms of TTK.

When home listeners played their phonograph records, they took part in an act of transduction, whereby the grooves on the disc were transformed into sound waves in the air. Sterne's focus on transduction as the central operation in sound reproduction has been a productive way to historicize modern audio devices and to explore discourses adjacent to sound recording such as the scientific study of hearing, regimes of education for the deaf, and the history of medical dissection. Those adjacent discourses tend toward the concerns of doctors, educators, scientists, and inventors, but consumers and manufacturers of records often located the materiality of sound reproduction not in the transduction achieved by the phonograph's diaphragm but in the phonograph needle. One advertisement declared that the needle was the "tongue" of the phonograph, suggesting that it was the site of the device's enunciation.[75] The needle was a significant component of the infrastructure of phonography during the Green Disc era and needs to be included in a material history of recorded sound.

CACTUS PETE

Walter H. Bagshaw established the Bagshaw Needle Company in Lowell, Massachusetts, in 1868. Bagshaw had learned how to manufacture comb pins in the English industrial town of Leeds, and his Massachusetts factory produced needles for the textile industry. In 1897 Bagshaw received an order for one hundred thousand needles that came not from a textile firm but from a Philadelphia company called Zonophone, one of Berliner's early rivals in the disc business. As the recorded-sound industry grew, the Bagshaw company grew with it, to become one of the largest manufacturers of phonograph needles in the world.[76] The scale of the needle market was apparent by the 1910s: the author of a 1916 article in the trade press breathlessly declared that, given the common assumption that the needle should be changed after every playback of a record, an ordinary American family used between twenty and twenty-five needles a day.[77] One Bagshaw advertisement showed a stream of needles pouring over the globe and boasted of shipping an order for 1.75 billion needles: "the largest single order on the face of the earth for talking machine needles."[78]

We can read this advertising image, against the grain of its original intention, as a representation of the environmental damage wrought by countless disposable steel needles. Bagshaw was, in fact, one of the pioneers of disposable consumer culture: the 1897 order from Zonophone came just five years after William Painter invented the disposable tin bottle cap and only two years after King Gillette's cheap, disposable razors revolutionized American marketing.[79] The phonograph industry was thus complicit in the birth of a throwaway culture of obsolescence that is the antithesis of contemporary green marketing practices. Steel needles were made to be used once and then thrown away, but the phonograph trade press reported on the surprising ways in which their consumers were reusing discarded needles: they were used to hang pictures on the wall, grate horseradish, clean dirty milk bottles, repair shoes, make tattoos, support window frames, plug mouse holes, and serve as grit on slippery streets.[80] The German military found an innovative use for old phonograph needles during World War I. At a French army hospital on the western front, a soldier's injured arm was found to contain steel phonograph needles that had exploded out of a trench bomb.[81]

Steel needles could tear through human flesh, and they could also damage shellac phonograph discs. It is not a surprise then, that one of the distinctive characteristics of the Green Disc era was a widespread consumer awareness of the costs of sound reproduction. Phonograph listening at this time was always active listening to the extent that playback required human exertion to wind the spring, place the record on the turntable, and select and mount the proper needle. Industry handbooks and trade-press articles advised consumers on how to choose the appropriate needle: thicker needles produced greater volume, for example; the music of brass bands was pleasing with a longer pointed "soft tone" needle; and "loud tone" needles should be used in small rooms with low ceilings.[82] We have grown accustomed to the idea that playback of a CD or MP3 file is the same every time we hear it, but the act of selecting and replacing the needle marked each playback as a unique sonic performance and one that always inflicted damage to the disc. The damage wrought by hard steel needles was easy to perceive: if the needle was too sharp, it would dig down into the bottom of the groove; if it was too blunt and wide, it would deform the sides of the groove. As a result, the average life of a shellac disc was estimated to be around 75 to 125 spins.[83] Sound reproduction during the Green Disc era was, to paraphrase Paolo Cherchi Usai's comments on the cinema, the art of sound destruction, with listeners doing the most damage to the recordings that they loved and played the most frequently.[84]

Listeners who wanted to maximize the frequency of playback and minimize the damage to their records had two alternatives to the destructive steel needles. One option was to invest in "semi-permanent" or jeweled needles that had a sapphire or diamond tip.[85] The Pathe Sapphire Ball, for example, was tipped with a polished sapphire purported to lengthen the life of the record because it did not dig into the disc's surface: an ad declared that "after a thousand performances, Pathe discs show no perceptible wear."[86] Edison introduced Diamond Disc records in 1912, meant to be played with a diamond-tipped stylus. Jewel-tipped needles did not have to be replaced as often as steel needles, but some consumers were concerned that they were not flexible enough to conform to the shape of the record's groove.[87] Needles made of natural fibers were a second, more flexible, alternative.

Frederick Durize Hall, the founder of the B&H Fibre Company, had initially been unimpressed by the sound of the phonograph, which he found to be tinny and harsh. Hall set himself the task of correcting these deficiencies by improving the connection between the sound box and the disc, a response that indicates how attention to the process of sound reproduction could center on the needle rather than the diaphragm. Hall searched for a natural material that could be shaped into a needle and would play records without any "scratching, hissing, [or] rasping sound." He tried many varieties of wood before settling on a particular type of Japanese bamboo that was suited to the task.[88] Hall was satisfied that the tone produced by his bamboo needles was "simply remarkable" and wrote that "the manner in which delicate shadings, too often obscured, are brought out is delightful indeed to the critical listener." Moreover, Hall claimed that his needles preserved the life of the record and could play a disc up to three thousand times without damage.[89]

Hall's bamboo needles met with great success and became the most prominent alternative to steel for many years, although they were not without competition.[90] Other companies at this time sold fiber needles made of various natural materials: needles were made from the thorns found on apple trees and South American shrubs; another company marketed needles made from the sharp horns of the dogfish; and in England the spines of the hedgehog were given favorable reviews.[91] Cactus needles were particularly popular with record enthusiasts during the first half of the twentieth century. The Tusko Company of Chicago manufactured phonograph needles made from Arizona barrel-cactus needles. The Permo Company of Oakland, California, marketed the Permatone cactus needle and in 1921 could proclaim that "the use of cactus in the manufacture of needles has long been regarded favorably by music lovers."[92] Given the assumption that fiber needles were gentle on records, it is not surprising that record collectors sought out cactus needles in the hopes that they would extend the life of their beloved 78s. Cactus needles were the subject of several cartoons that appeared in the *Record Changer*, a magazine for record collectors published during the 1940s. Gene Deitch published a series of comics in the magazine that documented the trials and tribulations of the record-collector community. In one, we see an assortment of "technical experts," including a figure labeled "Cactus Pete," who is shown cultivating a cactus plant to harvest its needles. In another, Deitch's comical jazz-collector character waters his cactus plant while incredulously asking a friend, "You use *needles* on your records?!"

Cactus Pete and his ilk were certainly a specialized cohort of enthusiasts, but their cultivation of cactus plants deserves to be remembered for several reasons. First, it is another example of vegetable actants in the Green Disc network, with cactus-growing jazz buffs mirroring the Indian *raiyats* who tended their kusum trees. Second, cactus needles—like all replaceable needles of the era—acknowledged the material costs of phonographic playback and did so in a form that was a biodegradable and sustainable alternative to the throwaway culture of steel needles.[93] Cactus needles might thus find a place in a convivial phonographic network that includes shellac discs and acoustic technologies of recording and playback.

Spring-wound, acoustic playback was one of the first aspects of the Green Disc network to disappear, since electric motors were sold as attachments to phonograph players in the early 1920s. An ad for the Johnson Electric Motor Company of Chicago announced the arrival of the electrical talking machine and claimed that two phrases that retailers would be hearing in the coming year were "Do It Electrically" and "Why Crank Your

Phonograph?"⁹⁴ In 1925 the first "fully-electric" record player—the Brunswick Panatrope—went on the market with an electric motor, a magnetic pickup, and a vacuum-tube amplifier and speaker.⁹⁵ Electric motors were marketed to consumers as a modern convenience that reduced physical exertion. In an ad for Shelton Electric Motors, we see the image of a well-dressed woman listening to an electric phonograph, reclining dreamily on a chair laden with luxurious pillows, her eyes half shut.⁹⁶ A few years later an ad for the Roberts Electric Phonograph Motor Company shows a woman and three children all comfortably seated on a sofa and chairs, listening to the phonograph. Ad copy reads, "The Electric Age Comes to the Phonograph Industry."⁹⁷

Though undoubtedly convenient, electrical playback meant that record listeners no longer participated in the energy costs of phonographic playback through their muscle power. Instead, the burden of playback was borne by electric power created by the burning of fossil fuels. The phonograph was one of a host of electric appliances that became commonplace in middle-class homes at this time. Benjamin Kline writes that American consumption of electricity rose from 57 million to 188 million kilowatt-hours during the 1920s, and, consequently, American power plants "consumed 42 million tons of coal, 10 million barrels of oil, and 112 million cubic feet of natural gas."⁹⁸ Given the decline in muscle-powered phonography, it may not be a coincidence that some of the best-selling records of the early 1920s were Walter Camp's Daily Dozens and the Wallace Reducing Records series, which led a sofa-bound populace through a regimen of home calisthenics.

Electrification meant that playback did not require the listener's muscle power and that recording did not require the studio performer's wind power. Western Electric demonstrated electric recording techniques to the industry in 1924, and a year later microphones replaced the recording horn in Victor's recording studios.⁹⁹ As has often been noted, the sensitivity of the microphone created opportunities for new modes of studio performance such as the popular "crooning" style of singing. Mark Katz argues that crooning was "only possible with the microphone, for without amplification such singing would be expressively flat and nearly inaudible."¹⁰⁰ Electric recording allowed for new protocols of popular singing and provided more frequencies of sound, more nuances of expression, and a fuller sense of the spaces in which a recording session took place. These are all admirable developments if the goal is sonic fidelity. If, however, the goal is a convivial phonography, then gains in fidelity are less significant than a loss of equilibrium in the network. That is, during the acoustic era, there had been a balance between power derived from fossil fuels and human exertion. Both sounds of relaxed crooners and images of reclining listeners illustrate the decline of human energy inputs in the phonograph network.[101] Critics of the 1920s and 1930s who complained that crooning was an "unmanly" or debased style of singing seem comically wrongheaded today, but perhaps the style merits a different kind of critique, as a symptom of increasingly fossil fuel–dependent and unsustainable practices of media production and consumption.

The transition from the acoustic to the electric era of phonography during the 1920s marks a departure from the optimal field of overlap on the Venn diagram described earlier. Nonetheless, the shellac disc continued to be the primary format for recorded sound for two decades after the introduction of electric recording. In fact, one eco-friendly attribute of shellac became most perceptible during the twilight years of the Green Disc era.

SAVE THE PIECES

Shellac shortages became a cause of concern for the phonograph industry during World War I, when the government required shellac for the production of munitions.[102] An even more dramatic crisis occurred with the onset of World War II, when the U.S. War Production Board rationed rubber, gasoline, sugar, and other scarce materials. Used in aircraft instrument panels and ammunition casings, shellac was among the materials deemed vital to military production. In April 1942 the board issued conservation order M-106, which forced record companies to consume only 30 percent of the shellac they had used the previous year. To make matters worse, the Japanese army took control of several shellac-producing areas in Asia, slowing exports to the West.[103]

Wartime shortages inspired new ways of enacting patriotic citizenship on the American home front, such as recycling, responsible consumption, and the cultivation of Victory Gardens. In addition to reducing their consumption, Americans were encouraged to take part in scrap drives for metal, rubber, paper, and fats.[104] The major record companies of the time—RCA-Victor, Decca, and Columbia—launched a campaign in 1942 to collect old shellac discs, though much of the work of collecting the discs fell to local distributors and retailers. Scrap barrels for discs were placed outside record stores, and scrap reminders were enclosed with bills and mailings. Consumers were encouraged to return old discs every time they purchased new ones. Jackson's Furniture Store in Oakland, California, announced that customers would be given a new record for every twelve old ones they brought in. "You can help the record manufacturers and keep them making records as before," the ad declared. "Your old discarded records will do just that, no matter how old and worn out they may be." Albright's record store in Annapolis, Maryland, announced that it would pay six cents a pound for shellac records, "broken or whole."[105]

The big record producers worked with a number of different organizations in the pursuit of scrap. They made agreements with theater operators so that patrons could pay admission in old records. They worked with urban ballrooms to host "disc nights," where customers were given credit for old records. A patriotic group of musicians called Records for Our Fighting Men dedicated itself to shellac salvage, and popular singers encouraged New York schoolchildren to take part in the scrap drive, presenting them with special diplomas when they had a reached their quota on old records.[106] Civic groups such as the Boy Scouts, the Red Cross, and the American Legion joined the drive as well. *Time* magazine reported that 1.5 million members of the American Legion and the Women's American Legion Auxiliary were canvasing the nation as part of "the greatest record hunt in history": "Corn cribs, set up on street corners in small Kansas towns, bulged with old phonograph records . . . [and] open-mouthed caricatures of Hitler, Mussolini and Hirohito on Manhattan's Times Square made inviting receptacles to throw discs into."[107] Some firms were even said to be enlisting the help of janitors to comb houses for old records.

The industry's active participation in the 1942 shellac drive can be seen as a precursor to green marketing initiatives of the current era. For one thing, it was an early example of the environmental design strategy in which customers are paid for returns. It also resembles the industrial practice of extended product responsibility (EPR), in which corporations are asked to factor ecologically responsible disposal into their business strategy.[108] EPR has been one of the solutions offered to address the problem of health hazards caused by discarded electronic consumer goods when they enter the waste system. The wartime shellac drive was a rare instance of media-industry EPR, and we should note that it was made possible by the particular characteristics of shellac as a reusable bioplastic. In other words, the fact that shellac records were easy to break made them amenable to recycling. "The cry of 'save the pieces' is going up in shops and among the customers," wrote a reporter in the *Baltimore Sun* in 1942. "No more will the graven discs go to waste. Record dealers all over town are beginning to ask for the pieces in exchange for a few pennies when a new record is purchased. . . . The pieces are turned back to the wholesaler by the retailer and then go back to the factory to be melted down in the manufacture of new records."[109]

Despite these resemblances to green marketing strategies, World War II scrap drives did not significantly slow American consumerism; neither did they spur the record industry to take EPR to heart in any sustained manner. Instead, the industry's primary response to wartime shellac shortages was to redouble its commitment to finding synthetic alternatives. The record industry had long experimented with using synthetic plastics instead of shellac. Cylinders made in the 1900s by the Lambert Company had contained celluloid, the first synthetically produced plastic, as did Edison's 1912 Blue Amerbol cylinders. The chemist Leo Baekeland was searching for a "more serviceable substitute for shellac" when he produced a synthetic resin that was marketed as Bakelite. Edison used Bakelite in his 1912 Diamond Discs.[110] In the wake of World War I shellac shortages, industry laboratories were said to be "hard at work day and night" in the effort to find an affordable shellac substitute.[111] The rationing of the 1940s gave new urgency to that effort. In 1942 the new record company Capitol shocked competitors by turning out a surprising number of discs, given the wartime reductions in supply. Capitol's secret was revealed to be a new disc manufacturing process that did not rely on shellac. As *Newsweek* put it, the company was actively searching for "chemical substitutes for the juice of the Indian lac bug."[112] Strong incentives for developing alternatives continued after the war, when price controls were lifted and the cost of shellac rose to a prohibitive level. It is not a surprise, then, that RCA-Victor introduced its first transparent, ruby-red plastic discs in 1945.[113]

RCA-Victor's discs were made of a synthetic compound of petroleum and chlorine called polyvinyl chloride (PVC), or "vinyl" for short, which was marketed commercially by the Union Carbide Company in the 1930s.[114] Peter Goldmark, the CBS researcher who played a central role in the development of Columbia's long-playing records, wrote that he had been looking for "a smooth, hard material to replace shellac," and he found it in vinylite, "a World War II era development" that had been used primarily in the manufacture of garden hoses.[115] It is easy to see why the industry saw vinyl as an improvement over shellac. Lighter and tougher than shellac, vinyl was considered to be "unbreakable." The sturdiness of vinyl had come in handy during World War II, when the material was used to produce "V disc" records for the armed forces, some of which had to be dropped to soldiers by parachute.[116] Vinyl was harder and finer than shellac and so allowed for more grooves to be pressed onto a disc, hence the material's importance for the development of long-playing records.[117] All of these facts made it self-evident that the introduction of vinyl records signaled a change for the better, one of many signs that postwar consumers were entering an era of "Better Living through Chemistry."[118]

The defining moment in the birth of the modern environmental movement—Rachel Carson's 1962 exposé of the chemical pesticide industry—was a provocative challenge to that optimistic narrative, and an eco-critical perspective emboldens us to question record-industry marketing rhetoric that would have us believe that the undeniable benefits of vinyl LPs came without any significant costs. Vinyl is generally made from petroleum, which is a nonrenewable resource. Nonrenewable resources like minerals and mineral fuels can only be used once, and the geological processes that form them are too slow to be sustainable. By contrast, shellac is a potentially renewable resource, given that the forest ecology that supports it is allowed to regenerate faster than the rate at which it is consumed.[119] The shift from shellac to vinyl records thus speeds the depletion of nonrenewable fossil fuels.

Whereas shellac is nontoxic and even edible, PVC has been called "the most environmentally pernicious plastic in use" due to concerns that it causes cancer among factory workers and releases deadly chemicals like dioxin into the food chain.[120] Greenpeace writes that of all the plastics, vinyl is "the most environmentally damaging. Throughout its lifecycle it requires hazardous chemicals for production, releases harmful additives and creates toxic wastes."[121] From the perspective of recycling and reuse, the fact that vinyl is "unbreakable" is a weakness, not a strength. Recall how scraps of shellac were reused in the production process and how old and broken shellac records were returned to dealers to be melted and remolded.[122] Less than 1 percent of PVC is recycled, and because products made of vinyl are difficult to repair, they are typically discarded instead of being reused. Historian Susan Strasser argues that the rise of plastic consumer products during the postwar era fostered "a relationship to the material world that required consumers to buy things rather than make them and to throw things out rather than fix them. Nobody made plastic at home, hardly anybody understood how it was made, and it usually could not be repaired."[123] This has implications for landfills, and nonbiodegradable plastics like PVC account for approximately 18 percent of the volume of municipal waste.[124] In other words, once records were made of vinyl, they became nonbiodegradable hyperobjects. In 1945 a writer for *Billboard* magazine wrote that the new plastic LPs were "ageless copies of the music that the family wants to keep forever."[125] The statement was correct but incomplete, since the ecological implications of producing millions of indestructible Mitch Miller LPs were not part of the discussion.

Columbia Records unveiled their 33⅓ rpm vinyl LPs at a 1948 press conference. The company presented its new format as a lightweight means of storing more sound than was previously possible. In its coverage of the event, *Life* magazine ran a photograph of Columbia's Peter Goldmark standing beside an eight-foot-high tower of "old-style" 78 rpm records that weighed more than three hundred pounds. To demonstrate the benefits of the new format, Goldmark held in his arms the equivalent amount of recorded sound in vinyl: a one-foot-high, thirty-pound stack of LPs.[126] This industry-choreographed photo opportunity made use of rhetoric similar to that used to portray recent digital music devices as thin and lightweight and cloud-based services as offering limitless storage space for dematerialized music files. Then, as now, the issue is not as simple as triumphalist industry marketing would suggest.[127] For green marketers concerned with the life-cycle analysis (LCA) of consumer products, the greenest devices are sometimes those that *reject* the miniaturization that leads to "thoughtless disposal."[128] If we look more closely at the case of the vinyl LP, we can see how the rhetoric of lightweight media formats and bountiful storage space encourages the escalation of consumption and obscures a number of significant ecological problems.

The much-heralded extended playing time of the LP can be viewed in the same manner that Nadia Bozak critiques the cinematic long take. For Bozak, the long take is a "signal of material excess and an ideology of material decadence," whereby the camera is left to idle, perpetuating habits of waste and overconsumption. "There is an ideology of limitlessness, expansionism, and unfettered expenditure built into this specific formal decision," she writes, "wherein the camera aperture is opened indefinitely and seemingly indefatigably." A similar ideology of unfettered expenditure is signaled by recording devices allowed to record the long unbroken sides of the new LPs. I am one of countless record fans who would cringe at the thought of a world without LPs containing the extended improvisations of postwar jazz musicians like John Coltrane and Bill Evans; the long-form comic routines of Mort Sahl, Lenny Bruce, and Bill Cosby; or the album-length musical cycles of postwar recording artists such as the Beatles, Van Morrison, or Marvin Gaye. Nonetheless, it is time to reinvest in the merits of "short media" in a manner roughly analogous to the way in which the "slow food" movement has reshaped popular attitudes about eating. The four-minute, single-track 78 rpm disc should be appreciated as the phonographic equivalent of what Bozak calls "cinematic thrift," whereby filmmakers repurpose extant films, repeat a single shot, or by some other means acknowledge the photographic image as "a valuable, potentially finite resource."[129]

There is a flipside to high-fidelity records as well as long-playing ones. Vinyl records were part of a postwar "revolution" in sound technology,

FIGURE 3. Peter Goldmark stands beside a three-hundred-pound tower of 78 rpm records while holding a thirty-pound stack of vinyl LPs. Eric Schaal, Life Picture Collection, Getty Images, Seattle, WA.

hailed for its stunning increase in sonic fidelity. Shellac was difficult to standardize, since batches of the material tended to contain various amounts of impurities that caused some of the pops and hisses that we associate with early phonograph records. Vinyl, on the other hand, had a high degree of uniformity from batch to batch and contained fewer additives than shellac, resulting in discs that had considerably less surface noise. A century of industry advertising has made it seem natural to base qualitative judgments about recorded sound on the faithful reproduction of a source event and the absence of "noise."

Scholars in the field of sound studies have demonstrated the extent to which discourses of sound fidelity were shaped by the specific historical context of the early twentieth century, making clear that it is only one possible criterion for assessing sound recordings.[130] The "impurities" in shellac were caused in part by material traces of the trees and insects that produced the bioplastic material needed for sound reproduction. In our culture, where "a speaking subject is jealously guarded as an exclusively human prerogative," the noise of the shellac can be appreciated for the way in which it resists the tendency for nature to become silent. "We require a viable environmental ethics to confront the silence of nature in our contemporary regime of thought," Christopher Manes argues, "for it is within this vast, eerie silence that surrounds our garrulous human subjectivity that an ethics of exploitation regarding nature has taken shape and flourished."[131] The pops of Green Discs can be heard not simply as noise to be eliminated but as an eco-positive attribute of shellac, giving voice to the kusum trees and reddish insects that provide a material base for the voices of Gilbert Girard or Enrico Caruso.[132]

What I hope has become clear is that there were a host of hidden ecological costs associated with the introduction of unbreakable, lightweight, long-playing, high-fidelity vinyl records. Moreover, an eco-critical perspective reveals the particular material benefits of shellac. The fragility of shellac encouraged extra care to be taken in sound reproduction, leading to a consumer ecology that included the cultivation of fiber needles and the acknowledgement of the material costs of playback. Shellac discs had the potential to remind listeners of the role played by nonhuman producers, and by extension the larger ecology of energy cycles, in the phonographic system. For these and other reasons, the Green Disc era should be revisited as the point of departure in the construction of a more convivial phonography.

Ivan Illich describes a historical pattern whereby technologies cross two thresholds. The first is a watershed that occurs when the desirable effects of a new discovery become "easily measured and verified," and new knowledge is applied to a "clearly stated problem." At a second watershed, technology becomes the means to its own ends and is used for the exploitation of society in the service of "self-certifying elites." Illich gives the example of transportation technology, writing that "it has taken almost a century to pass from an era served by motorized vehicles to the era in which society has been reduced to virtual enslavement to the car."[133] Illich is certainly painting with broad strokes (few technologies, for example, have the neat trajectory he postulates), but it is useful to think of the Green Disc era as a convivial sweet spot between two watersheds. The first marks the invention of sound recording, which allowed for the preservation of sounds in all their diversity and specificity and the development of a popular market for recorded sound. The second watershed marks the passing of the Green Disc era and the decline of a relatively low-impact and sustainable infrastructure.[134]

Over the course of this chapter I have mapped the Green Disc network in terms of the circulation of energy, the industrial transformation of raw materials, the transduction of sound waves into record grooves and back again, and the recycling of old records as reusable scrap. When we zoom back to consider the Green Disc network as a whole, the content of the network appears to be the process of transformation itself, be that the plasmatic play of sound, the material malleability of plastic, or the circulation of energy. If we were to reorient the network around the attribute of plasticity as opposed to fidelity, then we might pursue a convivial infrastructure that provides the maximum play of plastic transformation through the least amount of damage to the planet.[135]

As an emblem for that pursuit, I offer the humble lac insect, whose labor was essential to one of the first modern media industries and whose process of manufacturing is convivial in ways that human industry is not. Designers William McDonough and Michael Braungart write that "all the ants on the planet, taken together, have a biomass greater than that of humans. Ants have been incredibly industrious for millions of years. Yet their productiveness nourishes plants, animals, and soil. Human industry has been in full swing for little over a century, yet it has brought about a decline in almost every ecosystem on the planet."[136] Likewise, the industry of the lac insect was part of a sustainable natural energy cycle, as opposed to a human plastics industry that relies on "non-renewable geological capital."[137] Human observers thought that they were elevating insects by comparing them to Victorian industrialists, but the irony is that Mr. and Mrs. Lacca were way ahead of us in the implementation of convivial manufacturing. In fact, our nonconvivial industrial practices are a threat to the very existence of the lac insect. Anthropogenic climate change has caused temperatures to rise in lac-producing areas, leading to a drastic decline in the number of the insects. Lac insects and their host trees are vulnerable to changes in climatic conditions, and extremely hot weather is particularly hazardous to the former because at a certain temperature their "gummy domes" melt, suffocating the insects inside. Changing climate patterns have also caused shifts in seasonal patterns, allowing parasites on the lac to proliferate.[138]

I would like to end this chapter not with the Indian lac insect, however, but with the human laborers in the Indian shellac industry. The record industry's shift to vinyl placed the Indian shellac industry in a "severe crisis" that threatened the employment of millions of workers and small-scale cultivators.[139] The Indian government formed a committee in 1931 to counter the growing market pressure caused by the development of synthetic resins, but it could not stop the decline of the industry.[140] The rise of synthetic plastics resulted in the loss of valuable income for millions of Indian lac cultivators as well as an economic motivation for maintaining the health of the forest. Given the role of synthetic chemicals in the collapse of the shellac market, there is a terrible irony to the fact that one of the worst industrial accidents in world history took place in India and involved the company that first marketed PVC. On December 3, 1984, Union Carbide's chemical pesticide plant in Bhopal released more than forty tons of toxic gas, killing thousands of people and providing a horrifying demonstration of the costs of "Better Living through Chemistry."[141]

There is another form of contemporary Indian labor that may provide clues to a twenty-first-century practice of convivial phonography. India is one of the few countries that continues to produce hand-wound, acoustic phonograph players. These machines circulate globally, but the Western collector community denigrates them as "Crap-o-phones" or "Frankenphones," due to the fact that they are often composed of parts taken from various machines of different vintage. As this chapter has shown, we can appreciate these machines, not as second-rate knockoffs or quaint nostalgic bric-a-brac, but as TTK in action—signs of surviving ambimodern skills that should be understood and encouraged as we face what John Michael Greer calls the "deindustrial age."

As the supply of petroleum inevitably declines, Greer claims that Western populations will have to scale back their expectations and make do with technologies that work with available renewable resources. Greer suggests that his readers adopt an obsolete technology and learn how to use it before those skills are forgotten and have to be "laboriously reinvented decades in the future."[142] We do not need to subscribe to the most apocalyptic aspects of Greer's scenario to appreciate acoustic phonography as a lesson in green media practice. Recall Maxwell and Miller's provocative question to media scholars: "how much communication and entertainment media is enough to attain a system that serves everyone on the planet fairly without contributing to 'ecological suicide?'" If I had to answer that question with regard to sound media technology, I would begin with the Crap-o-phone and not the iPhone.

2. Birdland Melodies

A 1971 television commercial begins with an interior view of an open window at night. An orange cat saunters onto the outside windowsill and looks into the room. The next shot reveals the object of the cat's interest: a yellow canary chirps and hops about in a cage whose door is tantalizingly ajar. The cat licks its lips and jumps down onto the floor of the room. Suspense builds as shots alternate between the cat slinking forward in the half light of the room and the canary nervously ruffling its feathers. With an angry hiss, the feline charges out of the frame. Both the cat and the television audience are surprised by what happens next: what we thought was a live canary is revealed to be an image on a Sylvania color television set. As the cat makes futile jabs at the screen, a narrator explains, "You've been watching a dramatization of how real we think the picture is on Sylvania color television. The question was, how to tell you in a way you'd remember." A print version of the ad condensed the TV spot into the single striking image of a cat leaping at a television screen on which a canary appears to recoil in fright.

The commercial message of Sylvania's "Cat and the Canary" campaign is clear enough, but what interests me is the way in which the ad dramatizes a moment of interaction between a domestic medium and a domestic pet. In that regard, "Cat and the Canary" is an update of the famous Victor Records logo "His Master's Voice," which shows the dog Nipper cocking his head to listen to the recorded voice of his human owner.[1] "His Master's Voice" and "Cat and the Canary" portray a contact zone that existed between the interspecies ecology and the media ecology of the home, but how might we begin to write a history of that zone? The "Cat and the Canary" gives us a clue. Notice how the TV in the magazine version of the ad is transformed into a birdcage. The visual rhetoric of this image acknowledges, albeit unintentionally, that cage birds were precursors to television,

FIGURE 4. An advertisement for Sylvania color television sets, which appeared in *Saturday Review*, November 20, 1971, 42–43.

radio, and the phonograph as sources of sonic entertainment in the home. In the last chapter, I investigated the materiality of shellac discs to acknowledge the bugs in the phonographic system. This chapter examines a nineteenth- and early twentieth-century biotechnological apparatus that interlinked birds and sound technologies and that was eco-sonic to the extent that it fostered an appreciation of nonhuman nature and facilitated cross-species communication.

By beginning the chapter with the Sylvania and Victor ads, I want to signal that one of my goals is to engage with scholarly work on the media representation of animals. Akira Mizuta Lippit writes that animals have come to be experienced primarily though the media and so have shifted "from a body to an image; from a living voice to a technical echo."[2] Lippit is mostly concerned with the visual representation of animals, and he argues that it was cinema that "best embodied the transfer of animals from nature to technology." Notice, however, that despite Sylvania's emphasis on the color image, the TV spot gives the canary the "final word," since we hear it chirping after the image has faded to a corporate logo. The canary's chirp reminds us that amplifying horns and loudspeakers were just as important as screens in constructing the mediated "echo" of animal voices and that the analysis of animal representation needs an audio component. The case studies in this chapter explore the sonic representation of animals, but they also trouble Lippit's conceptual boundary between "living voices" and "technical echoes," because living birds functioned as recording devices, humans imitated birds as a genre of media performance, and sound technologies were used to speak to birds as well as to humans.

The scholarship on animal representation prompts us to consider animals as media content, but caged canaries are perhaps better understood as media infrastructure. Historians of technology have begun to investigate the "biotechnologies" created when humans transform organisms through breeding and training.[3] Donna Haraway writes that technologies are always "compound" in that they are composed of "human beings or parts of human beings, other organisms in part or whole, machines of many kinds, or other sorts of entrained things made to work in the technological compound of conjoined forces."[4] Songbirds were the biological components in a nineteenth-century compound technology of sound recording, and their training involved a form of cross-species sociality that should be included in histories of human interaction with domestic companion species.[5]

Haraway discusses cross-species sociality primarily in terms of the visual and tactile communication between humans and dogs. Sound was the primary medium of communication between humans and birds, and their interaction was often understood in terms of music and speech. Spoken language has been the primary yardstick by which humans have assessed animal communication, and so research has tended to focus on the extent to which animals can learn human language. Erica Fudge draws our attention to the implicit assumption in much research that human language is primary and wonders why more attention has not been given to the human ability to "speak" animal languages.[6] The featured performers in this chapter are artistic whistlers and bird mimics who dedicated their professional lives to the pursuit of that goal. The humble human whistle emerges as a form of zoosemiotic communication shared across species, as well as an interface between performers and early recording technology.[7] My study of twentieth-century phonographic whistlers and bird mimics has the added benefit of bringing a sonic dimension to the history of the American conservation movement.

You might hear this chapter, then, as a whistling trio between birds, humans, and sound technologies. Eldridge Johnson, the mechanic who became the head of Victor Records, famously stated that his first impression of the gramophone was of a "partially educated parrot with a sore throat and a cold in the head."⁸ It is not surprising that Johnson's initial point of reference for a domestic sound reproduction device was a parrot, since cage birds had been popular sources of sonic entertainment in American and European homes since the 1600s. In the previous chapter, I asserted that insects could be heard in the pops of 78 rpm records. To begin this chapter, I would like for you to listen for the piping of songbirds in the word "record."

RECORDERS

The verb "to record" has a number of meanings, two of which seem to pull in quite different directions. The word can describe the act of remembering, learning by heart, or committing to memory, but "to record" can also be used to describe the act of recalling, repeating, declaring, or bearing witness. The word thus exists in a field of tension between the *preservation* or *inscription* of information, and the *retrieval* or *performance* of it. Similarly, the noun "record" can be either a piece of information that has been preserved or the act of showing forth that information (as in "to bear record" or to go "on the record").⁹ The tension between these two meanings is resolved in one of the word's archaic uses, which is to describe the vocalization of young songbirds. The *OED* gives a 1754 example: "If any of the young birds or nestlings, before they can feed themselves, do *record* something of song, you will perceive the motion of their throats when they *record*."¹⁰ Birds learn and remember their song (they "record" it) by hearing themselves perform (or "record") it. Birdsong can be heard, then, as a fundamental tone underlying the multiple meanings of the word "record," since it activates and harmonizes much of the word's associational resonance.¹¹

The word "record" encompasses the acts of preserving and showing forth, and it also demarcates a sonic contact zone between birds and humans, both of whom rely on sonic communication to maintain the structure of their societies.¹² Some birds learn their vocalizations in a manner similar to the human acquisition of language. Biologist W. John Smith notes that both birdsong and language acquisition involve "critical periods before sexual maturity in which young individuals select a set of sounds that they will learn from the many available to them in natural circumstances."¹³ Just as human infants make babbling sounds as they acquire speech, so young birds make "rambling, soft vocalizations" as they "record" their songs, sounds that are referred to as a "subsong" or "plastic song."¹⁴ Not all species of birds have the same ability to learn. Some make their species-specific vocalizations even if they are deafened soon after birth, suggesting that little or no learning takes place. Others have a critical period during which they learn the only song that they will ever sing. A number of bird species, however, such as mockingbirds, starlings, and canaries, are "open-ended learners," capable of acquiring new songs throughout their lives.[15]

Humans have developed techniques for intervening in the learning process of open ended–learner birds. An 1857 handbook on cage birds advised that as soon as young songbirds begin to twitter ("or 'record' as it is called"), then it is time to "commence their education."[16] Trainers sometimes taught their young birds to sing by playing them melodies on a reedless wind instrument known as a flageolet, or "recorder." In 1718 J.-C. Hervieux de Chanteloup published a book in London that described how to teach cage birds musical airs on the flageolet. Around that same time a collection of tunes intended for that purpose was published in London under the title *The Bird Fancyer's Delight*, and it is still used in children's music education today.[17] The recorder was a technology for shaping the plastic song of birds to human ends, but the central components of the bird-recording apparatus were the songbirds themselves. One of the most popular songbirds imported into Europe was the canary.

The canary bird *(Serinus canaria)* gets its name from its original habitat in the Canary Islands, located off the northwest coast of Africa. Press accounts and articles in bird-fancier literature often printed a narrative that explained how the canary had first came to Europe. This "origin story" was often presented as common knowledge, and its outlines are as follows. Sometime in the 1400s a Spanish navigator happened to land on the Canary Islands. He took some native birds back to Spain, where they became popular pets among the Spanish aristocracy. Years later a European ship carrying a large number of canaries encountered a tremendous storm in the Mediterranean. The ship sank, but not before the crew freed the caged birds, who flew to the nearby island of Elba, where they thrived.[18]

Roland Barthes defines myth as a form of depoliticized speech that empties events of history while leaving a kind of "perceptible absence."[19] This is an apt way to describe the conventional narrative of the canary's arrival in Europe, because it empties that history of the violence of colonial conquest and commerce. The canary was, in fact, one of the first exotic birds to be brought back to Europe by merchants and explorers as tokens of colonial adventure. The proliferation of domesticated canaries was the result of the first encounter between European colonists and a culture of traditional, or "premodern," people. In the words of historian Alfred W. Crosby, the Canary Islands were "laboratories for a new kind of European imperialism."[20]

European raids of the Canaries for slaves began in the 1300s, but the arrival of a French expedition in 1402 marked the start of full-scale colonization, which was completed by the Spanish in a series of conquests between 1478 and 1496.[21] Jean de Bethencourt, the Norman adventurer who first invaded the islands in the 1400s, brought canary birds back to the courts of France and Spain, where they became fashionable courtship gifts: King Charles VII of France wooed his mistress with a canary in the 1440s.[22] European colonization of the Canary Islands was a long and violent process that resulted in the extermination of the indigenous people and their culture. To quote Crosby again, the native Canarians, or Guanches, were "the first people to be driven over the cliff of extinction by modern imperialism."[23] The colonization of the Canaries was a grim portent of things to come, and it is telling that Christopher Columbus passed through the islands on his way to America in 1492.[24] The Canary Islands soon became a hub in the traffic of slaves from Africa to the Americas.

Barthes argues that myth does not hide or deny painful truths but rather distorts or purifies them. We can hear the distorted echo of colonial conquest and the enslavement of the Guanches in the conventional narrative of the canary bird's arrival in Europe: in the tumult of the tremendous storm for example; the violence of the sinking ship; and themes of imprisonment and diaspora. We will return to the culture of the indigenous Canary Islanders at the end of the chapter, but, for now, we should note that the circulation of captive canary birds in Europe and later America followed colonial conquest and the traffic in captive humans. As such, the voices of canary birds were part of the soundscape of the "Black Atlantic" or "circum-Atlantic world," and their cheerful songs always contained dark undertones of imperialism, slavery, and genocide.[25]

The indigenous Guanches people might not have recognized the song of the domesticated canary, because Europeans became so adept at training the birds to sing in "unnatural" ways. It is to these training techniques that I now turn, and my analysis follows the route described by the conventional story of the canary's arrival in Europe, which typically noted that many of the birds were taken north to Germany, where the training of songbirds was said to have reached its "greatest degree of perfection."[26]

ROLLERS

It was a truism of the nineteenth and early twentieth century that Germany led the Western world in the training of domestic songbirds.[27] The German cage-bird industry was associated with the Harz Mountain region and, in particular, the town of St. Andreasberg. "The difference between a beautiful 'triller' of St. Andreasberg, and an ordinary 'screamer,'" wrote an author in

1873, was so patent that even an "unskilled ear" could detect it immediately.[28] St. Andreasberg had a reputation for clear mountain air and pure water, which made it a summer resort for those suffering from lung and throat ailments. That environment was also thought to have a "wonderful effect" on the song of the canary.[29] As we will see in the next chapter, mining was the principal occupation of the region, and miners and their families raised songbirds to supplement their meager income. In other words, the production of Harz Mountain songbirds was literally a cottage industry. In 1901 the *Ladies Home Journal* described a typical Harz Mountain cottage with a low ceiling, unpainted walls, unscrubbed floor, a stove in one corner, and numerous birdcages arranged on the walls.[30]

Canary fanciers in England and Belgium often bred birds for their exceptional size or color, but the Germans were known for producing the best singers.[31] German trainers achieved their results through a regimen that began with the careful control of the birds' sonic environment. Young male birds—and only males were thought to make marketable songsters—were prevented from hearing the natural song of their compatriots and confined in dark rooms or training cages so that their attention was directed exclusively to sound. At appointed times, an instructor bird was placed in a cage nearby to produce a model song for the student birds to imitate. The instructor was either a gifted canary or a songster of another species, sometimes a nightingale.[32] German trainers took part in a modern tendency to separate the senses to better understand and manipulate them. We might say that Harz Mountain training cages produced an avian "audile technique" akin to the skills acquired by humans who learned to listen to electric signals through earphones or carry on telephone conversations.[33]

Instructor birds and training cages were only two of the tools used by German trainers to mold their canary's voices. Some trainers taught melodies to their birds by whistling to them. One author declared that, though German trainers were "deficient in many of the graces of life," they could "whistle songs as correctly as another man can play them on a cornet or piano."[34] The flageolet was also employed to teach melodies to birds, as was a device called a serinette. Designed in France around 1730, the serinette was a small, hand-cranked barrel organ that blew air through a bellows to produce short tunes that were encoded with movable pins.[35] Serinettes appear in several eighteenth-century paintings, such as William Hogarth's *The Graham Children* (1742), which shows a young boy turning the crank of the device, happily gazing up at his pet goldfinch. A cat can be seen peering at the bird behind the boy's chair, in a period staging of a familiar domestic ecology. In Jean-Baptiste Chardin's *La Serinette* (1751), a middle-class

French woman sits in her parlor, a hand on the crank of her serinette while she looks intently at her pet canary in a nearby cage. These paintings suggest that the serinette was a sonic ancillary to the rise in pet keeping in upper-middle-class European homes.[36] Harz Mountain trainers employed the device as a way to produce marketable songbirds in large quantities. According to an 1873 account, German trainers used serinettes for "hours at a time, so that the bird hears and knows nothing else than these [tunes]; and is at last tempted to try its skill at the melody, out of sheer desperation."[37]

Trainers delegated some of the repetitive human labor involved in training songbirds to the serinette, as well as another device that was thought to improve the overall quality of the bird's vocalizing. Sometimes referred to as a "bird organ," this odd contraption was about the size of a grandfather clock, with water-filled cylinders put in motion by a weight-and-pulley system similar to the acoustic-recording machines described in the previous chapter. As the weight fell, it pumped a bellows that sent air through the cylinders to produce a number of distinctive sounds, one of which was described as being "a low, plaintive monotone that goes on and on, like the sound of water running over rocks, or the wind's motion in the trees." Birds exposed to the machine were said to listen "as if fascinated" and became "gentle and teachable."[38] One book claimed that there were several of these "song-machines" on the market, some of which could produce up to sixty different sounds for the birds to imitate.[39]

Harz Mountain cottages equipped with training cages, recorders, serinettes, and bird organs were nineteenth-century home recording studios in which the sounds deemed valuable to human listeners were molded onto the "plastic song" of open ended–learner birds. We might say that the Harz Mountain canary was a form of "phonography by other means." In fact, canaries were such effective recording devices that would-be trainers were warned to keep their serinettes in top condition, as the birds would imitate any squeaky or out-of-tune note they heard.[40] In other words, the bird-recording apparatus was sometimes criticized, not for a lack of fidelity, but for having *too much* fidelity, contrary to Michel Chion's assertion that "no one complains of nonfidelity from too much definition."[41] In this case, the birds recorded too well, mimicking not only the notes of the desired melody but also the specific timbre of an out-of-tune serinette, and sound professionals complained about excessive sonic definition.

The goal of many nineteenth-century training techniques was to produce an ideal bird called a "roller" canary. Rollers had several desirable qualities, the first of which was a "sweet, round, and full" tone, with no loud, harsh, short, or choppy notes.[42] The roller's song was valued for its length and variety, with the goal being a sound "like an endless stream."[43] One author wrote that the best canaries displayed "great variety and compass," their voices "now high and clear and sweet, then deep, low, resonant, inspiring. There are light and shade, foreground of brilliancy, and distant, subdued effects, but all one glorious masterpiece of song."[44] Some of the roller's various sonic effects were given names: the Bell Tour was reminiscent of "a little tinkling silver bell"; the Water Gluck was similar to "a little drop of water falling into water"; and the Water Roll was akin to "the gurgling, rushing, bubbling of a tiny brook, whirling and eddying over its pebbly shallows."[45] The earlier reference to "subdued effects" is indicative of a desire to create birds that produced mellow, soft, or relaxing sounds. St. Andreasberg canaries were said to be excellent gifts for sick or bedridden friends because their voices were so comforting and restful. One popular handbook explained that the song of a St. Andreasberg canary soothed "both mind and body," lifting the listener into "an Arcadia of rustling wings and entrancing melody."[46] Finally, the best roller canaries had been trained so thoroughly that they retained their recorded song for a long time.[47]

The sounds produced by roller canaries were well designed for their intended destination in middle-class homes. The urbanization and industrialization of the late nineteenth century had produced a new soundscape that sparked concern about the noise of modern life. Middle-class commentators and reformers hoped that the interior of the bourgeois home could be "a safe haven from a harsh world," in which one could "escape urban realities and attain a degree of separation and self-definition."[48] The St. Andreasberg canary's song was associated with the European countryside, pure air and clean water, bubbling brooks, tinkling bells, and the peaceful, evening tones of the nightingale and so harmonized with dominant notions of a tranquil domestic space. Caged canaries were organismal technologies that produced ambient music in the home, and they were prized by middle-class pet owners in part as an antidote to the noise of urban crowds, streetcars, construction, and street vendors.

Though the songbirds' final destination was in the private sphere, the trade had, by the mid-1800s, become a major public enterprise, and the Bell Tours and Water Glucks of roller canaries became part of the soundscape of major American cities like New York. German bird dealers began to send large numbers of canaries to New York on steam-powered ships around 1850. Few birds survived the transatlantic journey on sailing vessels, but steamships conveyed the animals "with speed and safety, and dealers were quick to avail themselves of the changed conditions."[49] One report claimed that ten thousand German canaries were brought to the United States in

1853, and sixty thousand in 1871. The U.S. market took an estimated hundred thousand birds a year by 1893. That number continued to rise between 1906 and 1916, with an average of three hundred thousand birds arriving on American soil annually.[50] German roller canaries were the most prestigious feathered imports, and Germans dominated the retail trade: an author noted in 1873 that if one were to investigate the ownership of New York City's bird emporiums, one would find that "everywhere it is the Germans who are found among the birds."[51]

The connection between German birds and German retailers reminds us that the mass immigration of European songbirds was occurring at the same time as the mass immigration of European people. Late nineteenth-century European immigrants brought their taste in music as well as their taste in birds, and the former had a marked effect on the early phonograph industry. William Howland Kenney argues that records served as "commercialized musical memories" for immigrants and that ethnic music functioned to maintain and reinforce "Old World values."[52] Kenney points to the market for opera records among Italian immigrants, but a similar argument could be made about roller canaries. Consider that the best roller canaries, those that were used as instructor birds, were sometimes referred to as "Campanini Canaries." "Campanini" was a reference to the opera singer Italo Campanini, a famous Italian tenor who toured Europe and America during the 1870s. Roller canaries and bel canto opera singers had much in common: both were praised for the clarity, consistency, and purity of their vocal tone; both were sonic souvenirs for an immigrant population; and both were beneficiaries of the "sacralization" of European classical music in late nineteenth-century America.[53]

Italo Campanini died in 1896, and his voice is not known to have been preserved by the phonograph. Campanini may not have recorded, but Campanini canaries had been recording in American parlors for many years. They established a niche in the domestic soundscape that would later be filled by sound technologies like the phonograph and records produced by Campanini's successor, Enrico Caruso.[54] An 1892 book on cage birds made an explicit comparison between opera singers and canaries: "among the musicians who come to our shores to charm us with their notes, the largest orchestra is that of the singing birds. They require very little of our money, and never demand an opera house as the only theatre worthy of their performance. A few dollars will buy one of these sweet singers, and a few more will build or buy an opera house for his performances."[55] This passage suggests that trained canaries could be understood as little opera singers performing in miniature opera houses during the decades before a similar rhetoric of "opera in the home" became a common trope of phonograph marketing. The contact zone between birds and the phonograph extended beyond the cultural field of opera, however, and in the next section we will listen to another type of recorded performance that tied a knot between birds, humans, and sound technology. We begin to unravel the twists and turns of that knot by attending to another origin story, this one recounting the birth of a song.

WHISTLERS

In 1855 a songwriter was sitting in his parlor, listening to the song of a neighbor's caged mockingbird. To his surprise, a second bird joined in the refrain. Captivated by the beautiful duet, he rushed outside to better appreciate the music and was shocked to discover that the second bird was in fact a "diminutive Negro boy" whistling along with the mockingbird's song. Inspired by this occurrence, the songwriter composed a tune for the boy to sing and whistle. The songwriter in this narrative was Septimus Winner, and the song that he composed was "Listen to the Mockingbird," one of the most popular compositions of the last half of the nineteenth century.[56]

The "Listen to the Mockingbird" origin story has the same mythic quality of "perceptible absence" as the popular narrative of the canary's arrival in Europe. In the words of a writer for an African American newspaper, a "shadow" seems to linger in the story. In fact, it resembles accounts of the origins of American minstrel-show routines that describe moments when "black sounds" fill the air and "fascinated white men understand for the first time that there is fame and money to be made."[57] As with those narratives, the "Mockingbird" origin story is intended to establish a white artist's authorship, but, as we look closer, the singular author fragments as if in a hall of mirrors. Winner published the song under the pen name "Alice Hawthorne," but the first edition of the sheet music from 1855 also gives credit to Richard Milburn, an African American street performer who worked in Philadelphia during the same years when Winner was a resident. Milburn was known as "Whistling Dick," and, by some accounts, he not only specialized in the whistled imitation of mockingbirds but composed the melody of "Listen to the Mockingbird" and performed it for many residents of the city. The *New York Amsterdam News* claimed that Winner simply transcribed Milburn's melody in exchange for five dollars. This would explain why the first edition of the sheet music gives the credit as "Melody by Richard Milburn, words and music by Alice Hawthorne." Subsequent editions of the sheet music refer only to Hawthorne.[58]

The origin story of "Listen to the Mockingbird" alludes to Milburn's role in the song's genesis but transforms him from a renowned adult performer to a diminutive "boy." The story works, then, to distort and obscure an American musical culture in which white middlemen like Winner claimed ownership of cultural material through their knowledge of musical notation and the economics of music publishing, areas of expertise that were, at that time, more easily accessible to white, middle-class, urban people.[59] By contrast, Milburn's talent for whistling relied on what Raymond Williams calls "immediate human physical resources" and so did not require large investments of capital. In the words of a 1910 essayist, "the human whistle is the most delightfully informal of instruments."[60] A working-class African American street performer in 1855 may have lacked the capital necessary to acquire the training and equipment needed to advance in the field of music publishing or classical music but could, with dedication and talent, become a skilled whistler. The "Listen to the Mockingbird" origin story prompts us to appreciate the whistle as a no-wattage minimal medium of sonic communication.

Whistling Dick may not have had Winner's skills of musical notation or access to the sheet-music publishing industry, but if his career had continued to the turn of the century, he might have made an end run around them both and brought his whistling talent to a national audience through the medium of recorded sound. Another African American street performer did just that. Thirty-five years after Winner first published "Listen to the Mockingbird," George Washington Johnson, the first African American recording artist, released whistling records that were some of the earliest blockbusters of the phonograph industry.[61] Johnson was born in Virginia in the 1840s and after the Civil War moved to New York, where he became a street musician. Like Richard Milburn, Johnson was known for his whistling skill, and his repertoire included "Listen to the Mockingbird." He was hired by the New Jersey Phonograph Company in 1890 and began a remarkably successful career as a recording artist. Johnson is best known for "The Laughing Song," but his other signature tune was a number titled "The Whistling Coon," which was written in the racist "coon song" style by the vaudeville performer Sam Devere.[62]

Both "The Laughing Song" and "The Whistling Coon" juxtapose verses of Johnson singing painfully racist lyrics with choruses in which Johnson leaves the realm of spoken language to perform ecstatic vocalizations, either laughter or whistling. Johnson's records enact a distinction made by Lindon Barrett between a "signing voice" associated with Euro-American culture, whiteness, literacy, and disembodiment and a "singing voice" often understood as the site of embodiment and blackness.[63] Johnson's best-selling records perform the singing/signing distinction through their verse-chorus structure and thereby work within the limited stylistic options available to African American performers at this time while simultaneously struggling to transcend them. Johnson's records were extremely successful and helped to forge a strong association between whistling and minstrel stereotypes, as can be heard on Edison recordings such as Dan W. Quinn's "Whistling Rufus" (1902); S. H. Dudley's "The Merry Whistling Darkey" (1907); Billy Golden and Joe Hughes's "Whistling Pete" (1911); and Ada Jones's "Whistling Jim" (1913).

The proliferation of whistlers on early phonograph catalogs may have been encouraged by Johnson's success and the lingering popularity of the minstrel show, but it was also a mode of performance that was well suited to the strengths and limitations of acoustic-era phonography. As noted in the previous chapter, performers during the early decades of the phonograph industry often had to record their material again and again. The human voice tends to fail or crack after extended use due to exhaustion or illness, but the whistle is a remarkably resilient and durable mode of expression. Professional whistlers boasted of their ability to deliver a flawless performance even when stricken with a severe head cold that would sideline a singer. Moreover, the whistle's loud volume and high pitch complemented acoustic recording's "limited frequency range and need for bright and directed tones."[64] Amateur recordists were encouraged to begin their experiments by making a whistling record: "there is no doubt," wrote the author of a popular guide to home recording, "that one of the easiest sounds to record is that of whistling."[65]

The whistle thus provided a sturdy interface between human performers and the technological affordances of the acoustic era, but it was also a contact zone between humans and birds. In fact, if we listen again to "The Whistling Coon" we will hear that Johnson's exuberant choruses feature the trills and piping of birds. In other words, apart from being a singer and whistler, Johnson is a talented bird mimic. His whistling skills are best heard on a haunting solo performance of "Listen to the Mockingbird," recorded for Berliner in 1896.[66] Johnson begins with the melody of the well-known song but elongates and distorts it, sometimes looping and repeating short phrases, other times dropping it entirely in a flurry of birdcalls. Despite these frequent shifts in register, the performance has a powerful rhythmic momentum that Johnson creates using only his whistle. The groove is so assured, in fact, that by the middle of the record, Johnson omits notes from the melody while still implying them, creating the illusion that he is performing a duet with himself. We might say that Johnson's "Listen to the Mockingbird" allows the "singing voice" free reign, while also blending together the voices of Winner, Milburn, Johnson, and even the mockingbird in a display of what the literary theorist M.M. Bakhtin might call "a genuine polyphony of fully valid voices."[67]

The fact that Johnson includes birdcalls in his polyphonic phonography reminds us that while whistling is a mode of communication available to most humans regardless of social class, it is also a mode of zoosemiotic communication that humans share with birds. With that in mind, recall the scene described in the origin story of "Listen to the Mockingbird": Septimus Winner stands in shock at the sight of a caged mockingbird and a young boy whistling together. Whatever legitimating functions this story might be serving, it is also a parable of cross-species communication along the lines of "His Master's Voice" and "Cat and the Canary." By this reading, the whistle functions like Nipper's phonograph or the Sylvania television set as a medium that brings different species into dialogue.[68] Johnson's version of "Listen to the Mockingbird" encourages us to recognize the bird's active participation in the scene, which, in turn, makes questions of authorship even more complicated. Mockingbirds are, after all, open-ended learners known for their acts of mimicry. Perhaps the caged mockingbird that Winner overheard was whistling a tune that had been "recorded" onto it by someone playing a recorder or serinette. Maybe the mockingbird's song contained imitations of other songbirds in the area, or even melodies that it had heard being performed by Richard Milburn on the streets of Philadelphia.

What is certain is that Winner and Milburn's "Listen to the Mockingbird" became a staple of early record-industry catalogs, and though Eldridge Johnson compared the early gramophone to a partially educated parrot, many consumers first experienced it as a whistling mockingbird. George Washington Johnson's successor as the premiere professional whistler of the phonograph industry was Joseph Belmont, who was born in Shamokin, Pennsylvania, in 1876. He began whistling and playing piano on the stage as a teenager and was sometimes billed as the "Human Bird." Belmont made his first records for Columbia in 1894, and by 1900 he was established as "one of the most popular of all recording artists."[69] Several phonograph records depict his stage act. *The Robin and the Wren* (Edison, 1914) begins with a short orchestral vamp followed by the sounds of an audience applauding, prompting listeners to assume that they are hearing a vaudeville performer taking the stage. Belmont announces, "many in my audiences believe I have something in my mouth with which I produce my bird imitations." He assures the crowd that this is not the case and even invites an audience member onto the stage to verify his assertions. Belmont explains that he whistles by placing his tongue against his front teeth, then gives a demonstration. With these preparatory comments out of the way, Belmont launches into the heart of his act, which consists of alternating spoken announcements and whistled bird imitations. On the record *Bird Imitations* (Edison and Lambert, 1902), we hear Belmont's impressions of a whip-poor-will, wren, robin, canary, and mockingbird.

Before I say more about Belmont's records, recall that in the previous chapter I referred to the early phonograph mimic Gilbert Girard as an avatar of the plasmatic qualities of phonography. Girard's records were eco-sonic, I argued, because they acknowledged recorded sound's reliance on plastic. Girard's records are also pertinent to the concerns of the present chapter because they feature performances of cross-species mimicry. Girard was best known for his ability to aurally morph into animals. Publicity images show his head on the body of a dog, and press accounts describe his conversations with zoo animals, referring to him as the "phonograph menagerie." A 1923 story in the *New York Tribune*, titled "The Man Who Comes Nearest to Dr. Dolittle," describes Girard as "the talking machine linguist in furred and feathered languages" who has a "speaking acquaintance with the birds and animals of the Bronx Zoo and the Central Park menagerie." An accompanying illustration shows Girard sitting on a chair in a large cage, cupping his ear to listen to a crowd of animals around him. The caption reads, "The talking machine linguist takes an oral language lesson from his friends of the Bronx Zoo."[70]

Girard's records put the plasmatic quality of phonography in the service of cross-species transformation, as did Joseph Belmont's quick change between spoken announcements and bird whistles. George Washington Johnson's "Listen to the Mockingbird" features a polyphonic blend of voices, but Belmont's records—and those of many subsequent mimics—use two formal strategies to separate bird and human vocalization. The first of these formal patterns is a sonic captioning whereby human language labels the nonlinguistic whistle that follows. "A robin chirps through the day like this," Belmont says, and pipes a happy tune. "In the evening, this way," and he follows with a rolling chirp. The final sequence of Belmont's 1902 recording *Bird Imitations* works in a different way, however. Belmont announces that he will depict the "various sounds in a bird store when a street piano plays in front of the door" and then recreates that soundscape with whistled chirps and a rollicking piano accompaniment.[71] The bird store sequence of *Bird Imitations* depicts a multispecies collaboration that involves not the alternation of human language and aural image but instead the sonic superimposition of birdsong and human music.[72] The aural world of birds is superim-

FIGURE 5. The animal mimic Gilbert Girard, master of the plasmatic possibilities of phonography.© Victoria and Albert Museum, London.

posed onto the aural world of humans, but those worlds are kept separate in that they do not emanate from the same performer's body. We might say that sonic captioning polices the temporal boundaries of bird and human vocalization, and sonic superimposition polices the spatial boundaries, the latter allowing for the simultaneity of music and birdcalls, albeit not produced by the same throat.

Belmont's sonic superimposition of birdcalls and music can be heard on a Victor record that was one of the first discs to be pressed with content on both sides. This 1909 release is "double-sided" in more ways than one. There are grooves on both sides of the disc, of course, but the two sides also feature different traditions of turn-of-the-century whistling as well as different protocols of gender display. On side A, Belmont warbles "The Birds and the Brook" with the Victor Orchestra. Side B features the song "In Venice" as whistled by Alice J. Shaw, the first celebrated female whistler. I have drawn on Raymond Williams's notion of "immediate human resources" to describe the whistle as a mode of communication available to everyone, but Jan Radway urges caution when taking certain bodily resources as "unproblematic schema for discriminating cultural forms that are somehow more fundamental or popular."[73] Some modes of communication, like the whistle, may require less training and capital than others, but none are outside of the realm of social power. Nineteenth-century African American performers might have felt compelled to whistle to comply with racist stereotypes and stage conventions. Nineteenth-century women, on the other hand, were often denied access to that communicative resource.

The prevailing wisdom on the subject of female whistlers at this time was summarized in the well-known proverb, "Whistling girls and crowing hens, always come to some bad ends." The proverb conjures another cross-species duet, this time for the purposes of naturalizing and enforcing gender norms. Only roosters should crow, the saying suggests, and only men should whistle, with "whistle" standing in for any kind of assertive or public vocalization. The "whistling girls" proverb hints at the consequences that could follow for women who disregarded gendered norms of communication. Just as noisy hens were likely to be the first on the chopping block, so women were reminded of the violence that could result from being too vocal. In 1924 a middle-aged woman recalled hearing the proverb frequently as a young girl and feeling afraid that her head would be chopped off if she were caught whistling.[74]

Despite the prevalence of this proverb and the threat that it implied, an "epidemic" of whistling spread among American women during the last decades of the nineteenth century.[75] The aforementioned Alice J. Shaw, also known as "La Belle Siffleuse," had much to do with this craze for female whistlers. A writer for *Harper's New Monthly Magazine* was almost certainly thinking of Shaw when he wrote that, contrary to popular expectations, a certain "whistling girl" had not come to a bad end but instead was "a girl of spirit, of independence of character, of dash and flavor," and whistling had brought her money and "blown her name about the listening world. Scarcely has a non-whistling woman been more famous."[76] Shaw was born Alice Horton in Elmira, New York, and described herself as something of a nonconformist. "I was regarded as a good deal of a tomboy," she said, "and could toss a ball or fly a kite with the best of them." She also loved to whistle and drove her mother "all but distracted" by whistling about the house.[77]

Compelled to provide income for her family, Alice took the advice of society friends and began to study music with a well-regarded Italian music instructor who cultivated her whistling. She made her first public appearance in 1886 as part of the entertainment at a teachers' association event and was such a success that she was asked to perform at Steinway's Hall in New York City.[78] Soon thereafter she became the talk of high society. In April 1887 she traveled to England, where she whistled at concert halls and private gatherings before notable figures such as Sir Arthur Sullivan and the Prince and Princess of Wales. On her return to the States, she made a number of well-publicized appearances and garnered considerable press coverage. A reviewer who heard her at the Music Hall in Cincinnati wrote that "she puckered up her lips and the first note was as pure as liquid gold."[79] She was very popular with female audiences, many of whom began to emulate her. By one account, Shaw's fame had exercised "a wonderful effect upon the young women of New York," and a writer in Boston claimed that, thanks to Shaw, "it is no longer considered vulgar for a woman to whistle, so young ladies are now giving up the mandolin and devoting their leisure hours to learning to whistle familiar melodies to a piano accompaniment."[80]

Shaw went on to have a long career on the variety stage, in later years performing with her twin daughters, Ethel and Elsie. The "liquid gold" of Shaw's whistle was also poured into the grooves of phonograph records. In fact, Shaw was making recordings before either George Washington Johnson or Joseph Belmont. While on a tour of England in 1888, Shaw attended a party where Thomas Edison's London representative, George Gouraud, was exhibiting the second phonograph machine to be sent from America. Shaw's whistling was recorded onto a cylinder and played back "with astonishing accuracy." A reporter present at the event observed that the device benefited from the fact that Shaw's whistle had a louder and "more intense character" than either speech or song, another example of the whistle's privileged status in early phonography.[81] In subsequent years Shaw made popular records for Edison and Victor, such as the double-sided record described earlier, where we can hear her elegant, precise style, which some critics praised for its rejection of the kind of bird mimicry and promotional ballyhoo associated with the popular stage. Shaw was said to have made whistling "an art that would stand or fall upon the plain and simple question of musical merit. She relied upon no adjuncts of variety show mimicry or trickery; she depended not upon society favor or managerial booming."[82]

Shaw and subsequent female whistlers should be added to histories of turn-of-the-century women's culture as well as sound culture, since they were successful performers and recording artists who expanded the range of permissible female vocalization. The "racy, modern, whistling girl" might be seen as the phonographic equivalent of the cinematic serial queen, since both utilized the modern media to intervene in performance traditions commonly considered to be the province of men.[83] Shaw managed that intervention by emphasizing her classical music credentials and downplaying any similarity to vaudeville bird mimicry, but she was described in avian terms nonetheless.[84] Her whistling was often compared to birdsong, as when a Boston reviewer declared that Shaw made the music hall where she appeared echo "with the flute-like notes of the woods and the meadows when birds fill the air with joyous song." A London reviewer claimed that Shaw had a "whole aviary" in her mouth and mused that her soul had previously inhabited a nightingale that had been "brought up in a family of thrushes, with a bevy of quails upstairs, and a cluster of canaries over the way."[85] In the wake of Shaw's success, another female whistler was inspired to open a school of artistic whistling that synthesized Belmont's bird mimicry and Shaw's concert hall performances.

Like Alice Shaw, Agnes Woodward liked to whistle as a girl but gave it up under pressure from her parents. After her father died, Woodward moved with her sick mother to Los Angeles, where she rediscovered her childhood talent and established the California School of Artistic Whistling. Her school attracted female students as well as national press coverage, and she outlined her teaching method in the 1923 book, *Whistling as an Art*. Woodward begins her book with the assertion that whistling is both an art and an educational tool that aids the study of bird life.[86] In fact, Woodward developed her method through the close observation of birds. After arriving in Los Angeles, she spent many days roaming the California foothills and canyons, delighted by the "music of the birds." She became so interested in birds and their songs that she rented a shack in the mountains, where she began to annotate birdcalls and learn to whistle them.[87] Such was the genesis of the Woodward Method of Bird Whistling, which integrated birdsong into musical compositions through a system of graphic notation that utilized onomatopoeia, alphabetic writing, musical scores, and linear depictions of sound that resemble the grooves on a phonograph record.[88]

Woodward preserved the sounds of birds with her written method, but she did not make any phonographic recordings of her own whistling. Her star pupil did, however, and continued Woodward's engagement with bird life. Margaret McKee joined Woodward's school as a young girl and was making public appearances by the time she was fifteen.[89] One press account declared that McKee was "born with an innate love of nature and especially bird life," and as a child she had attracted notice for her bird imitations. "She would go out alone for hours into the fields and the woods and listen to the chirp and song of her feathered friends, returning home with their calls and songs in absolute imitation."[90] She was given the title "Queen of the Whistlers" by the world-renowned actress Sarah Bernhardt, who was impressed by her rendition of "Listen to the Mockingbird." During a public concert in 1919, she performed a whistling solo titled "Woodland Songsters," which the program declared would allow listeners to hear "the spring songsters warbling, trilling, chuckling, calling to each other from out of the leafy groves and answering in love-notes from distant boughs."[91] McKee made a number of records for Victor in the early 1920s, such as *Tweet, Tweet* (1923), *The Boy and the Birds* (1923), and *The Whistler and His Dog* (1925), and was the subject of a Warner Brothers Vitaphone sound film in 1927.[92]

Woodward and McKee wedded artistic whistling to the study of the natural world, but they were not the only women hiking through the American countryside in pursuit of birds at this time. In fact, their engagement with avifauna should be placed in the context of women's role in the bird conservation movement.[93] Though early conservation is most typically associated with men like Theodore Roosevelt and John Muir, and with public debates about the National Parks and the protection of the American bison, a crucial factor in raising public awareness about the preservation of wildlife at the end of the nineteenth century was concern about the use of bird feathers as decoration on women's hats.

By the 1880s hundreds of thousands of birds had been killed to provide feathers, wings, and bodies to the hat industry.[94] Public concern over the slaughter of birds for their plumes led to the mobilization of the first bird-protection organizations. George Bird Grinnell founded the Audubon Society in 1886, and a special issue of the journal *Science* that year called for the protection of native birds. Women were central to the rhetoric of the movement because of their consumption of hats. An essay in the 1886 issue of *Science* declared that women held the power to determine the fate of birds through their consumer choices: "Let our women say the word, and hundreds of thousands of bird-lives every year will be preserved."[95]

Women were the target of the movement's rhetoric, but they were also key players in creating it, especially in its second phase. Grinnell's Audubon Society faltered in the 1890s, but was reenergized by regional Audubon Societies, which were often formed by women. One of the first local Audubon chapters was organized at the all-female Smith College, where hundreds of women took part in nature walks and renounced the wearing of feathers.[96] The influential Massachusetts Audubon society was founded in 1896 by Harriet Hemenway, a Boston socialite and philanthropist. Hemenway had been shocked by an account of Florida herons killed for their plumes, and she worked to turn Boston society women against wearing feathered hats.[97] Mabel Osgood Wright helped to create the Connecticut Audubon Society and later became an associate editor for the Audubon magazine *Bird-Lore*, as well as the author of the popular guide, *Birdcraft* (1895), which was reprinted nine times.[98] Many middle- and upper-class American women took part in bird clubs, local Audubon Societies, school "bird days," and bird-observation field trips, with the goal being to stimulate enthusiasm for "living rather than dead plumage."[99]

Female whistlers and birdsong enthusiasts like Woodward and McKee add an audio dimension to this era of conservation history. Birdsong took on a certain rhetorical weight in the bird-protection movement since it was an index of the beauty provided by living animals as opposed to the visual beauty of dead ones displayed as a hat or trophy. An influential early critique of the hat trade appeared in *Harper's Bazaar* in 1875 and referred to the birds on women's hats as "only ghosts of birds, mute warblers, little captives deprived of life and light and song."[100] In the famous 1886 issue of *Science*, an aesthetic argument for preserving birds was based on their grace in movement and their "melodious voices."[101] The movement sponsored bird-related events, organizations, and educational initiatives that created new opportunities for bird-friendly performers, and bird mimics and artistic whistlers filled that niche admirably.

A number of male whistlers combined the message of conservation with their talents. Among them, Edward Avis and Charles Crawford Gorst performed under the auspices of the National Audubon Society, the Burroughs Nature Club, and fund-raising initiatives to save the passenger pigeon.[102] Avis was born Martin E. Sullivan in 1873 in Enfield, Connecticut, and, like McKee, developed a keen appreciation of nature as a child, with birds a particular interest. According to one account, the young Sullivan would go into the woods with his violin and strike up a chorus with the birds.[103] By the early 1910s he was making appearances as a bird mimic in New England under the name "Edward Avis," and press coverage sometimes referred to him as "The Bird Man."[104] Gorst was also said to be captivated by birds as a boy and learned to sing their songs "so perfectly that the little songsters would answer and fly to him." Gorst studied ornithology in college and joined the American Ornithologists' Union, one of the first organizations to recognize the threat that human society posed to birdlife. During postgraduate work, Gorst's public performances of whistling and bird mimicry became so successful that he made it his vocation.[105]

Gorst and Avis combined birdcalls with projected images of birds in their natural habitat. Gorst displayed his own pastel paintings of birds in illustrated lectures on "bird anatomy and habits," which he accompanied with fifty different birdsongs.[106] Avis projected photographs and motion pictures of birds. He would "throw a forest scene on the canvas, locating different birds on opposite sides of the picture, and then most perfectly mimic their answering voices as they sang to each other."[107] Despite this visual component, Avis was primarily an aural artist, and in one number he depicted a peewee singing in unison with the organ of a country church, whistling the part of the peewee and simultaneously imitating the organ on his violin in an act of sonic superimposition. Avis also impressed audiences with aural effects that produced the illusion of spatial depth, as when he used variations in volume to depict a meadowlark receding into the distance.[108]

Reviews suggest that Avis's audiences frequently had the sensation of being transported from the city into natural spaces. One reviewer claimed that Avis took the audience "into the very midst of the forest and meadowland"; another that the lecture hall was transformed into "the edge of the forest enchanted"; and a third declared that attending Avis's recital was "like going out into the country and wandering through green fields and along the banks of gently flowing streams."[109] These quotes demonstrate that Avis's birdcalls, like the sounds of the roller canary, conjured an imaginary natural environment that served as an antidote to urban living. Avis's act also shows that birdsong functioned as a temporal architecture for many turn-of-the-century Americans. A 1916 program indicates that Avis organized his birdcalls according to particular times of day, with sections dedicated to "twilight hymns," "morning concert," "Noonday concert," "Vesper songs," and "Nocturnal sounds."[110] Avis's stage performances indicate the range of meaning that could be conveyed by birdcalls at the turn of the century: they were aural anchors to natural spaces, keynotes that situated listeners in a temporal architecture of shared experience, and signs of familiar aural personalities that were communicative resources for performers and audiences.[111]

Given all of that, it is not surprising that the phonograph industry was interested in marketing the vocal talents of performers like Gorst and Avis. Gorst made records for Edison and Victor between 1914 and 1916, and Columbia Records released several Avis performances in 1919–20. Many of Gorst's and Avis's records feature the kind of sonic captioning heard on Joseph Belmont's discs, with spoken announcements followed by whistled imitations of native birds. Avis adapted this structure to the form of an illustrated children's book on a record made in collaboration with Howard R. Garis, the creator of the Uncle Wiggly books. Titled *Bird Calls with Story*, Garis narrates the tale of the rabbit Uncle Wiggly, while Avis provides aural illustrations of a robin, whippoorwill, oriole, and cricket. Phonograph records also captured Avis's depth illusions, as when he announces, "The robin sings his evening song from the top of a tall tree," and then gives a loud whistle. "Another robin answers from a distance," he says, and a quieter whistle gives the impression of distance. The title of Avis's record, *An Evening in Birdland* (1920), indicates that the temporal architecture of birdsong was imported to the medium of phonography as well. On that disc Avis enacts a "woodland concert" given from sunset until nightfall, featuring all the "familiar sounds in the woods at the close of a day in June." Record-industry marketing of this era frequently claimed that records could transform the listener's living room into a concert hall. *An Evening in Birdland* transformed the listener's living room into "the edge of the forest enchanted" through the performance of sounds with visceral ties to specific times, places, and seasons ("the woods at the close of a day in June").

Records like Avis's *Birdland Melodies* and *An Evening in Birdland* aimed to foster an appreciation of the natural world and relied on the close observation of animals. The cross-fertilization of wildlife conservation and bird mimicry was even more explicit in the career of another phonographic whistler of this era. Charles Kellogg was born in 1869 in Spanish Ranch, California, located in the scenic Sierra Nevadas. Kellogg portrayed himself as a "child of nature" who had been raised by "a faithful Indian squaw" and claimed to have spent his youth roaming the woods and learning about the natural world from the Paiutes who lived in the area. This upbringing made him, according to one reporter, "a white woods creature who could hear and see things other whites could not."[112]

Kellogg's public persona as a "white woods creature" took shape in the decade just prior to the release of the book *Tarzan of the Apes* (1912), and, like Edgar Rice Burroughs's iconic hero, Kellogg presented himself as a "nature man" who had learned the language of animals. Kellogg described his love of listening to birds and insects as a youth and even claimed to talk to them "in their own language." In a 1911 interview he stated that he had created a dictionary of the language of the hearth cricket.[113] Whatever the extent of Kellogg's cross-species communication, it is certain that he channeled his intimate knowledge of wildlife into a stage performance that brought him national recognition. Kellogg began his career as a performer on the Chautauqua circuit in the 1890s and was appearing on the vaudeville stage by the early 1910s, where he combined bird imitations with the enactment of traditional skills like starting a fire by rubbing two sticks together.[114]

Other bird mimics were billed as the "Bird Man" or the "Human Bird," but Kellogg was depicted in the press as an actual physiological hybrid, born with a bird's syrinx in addition to human vocal cords.[115] A promotional program for one of his appearances explained that nature had selected Kellogg for his work, for at the age of three he discovered that he was endowed with the "unique and famous gift of bird warbling." Scientists had measured the vibrations of his bird-tones, the promotional text continued, and determined that he had "a range of over ten octaves, three higher than the human ear can appreciate." Those higher vibrations were said to be intelligible to birds, meaning that Kellogg's vocalizations were "not what might be called imitations, but *reproductions,* for to all appearances the methods and results are identical with those of the birds."[116] "I do *not* imitate the birds," Kellogg told an interviewer. "I sing bird songs, because I have the vocal apparatus of a bird."[117]

There is certainly an element of Barnum-esque ballyhoo to such claims, but Kellogg had the respect of well-regarded nature conservationists. He was friends and traveling companions with the famous naturalist, writer, and Sierra Club founder John Muir, as well as with the popular nature writer John Burroughs.[118] Kellogg spoke about his desire to spread "a love for nature and the great outdoors." "There are thousands and thousands who dwell in the great cities who hardly know the appearance of a green field, of a copse or of a woodland stream," he told a Minneapolis newspaper in 1913. "There are thousands who are utterly ignorant of bird lore: utterly ignorant of nature's varying moods." "I come into the artificial atmosphere of a theater," he said, "because I feel that I have a message for these people."[119] Passages of his 1930 autobiography articulate a proto-ecological sensibility, as when he describes trees as "living, breathing, life-holding, moisture-holding creatures to bless the earth" or urges campers not to kill snakes but to appreciate them as "silent workers" who balance the insect and rodent population.[120]

Kellogg's intermingling of self-promotion and conservation is perhaps best embodied in the unusual vehicle that he referred to as his "travel log." Brokenhearted at the "terrible devastation" that the lumber industry had wrought on California forests, Kellogg determined to convey the "greatness and beauty" of those forests to the world so that "all could help in saving them." Since the world could not come to the forest, Kellogg took the forest to the world in the form of a twenty-two-foot, thirty-six-ton section of a giant redwood tree that he hollowed out and put on the back of a Nash Quad truck. Kellogg equipped his travel log with a closet, kitchen, lavatory, beds, electric lights, running water, and a fireplace, and he and his wife, Sandi, took this "motor house" on a tour of the 162 cities on the Keith and Orpheum vaudeville circuit. Everywhere he went, he used his act as a means to spread the message, "Save the Redwoods."[121]

Kellogg's message of conservation was circulated to the nation in the form of his quirky travel log, and his bird "reproductions" were circulated to the nation on his equally quirky phonograph records. Kellogg was eager to bring his talents to the phonograph and even made the fantastic claim that he had made his first recordings of wild California birds in 1892, using the thorn of a rose to record onto the skin of an onion.[122] Like Edward Avis, Kellogg tended to situate his birdcalls in specific times and places. *Songs of Our Native Birds* (Victor, 1915) prefaces the sound of the cardinal with Kellogg's statement that it is the "first bird voice that greets me in the spring of the year," and before the loon we are told that it is best heard "from over the lake on a moonlit night." Like Belmont, Gorst, and Avis, Kellogg structured his records with the back and forth of sonic captioning, but he mobilized that form in novel ways. *Sounds of the Forest* (Victor 1917) extends the conventional bird mimic repertoire to include crickets, frogs, and the "love note" of the moose. One sequence of the record uses sonic captioning to classify several different expressions of animal emotion. "Who that hears can doubt that the creatures all about us can voice emotions as varied as those of the human heart," he announces and then demonstrates the point by imitating a baby chicken's vocalizations of contentment and fear.

Kellogg tends to enact sonic captioning, but only to break down the boundaries that the form creates between spoken announcement and aural image. In his autobiography, he described visiting a marsh on the Gulf of Mexico, where he took part in "bird conversations." "As they talked back and forth, one to another, with their raucous voices," he wrote, "I imagined they were telling stories to each other ... every time a bird would say something that sounded like real words, I would say the same thing, and they would seem to understand and answer back."[123] Kellogg integrated this experience into his stage act, as can be heard on *Songs of Our Native Birds*. He begins the sequence by explaining that through "easy imagination," one can understand the language of marsh birds, and then he proceeds to introduce various birdcalls with their linguistic approximations: "watch out, watch out," "what for," "well, well, well," "come over here," "I want to come home." Kellogg's record strives to make birds understandable through an act of intentional anthropomorphism cultivated as a deliberate strategy for communicating with the nonhuman world, and, like George Washington Johnson's "Listen to the Mockingbird," Kellogg's is a plasmatic and polyphonic phonography that creates a vocal bridge between human language and birdcalls.[124]

The marsh sequence of *Songs of Our Native Birds* presents bird vocalization through the filter of human speech, but another recorded sequence disarticulates birdcalls from human meaning entirely. Toward the end of *Sounds of the Forest*, Kellogg describes the strange sounds heard at nighttime in a marsh, each of which conveys a "marshland intelligence" to another creature. Rejecting the conventional approach to sonic captioning, he declares, "I shall not name the call, but give it, to play upon your imagination." What follows is a wild cacophony of vocal effects with no spoken captions. Roland Barthes characterizes written captions as a "parasitical message" that burdens the photographic image, loading it with "a culture, a morality, an imagination."[125] Following Barthes, one might argue that the tradition of bird mimicry embodied by Belmont, Gorst, and Avis yoked the aural image of birds to the domain of human speech. The end of *Sounds of the Forest* presents an aural image unmoored from human language in a sonic depiction of wilderness in which birdsong is recognized as a language but allowed to remain untranslated.

Sounds of the Forest is certainly an exceptional case, but the entire genre of recorded whistling and bird mimicry is eco-sonic when it emerges from the observation of and interaction with birds and aims to foster a deeper appreciation of them. The 1910s were the golden age of phonographic whistlers and bird imitators, when record catalogs listed numerous "Whistling Records," "Records with Whistling Effects," and "Records with Bird Effects."[126] It has become a truism that the phonograph replaced the piano and pianola in American homes, but the phonographic aviary of the 1910s suggests that the recorded-sound industry also found ways to substitute for the everyday pleasures of listening to birdsong. During the acoustic era, the phonograph was a "whistling machine" almost as much as it was a "talking machine," but records tended to present the "technical echo" of birds as performed by human stand-ins. In the late 1920s, new electric technologies allowed birds to speak for themselves.

CHOPPERS

Joseph Belmont's career as the foremost whistler of the early phonograph industry was brought to an abrupt end when a dentist in Australia carelessly filed away part of his front tooth. Determined to remain in show business, Belmont purchased a troupe of twenty-three birds and trained them to sing on command, returning to the stage as the director of a "canary opera." Belmont's new act appeared in the 1929 Ziegfeld's Follies, and that same year Columbia released a record of *Joe Belmont's Group of Real Feathered Songsters*. The Columbia record picks up where the "various sounds in a bird store" sequence on his *Bird Imitations* record of twenty-five years earlier had left off. Recall how that sequence had featured the sonic superimposition of birds and a street piano. The 1929 *Real Feathered Songsters* record is entirely in the mode of sonic superimposition, with the chirps of Belmont's canaries layered over a delicate piano that plays a medley of popular songs, including, of course, "Listen to the Mockingbird."[127]

Belmont's career makeover from bird imitator to bird trainer occurred during the decade when acoustic-recording technologies were replaced by electric ones. Few recordings were made of actual birds during the acoustic era, which is not a surprise once one considers the difficulty involved in isolating and amplifying the calls made by wild birds or in training domestic birds to perform on cue in the studio. Exceptions that prove the rule are 1914 Victor releases credited to "Karl Reich of Bremen" or "Reich's Aviary," with titles like *Canary and Thrush Duet, Song of a Sprosser,* and *Actual Song of the Canary Bird*. Karl Reich was a famous canary breeder from Bremen, Germany, and made phonograph recordings of his birds in the early 1910s to send to friends. According to historian Tim Birkhead, Reich painstakingly trained his birds to perch inside the horn of the recording machine to ensure clear recordings.[128] Reich's Victor discs have a certain haunting beauty, but they also contain stretches during which the birds are barely audible, demonstrating the difficulty of producing marketable recordings of live birds at this time and the corresponding practical necessity of hiring humans to chirp in their place.

Electric technologies allowed for a new degree of precision and clarity in the recording of birdsong, and ornithological researchers at Cornell University seized that opportunity by using portable recording equipment and parabolic microphones to record birds in the wild. The researchers made their recordings available to the public on phonograph records such as *American Bird Songs* (1942), which demonstrated that, in an era of electric recording, birds no longer needed human intermediaries to make their voices heard in the modern media.[129]

Microphones and loudspeakers also made possible new approaches to the training of cage birds. Nineteenth-century trainers had used weight-and-pulley bird organs and serinettes to mechanize the learning process, and a few plucky pioneers had experimented with acoustic phonograph players in that capacity as well.[130] Mechanized bird training was given a new degree of systematization with the proliferation of electric sound technologies, as can be seen in the history of the Hartz Mountain Company. Max Stern arrived in the United States from Germany in the early 1920s and brought with him a shipment of canaries that he sold to the John Wanamaker Department Store. Stern continued to import German canaries to his pet store in New York and in 1926 he founded the Hartz Mountain Company, which sold birds through mail order and chain department stores like Sears and Roebuck. By 1934 Hartz Mountain had become the largest livestock importer in America.[131]

The mass distribution of songbirds created the need for a similar scale of bird training. Hartz's birds were supplied by the Odenwald Bird Company, which was operated by Max's brother Gustav Stern. A 1947 article in the *Saturday Evening Post* claimed that Odenwald had transformed an "Old World craft to big business" and relocated the center of canary production from Germany's Harz Mountains to a single building in America that was the site of "one of the oddest assembly lines—and certainly the most musical—that has ever existed anywhere." Odenwald's "canary factory" was housed in a three-story building that boasted a thoroughly mechanized operation with thousands of birdcages designed for easy cleaning and a system of loudspeakers used to train the birds to sing. In an update on nineteenth-century training cages, Odenwald's best singers were kept in the dark until an appointed time, when they were placed in front of a microphone near a sunny window. Their exuberant song was then piped through the factory's loudspeakers to be heard by thousands of feathered students.[132] Odenwald combined Old World training techniques and Fordist efficiency to mass-produce the trained canaries needed to supply America's chain stores.

Loudspeakers broadcast the song of Odenwald's instructor birds through the factory, and Hartz took the logical next step and plugged that amplification system into the national radio networks. The Stern brothers sponsored a network radio show that was intended to advertise their pet products and showcase the skills of their trained canaries. *Hartz Radio Canaries* originated from New York station WOR and was broadcast in the late 1930s and early 1940s on the Mutual Network. The show featured the vocalizations of six Odenwald canaries, which were superimposed over a musical accompaniment of organ and violin.[133] The Odenwald canaries were not radio's only feathered songsters. American Bird Products, another canary food company, sponsored a show called the *American Radio Warblers*, which debuted in 1927 and was broadcast from Chicago's WGN.[134] *American Radio Warblers* had a similar format as *Hartz Radio Canaries*, with a chorus of birds chirping over easy-listening tunes. *Variety* wrote that the show appealed to "those who love canaries and mellow nostalgia and are in the market for bird food."[135] The warblers made personal appearances around the Midwest, traveling in a special portable studio. In 1935 an Iowa newspaper urged readers to see the "feathered songsters of the air" in their miniature studio. Visitors could also talk to a "bird counselor," who accompanied the birds, and even buy understudies of the famous warblers for $6.95 apiece.[136]

If the 1910s were the golden age of phonographic whistlers and bird mimics, the 1930s and 1940s were the golden age of radio warblers, but not all listeners found the sonic superimposition of bird and human performances to be harmonious. In 1940 a *Billboard* review described *Hartz Radio Canaries* as "a batch of canaries who warble their brains out" over music accompaniment. "According to announcement," the birds sang songs like "Swanee River." "We are not quite sure whether the birds really delivered these tunes," the reviewer quipped, although "the general mélange was rather pleasant."[137] The radio warblers' sonic mélange may not have been entirely convincing as human music, but that critique misses the more interesting point that the show had developed a format that addressed both human and avian listeners. Indeed, episodes of *Hartz Radio Canaries* sometimes began with the sound of chirping birds and barking dogs, followed by the announcement, "Just listen to our pets—they're calling your pets from coast to coast!"

Hartz Radio Canaries and *American Radio Warblers* addressed their feathered listeners as vocal students. A 1937 article on the warblers explained that bird owners should situate their pets within easy hearing distance of the radio and claimed that birds would listen with interest and then join in with the broadcast, in the process learning some new trills and melodies.[138] The radio set functions here as an automated update on the serinette or bird organ. Hartz and American Bird Products also released phonograph records to supplement their broadcast training sessions. The liner notes on a "Hartz Mountain Master Canaries" disc recommended that canaries be placed near the phonograph and allowed to hear the record several times a day. "Your canary will begin to imitate the notes he hears on the record. In no time, he'll be singing right along."[139] The content of the Hartz and Radio warblers records was similar to the content of the radio shows, and a particular emphasis on the waltzes of Johann Strauss continued the long association between trained canaries and European musical culture.

Midcentury radio warblers could still conjure associations with the Old World charm of a Viennese waltz, but the new training techniques used by companies like Odenwald exacerbated a break from nineteenth-century traditions. Canaries trained in America were making different kinds of sounds, so different, in fact, that American birds of the late-1920s were given a new

FIGURE 6. Phonograph record released by the Hartz Mountain Company. Photograph by Henry Smith. Reprinted by permission from Emanuel Stern.

designation: they were not "rollers" but "choppers." According to one 1928 account, the 1920s marked a "big change in the demand for canaries": "People are now buying the birds that make the loudest noise; they no longer seem to consider the quality of the tone." The author was among many to link that change to the American craze for jazz music. Where previously the ideal bird had been the roller who gave a "low sweet sound," now consumers wanted "the loud chopper that makes a good ear-splitting noise warranted to drown out the baby on his worst days."[140] In 1934 the president of the Greater Chicago Cage Bird Club noted a preference for "the 'jazz singer' canary rather than the roller or 'opera singer' canary." He accounted for this by observing that birds now had to compete with radio and "other noises in the modern home."[141] Five years later a writer for *Collier's* referred to choppers as the "Benny Goodmans" and "jitterbugs" of the canary world.[142] Even the Stern brothers at Hartz Mountain were said to be "a little embarrassed" by the loud song of their choppers. They had resigned themselves, however, to the fact that "Americans like their canary cadenzas strong." The "soft-voiced, sweet-singing" roller was increasingly found only in "a few German settlements." America had become the "land of the chopper, who trills loud and long."[143]

The shift from "roller" to "chopper" is an example of what Donna Haraway calls a "metaplasm": an alteration in language that is also a recalibration of companion-species relating.[144] The new name given to domestic canaries was part of a constellation of changes that involved the ways in which birds were trained and sold, the sounds they were encouraged to make, and the aural environment in which they were situated. The midcentury canary metaplasm was produced in part by the introduction of electric sound technologies and was aligned with similar changes taking place in the phonograph industry. Record buyers, after all, had developed a preference for Benny Goodman over Caruso around this same time, and the rise of the quintessentially American choppers corresponded with a larger decline in the influence of European high culture.[145]

During the ten years prior to 1915, most of the canaries imported into the United States had come from Germany. World War I led to a decline in German imports, from an average of more than a thousand birds per day in 1914 to about ten thousand for the entire year of 1918. In the last years of the 1910s, the flow of German canaries had virtually ceased.[146] The German export market returned to a limited extent during the 1920s but declined again with the rise of German fascism. When Hartz published a handbook on canaries in 1936, it carefully avoided any mention of Germany, instead referring to the origins of their training methods in a tradition of "European breeders" based in the "European mountains."[147] One survey showed that the American canary population had dropped by 60 percent between 1939 and 1943, falling from one out of four families owning a bird to one out of ten.[148] Gustav Stern declared that World War II decimated the German industry. "In all of Germany I do not believe there are a thousand birds," he said. "It will take years for the trade to come back, if ever."[149]

American chopper canaries supplanted German roller canaries during the same decades when American popular music supplanted German art music on the cultural landscape, but this was the last time that bird media and sound media developed along parallel tracks. During the postwar decades the home hi-fi stereo became more technologically sophisticated, and innovations like semipermanent needles meant that the device required less care and attention. As a result, it was treated less like a pet and more like an appliance, and it became increasingly difficult to understand the birdcage and the phonograph as belonging to the same class of objects. Meanwhile, the sale of domestic songbirds declined, in part due to the nature preservation movement, which changed American attitudes toward birds. Historian Robin Doughty writes that, as the twentieth century progressed, more and more Americans came to the conclusion that birds should be observed "out of doors in their own haunts, not in aviaries," and the caging of birds came to be seen as akin to bear baiting and dog fighting, a "brutish behavior, unworthy of the cherished American values of individual freedom and compassion for the weak."[150]

During the same years that it became less fashionable to have a caged songbird in the parlor, it became less common to hear whistling on popular records. Professional whistling peaked in the 1910s but continued well into the 1930s, when several popular swing bands featured whistlers: the Horace Heidt Orchestra had Fred Lowery, for example; and the Ted Weems Orchestra had Elmo Tanner. Gene Austin's recording of *My Blue Heaven* (Victor, 1928) was one of the best-selling records of the first half of the century and featured a stunning whistling solo by Robert MacGimsey. Iconic singers of the 1920s and 1930s were also whistlers, as demonstrated by Al Jolson's manic whistle solo in *The Jazz Singer* (1927) and Bing Crosby's whistle on signature numbers such as "Where the Blue of the Night" (1932) and "White Christmas" (1942).

By contrast, popular singers of the postwar era, like Frank Sinatra, Elvis Presley, and the Beatles, tend not to whistle. The decline in whistling may have something to do with the slow fade of minstrel show conventions or the emergence of new singing styles in which performers were more like Method actors delivering lines of dialogue than vaudeville stage performers with an assortment of ear-grabbing shticks. There were fewer songbirds in American parlors and fewer popular records that included bird imitations. But the home hi-fi still chirped and trilled; only in the postwar era, those sounds were made by the beeps and blips of space-age mood music.

Green media archaeology helps us to appreciate songbirds as no-wattage biotechnologies of aural entertainment, and one final origin story suggests how they can be heard as precursors to influential genres of contemporary recorded music. In early 1975 the rock musician Brian Eno was confined to his bed as he recovered from a traffic accident. His friend Judy Nylon paid him a visit and brought along a record of seventeenth-century harp music. The record was still playing when she left, and Eno realized that the volume on the record player was so low that he could barely hear the music above a rainstorm outside. He later recalled how only the loudest notes of the music were audible, "like little crystals, sonic icebergs rising out of the storm." He was forced to continue listening in this manner, however, since he couldn't get up to adjust the volume. To his surprise, Eno gradually became "seduced" by this listening experience: "I realized that this was what I wanted music to be—a place, a feeling, an all-around tint to my sonic environment."[151] It was this epiphany that inspired Eno to create the album, *Discreet Music* (1975), which effectively created the new genre of ambient music.

The first point I'd like to make about this story is that, a century earlier, Judy Nylon would likely have brought a roller canary to soothe her friend's convalescence. Eno's ambient records are typically compared to the works of John Cage and Erik Satie, but they can just as easily be placed in a history of domestic sound that includes roller canaries, whose songs were "like an endless stream" and bird organs that emitted "a low, plaintive monotone that goes on and on." In Karin Bijsterveld's terms, both Eno's ambient music and the ideal roller canary's song were a sensuous and comforting "multitude of variable sounds that filled the environment" with a "continuous, soft drone."[152] In other words, both were intended to add an "all-around tint" to domestic spaces. Midcentury canary-training records by the "Hartz Mountain Master Canaries" should be added to the history of ambient music and appreciated as sonic souvenirs of a brief era when bird media and sound media were close enough to overlap.

Eno's ambient music has proliferated since 1975, but the keeping of songbirds in the American home has declined. There was a gendered dimension to that decline. Historians of sound technology have argued that postwar hi-fi culture was typically associated with fantasies of the male "bachelor pad" and served as a male escape from family "togetherness."[153] Roller canaries provided avian ambient music in the home but lacked the masculine aura of tinkering with electronics or the allure of *Playboy*-esque modern product design. In fact, songbirds had long been associated with femininity, and even in the nature-conservation community men who worked to save birds were "subject to potential scorn by those who saved big game, forests, and mountains."[154] Another factor in the decline of pet songbirds, then, had to do with changing dynamics of gender in relation to the domestic soundscape. One indication that domestic songbirds were understood to be both feminine and outdated in the postwar era can be found in Warner Brothers' popular series of Tweety Bird cartoons. Begun in the late 1940s, these cartoons depicted the canary owner as an out-of-touch old granny who wore turn-of-the-century fashions and drove an antique car. Granny was a supporting character, of course, and the main event was Sylvester the cat's pursuit of Tweety Bird in a comic adaptation of the domestic ecology portrayed in Hogarth's painting of *The Graham Children*.

We have come full circle, then, back to the 1971 Sylvania "Cat and the Canary" advertisement, which might now be read as symptomatic of the disarticulation of bird media and sound media in the popular imagination. After all, the hook of that ad depends on the audience being surprised by the association of a birdcage with television, their conjunction presented as a category error that could only be made by a dumb animal. I hope that this chapter has demonstrated that there are benefits to rearticulating bird media and sound media. Nineteenth-century practices of songbird training allowed for an everyday knowledge of animal life and might serve as a blueprint for more eco-sonic practices of the future.

Much of this chapter has described how humans have intervened in bird communication, but I'd like to conclude by asking if influence could flow in the other direction as well. That is, can birds participate in human communication? To provide an example of how they can, we must return to *Serinus canaria*'s natural habitat. By a remarkable coincidence, the Canary Islands are the home not only of the bird species that became the Western world's favorite feathered songster but also of one of the world's few existing whistle languages.

TALKERS

Recall that the population of the indigenous people of the Canary Islands was decimated by the European conquests of the fifteenth century. Of the few remaining aspects of the Guanches' culture that survive, one is a whistle language called Silbo Gomero, which is still used on the island of La Gomera. With a greater sonic range than the voice, whistling is particularly useful on that island, where steep mountains and valleys isolate communities and make travel difficult.[155] In 1402 a French visitor was amazed at the Guanches' ability to communicate across great distances by their whistling and recounted how they were able to convey information to remote villages.[156]

Centuries later the settler population had adopted the whistle language, as indicated by a 1904 article in the *Boston Daily Globe*, which gives a vivid account of Silbo Gomero in action. Two British tourists described their encounter with a Gomeran muleteer who placed two forefingers in his mouth and produced a whistle that seemed to "rise and swell, shriller and louder, and shriller and louder yet ... speeding like an arrow of sound far away into the distance, over the deep ravines and up the stony terraces, right into the heart of the hills." The whistler then stopped and listened for a reply:

> From some invisible creature hidden among the heights, comes a tiny silvery reply, thin as the ghostly shrilling of a bat or the distant pipe of a mosquito. The call has been answered. The muleteer listens, with his head cocked on one side like a fox terrier, to locate the sound, and when it stops he begins to talk in whistles, evidently using the echoes of the rocky mountain walls to catch and toss onward his calls with wonderful skill. It seems to be a sort of morse whistling code, elaborated into long calls, short calls, high and low calls, dropping and rising inflections and curiously articulated calls like a mingling of bird notes and human words.[157]

The muleteer explains that his interlocutors had communicated to him that they were hoping to sell a cow, which is confirmed when, after a short time, the tourists are met by two men who bring their animal in the hopes of making a sale.

The first thing we should note about this account is the way in which it conveys a sense of wonder at the muleteer's ability to communicate at a distance. Note the supernatural terms with which the author describes the interaction: "invisible creature" and "ghostly shrilling." This is the kind of language that media scholars have associated with early encounters with communication technologies such as the radio, telephone, or telegraph. Silbo Gomero functions here as "telephony by other means," with the whistle as a minimal form of amplificatory media that extends the range of communication beyond the reach of the voice. A 1976 survey found that the residents of La Gomera referred to Silbo Gomero as their "telefono."[158]

The indigenous Canarians were not the only traditional people to develop minimal practices of amplificatory media. Anthropologists have documented the use of whistle languages in North America by the Kickapoo, Mazateco, and Tepehua peoples.[159] The bird mimic Charles Kellogg spoke of a system of "woods radio" used by Native American people to communicate over long distances by drumming on hollow trees or whispering into lakes or rivers in such a way that the water carried the message.[160] In 1924 members of the U.S. Forestry Service encountered a tribe of native people in the Siskiyou Mountains of northern California who used whistling to communicate. Forest rangers heard "uncanny whistlings" over the telephone lines that connected their mountain outposts, and a ranger was sent to investigate. At a remote station, the ranger met a group of Native Americans who "conversed only with staccato whistlings." The native people explained that they had observed rangers using the telephone and had experimented with it themselves, hence the mysterious sounds heard over the lines.[161]

The Gomeran "telefono," woods radio, the Siskiyou whistlers: all are minimal practices of sonic communication at a distance. In the last chapter I argued that phonography of the Green Disc era could be understood as a network for the movement of plastic form. I submit that the constellation of bird-media devices and practices of this chapter be understood in terms of communication at a distance, with "distance" understood in three different registers. The first register is distance in time, as in durative forms of recording that use devices and techniques to manipulate the plastic song of birds. The second register is distance in space, as in the whistled "arrow of sound" that the muleteer sent across the valleys of La Gomera. We are in familiar territory thus far, since the modern media have often been described in terms of their ability to "collapse" time and space. The third register of distance explored in this chapter moves into different territory or, more precisely, into territories of difference. This register has to do with the distance between categories of difference, in particular, species difference.

These registers exist in dynamic interrelation such that a dramatic showing in any of them can result in a sense of astonishment or wonder. As cultural historians and media scholars have argued, media technologies often create a sense of astonishment when they are new, when they are made "old" by the introduction of new devices, or through various discursive means (such as avant-garde practices of distanciation). The three registers of communication at a distance provide another matrix for understanding media's capacity to astonish. Telephones allow for communication across the globe and recordings allow utterances to endure over large expanses of time, but equally impressive is the ability for a technology to allow for a meaningful interaction with nonhuman creatures, even if that interaction takes place in the present moment or in one's own backyard or front parlor. The Siskiyou people's whistle language might not have traveled as far as the Forestry Service's telephone wires, but it could do something just as stunning. Press reports of the ranger's encounter described how, at a "whistled command" from the Native Americans, birds fluttered down from the trees to eat food that the people had scattered.[162]

Teasing out these various registers of mediated communication at a distance can help us notice when they interact or overlap, as when the Gomeran muleteer's communication across spatial distance is described with the language of species difference: notice the author's references to bats and mosquitoes, for example, and the mingling of "bird notes and human words." The muleteer is even said to cock his head to listen like a fox terrier, that is, like Nipper in "His Master's Voice." Birds, humans, and technologies are intertwined, as are registers of space, time, and difference. "Woods radio" and whistle languages like Silbo Gomero are minimal media and traditional technological knowledge that are important to understand and preserve because they help us to appreciate the potential for media technologies to facilitate communication with nonhuman others. In fact, when humans speak in whistle languages, birds can talk back. Wild blackbirds have reproduced human calls, for example, and crested larks have intervened in the whistled signals used by shepherds to direct their dogs.[163] Perhaps the Canarian whistle language was used to bridge the gap between *Homo sapiens* and *Serinus canaria* as well as between the steep valleys of La Gomera.

In our fascination with modern sound-media technologies, we have neglected this other kind of mediated communication. What if the cross-species potential of the Gomeran telefono had been given the same research budget as Bell's telephone or Marconi's radio? Where might that technology have advanced by now? The bird mimics and phonographic whistlers of the early twentieth century were "first users" of media technology and should be revisited as researchers in this domain of eco-sonic media culture. The bird mimic Charles Gorst described his joy in using sound to enter into the social world of wild animals, if only for a moment:

> In silent woods I have sung and started a general chorus. The Brown Thrasher has flown to me for a singing contest. The hawk has answered my scream and swooped at me. I have called a maiden Redstart away from her lover and brought him in anger after her. Like a baby Song Sparrow I cried for food; its fidgety mother brought me a green worm! On a solitary Canadian lake my imitative laughter decoyed a pair of swimming grebes to me through the reeds. I have stood in the dusk of a giant redwood forest and called the Varied Thrush down a long pillar of light from the wood's high roof. In Florida when I mocked a Mockingbird I brought upon him an undeserving beating from another! ... In the cool twilight of northern woods I have stood beside vine-wound columns under high green arches and sung heavenly evening hymns with Hermit Thrushes. From a high cliff, on a black autumn night, I have called up to migrating birds and heard a circling voice come down and murmur, "Are you there? Come with us!" And I have longed to go.[164]

Gorst's litany of social encounters with animals lends credence to Erving Goffman's assertion that social interaction catches humans "in just that angle of their existence that displays considerable overlap with the social life of other species."[165] At a time when one in eight bird species is threatened with extinction, Gorst and his cohort's ability to explore that area of overlap and translate that experience to a wide media public are valuable skills indeed.[166] Gorst heard migrating birds beckoning him to join them, but now, on the other side of a century that has seen the acceleration of the planet's sixth great extinction, we might have more in common with the sentiment expressed by the environmentalist Paul Shepard, who writes that "as human numbers increase and the Others recede," it becomes our last passionate desire to make contact with an intelligence besides our own, and many of us "feel like calling, as the birds fly away, 'Come back! ... Hear me!'"[167]

3. Subterranean Signals

In the previous chapter I made passing reference to the fact that male canaries were trained as singers more often than females because of the former's more frequent vocalizations. The less garrulous females were preferred, however, when it came to another kind of biotechnological media device. The flow of German canary songsters into the United States may have slowed to a trickle during World War I, but thousands of "canary heroines" made the reverse journey, traveling from the United States to Europe to be used by the military to detect dangerous gas in tunnels and trenches. Female birds were chosen for these purposes because the noisier males were more likely to betray a unit's position to the enemy.[1] This practice was a variation on the well-known "canary in the coalmine" long utilized in the mining industry. The Harz Mountain region of Germany had been the site of silver mining since the 1500s, and miners there learned how to bring small birdcages into the pit and keep an eye on the birds to see if they fell unconscious, a warning that the air was unsafe.[2] By the early 1920s portable birdcages had been designed with a glass window for observing the canary and an oxygen tank to revive the bird in case of emergency.[3] These portable, handheld birdcages bear a physical resemblance to transistor radios, but they were biotechnologies of remote sensing rather than outlets for audio entertainment.[4] Birdcages taken into the trenches or mines are part of the history of portable media technology, and in this chapter I bring an eco-critical perspective to that history through the consideration of a family of devices that includes the divining rod, Geiger counter, and metal detector.

Portable devices of remote sensing (henceforth divination media) should be added to the eco-media agenda for two reasons: first, they allow users to experience both a sense of place and a sense of planet; and second, they have

Subterranean Signals / 81

FIGURE 7. Portable birdcage for use in the mining industry, circa 1920s. Science Museum, Science and Society Picture Library, London.

been integrated into practices that are an alternative to consumer culture. Ursula Heise notes that American environmentalists have tended to celebrate the sense of place that comes from immersion in the natural landscape. Heise warns that not all individuals and communities have the same access to "back to the land" initiatives, and she challenges environmentalists to shift their cultural imagination from a single-minded emphasis on place to a "sense of planet," understood as the means by which individuals and groups envision themselves as part of the "global biosphere." Heise argues that media technologies play a key role in helping people to grasp "biospheric connectedness," as in the case of iconic photographs of the earth taken from outer space and Google Earth, which allows users to play with geographic scale and perceive the planet as a "complex set of ecosystems."[5]

I am not as skeptical as Heise about efforts to foster a sense of place, and I agree with Carolyn Merchant that the bioregionalism movement offers "a program of change toward a sustainable way of life."[6] Heise's critique is trenchant, however, and I share her desire to avoid romanticizing a narrow sense of the local that denies cultural difference or turns away from the kind of global outlook essential to social and environmental activism. It is for that reason that I have followed Heise's lead and sought out sound media practices that can do justice to the fact that places are "inexorably connected to the planet as a whole" and that planetary wholeness encompasses "vast heterogeneities."[7] Doreen Massey makes a similar point when she argues that a sense of place is constituted by a "particular constellation of social relations, meeting and weaving together at a particular locus," but that some of those social relations "go beyond the area being referred to in any particular context as a place."[8] Portable media can realign the constellation of social trajectories that intersect at a particular place and bring planetary relations into that mix when they produce signals from above or beneath the earth.[9]

In addition to this recalibration of place and planet, divination media can foster material practices that are an alternative to consumer spending. As we shall see, postwar metal-detector hobbyists spent their leisure time locating and unearthing the throwaway material culture of a previous era rather than buying and discarding new consumer goods. Treasure hunters thus engaged in a cultural practice that was a hybrid of scavenging, amateur archaeology, and volunteer recycling. Recent scholarship has shown the economic and environmental benefits of the scavenging that takes place in the developing world.[10] Postwar treasure hunters made salvage and reuse a popular pastime, and they should be appreciated for developing what Kate Soper calls an "alternative hedonism," that is, an "anti-consumerist ethic" that has little to do with advertising or shopping and appeals to the "gratifications of consuming differently."[11] The sonic scavengers of this chapter join my roster of models for a more sustainable sound media practice of the future, and green-media archaeology lays a foundation for that future by excavating the history of divination media and its ties to early modern technoculture.

The divination media at the heart of my analysis are twentieth-century metal detectors and Geiger counters, which provided feedback to users by means of sonic signals heard through headphones and so are best understood as a form of sound media. Scholars in the field of sound studies have tended to examine mobility and portability in relation to devices like the

Apple iPod and Sony Walkman and, less often, museum audioguides and experimental "soundwalks," like those created by the Canadian artist Janet Cardiff. Scholars have often been pessimistic about many forms of portable sound, arguing that users are encased in "psychic cocoons" and oblivious to their surroundings.[12] This scholarship can also assume that portable media practices occur only in urban spaces and are best compared to the cinematic soundtrack: note, for example, the oft-repeated assertion that portable music creates a "soundtrack to the city."[13] The metaphor of the soundtrack to the city describes one experience of portable sound media, but not the only one, and divination devices were often used on the margins or outside of the metropolis and have connected people to the lived environment in ways that have little to do with the cinematic soundtrack.

Another way in which scholars have discussed portable media is in terms of the ways in which portable digital technologies enable data to be layered over geographic places, variously described as "urban information overlay," "augmented" space, or "hybrid" space.[14] Lev Manovich's examples of augmented space are global-positioning systems, airport check-in procedures, and the retrieval of product information in retail stores, although, notably, he posits Janet Cardiff's audio walks as "the best realization" of the phenomenon.[15] My investigation of divination practices challenges the "strategic amnesia of digital culture" by exploring the eco-critical potential of predigital mobile sound media used in rural as well as urban spaces and its association with cultural discourses beyond those associated with film, popular music, or consumer culture.[16]

In the last chapter I described whistling as a form of minimal media, requiring only the resources of the human body. This chapter begins with another form of minimal media: the forked stick used in "rhabdomancy" (divination with a rod). Proposing that a twig is a media technology in the same sense as network broadcasting or Hollywood cinema requires some explanation. Lisa Gitelman defines media as "socially realized structures of communication, where structures include both technological forms and their associated protocols, and where communication is a cultural practice, a ritualized collocation of different people on the same mental map, sharing or engaged with popular ontologies of representation."[17] Though certainly minimal in its technological form, the divining rod is a medium by Gitelman's definition: it is the technological component of a structure of social communication in which users encounter the world through an embodied, mobile practice that intertwines sensory experience, physical space, and a set of shared mental maps that, as we shall see, consist of local folklore and traditional beliefs about the subterranean world.

The fact that media scholars have overlooked divining devices may be due to the fact that divination can appear to be an occult practice rather than a technological one, and, aside from Jeffrey Sconce's work on "haunted media," there has been little theoretical traffic between media studies and the occult.[18] The sound-based divination described in this chapter can supplement Sconce's research and serve as a counterpoint to Jonathan Sterne's account of the emergence of rationalized listening. Sterne argues that telegraph operators and the users of stethoscopes embodied an "audile technique" characterized by "logic, analytic thought, industry, professionalism, capitalism, individualism, and mastery" and offered a counternarrative to accounts that posited "sight as the sense of intellect and hearing as the sense of affect." Sterne shows how the use of the stethoscope to diagnose—a technique known as "mediate auscultation"—marks the articulation of hearing to reason.[19] In this chapter I am interested in practices that might run counter to Sterne's counternarrative. Twentieth-century divination often took the form of an "occult auscultation," whereby techniques of listening probed the environment for hidden treasures or resources. One of the earliest accounts of divination comes from the same geographic location that was the center of the international trade in singing canaries: the Harz Mountains of Germany. We begin this chapter, then, with a return to the Harz Mountains and the miners who worked beneath them—not to listen to the exquisite sounds of their roller canaries but to observe their use of the divining rod.[20]

THE METALLOSCOPIC IMAGINATION

Large-scale mining operations were an essential ingredient in the emergence of modern technological culture. Mining required investment and absentee ownership and so was closely bound up with the development of modern capitalism. The extractive industries also spurred technological developments that became integral to the industrial revolution: the steam engine was developed to drain groundwater from mines, and early locomotives were employed to haul ore.[21] It is not surprising then, that ecologically minded historians have tended to cast mining as a kind of "original sin" of Western culture that marks a shift from a medieval economy based on renewable energy sources such as wood, water, wind, and animal muscle to one based on nonrenewable metals and nonsustainable carbon energy sources. Lewis Mumford claimed that mining upset the balance between nature and human needs: agriculture brought "cumulative improvements to the landscape," he wrote, but mining passed "from riches to exhaustion, from exhaustion to desertion" and so was the epitome of "human discontinuity, here today and gone tomorrow, now feverish with gain, now depleted and vacant."[22] Carolyn Merchant connects the rise of mining to the eclipse of an organic theory of nature that cast the earth as a nurturing mother who gave birth to stones and metals within its womb. Beliefs such as these, Merchant argues, served as constraints against mining.[23]

Miners enacted a new attitude toward nature and a new kind of human relationship with the subterranean world, and their work spurred the desire for more accurate means to perceive the unseen depths of the earth. The divining rod was an early modern tool of remote sensing that aided in that pursuit. Georgius Agricola's 1556 compendium of sixteenth-century mining methods, *De re metallica*, contains many images of modern metallurgical technologies and intricate mechanical contraptions. Among those images, however, we also find several illustrations of miners engaged in rhabdomancy. Agricola writes that miners would "cut a fork from a hazel bush," grasp it with their hands such that the clenched fingers were held upward, and then "wander hither and thither at random through mountainous regions." The twig was said to twist and turn when the miner was over a vein of ore.[24]

The first thing to notice about these images is that the diviners were men. In an era when female practitioners of magic were in danger of being persecuted for witchcraft, divination was a form of male magic amenable to emerging notions of science and the capitalist exploitation of the natural world.[25] Divination can be understood as a male-dominated culture of magic, but also as a form of media. That is, when placed in the context of Agricola's book, the divining rod is the media component of a modern technological network whose aim was to explore the depths of the earth: as the author of a 1693 book on rhabdomancy put it, the rod provided knowledge about the subterranean world as though "the earth were crystal" or there were a "window to look into it."[26]

When understood as a media device, the divining rod alerts us to a history that runs parallel to what Charles Musser calls "screen practice." Musser begins his history of screen practice with the catoptric lamp of the German-born Jesuit priest and scientist Athanasius Kircher (1601–80). Kircher's work provides Musser with a "decisive starting point" for a form of modern spectatorship distinct from an earlier era of the "pre-screen," when projected images were presented as magic and used to manipulate spectators.[27] Kircher's intellectual production encompassed far more than protocinematic devices, however, and he also wrote about acoustics, talking statues, hearing instruments, mechanical musical devices, and divining rods.

FIGURE 8. Depiction of rhabdomancy in Georgius Agricola's *De re metallica* (1556; repr., New York: Dover, 1950), 40.

Kircher's interest in talking statues and divining rods reminds us that screen practice is only one branch on the media family tree, and green-media archaeology encourages us to consider its alternatives.

In his 1641 work *Magnes sive de arte magnetica*, Kircher sought a "purely scientific" investigation of rhabdomancy and referred to divining rods as "metalloscopia." Kircher stated that he had "witnessed and made innumerable experiments" concerning the efficacy of the rod. In one case, he tested rods made of different varieties of wood by balancing them on a pin and discovered that they did not move without the contact of a human operator. According to the author of an exhaustive review of the literature on divining rods, Kircher's experiment marked the first assertion that unconscious muscular action was the primary mechanism of the rod's mysterious movements.[28] Nonetheless, Kircher's faith in the efficacy of the rod tempers any urge to draw a hard and fast line between modern and premodern technological practices. In fact, rhabdomancy retained strong occult overtones into the seventeenth century, when it was used to identity criminals, to ascertain the fidelity of spouses, and to determine the location of property lines.

German miners brought the divining rod to England during the reign of Elizabeth I (1558–1603), and the European tradition of rhabdomancy came to the eastern United States with eighteenth- and nineteenth-century immigrants.[29] Divination practices were the topic of considerable discussion in nineteenth-century American periodicals, as when a writer in 1826 claimed that there were "many decided friends of the divining rod" in America and pointed as evidence to the frequency with which public journals contained letters from "respectable correspondents" who maintained its "truth and integrity."[30] Nineteenth-century accounts of American rhabdomancy show a continuity of practice with the sixteenth-century miners described in *De re metallica*. As in Agricola's day, the percentage of American specialists in the art was said to be overwhelmingly male, and they used an approximately two-foot forked branch from a tree whose bark was smooth and whose fiber was elastic: often a peach, cherry, or witch hazel. Two ends of the three-pronged branch were held such that the operator's palms were turned upward. The divining rod was thus characterized by a "fit" between hand and device, which Heidi Rae Cooley finds in the electronic handheld devices of our own era. Cooley describes a "tactile vision" involving hands, eyes, and devices that enables a "more direct and vital mode of experiencing one's surroundings."[31] The rod relied on a similar "fit" and was sometimes visually represented placed snugly in a pair of disembodied hands. Diviners engaged in a mode of tactile vision, moving with a "slow and creeping step" until the rod tugged downward, marking the location of water or ore.[32]

Nineteenth-century American commentators associated rhabdomancy with rural, uneducated people. In an 1850 article, we read that "a large portion of the simple-hearted people in the agricultural districts of the country" believed in the powers of the divining rod "for the discovery of water, mines, or hidden treasures."[33] To the extent that the rod's tactile vision was used to locate hidden treasure, rhabdomancy was part of a tradition that had been shaped by hermetic thought, medieval alchemy, and legends about buried treasure hidden in the American landscape by pirates, early Spanish explorers, or America's ancient inhabitants.[34] Divining rods were used to locate hidden treasure, which then had to be wrested away from guardian spirits believed to be the ghosts of men or animals sacrificed by the treasure buriers. Treasure seekers fended off such supernatural entities by laying out protective magic circles, wielding enchanted objects, making ritual incantations, and even spilling the blood of animals. Once the excavation of the treasure site began, there was a strict rule of silence based on the belief that any spoken word might unleash angry spirits or cause the treasure to sink into the earth.[35]

Washington Irving's 1824 short story cycle, "The Money Diggers," provides a vivid illustration of the horizon of popular imagination surrounding American divination during this era. Irving begins "The Money Diggers" by recounting the legend that the pirate Captain Kidd buried his treasure somewhere around Manhattan Island. Search parties had long sought Kidd's loot, but at just the moment when the diggers thought that the treasure was within their grasp, "the earth would fall in and fill up the pit, or some direful noise or apparition would frighten the party from the place; and sometimes the devil himself would appear and bear off the prize." Irving moves from these traditional folk beliefs to the tale of Wolfert Webber, a "burgher" of Manhattan descended from a long line of Dutch cabbage farmers. The city around the Webber farm had grown so rapidly that Wolfert found himself "a kind of rural potentate in the midst of a metropolis." As a result, he grew poorer while the city around him grew richer. While ruminating on this sad state of affairs, Wolfert hears a local storyteller recount the tale of pirates burying treasure in the area, and he immediately perceives his environment in a new way: "the soil of his native island seemed to be turned into gold dust; and every field to teem with treasure." By comparison, the venerable Webber farm now filled Wolfert with disgust at "the narrowness of his destiny."[36]

Spurred by vivid dreams, Webber becomes convinced that there is treasure buried in his cabbage fields, and though he digs relentlessly, he finds nothing and ruins his crop in the process. More desperate than ever, Webber hires "Black Sam, the old negro fisherman," to guide him to the spot where, according to local lore, a spirit known as "Father Red-cap" guarded a cache of pirates' gold.[37] As described by Irving, Sam the fisherman is not only a guide into the region's legendary past but also a kind of intermediary between the area's human and nonhuman denizens: we read that Sam had led "an amphibious life," that he was "like a shark" or a "solitary heron." Irving is certainly playing on racist stereotypes that portrayed African Americans as being somehow closer to nature than whites, but Sam is also portrayed as an expert in locally embedded knowledge and experience. Irving writes that Sam was so well acquainted with "every hole and corner of the Sound" that he "knew all the fish in the river by their Christian names."

The two men reach the ruins of an old Dutch dwelling, which they assume to be the haunted abode of Father Red-cap. A gothic mood pervades the scene, as Sam leads Wolfert down an overgrown lane, where wild vines, garter snakes, toads, and catbirds seem to stand guard over the treasure. A skull rolls on the ground, and the evening light fosters a "lurking feeling" of awe and superstition.[38] Wolfert vows to return to Father Red-cap's turf and enlists the aid of the town's "High German doctor," Dr. Knipperhausen.

We read that the doctor spent his youth among the Harz Mountains of Germany, where the miners had taught him about "the mode of seeking treasure buried in the earth." Under Knipperhausen's guidance, Wolfert learns that one must dig for money only at night and under the auspices of certain ceremonies and mystic words. Above all, one must make use of the divining rod. The three money diggers make a nighttime journey to the location of Sam's mysterious encounter. Wolfert holds a lantern while Knipperhausen operates the rod, which slowly turns to point at one spot. The doctor orders the party to remain silent to prevent the "evil spirits which keep about buried treasure" from doing them any harm. Knipperhausen draws a circle around the point indicated by the rod, lights a fire and burns herbs, reads passages from a book written in German, and then orders the digging to begin. Warmed by a "stone bottle of good Dutch courage," they dig until they hit something that makes a hollow sound. In his excitement, Wolfert carelessly breaks the rule of silence, exclaiming that they have found a chest of gold. At that moment a sound from above the pit interrupts their celebration. Webber thinks he sees the "grim visage" of a pirate and drops the lantern, causing the diggers to run for their lives, convinced that they are being pursued by a "legion of hobgoblins."[39] This comic scene is illustrated in John Quidor's 1832 painting, *Money Diggers*.

Irving's tale of Wolfert Webber throws into relief some of the salient aspects of American rhabdomancy during the mid-nineteenth century. We get a demonstration of the rod, which is explicitly tied to German miners and traditional lore about guardian spirits. The story also makes reference to chests of money that fall into the earth if the diggers violate a ritual practice. Historian John L. Brooke connects such beliefs to the concept of "metallic growth," which held that the transmutation of the four elements in the earth produced two "exhalations," one that was fiery and produced stones and one that was watery and produced metals. The divining rod's ability to detect both water and metals made sense by this logic, since the two were materially related. Treasure hunters in seventeenth-century Germany believed that vapors released during the genesis of minerals moved upward and formed a sympathetic relationship with trees and bushes, hence the behavior of wood taken from specific trees could indicate the location of specific ores.[40] When placed in the context of beliefs such as these, rhabdomancy provided practitioners with a tactile sense of the kind of planetary networks depicted in Athanasius Kircher's seventeenth-century illustrations of subterranean fires.[41]

Irving's depiction of the guardian spirit Father Red-cap also has a venerable pedigree. Brooke claims that such figures betray a "residual belief in the spiritual powers inherent in metals," which in the German tradition were personified by gnomes and mine spirits.[42] In his 1556 book Agricola stated that "demons of ferocious aspect" could be found in some mines and had to be "put to flight by prayer and fasting." Agricola also described two-foot "little miners" who idled about in mine tunnels and sometimes threw pebbles at workmen. In his commentary on this section of Agricola's text, mining engineer (and future U.S. president) Herbert C. Hoover explained that "neither the sea nor the forest so lends itself to the substantiation of the supernatural as does the mine": "The dead darkness, in which the miners' lamps serve only to distort every shape, the uncanny noises of restless rock whose support has been undermined, the approach of danger and death without warning, the sudden vanishing or discovery of good fortune, all yield a thousand corroborations to minds long steeped in ignorance and prepared for the miraculous through religious teaching."[43]

The same might be said about nineteenth-century money-digging expeditions like the one conducted by Wolfert, Sam, and Dr. Knipperhausen. Childhood exposure to treasure tales, long hours of nighttime digging by flickering lanterns, and a generous supply of alcohol (recall Wolfert and company's bottle of "good Dutch courage"): all of these could serve to trigger group hallucinations and memorable experiences, if little actual treasure. Historian Alan Taylor notes the practical utility of some of the arcane procedures of money digging in such a context. The rule of silence, for example, helped to "put a lid on expressions of doubt and futility, and thereby kept a party at their task."[44] What is more, any verbal expression of doubt or frustration could become the scapegoat for a digging crew's failure to find the promised treasure.

It is easy to become enchanted by the occult dimensions of rhabdomancy, but what I find most compelling are the ways in which the practice served real social needs by connecting people with their local environment at a time when powerful forces were pulling in the opposite direction. Diviners were ostensibly pursuing buried treasure, but they also enacted local folklore such that they experienced an encounter with an area's previous inhabitants. In the case of Irving's "The Money Diggers," Wolfert and his party enact local legends about pirates and early settlers by moving into previously inhabited spaces at the edge of town. In this instance, rhabdomancy becomes what Bruno Latour calls a "localizer": a means by which places were placed, and locals were localized.[45]

Recall Doreen Massey's definition of place as a constellation of social relations woven together at a particular location but stretching beyond it.[46] Places can also be defined by social relations that stretch beyond the present moment in time, and the use of the rod in treasure-hunting expeditions like Wolfert's worked to forge a lived connection between current and previous inhabitants of a place. In other words, rhabdomancy constructed what Michel De Certeau calls a "haunted" space saturated with social and cultural meaning, as when local legends haunt urban spaces by opening them up to "something different." We might say that the rod created a form of predigital augmented space by laminating a layer of historical data onto physical space.[47]

To the extent that rhabdomancy provided practitioners with an embodied experience of local place, it was useful for rural people negotiating the transition to a modern capitalist economy.[48] Taylor argues that treasure seeking occurred at "the murky intersection of material aspiration and religious desire" and functioned as both a "materialistic faith" that was an alternative to an "unsatisfactory abstract religion" and a "supernatural economy" that was an alternative to a disappointing natural one. In his discussion of supernatural economy, Taylor draws on the work of anthropologist George M. Foster, who argued that peasant societies tend to have a "limited good" worldview. In such a society, the desired things in life are thought to exist in finite quantity and are always in short supply, so improvements in one's social position always come at the expense of others. Building on Foster's work, historians Johannes Dillinger and Petra Feld write that in societies with a limited good worldview, treasure tales function to reduce conflict by accounting for wealth that could not be explained in other ways.[49] Treasure hunting was an accepted form of economic initiative for people who still adhered to the concept of a limited good but who also sought to improve their financial situation. The practice thus marks the "slow transition from an agricultural society to a bourgeois society dominated by a newly emergent market economy."[50]

The conclusion of Washington Irving's tale of Wolfert Webber provides an illustration. Recall how Wolfert had found himself a "rural potentate" in the midst of the metropolis and became dissatisfied with his family's agricultural heritage. Webber turns to money digging as a means to gain the kind of rapid and unlimited wealth that his cabbages cannot provide. Irving clearly wants us to see the comic futility of such an approach, and at the end of the story he contrasts it with a different, though equally rapid and unlimited, mode of economic growth. Distraught at the failure of his money-digging enterprise, Wolfert learns that "the corporation" of the city is to build a new street through the center of his cabbage garden. His lawyer explains that the economic consequences of the road construction will make Webber a very rich man. In the end then, Wolfert's "golden dream was accomplished": "he did indeed find an unlooked for source of wealth; for, when his paternal lands were distributed into building lots, and rented out to safe tenants, instead of producing a paltry crop of cabbages, they returned him an abundant crop of rents; insomuch that on quarter day, it was a goodly sight to see his tenants knocking at his door, from morning to night, each with a little round bellied bag of money, the golden produce of the soil."[51]

"The Money Diggers" charts a transition from wealth derived from farming to the seemingly unlimited "golden produce of the soil" that is the result of property ownership and land speculation.[52] Seen in this light, "The Money Diggers" becomes a parable of what cultural critics have referred to as the "deterritorialization" or "disembedding" characteristic of modernity.[53] Anthony Giddens argues that the advent of modernity gave rise to a dynamic whereby geographically and socially situated places became "increasingly *phantasmagoric*" in the sense that locales became "thoroughly penetrated by and shaped in terms of social influences quite distant from them."[54] Giddens refers to the separation of place and space as the "disembedding" of social relations from local contexts of interaction and their subsequent restructuring across indefinite spaces.[55]

Massey warns us that historical arguments about the spatial disruptions of modernity can rely on the questionable assumption that premodern or non-Western societies existed in a state of isolation.[56] Nonetheless, Giddens draws our attention to a historical shift in the constellation of lived social relations, and Irving's account of Wolfert's transformation from cabbage farmer to landlord dramatizes the lived experience of a temporal and spatial disembedding: temporal in the disruption of the Webber family genius and spatial in the reconfiguration of the Webber estate from a space enriched by the fecundity of agriculture to an abstract plot of land given value by decisions about the urban grid made by a distant "corporation." "The Money Diggers" thus depicts one experience of global modernity—the penetration of "locally situated lifeworlds" by "distant events, relations and processes."[57]

Notice how practices of divination play a transitional role in this transformation. Rhabdomancy provides Webber with a set of practices that allow him to imagine a means to produce wealth above and beyond the narrow destiny of agriculture, but which is nonetheless grounded in local experience. Rhabdomancy and finance are presented as Wolfert's two avenues to postagricultural wealth, and though Irving ostensibly mocks the superstitious belief in the divining rod, the thematic structure of the story reveals the degree to which divination and capitalist development could be seen as competing forms of supernatural economy. We can read Irving's critique of money digging against the grain, then, and see the divining rod not as a comical detour on the path to capitalism but as a means to resist one kind of spatial and temporal disembedding characteristic of modernity by reasserting a sense of place constructed from the repertoire of local history. Rhabdomancy was an embodied practice that allowed Webber to negotiate local place and traditional knowledge (embodied by Sam and the doctor) and to encounter a landscape populated by Dutch settlers, pirates, and even the nonhumans who lived on the edge of human habitation: the snakes, toads, and catbirds that guarded Father Red-cap's treasure.[58]

In sum, "The Money Diggers" illustrates how nineteenth-century rhabdomancy could create both a sense of place (through an engagement with local treasure lore) and a sense of planet (through a tactile experience of the subterranean signs of metallic exhalation). I have been emphasizing the potentially eco-positive aspects of divination, but there is little doubt that the practice was often the province of hucksters and confidence men, and it is easy to understand why Irving and many of his contemporaries held it in contempt. The rural, working-class social position and occult overtones of rhabdomancy made it an easy target for well-educated and science-minded critics. In 1826 a writer for the *American Journal of Science and Arts* concluded that the art of locating water and ore with a "succulent twig" was an offense to reason that deserved universal reprobation.[59] Ironically, the same science journals that attacked rhabdomancy were, by the end of the century, championing devices that they heralded as "scientific" divining rods.

METALLOSCOPE TO METALLOPHONE

The technological component of rhabdomancy underwent a significant change during the late nineteenth century, when the hazel twig began to be replaced by new electronic devices. It is difficult to demarcate the transition from traditional divining rods to their electrically powered functional equivalents, in part because a number of turn-of-the-century devices were said to locate water or minerals through scientific means. Despite the claims of their inventors, none of these "galvanometers," "magnetometers," "phonendoscopes," "electro-terreohmeters," and "electro-geodetic mineral finders" seem to have produced results much more reliable than the traditional forked twig.[60] The line between pre- and postelectrical divination is also blurred by the fact that many nineteenth-century commentators believed that the actions of the rod were the result of a circuit of "galvanic electricity" that linked negatively charged underground waters, the positively charged atmosphere, and the arms of the diviner.[61] In this view, the divining rod was an electrical device long before it was hooked up to any batteries.

There was, nonetheless, a marked shift in the form and practice of rhabdomancy when diviners began to use devices descended from David Hughes's 1879 induction balance. Hughes, who invented the carbon microphone in 1878, discovered that when metal was passed across the gap between two electrical coils, it disturbed electrical induction, and that disruption could be made to trigger an audible tone.[62] Alexander Graham Bell experimented with an electronic metal detector based on these principles. Bell's device gained nationwide press coverage when he used it in an attempt to locate a bullet that had lodged in the body of U.S. president James Garfield after an attack by an assassin in 1881. In the weeks after the attack, Bell tried to find the bullet during two tests of his induction balance, neither of which met with success. Bell later attributed his failure to the interference caused by steel springs in the president's mattress.[63]

Use of the induction balance turned from the pursuit of metal in the human body to metal in the earth. As early as 1880 the journal *Scientific American* proposed using the induction balance for metal prospecting.[64] In 1882 Bell conducted experiments with a portable induction balance that produced sound in a telephone receiver, using the device to locate iron wire buried under the ground. Bell made a sketch of the portable induction balance, which depicted a human figure supporting the triangular frame of the induction coils in one hand and holding a telephone receiver toward his head with the other.[65] To contemporary eyes, Bell's figure appears to be a hybrid of a telephone conversationalist, a portable stereo user, and a mobile radio tower. Bell's linkage of mobile divination and sound technology was prescient, and this image seems to embody what William J. Mitchell describes as the dynamic, whereby network "functions that were once served by architecture, furniture, and fixed equipment are now shifting to implanted, wearable, and portable devices." Bell's sketch shows an early glimpse at an "electronically nomadized world" in which a smartphone user might be described as "a two-legged terminal, an ambulatory IP address, maybe even a wireless router in an ad hoc mobile network."[66] By the turn of the century a number of portable induction balances equipped with telephone receivers had been demonstrated for the popular press.[67]

FIGURE 9. Alexander Graham Bell's 1882 sketch of a portable induction balance. Alexander Graham Bell Family Papers, Manuscript Division, Library of Congress, Washington, DC.

The presence of Bell and Hughes in the foregoing historical narrative indicates that the emergence of "scientific" divining rods was closely tied to research on sound technologies like the microphone and the telephone. As a result, popular divination shifted from the tactile vision of the rod to the audile technique of the induction balance. A 1904 article titled "The Gold Finder" described how the electrical waves from an induction balance could make mineral deposits audible to someone listening through a telephone. The sound produced by the device normally made a "gentle tap-tap-tap" that was intensified when the device came into contact with ore: "The prospector moves his telephone about the field hither and thither, listening for a moment at each fresh pitch, until suddenly he hears this intensified tap-tap-tap. Then he knows that he is just above the lode."[68] Accounts like this one mark a transition from Athanasius Kircher's metalloscope to a twentieth-century metallophone that *sounded* the subterranean world and so extended the reach of the sonorous envelope of the earth.[69]

Despite their modern design and scientific pedigree, electric divination devices could be mobilized for the same purposes as the divining rod. In the wake of Bell's much-publicized experiments on President Garfield, a reporter asked Thomas Edison if the induction balance could be "a handy thing for seekers after Capt. Kyd's [sic] buried treasures." Also note that, in an 1892 article on the induction balance that had the title, "Unscientific and Scientific Divining Rods," the author felt the need to debunk the persistent popular belief in rhabdomancy before offering a number of "scientific divining rods" in its place. A decade later an essayist wrote that electronic inventions had resulted in a "modern divining-rod" based on "scientific principles." "Once again science has followed in the track of an 'old wife's tale,'" wrote another author in 1904: "What the quack professed to do with a hazel wand the scientist has actually accomplished, only, instead of a hazel wand he uses an electric battery and telephone." As late as 1917 a newspaper article compared metal detectors that worked by means of "modern magnetic current" to "the forked hazel stick of the old-fashioned dowser" and concluded that "science is now said at last to have found a sure method of locating mineral wealth hidden in the earth."[70] Popular discourse thus frequently placed users of the divining rod and the scientist-inventor in the same category and described them as pursuing similar goals, with scientists following a script that had been rehearsed by diviners.

Though electric metallophones received press coverage at the turn of the century, they did not become popular commodities until the years after World War II. Metallophones entered the American consumer marketplace in two waves during the postwar decades, the first of which occurred in the 1950s, when tens of thousands of Americans took part in what was called "the greatest metal hunt ever known to man."[71] That hunt relied on a metallophone that evolved, not from Hughes's induction balance, but from a device that detected radioactive particles.

ATOMIC-AGE ALARM

A 1913 article on the divining rod referred to the "surprising discoveries" that had been made in recent years regarding atomic radiation, and the author wondered whether these discoveries might provide an explanation for the actions of the rod: perhaps its movements were due to the "radioactive influence" of underground waters acting on the person who held it.[72] Ernest W. Rutherford was a pioneer nuclear physicist who was responsible for many of those "surprising discoveries," and in 1908 he and his assistant Hans Geiger designed the first version of a tool that indicated the presence of radioactive particles. Geiger continued to refine the device, which came to be known as a "Geiger counter," and portable models were available on the American consumer market by the 1930s.

The sound of the Geiger counter was first heard by many Americans on radio broadcasts in the late 1920s. The *New York Times* announced in 1929 that radio listeners could hear a demonstration of "the smallest voice known to science, that of the electron," and compared the sound to "hail stones dashing against a window pane in a Summer shower."[73] Two years later the demonstration of a Geiger counter was described as the process by which cosmic rays were translated into clicks that had the rhythmic regularity of a ticking clock.[74] Other press reports compared the sound of the device to "peas being dropped slowly into a pan," "a snare drum," a "panful of frying eggs," or "distant, intermittent rifle fire."[75] The range of metaphors that reporters mobilized to describe the sonification of invisible radiation suggests the novelty of the experience. These early demonstrations established an association between the Geiger counter and radio that was rearticulated in the postwar era, as we shall see.

Sales of Geiger counters skyrocketed in the late 1940s, when the U.S. Atomic Energy Commission established set prices for the newly valuable mineral uranium and offered cash rewards for significant discoveries. The result was what the popular press referred to as the "uranium rush," in reference to the American "gold rush" of a century earlier.[76] In 1849 prospectors had brought divination practices with them to the western United States on their search for gold and silver. The ability to locate water and ore was a valuable skill in those dry, hot regions, and, according to one nineteenth-century writer, it was in the West that diviners obtained celebrity.[77]

In 1949 a new generation of prospectors headed to the deserts of Colorado and Utah in search of uranium and were equipped, not with a forked twig, but with a portable Geiger counter. Retail sales of Geiger counters jumped 75 percent in 1950, with most sales reportedly going to hobbyists intent on doing "a little uranium prospecting on their vacations."[78] In 1955 *Popular Mechanics* magazine asked its readers, "if you're looking for a vacation in the open with adventure thrown in, why not consider prospecting for uranium?" Amateur prospectors were inspired by well-publicized success stories, like Charlie Steen, for example, who found 30 million dollars' worth of uranium in Utah; and Dorothy Madigan, who took a cheap Geiger counter on her vacation and discovered uranium deposits in an abandoned feldspar mine.[79] Geiger counters provided feedback primarily through sound, and some models even combined the functions of radiation detector and radio receiver. A 1957 article in *Popular Mechanics* explained that treasure hunting can be a "lonely, monotonous business," and so a special kit was designed to provide not only a sensitive Geiger counter but also "an entertaining companion; one who will not ask for a cut of the 'take' in the event of a strike—a portable radio."[80]

As this do-it-yourself kit indicates, the "uranium boom" overflowed its banks as a vacation pastime and flooded the plains of popular culture: references to Geiger counters and uranium prospecting appeared in books, magazines, and board games. An article in *Life* featured a full-color photo of a family standing in front of a desert backdrop adorned in the latest uranium prospecting fashions. Mother wears an orange jumpsuit and leans on a shovel, a young girl is dressed in a matching "Diggerette Jr." suit, and Father smiles in the background, clutching a portable Geiger counter and wearing a pair of headphones.[81]

Numerous American radio and television series dedicated episodes to uranium prospecting. In August 1954 radio listeners heard Fibber McGee purchase a Geiger counter and head to Utah. On the *Burns and Allen Show* episode "The Uranium Caper" (1955), George's neighbors mistakenly believe that he has found uranium, and, similarly, the soldiers on *The Phil Silvers Show* are convinced that they have made a "Big Uranium Strike" (1956). Jack Benny follows Don Wilson to the desert to search for uranium on "Jack Hunts for Uranium" (1955), and Andy gets a demonstration of a Geiger counter during the *Amos 'n Andy* episode "The Uranium Mine" (1955). In an episode of the *Lucy-Desi Comedy Hour*, titled "Lucy Hunts Uranium" (1958), Lucy (Lucille Ball) and her friends equip themselves with Geiger counters, headphones, and prospecting clothes and head for the desert in search of uranium.[82] Images of Lucy, Ricky, Fred, and Ethel pacing across the desert landscape attending to their earphones illustrate how amateur prospectors fused the clicking sound of Geiger-counter feedback with the visual experience of the landscape of the western United States, in an update on rhabdomancy's negotiation of place and planet.[83]

The "uranium boom" was relatively short-lived, and by the end of the 1950s amateurs equipped with Geiger counters had been replaced by professional prospectors, geologists, and geophysicists.[84] By that time the clicks of the Geiger counter had become associated with fears about the radioactive fallout that would accompany a nuclear war. *Popular Science* described the Geiger counter's sharp metallic clicks as the "atomic-age alarm" and told readers that their safety might soon depend on it.[85] The chattering of the Geiger counter was a Cold War "earcon," containing symbolic meaning far exceeding the contours of its sound wave.[86] Uranium prospectors of the 1950s experienced that sound as one component of the first hobbyist culture to be convened around a metallophone, and the tiny clicks that they heard were echoes of a "logarithmic increase in the actions of humans as a geophysical force" ushered in by the nuclear age.[87] A second wave of postwar metallophone culture occurred when electronic metal detectors became available as affordable consumer goods.

GLITTERING PROSPECTS

As we have seen, Alexander Graham Bell used a portable induction balance to locate buried wire in 1882, and similar devices were being used to hunt for gold at the turn of the century. The induction balance did not find a niche in American popular culture, however, until several decades later. War played an important role in the technology's development. After World War I, portable induction balances were used to locate unexploded shells in European battlefields being reclaimed for agriculture.[88] Small-scale production of electronic metal detectors for the consumer market began in the 1930s. Gerhard R. Fisher, a German electrician who worked as a research engineer in Los Angeles, founded Fisher Research Laboratory in 1931. A few years later he and four employees began producing a "Metalloscope" in a garage behind his home in Palo Alto.[89] The manufacture of devices like Fisher's Metalloscope increased significantly when the U.S. military contracted with the Hazeltine Corporation of New York in 1941 to produce the SCR-625 mine detector.

The SCR-625 consisted of a six-foot exploring rod, a search coil mounted under a wooden disc, earphones, and dry-cell batteries carried in a canvas sack. The unit's earphones produced a low hum that rose in pitch in the presence of metal buried less than twelve inches below the surface of the ground. Soldiers walked forward and swung the search coil in such a way that the device was called an "outdoor carpet sweeper." The SCR-625 was used successfully by the Allies during the 1942 North Africa campaign, but it proved to be less reliable during subsequent initiatives. In 1943, iron in the Italian soil confused the device, and the Germans began assembling mines in wooden boxes to avoid detection.[90] Despite these setbacks, the SCR-625 became an iconic military tool of the period. In 1944 the *New York Times* wrote that metal detectors were one of the ten most "vital weapons" of the war, ranking with tanks, hand grenades, and flying fortresses.[91] The strategic and symbolic importance of the metal detector is indicated by a "Sad Sack" comic printed in a 1944 *Yank* magazine: we see a long line of tanks waiting patiently behind a single soldier equipped with an SCR-625.

After World War II the military sold millions of dollars worth of surplus electronic and radio equipment to the public, including walkie-talkies, radio sets, field telephones, radar devices, and mine detectors.[92] Several years after surplus military detectors began to make their way into American homes, they were joined by a number of cheap, lightweight, transistor-based models. Charles Garrett led the way in expanding the postwar consumer market for metal detectors. Garrett had been an electrician in the U.S. Navy and established a business manufacturing metal detectors in 1964.[93] Metal detectors of this era provided sonic feedback in several ways: beat frequency models emitted a series of sonic pulses that increased or decreased in speed, and transmitter-receiver detectors produced a constant drone that changed in pitch or loudness. Detectors were also equipped with meters that visually indicated the presence of metal, but hobbyists argued that these were of limited utility. One author pointed out that it was difficult "to search an area while keeping an eye on a meter. Therefore, meters are most often used to double check a slight audio signal." "The needle doesn't afford much help," wrote another, "but one can learn to tell from the sound what kind of metal has been located."[94]

Handbooks aimed at the hobbyist market warned that considerable skill was required to combine movement, vision, and hearing in the operation of a metal detector. To master this multisensory media practice, novices were encouraged to undergo a period of training for their "ears, eyes, and reflexes." This typically involved a series of graded exercises during which coins where hidden under carpets, then in a backyard lawn, and then underground. By completing such exercises, the modern diviner could learn to recognize all the various "notes" by which the device sonically indicated buried objects. One had to learn how to "read" the audio signal, wrote one author, who went on to describe how a coin near the surface of the ground gave a "sharp" signal while a deeply buried axe head gave a "weaker, more diffused" one.[95] The combination of sonic feedback and mobile visual observation in pursuit of buried metal could be the source of pleasure: one writer recounted how "tension mounts with each swing of the metal detector over the ground. Adrenaline surges through the nervous system when the instrument sends out a high-pitched whine—an indication metal is buried in the soil."[96] The discovery of a promising sonic signal culminated in the intensification of the tactile element of the practice, as the operator dug into the earth and recovered any buried artifacts to be found there. In short, metal detecting could be a rich multisensory media practice that existed at the intersection of the audible, visible, ambulatory, and tactile.[97]

By the late 1960s the pursuit of such multisensory pleasures had blossomed into a full-blown popular pastime. In 1966 the *Los Angeles Times* reported that affordable devices were making metal detecting "as popular as surfing."[98] Seven years later the *New York Times* described "a growing band of amateurs" equipped with cheap metal detectors who were prowling the nation's beaches, woods, and parks.[99] This "band of amateurs" took part in what Kristen Haring calls a technical hobby, a form of "productive recreation" that takes a machine as its focus.[100] The hobbyist community distinguished among a number of user groups: "coinshooters" searched for coins; "treasure hunters" were dedicated to the pursuit of large caches of lost or hidden wealth; "rockhounds" were interested in rare minerals; and "beachcombers" searched for valuables on public beaches.[101] Despite this diversity, hobbyists formed a national public constituted by national and local organizations, special events, and the publication of periodicals and guidebooks. The National Treasure Hunters League had approximately 30,000 members in 1976, and the league's president estimated that there were 250,000 Americans using metal detectors.[102]

In addition to joining national or regional clubs, enthusiasts took part in conventions like the three-day International Treasure Hunters show, where attendees brushed shoulders with the authors of popular guidebooks and examined the finds of fellow treasure hunters.[103] In addition to these special events, enthusiasts could stay engaged with the metal-detecting community year-round by subscribing to magazines such as *True Treasure, Lost Treasure,* and *Treasure Hunter.* They could also buy handbooks such as Frank L. Fish's *Buried Treasure and Lost Mines* (1961), Art Lassagne's *Metal Detector Handbook* (1967), E. S. LeGaye's *Electronic Metal Detector Handbook* (1969), Norman Carlisle and David Michelsohn's *Complete Guide to Treasure Hunting* (1973), and Karl Von Mueller's *Treasure Hunter's Manual* (1974).

Historians of sound media should appreciate the fact that thousands of earphone-clad, metal-detector hobbyists were taking part in a popular culture of portable sound that predates the 1979 introduction of the Sony Walkman. Furthermore, this was an audio culture that had less to do with the construction of a "soundtrack to the city" than with rhabdomancy's recalibration of local place. Indeed, metal-detecting guidebooks encouraged practitioners to undertake careful research into local history. Frank L. Fish wrote that "the first step of any treasure hunt is the accumulation and study of all available data relative to the proposed search." A *Popular Science* article from 1963 explained that the most successful treasure hunters found valuable objects through historical study, poring over "old maps, town records, tax assessments, old newspaper accounts, and historical books": "Pinpointing the precise location of an old hotel, a stage-line office, or Wells Fargo stop is a big advantage." The author of a 1975 *New York*

Times article agreed that research was required to discover the best sites and suggested consulting long-time residents, old maps, and local librarians about the sites where carnivals, fairs, or meetings had been held.[104]

As in Wolfert Webber's day, the study of local history could move into the realm of folk legend and treasure lore. Washington Irving's treasure tales were dominated by pirates, Native Americans, and Dutch settlers, but postwar treasure tales tended to evoke the iconography of the American West: photographs showed treasure seekers in western landscapes; metal-detector units had trade names like "Bounty Hunter," "Prospector," and "El Dorado"; and treasure literature often featured images of the Old West, tales of lost Spanish gold, western gold miners, abandoned ghost towns, and the buried loot of western outlaws.[105] Western themes permeate one of the most popular and enduring treasure-hunting guidebook of the postwar era: Frank L. Fish's *Buried Treasure and Lost Mines*). Fish's book contains descriptions of ninety-three caches of lost treasure, many of which indicate a lingering belief in the volatility of metals and guardian spirits. Fish writes in the introduction to the book that beneath the earth could be found "rotting chests of riches" like "Aladdin's legend come true" and that "the ghosts of long-dead prospectors, robbers, miners, and adventurers still haunt their sandy mounds and earthy tombs, ever guarding their wealth." In his tale of the "Lost Dutchman Mine," Fish explains how a party of early Spanish explorers discovered a gold mine but were attacked by Native Americans enraged at their trespassing on sacred ground. Two of the Spaniards survive, only to be killed by the eponymous Dutchman, who dies before claiming the mine's riches, leaving behind a mysterious map.[106] The tale of the "Lost Dutchman Mine" is its own act of excavation, revealing the rich sediment of historical social relations that could be drawn on to constitute a sense of local place in the American West. When tales such as this became mental maps for metal-detecting expeditions, they served, like the legend of "Father Red-cap," as localizers that allowed diviners to retrace the steps of an area's previous inhabitants.

Just as Wolfert Webber's discovery of treasure lore had made the soil of his native land gleam with gold dust, the combination of historical research and divination with the metal detector changed how hobbyists perceived their everyday environment. Domestic spaces, for example, were reimagined as "a multitude of niches and recesses for lost and hidden articles."[107] Treasure hunters were advised to explore old homes, paying attention to the spaces underneath stairways, removable sections in floors and walls, the stones under the fireplace, the back of mirrors and picture frames, and the inside of door locks, where children tended to place small toys and coins. In the outdoor spaces around a dwelling, treasure seekers developed an eye for unusual landmarks where people might have hidden valuables: a spot halfway between a house and a barn, the center of a triangle formed by three trees, the area near an old fencepost.[108] Like their nineteenth-century predecessors, postwar diviners opened fissures in the local environment where the exhalations of history might emerge and crystalize, to be grasped by the diligent treasure seeker.

To the extent that they explored ruins and excavated historical artifacts, hobbyists resembled amateur archaeologists. Professional archaeologists were ambivalent about this growing cohort of competitors. Joan Allen dedicated a chapter of her guidebook to the "strained relations" between treasure hunters and archaeologists and explained that archaeologists saw metal-detector hobbyists as "greed crazed and totally ignorant vandals."[109] Similar tensions are illustrated by a *New York Times* article that described how a Civil War battleground in Virginia had become a battleground between archaeologists and metal-detector enthusiasts, both of whom sought the site's historical objects.[110]

Archaeologists and hobbyists shared an interest in historical artifacts, but where the former sought to treat them with a certain scientific detachment and place them in a climate-controlled museum display, the latter wanted to revel in what David Lowenthal describes as the "existential concreteness" of the relic as history.[111] That is, hobbyists wanted to locate relics, dig them up, handle them, and take them home. Recall Alan Taylor's claim that nineteenth-century treasure seeking provided a materialistic faith that was an alternative to unsatisfactory abstract religion. We might say that twentieth-century metal detecting provided a materialistic archaeology that was an alternative to an unsatisfactorily abstract historical science. In other words, hobbyists made history tangibly present in an embodied practice that charged places and artifacts with the mysteries of the past.

Rhabdomancy's power as a localizer and the continuing tensions between amateur treasure hunters and archaeologists are dramatized on the National Geographic Channel's reality television show *Diggers* (2012–), which is part of a cycle of metal detecting–themed shows that also includes Spike TV's *American Digger* (2013–) and the Travel Channel's *Dig Wars* (2013–). *Diggers* follows the exploits of two "extreme metal detectives," Tim "the Ringmaster" Saylor and "King George" Wyant (aka "KG"), who, according to the show's publicity, "scour the country for relics, riches, and lost pieces of American history, while spreading a healthy dose of laughs along the way."[112] The laughs arise primarily from the infectious enthusiasm that the diggers display when they make a discovery, as well as a set of ridiculous but memorable catchphrases.

Episodes of *Diggers* confirm that sound remains a central feature of the metal-detecting experience. KG and the Ringmaster are typically shown wearing large headphones and walking with the "slow and creeping step" of the classic diviner. The opening title sequence of the series begins with the sound of the detector, and throughout individual episodes the hosts refer to the various "high tones" and "mid tones" produced by modern detectors. There is clearly a visceral pleasure to the aural component of the practice, and the hosts frequently make comments about an "awesome sound" or remark that a particular area of ground "sounds awesome" or even wax poetic about a tone being an angel singing in their headphones.

The interconnection of rhabdomancy, local history, and treasure lore is enacted on *Diggers* as well. Episodes of the show take place in western ghost towns and old gold-rush mines or center on folk heroes like Wyatt Earp, Bat Masterson, Bonnie and Clyde, and Blackbeard the pirate. In the first episode of the second season, the hosts are thrilled to discover coins and bullet shells that date from the era of Billy the Kid. In an episode from the third season, the team looks for pirate treasure in North Carolina. When KG finds a musket ball, he exclaims that it "could have been fired by Blackbeard." When they come across a giant cypress tree, the diggers assert that it "could have been" the legendary lookout tree where Blackbeard was said to watch for ships coming up the Tar River. An old belt buckle and button "could have" fallen off of Blackbeard's coat, and a strange metal object "could have" come from the bottom of one of the pirate's trademark pistols. Here and elsewhere, the hosts use the past conditional tense to speak of what "could have been" to create a clearing in the imagination where objects and places might take on heightened meaning. In the process the hosts construct an encounter with previous inhabitants through a set of objects most would consider to be garbage. The everyday spaces of a ranch or the shade beneath a North Carolina cypress tree become "haunted" spaces, saturated with local legends that make them alive to the past.[113]

KG and the Ringmaster's imaginative play with the conditional tense is usually brought down to earth by local historians and archaeologists who pass judgment on the diggers' finds. On the Blackbeard episode, for example, we learn that what "could have been" part of the pirate's pistol is actually the bottom of a furniture leg. It is notable that the presence of these historical professionals on *Diggers* was the result of protest from the archaeological community. There was considerable controversy surrounding this and other metal-detection shows, including an online petition by "Concerned Archaeologists and Their Supporters" that asked the cable channels to pull these programs because they promoted the "looting and disrespect of our national heritage."[114] The National Geographic Society convened a workshop with the goal of making *Diggers* more palatable to archaeologists and announced that, based on feedback from the event, they would include a supervising archaeologist during shooting, present archaeologists onscreen discussing the historical significance of found items, and downplay the monetary value of the objects, which was thought to encourage looting.[115]

The negotiation surrounding *Diggers* shows the continued tensions between amateur and professional approaches to history. The professionals get the final word on the show, but they can't help but appear as killjoys whose main function is to drain the pleasure from history and short-circuit the enchantment of local places. The tension enacted on *Diggers* resembles the contrast that Walter Benjamin makes between the knowledge gained from traditional storytelling and modern networks of "information": where the former borrowed from the miraculous and possessed a certain authority, even if it was not "subject to verification," the latter laid claim to "prompt verifiability" and was required to sound plausible. The archaeologist's claim that the object is a furniture leg is verifiable and plausible, but the digger's claim that it is Blackbeard's pistol can inspire the astonishment and thoughtfulness that Benjamin compares to seeds of grain that "have lain for centuries in the chambers of the pyramids shut up air-tight and have retained their germinative power to this day."[116]

I have been arguing that metal-detector hobbyists experienced a sense of place when they acted as amateur historians, folklorists, and archaeologists, but did they experience a sense of planet? It is safe to assume that few postwar hobbyists retained a belief in metallic exhalation, but occult discourses surrounding divination practices did continue into this era. The author of a 1967 guidebook asserted that metal detecting had "an aura of mystery and superstition," and despite its "scientifically sound methods and instruments," many people still considered treasure hunting to be in the realm of "the occult arts."[117] Traditional techniques of dowsing for water with the divining rod continued to be practiced during the postwar era (as they are today), and the American Society of Dowsers, an organization founded in 1961, reportedly had a membership of close to thirty thousand in 1968.[118] Communities of dowsing and metal detecting have often overlapped, as when treasure-hunting magazines featured advertisements for dowsing classes, or when articles in the popular press moved seamlessly from talking about one type of divination to the other. Given this fluidity of practice, it is safe to assume that some postwar treasure hunters were still hearing the whispers of planetary forces in their earphones.

We might say that the subterranean signals heard by postwar diviners only went so deep, but the practice could bring users into contact with a "bioregional" scale of interaction when hobbyists took themselves into wilderness or semiwilderness spaces.[119] Recall how Wolfert Webber's treasure hunting took him to the edges of urban space, where he encountered snakes and catbirds. Hobbyist guidebooks frequently praised treasure hunting for the way in which it brought users into natural landscapes. LeGaye dedicated his book to those who "love the outdoors" and concluded by declaring, "Never mind getting rich; never mind finding the big one! Just get out in the fresh air, get a suntan, feel the thrill that comes from hearing your detector's response when working new ground! Get out and enjoy! Get out and live!"[120] Von Mueller urged readers to get "away from all of the frantic city excitement" and wrote of how "the mountains and the desert have a mysterious way of entwining you with an invisible cloak of quiet excitement and a new way of life."[121] As these quotations indicate, treasure hunters may have been amateur historians, but they were also technophiles who took their gadgets into the countryside.

Portable sound devices that are taken into natural spaces create a contact zone between two material ecologies. Media scholar Frauke Behrendt describes this dynamic in terms of the ecological concept of "ecotone": the zone of transition between different biological communities, such as forest and grassland, where there is often increased variety and diversity. Behrendt refers to mobile smartphones as technological "edge species" that operate between "the techno-ecosystem of our cities and the natural ecosystem of our countryside and landscapes" and argues that the sounds produced by portable media allow users to move through natural spaces while listening to media signals and so inhabit both systems at once. Smartphones are not the first sound technologies to be taken into natural spaces. In fact, spring-wound record players of the acoustic era were marketed for use on camping trips and vacations. The cover of the June 1906 Victor Records catalog features an illustration of a young couple listening to their acoustic phonograph while floating in a canoe.[122] Here we find another argument for why the Green Disc era was "green": no-wattage sound technologies could become "edge species" that were enjoyed in green spaces. Treasure hunters belong in the history of portable sound devices, along with outdoor phonographic excursions and the smartphones and digital GPS systems described by Behrendt.[123]

What I hope becomes clear is that divination practices can be a powerful means of interweaving the experience of multiple spatial scales, as when practitioners toggle from the moment-to-moment monitoring of personal space, to encounters with local place and traditional lore, to the interaction with natural habitats, to the intimation of planetary depths that comes with the perception of underground veins of water or minerals. Alexander Graham Bell's sketch of his portable induction balance is a fitting symbol for the way in which this nesting of spatial experience is manifested in a hybrid of sound technology and the ambulatory human body. Sixteenth-century German miners, nineteenth-century American diviners, twentieth-century uranium prospectors, and metal-detector hobbyists all tuned in to subterranean signals and so, to one degree or another, experienced a sense of the planet. The eco-cosmopolitan potential of the practice was usually drowned out by the louder appeals of quick wealth, amateur history, or enervating weekend pastime, but beneath those dominant melodies hummed a quiet yet persistent planetary pedal note that an eco-sonic agenda aims to amplify.

SONIC SCAVENGERS

Metal detectors became popular commodities in the postwar decades, but they had an ambiguous place in consumer culture. When mobilized as part of a vernacular practice of scavenging, they pulled against the grain of a commodity culture that has become increasingly geared toward maximizing the sale of goods that are "made to break."[124] Hobbyist books and magazines often contained photographs of smiling treasure hunters standing proudly over the motley assortment of the discarded objects that they had discovered. The "golden produce of the soil" for these treasure hunters was the disposable material culture of the past: old bottles, coins, buttons, and fragments of antique guns.[125] Green marketer John Grant argues that one of the best ways to challenge the throwaway culture of planned obsolescence and overconsumption is to encourage people to treasure their objects, either through practices of collecting or by investing them with personal memory. Grant writes that "the ultimate nondisposable good is something you make yourself."[126] Metal-detecting hobbyists created nondisposable goods, not by crafting or collecting them but by unearthing them.

The television series *Diggers* demonstrates not only that discarded objects can be reinvested with value but also the high degree of affect that could accompany that operation. One critic complained that the show's hosts seemed to have "a grande mal seizure" every time they found an old coin or colonial-era button.[127] Their reactions to making a discovery can certainly seem hysterical, but in my opinion it is no more ridiculous than the expressions of sexual bliss seen in advertising images of bikini-clad models eating a cheeseburger or the spasms of game-show contestants after they learn that they have won a new car. Eco-minded media critics should note that when KG climbs a tree or the Ringmaster rolls down a hill after unearthing a discarded artifact that has little or no monetary value, they are enacting a form of "alternative hedonism."[128]

Metal detectors were the media component in a vernacular practice of scavenging and recycling in which the pleasure of finding and excavating discarded artifacts was an alternative to purchasing new ones, and disposable objects were transformed into treasured historical relics. Scavenging has emerged on the environmental agenda; academic studies have reported that the practice creates jobs, reduces poverty, supplies inexpensive materials to industry, conserves natural resources, helps to keep the urban environment clean, and extends the lives of dumps and landfills.[129] Notably, scavenging has often been considered an issue related to women's quality of life, since women in developing countries have tended to be responsible for family provision and waste management.[130] Understanding metal-detector hobbyists as scavengers suggests the potential for technologies of augmented space to do more than expedite airport check-ins or retrieve product information in department stores.[131] Green activists might look for new allies in the treasure-hunting community, with a goal of opening up divination practices to new users, new stories, and new signals, to develop an alternative and more politically engaged culture of green divination.[132]

Scavenging tends to increase during times of scarcity, and it is not a coincidence that the rise of metal detecting in the United States during the 1960s and 1970s coincided with a constellation of economic crises.[133] David Hesmondhalgh describes this period as marking the "Long Downturn" in the American and European economies, and David Harvey characterizes it as a crisis in the Fordist-Keynesian regime of accumulation that had formed the basis for the postwar economic boom.[134] Americans experienced the economic crisis in the form of a long period of inflation and unemployment ("stagflation") that "eroded the foundations of middle-class stability."[135] If all this weren't enough, there was a simultaneous crisis in the nation's subterranean wealth: American oil production peaked in 1970 and began a "long decline that has continued to the present."[136] The United States became more and more dependent on imported oil and lost the ability to stabilize world petroleum prices, setting the stage for a crippling OPEC embargo and soaring energy costs.[137]

As the economy stagnated and America's fields of "black gold" dried up, metal-detecting guidebooks and periodicals promised readers that the American soil was still as fecund as ever.[138] In fact, Americans reading this literature might have concluded, like a starry-eyed Wolfert Webber, that the soil of their native land had turned into gold dust. Von Mueller assured readers that "there is treasure lost, buried, or hidden in every county and parish of these United States and some of it is found every day." LeGaye wrote that "there are uncounted tens of thousands of treasures scattered across the land," and a 1973 guide estimated that the treasure buried in the United States was worth $4 billion.[139] It is extremely unlikely that all of the earth's treasures will ever be found, wrote Art Lassange, because "there are just too many of them," and their supply is "constantly being replenished."[140] In 1979, the year of President Jimmy Carter's famous "crisis of confidence" speech, a metal-detector enthusiast gushed that America was "positively strewn with treasure": "hidden from sea to shining sea are billions of dollars worth of the stuff. And nearly all of it is there for the taking."[141]

It is easy to dismiss the utopian visions of postwar metal-detector publications such as these as a denial of the harsh economic realities of the time. In this view, hobbyists were literally burying their heads in the sand, participants in a wave of 1970s nostalgia that Lowenthal claimed was fueled by Americans' mistrust of the future.[142] I want to suggest another possibility: that divination hobbyists were pioneers in the use of sound technologies to "make do with less" during a time of economic crisis and resource scarcity. These types of practices are important to understand and appreciate as we face an era in which natural resources are being rapidly depleted, and when there may be more scarce materials in discarded mobile phones than in the hidden depths of the earth.[143] Indeed, the cycle of metal detecting–themed reality TV shows coincided with a resurgence of the practice spurred by the 2008 financial crisis. In 2011 the *Wall Street Journal* reported that the skyrocketing price of precious metals had created a boom in the metal-detector trade.[144] Treasure tales and acts of rhabdomancy aided in the transition from an agricultural to a market economy. Perhaps practices of green divination can aid in the bumpy transition to a postcarbon economy of salvage, conservation, and reuse.

4. Radio's Dark Ecology

Orson Welles once referred to radio as an "abandoned mine." It was the 1970s when Welles made this remark, and he meant to convey his belief that radio had been the victim of "technological restlessness," abandoned by artists and audiences before all of its riches had been discovered. Welles's metaphor is a convenient bridge between the discussion of mining culture in the previous chapter and the project of the present one, which is to embark on an eco-critical investigation of radio theater. Given the central role played by mining operations in the history of industrialization and environmental degradation, Welles's linkage of radios and mineshafts reminds us that media technologies, no matter how much they may appear to exist in the immaterial airwaves, are always reliant on a material infrastructure that draws on finite resources.

In the same interview Welles made an implicit argument about media history. Just before his comment about radio, Welles claimed that theater, though still a source of "joy and wonder," was no longer "hooked up to the main powerhouse."[1] Welles was asserting that forms of modern media had taken the niche previously filled by the theater, but his choice of metaphor encourages us to hear another claim in this statement: that old or residual media technologies may be preferable to dominant ones to the extent that they are disengaged from the "main powerhouse," that is, the less energy and resources that they require. Radio stands as a case in point, as both a quintessentially "old medium," long understood to have been supplanted by television, and at the same time a "rugged and inexpensive technology" that can function "where topography, poverty, or politics limit access to television, computers, or electricity."[2] Radio has comparatively small energy requirements, meaning that receiving sets can be powered by hand cranks or solar cells. At least one radio station—KTAO in New Mexico—is powered entirely by the sun.³ Furthermore, the costs of production are lower than in film and television because radio plays tend to have small casts and forgo the costs of makeup, costume, and set construction. Radio should have a central place in a green-media agenda that aims to provide content to the largest number of people at the lowest cost to the planet's resources.

Much could be said about radio infrastructure along the lines of my analysis of phonography in chapter 1 or about radio's part in the history of portable sound, extending the discussion in chapter 3. Observations of this kind can be found in the analysis that follows, but the main thrust of this chapter is toward the goal stated in the book's introduction to *hear* the ecological potential of sound media as well as locate it in material objects and cultural practices. The analysis of sound-media texts has a place in an "up, down, and sideways" study of eco-sonic media along with analyses of infrastructure, devices, and protocols of use. Over the course of the previous three chapters, I have gestured toward what might be called an eco-sonic poetics: recall my suggestion that the noise of shellac discs could be heard as the voice of a forest ecology, or that plasmatic sounds acknowledge the use of plastic materials in sound production, or that phonographic whistlers and bird mimics are a form of zoosemiotic media communication. In this chapter, I bring my investigation of eco-sonic poetics to radio theater to identify some of the formal techniques, genres, and narrative themes available as expressive resources for ecological critique in that mode of sound production.⁴

Orson Welles's quip about the "abandoned mine" orients our first step toward a green-radio aesthetic. When understood in the most literal of terms, Welles is saying that radio is a very dark place. In fact, radio has long been described as having a special affinity for darkness. For Richard J. Hand, radio is "characterized by darkness" and for Andrew Crisell, radio is adept at conveying action that takes place "in utter darkness." Nadia Bozak draws our attention to film's reliance on energy-expensive artificial light and calls for a "sunless cinema" that relies less on light and more on darkness. Theorists like Hand and Crisell alert us to the fact that the original "sunless cinema" is radio.⁵

Hand asserts that radio's darkness makes it "ripe for horror," and other commentators have described radio as a "necropolis riddled with dead voices" or broadcast voices as "skeletonized."⁶ It is not a surprise, then, that some of the darkest of media genres—horror, crime thrillers, science fiction, and noir—have played a prominent role in the history of American radio theater. Tellingly, one of the most popular horror anthology series of American network radio was titled *Lights Out* (1934–47). A tendency toward literal and figurative darkness makes radio an ideal platform for a mode of ecological aesthetics that Timothy Morton calls "dark ecology," which lingers "in the shadowy world of irony and difference" and includes "negativity and irony, ugliness and horror." "The more ecological awareness we have," Morton writes, "the more we experience the uncanny," with the result that ecological art need not be limited to depictions of picturesque wilderness or uplifting accounts of charismatic animals.[7]

Another theme of Morton's work is that "the end of the world has already occurred." Morton shares environmental activist Bill McKibben's view that the earth that we knew is gone in the sense that humans have irrevocably altered the planet, a process that began with the large-scale burning of fossil fuels during the Industrial Revolution and has become dramatically more apparent in the era of global warming. "We have traveled to a new planet," McKibben writes, "propelled on a burst of carbon dioxide."[8] In this chapter, I attend to the dark ecological aesthetic that manifests in radio plays that depict the end of the world in the form of environmental crisis, the collapse of human society, planetary destruction, or species extinction. Such dark ecosonic texts offer models for listening to and creating sound media that can help us to cope with an ecological catastrophe that has already happened.

Morton's concept of "dark ecology" orients my exploration of radio's shadowy soundscapes, but my principal guide in terms of critical method is the literary theorist M. M. Bakhtin, who had a predilection for metaphors like voice, dialogue, accent, and polyphony, making him a decidedly sonic thinker. Moreover, Michael J. McDowell argues that his theory is "the literary equivalent of ecology" due to its focus on dialogic forms in which multiple voices or points of view interact.[9] In other words, Bakhtin's theory is both "eco" and "sonic." Bakhtin was interested in how dialogic relationships exist across time and wrote that texts begin to "sound in a different way" when social languages change. Adaptations of a text may strengthen the original intentions of an author or pull it in entirely new directions, actualizing a potential already available to it.[10] Bakhtin referred to this process of creative adaptation as reaccentuation, and it is pertinent to this chapter, first, because some of the broadcasts that I examine are adaptations of literature, and, second, because I reaccentuate my chosen texts by forging intertextual connections that may not have been intended by the original authors or perceived by its audiences but that actualize their potential as eco-critical sound art.[11] Specifically, I foster a dialogue between radio plays, American environmental literature, and eco-criticism.

Neil Verma writes that a radio play "is a story but it also must conjure a place," and I have chosen my case studies in part by the kinds of places that they represent.[12] Bakhtin's work becomes useful here as well, since his theorization of the relationship between literary spaces and the lived environment aids in the pursuit of what Ursula Heise calls a "properly ecological approach" to the study of the media, one that considers how media environments "relate to other types of environments."[13] During the same years that Orson Welles was starting his illustrious radio career, Bakhtin wrote a well-known essay in which he defined the term "chronotope" as "the intrinsic connectedness of temporal and spatial relationships that are artistically expressed in literature." Chronotopes such as "the road" were, for Bakhtin, the "organizing centers" for narrative events and literary genres, as well as a vital link between literary works and the lived experience of a particular historical time and place.[14]

The radio plays described in this chapter are all organized around spatial as well as temporal "Ends of the Earth." That is, they take place at the polar regions or on oceanic islands and also feature themes of extinction, social collapse, and planetary catastrophe. Bakhtin's notion of the chronotope directs our attention to the interpenetration of media space and geographic space and alerts us to the importance of the poles and islands in our experience of the temporality of the climate crisis. As is well known, warming temperatures melt polar ice, which leads to rising sea levels that threaten to flood coastal lowlands and island nations. To borrow an idea from the previous chapter, the poles and islands have become the "canary in the coalmine" for global warming.[15] You might imagine this chapter, then, as a descent into the abandoned mine of radio, but the farther down we go, the more we find ourselves emerging at the far-flung corners of the globe. It seems fitting that we begin our descent with a broadcast by Welles himself.

DEVIL'S SYMPHONY

The Mercury Theater's production of "War of the Worlds" on October 30, 1938, is probably the most famous radio program of all time. The show has continued to fascinate listeners, not only due to the panic that it incited but also because of its gripping enactment of the collapse of human society. The broadcast simulates radio news coverage of an invasion by an army from the planet Mars and builds to a climax midway through the show when a reporter speaks from a rooftop in New York City. Conceding that the U.S. Army and Air Force have been wiped out, the reporter describes five massive alien machines crossing the river into the city and the panic in the streets below, where people leap into the river "like rats." "This is the end now," he says, coughing in smoke and gas before passing out, leaving his live microphone to transmit the sounds of distant air-raid sirens.

Jeffrey Sconce claims that the "War of the Worlds" broadcast gains much of its power from the way in which it simultaneously depicts catastrophe at the level of the social body, the military, and the media infrastructure.[16] The notoriety of the "Panic Broadcast" has obscured the fact that the Mercury Theater staged a similar collapse three weeks earlier. On October 9 the Mercury Theater performed an adaptation of Edward Ellsberg's *Hell On Ice* (1938), which depicted a failed attempt by an American expedition to reach the North Pole in 1879. "Hell on Ice" is notable among the Mercury's radio broadcasts in a number of ways: it marks the debut of the writer Howard Koch, who became a regular on the series, scripting "War of the Worlds" three weeks later, and it is the only show to be based on a "stirring adventure of recent history" as opposed to classic literature. "Hell on Ice" also stands out among the Mercury oeuvre as a proto-environmental critique. That is, like "War of the Worlds," "Hell on Ice" enacts the collapse of human society, but where the October 30 broadcast was a science fiction thriller that tapped into public fascination with the possibility of life on Mars and anxiety about the looming war in Europe, the October 9 show used historical fiction to dramatize the folly of human attempts to master the natural elements and extend the reach of Western industrial society across the globe. As such, "Hell on Ice" is not only a masterpiece of audio theater but a powerful eco-sonic critique.

"Hell on Ice" tells the story of the first attempt to reach the North Pole by way of the Bering Strait. The expedition was cosponsored by the U.S. Navy and James Gordon Bennett, the owner of the *New York Herald*, and its aim was to send the ship *Jeannette* along a warm, northerly ocean current to the shores of the mysterious Wrangel Island in the Arctic Ocean, which some believed was the tip of a vast continent that stretched to Greenland.[17] Hopes for the *Jeannette* expedition were high, and a columnist for the *Washington Post* wrote that if successful, it would be "the triumph of the nineteenth century."[18] Captain George Washington DeLong and a crew of thirty-one men left San Francisco to great celebration on July 8, 1879, but the voyage did not go as planned. The *Jeannette* made safe passage into the Arctic Ocean and came within sight of Wrangel Island, but the ship became trapped in the ice on September 5, 1879, and remained stuck there for two years before being crushed by ice floes on June 11, 1881. The crew abandoned the shattered ship and made a desperate flight across the ice to open water, where they packed into three lifeboats and steered a course for Siberia. One boat was lost at sea with all its passengers, and the other two were separated in a storm before reaching land. Of those two, the party led by Captain DeLong froze to death in the Lena Delta. A search party led by the *Jeannette*'s engineer George Melville discovered their bodies on March 24, 1882, and their unhappy fate was soon front-page news across the nation.

Despite the tragic outcome of the expedition, there was much to the story of the *Jeannette* that might have appealed to Welles and the Mercury Theater. Welles was fascinated with literature "of and about the 1890s," as demonstrated by his adaptations of Booth Tarkington's *Seventeen* (1916) and *The Magnificent Ambersons* (1918).[19] Ellsberg's *Hell on Ice* also lent itself to the Mercury's "first-person" approach to radio narrative, drawing as it did on the journals of the *Jeannette*'s officers. Moreover, Ellsberg's is a surprisingly radiogenic book, with many vivid descriptions of sound. We read that the "unearthly screeching and horrible groanings" of the ice pack are "like the shrieking of a thousand steamer whistles, the thunder of heavy artillery, the roaring of a hurricane, and the crash of collapsing houses all blended together." Ice floes part "with roars like thunder, forming a deep bass background for the 'high scream' of the flintlike ice of grating icebergs, the whole echoing across the pack to us in a veritable devil's symphony of hideous sounds."[20] The Mercury Theater's adaptation of *Hell on Ice* grants considerable airtime to recreating that "devil's symphony," with stunning sequences depicting the ship's engines straining against the ice, floes that shriek and drum on the ship's hull, and the piercing Arctic wind.

Raucous sequences such as these stand out against the backdrop of the eerie polar silence. Indeed, the ice-covered Arctic Ocean is what R. Murray Schafer calls a "hi-fi soundscape," in which "discrete sounds can be heard clearly because of the low ambient noise level."[21] Ellsberg's book dramatizes the stark contrasts possible in a hi-fi soundscape, as when the thunderous grinding of ice floes comes to an abrupt halt, leaving the crew in the "deathly Arctic silence." The stillness is broken by the incongruous banality of the bosun's pipe, followed by his call "All hands! Lay below for breakfast!"[22] The Mercury broadcast depicts this uncanny episode in an early example of what would become one of Welles's signature approaches to sound: his use of "overdetermined bookends," whereby striking sound events and sonic contrasts are reserved for the beginning and ending of a sequence.[23]

The frozen world of "Hell on Ice" has many expressive possibilities for the Mercury's sound-effects crew, but it is also a showcase for composer Bernard Herrmann.[24] John Houseman claimed that Herrmann had a repertoire of music for the Mercury broadcasts, one of which was "frozen music" used for "gruesome effects."[25] Herrmann's frozen music is first heard when the ship becomes locked in the ice, and it signals a shift in the show's narrative emphasis to themes of frozen time, stasis, immobility, and deadening routine. The slow, queasy, pendulum-like movements of Herrmann's score make the perfect accompaniment to Captain DeLong's June 21 journal entry, read on the broadcast by the actor Ray Collins: "The absolute monotony; the unchanging round of hours; the awakening to the same things and the same conditions that one saw just before losing one's self in sleep; the same faces; the same dogs; the same ice; the same conviction that tomorrow will be exactly the same as today, if not more disagreeable."[26] Here and elsewhere in the broadcast, Herrmann's frozen music serves multiple functions: it is sonic set design that portrays the bleak scene of the Arctic ice pack; it casts a mood over that setting, much as expressive lighting might lend cinematic mise-en-scène with a sense of dread; and it provides commentary on the emotional life of the crew, who struggle with the soul-crushing monotony of life on the pack.[27]

What becomes clear is that Ellsberg's book was a remarkably inspired choice of source material for the Mercury Theater, and the resulting broadcast is certainly great radio, taking full advantage of the medium's expressive resources.[28] We should appreciate "Hell on Ice" not just for its aesthetic achievement, however, but also for its social critique. As with other Welles projects, "Hell on Ice" questions America's passage to an industrial and imperial society.[29] There is an ecological as well as a social critique to "Hell on Ice," but to fully hear it we need to broaden the intertextual field to include not only the works that Welles adapted but a few that he did not. One text in particular might have made an ideal source for Welles's concept for a *First Person Singular* series, as it is the most famous first-person singular account of nineteenth-century American literature: Henry David Thoreau's *Walden* (1854). Bringing *Walden* into the orbit of "Hell on Ice" reorients the matrix of texts in which "Hell on Ice" is situated and allows us to hear Welles's broadcast in new ways.

Walden initially suggests a narrative of adventure (the individual in the wilderness) but then quickly abandons it for descriptions of everyday life on Walden Pond. Robert B. Ray claims that Thoreau had little gift for narrative and that "going to Walden appealed to him because there *nothing could happen*." *Walden* is the first-person account of an adventure story in which nothing happens, and as the narrative interest fades, it is replaced by Thoreau's poetic descriptive passages and biting social commentary.[30] Bakhtin might have described this as a tension between two literary chronotopes, the adventure novel and the idyll. Adventure novels, Bakhtin wrote, tend to be composed of a series of short, discreet, temporal segments that exist outside of historical time and require an "abstract expanse of space" with little cultural specificity. By contrast, the idyllic chronotope blends natural, cyclic time with the "everyday time" of a pastoral or agricultural life in which human events are fastened down to a familiar territory "with all its nooks and crannies, its familiar mountains, valleys, fields, rivers and forests, and one's own home."[31] *Walden* suggests the chronotope of adventure before settling into the idyllic mode.

Captain DeLong's journals of the *Jeannette* expedition required a similar rerouting of narrative expectations, as the intrepid conqueror of the pole found himself immobilized in the ice. DeLong wrote in his journal that, given the "popular idea" that "daily life in the Arctic regions should be vivid, exciting, and full of hair-breadth escapes," the account of his voyage was sure to be found "dull and weary and unprofitable."[32] Immobility, routine, and unprofitability were a blessing to Thoreau, and he even contrasted his "experiment" on Walden Pond to the adventures of Arctic explorers like John Franklin and Martin Frobisher. Where they had explored the earth's higher latitudes, Thoreau implored readers to "explore your own higher latitudes. . . . Explore thyself."[33] DeLong could not follow Thoreau's example and move into the idyllic mode, not that he didn't try. In his journal entry of January 13, 1880, DeLong begins to describe "the perfect picture which nature gave us of a midwinter night," but he freezes up as he tries to expand on that sentiment: "to turn around and look at the ship was to feel that she had dropped out of fairy-land in her pure whiteness, and was too—Well, I can't say what I want to. These outbursts are too much for me; I commence them, and cannot finish them; I seem to know the tune, but can never remember the words."[34]

My point is not to fault DeLong for failing to be a poet but instead to see how "Hell on Ice" and *Walden* share a certain narrative problem or, more precisely, a "lack-of-narrative" problem. When Welles adapted DeLong's journals (via Ellsberg), he responded to that problem in part by recourse to character study. On the Mercury broadcast, the *Jeannette*'s thwarted mission opens up the possibility for brilliant dramatic scenes: the interaction among engineer Melville (Welles), DeLong (Collins), John Danenhower (Joseph Cotton), and reporter Jerome Collins (Howard Smith) during the crew's first Christmas on the ice; Melville's encounter with the seaman Erikson (Karl Swenson), who is losing his reason; the escalating tensions between DeLong and Collins; and Melville and DeLong's final conversation about their chances of survival on the ice.[35]

Taking a detour through *Walden* provides a new perspective on the structure of "Hell on Ice," but Thoreau's book is best known, of course, as a classic of American environmentalism. It may seem pointless to speculate about what Thoreau might have written had he been keeping a journal on board the *Jeannette*, but by a remarkable coincidence, another icon of the American environmental movement nearly did just that. The nature writer and Sierra Club founder John Muir was a passenger on board a government ship that was sent to look for the missing *Jeannette* in 1881. Radio fans familiar with Welles's colleague at CBS Radio, the writer-producer Norman Corwin, will take pleasure in the fact that the name of Muir's ship was the *Corwin*.[36] Muir was eager to travel on the *Corwin* as a chance to continue his study of glaciers and their role in shaping the landscape of the polar region during the last ice age. In the introduction to the book of Muir's *Corwin* journals, Bill McKibben writes that Muir "could look on what others saw as wasteland and sense its sublimity."[37]

Muir's Arctic writings contain passages that operate not in the abstract space and ahistorical time of the adventure story, nor in the mode of the idyllic everyday, but instead in what I want to call planet-time: a spatiotemporal dynamic in which place is experienced in relation to a scale beyond the human, and spatial immobility coincides with a present moment that expands to include the distant past or the distant future. Muir described standing before an Alaskan glacier, where he contemplated "the earth-sculpturing, landscape-making action" of glaciation and came to the realization that "the world, though made, is yet being made; that this is still the morning of creation; that mountains long conceived are now being born, channels traced for coming rivers, basins hollowed for lakes."[38] Muir took part in a tradition of the Romantic sublime, which allowed him to perceive the spaces of the frozen North not as an unprofitable wasteland but as a window onto deep time. If we listen closely, can we hear some of Muir's sentiments in Welles's "Hell on Ice"?

Listening for an ecological critique in the Mercury broadcast prompts us to hear Herrmann's frozen music as a sonic cue of planet-time, its eerie monotony signaling nonhuman scales of experience.[39] Likewise, the show's sound effects become more than a display of modernist radio technique; they are a means to give voice to nonhuman nature in a way that creates dissonant harmonies with human endeavors. Notice how the expedition is made to seem insignificant by the thunderous sounds of the "endless miles of surging ice" that snap the *Jeannette* to splinters. Or consider how, during DeLong's last divine service on the edge of the ice pack, the sound of the men singing a hymn is gradually drowned out by a crescendo of roaring Arctic wind. In these sequences the broadcast uses sound to play with spatial scale, performing a kind of auditory zoom from place to planet that works to diminish the human.[40] The conclusion of the show does something similar, but in a temporal register, as Melville describes burying DeLong and his men at a desolate spot overlooking the Arctic Ocean, where the winds wail an "eternal dirge."[41]

There is a painful irony to this conclusion, which asserts that the wind and ice of the Arctic are unchanging and eternal, for we have come to understand that the polar climate does indeed have a history and that humans now shape it in profound ways. "Hell on Ice" thus begins to "sound in a different way" in our own era, as public attention is again focused on the Arctic, not as the last frontier of heroic exploration but as the most tangible evidence of global warming.[42] As temperatures rise in the Arctic, we are forced to contemplate another kind of polar "hell," one represented not by an impenetrable wall of ice but by the thinning and disappearance of the ice pack, with all its intimations of environmental catastrophe.[43] I hear all of this in the roaring and shrieking of the wind and ice in the Mercury's October 9 broadcast, especially once I am prompted by the work of Thoreau and Muir. Indeed, it is now Muir's voice that I hear, with its planetary perspective, when Collins, as DeLong, speaks the line that the *Jeannette*'s captain wrote on September 6, 1879, the first day that the ship became frozen in the ice: "This is a glorious country to learn patience in."[44]

THE SOUL OF INERTNESS

Historian Aaron Sachs writes that the failure of the *Jeannette* expedition was painful to the American public because it seemed to reinforce "the insignificance of human striving in the face of nature's overwhelming power."[45] It is not surprising, then, that the *Jeannette* faded from public memory rather quickly, particularly once subsequent expeditions to the North Pole proved successful. In 1909 both Robert Peary and Frederick Cook claimed to have reached the northernmost latitude. Historian Lisa Bloom argues that polar explorers like Peary and Cook embodied turn-of-the-century ideals of masculinity in America and that the Arctic was a crucial site where the United States sought to establish itself as a "great imperial power."[46] Given this cultural context, we can appreciate all the more the critical bite of Welles's production of "Hell on Ice," which pulled against the prevailing currents of American ideologies of masculinity and expansionism.

The poles were ideal sites to perform heroic masculinity because they were thought to be desolate and dangerous regions, but turn-of-the-century explorers did not face them empty-handed. The *Jeannette* was fitted with an electric generator and arc lights provided by Thomas Edison, meant to illuminate the ship and produce a beneficial moral and physical effect on the men.⁴⁷ Alexander Graham Bell gave DeLong a telephone so that communication could be established between the ship and parties on the ice. The device's thin copper wires broke in the cold, however, and so it was used only on board the ship.⁴⁸ Polar explorers of the 1900s took advantage of the portability of acoustic phonography and brought record players on their expeditions. Peary wrote a letter to the Columbia graphophone company to report that their machine had provided "a distinct and agreeable break in the atmosphere of cold and gloom which surrounded us." Robert Scott took two gramophones with him on his ill-fated final voyage to the South Pole and wrote that "hardly a night passed without a gramophone concert." When they returned from the polar regions, Cook, Peary, and Ernest Shackleton even became recording artists, narrating scenes from their travels for the major phonograph companies.⁴⁹ We might say that polar exploration and the phonograph industry had a mutually beneficial relationship, with the former demonstrating the latter's durability and reliability, and the latter bringing reassuring sounds to far-flung and inhospitable territories.

Recall from chapter 1 that the era of acoustic phonography came to an end in the 1920s. That decade also marked a turning point in the technology of polar exploration, as dog sleds were replaced by airplanes, and acoustic phonographs were supplemented by wireless radio sets.⁵⁰ No figure embodied that transition more vividly than the aviator and explorer Richard E. Byrd, who first demonstrated the utility of radio during his 1926 airplane mission over the North Pole. The achievements of previous explorers had taken months to reach the rest of the world, but Byrd's flight was communicated by radio almost instantaneously, heralding a new era of global communication.⁵¹ Remarkable as the 1926 flight was, it was only the first act of Byrd's media celebrity. His Antarctic expedition of two years later surpassed it in notoriety and became one of the first modern multimedia events, covered by newspapers, radio networks, and even Paramount Pictures.⁵²

Highlights of Byrd's 1928 expedition to Antarctica included his flight over the South Pole in a three-engine plane and the discovery of mountains that he named the "Rockefeller Range."⁵³ The American public was fascinated by accounts of daily life at Byrd's base camp on the Ross Ice Shelf, which was known as "Little America." The camp was mostly underground and visual representations of it tended to emphasize its three radio towers.⁵⁴ This is fitting, given that the American public experienced Byrd's expedition largely through the radio. Byrd told the press that, next to food and navigational instruments, radio was his "most necessary equipment."⁵⁵ Every member of the expedition was trained in Morse code, and every party that left the base had shortwave transmitters and receiving sets.⁵⁶ As

FIGURE 10. Radio towers dominate visual representations of Richard E. Byrd's Antarctic base camp, Little America. Papers of Admiral Richard E. Byrd, Byrd Polar Research Center Archival Program, Ohio State University, Columbus.

they did with the phonograph, radio companies promoted their association with Byrd as a sign of their product's durability and dependability. Advertisements for Hammarlund Condensers bragged that their product was chosen by Byrd for their "ruggedness and simplicity"; an ad for Durham resistors featured the illustration of a letter from Byrd's radio engineer stating that the components could be relied on for "perfect performance under even the most adverse conditions"; Burgess radio batteries claimed to have shared "the hardships and the glory" of Byrd's polar flight; and Cardwell condensers declared that they had gone "over the pole" with Byrd, "where the failure of a single instrument might mean disaster."[57]

Radio also brought the sounds of America to Little America in weekly broadcasts sent to Byrd from the United States. American audiences listened to these ostensibly point-to-point communications, which included personal messages to members of the crew, statements by prominent politicians, and the sounds of the "throbbing life of New York" in the form of performances by popular musicians and comedians.[58] Radio also allowed Byrd a disembodied presence back in America, as when he sent electric signals to Los Angeles to switch on lights at a National Radio Show and to Philadelphia to illuminate a bust of Benjamin Franklin at the Poor Richard Club.[59]

The establishment of communication between America and Little America was a showcase for radio's capabilities. As one reporter put it, news from Little America was carried by "the modern Mercury" at 186,000 miles a second to tell "the story of his endeavor while the endeavor is being made." Radio brought "the Land of the Blizzard one-twentieth of a second from New York," wrote another, and so had shown "Marconi's invention capable of wonders never before revealed."[60] Radio's ability to reach Little America demonstrated what Rudolf Arnheim called "the great miracle of wireless": "The omnipresence of what people are singing or saying anywhere, the overleaping of frontiers, the conquest of spatial isolation."[61] Here was another example of the symbiotic relationship between polar exploration and sound media: Byrd demonstrated radio's global reach, and radio enacted a new kind of spatial adventure suited to the media age.

The "modern Mercury" of radio was not always so sure-footed, however. When the Byrd expedition left the Ross Ice Shelf and headed for home in March 1930, its first port of call was Dunedin, New Zealand, where Byrd spoke to Schenectady, New York, via the "most elaborate radio broadcasting hook-up ever attempted."[62] Press accounts described how the broadcast relied on one of the longest radio networks ever constructed, consisting of three transmitters, miles of wires, and submarine cables. Byrd's voice in Dunedin was sent over five hundred miles of cable to Wellington, where a station sent it on long-wave frequency to Sydney, Australia. From Sydney, Byrd's voice was transmitted by short wave to Schenectady, where the signal was wired into the broadcast transmitter of the nationwide NBC network.[63]

The Dunedin-Schenectady hookup was successful, but it was not without some rather revealing problems. For one thing, the content of the conversation did not strike all listeners as commensurate with the immensity of the effort. Consider a parody of the event published in several newspapers, which took the form of a mock dialogue between Byrd and Adolph Ochs, publisher of the *New York Times*:

    ADMIRAL BYRD— Hello. Can you hear me?

        MR. OCHS— It is certainly wonderful to hear the sound of your voice, Commander. How are you?

    ADMIRAL BYRD— I'm pretty well. How are you, Mr. Ochs?

        MR. OCHS— Yes, it is about 8 a.m. here. I can hear everything you are saying.

ADMIRAL BYRD— Hello. It's lovely weather here, too.

MR. OCHS— It is my privilege to welcome you back to civilization. You have made the world smaller by increasing our knowledge of it and man's triumph over the barriers of nature. You have added an empire to the * * *

ADMIRAL BYRD— I'm fine, thanks. How are you? You are coming over perfectly.[64]

Despite Byrd's and Ochs's repeated assurance that all was working perfectly, some listeners seem to have heard otherwise. The newspaper parody punctures the rhetoric of radio's perfect transmission and offers a subtle critique along the lines of Thoreau's comment concerning the construction of a telegraph wire from Maine to Texas: "Maine and Texas, it may be, have nothing important to communicate."[65]

Another problem arose from the fact that the voices of the interlocutors were sometimes drowned out by static that newspaper writers compared to the sounds of nature. One reporter spoke of "surging, rushing sounds" akin to "a giant surf beating against a rocky coast"; others wrote of "volcanic noises," "the yelping of sledge dogs and the savage crunching of polar ice," "storms," "avalanches," and "a mighty sealike roar."[66] It is as though listeners heard the static as the vast natural spaces that existed between New York and New Zealand, giving voice to the planetary forces that the conversational framing of the broadcast aimed to conceal.

In a certain sense, these accounts were correct: the static did give voice to the nonhuman nature in the network. In the days before the broadcast, commentators worried that the long-wave connection between Wellington to Sydney was the link in the chain that might cause problems, since the long-wave signals would be occurring during a season when electrical storms were frequent, creating the possibility for magnetic disturbances interfering with the radio signal.[67] In other words, some of the static that listeners heard was a sonic index of planetary scale caused by electromagnetic waves emanating from distant lightning strikes.

When atmospheric disturbances such as these are converted to sound by telephone and radio technologies, they are known as "whistlers," "sferics," or "natural radio." Douglas Kahn describes how Alexander Graham Bell's assistant Thomas Watson was one of the first people to listen to the snaps, chirps, and whistles of natural radio over telephone wires in 1876.[68] Three years later Captain DeLong described hearing "singing or humming sounds" on the *Jeannette*'s telephone wires, sounds that resembled "the buzz of a bee, or the whiz of a mosquito," which he knew to be caused by electrical storms.[69] Kahn argues that sferics are "globe-trotting signals" that bounce between the earth and the ionosphere to become "emissaries of earth magnitude."[70] The static heard on Byrd's New Zealand broadcast was another emissary of planetary magnitude, subtly undermining the official declaration that radio and polar exploration were making the world smaller.

There was another emissary of planetary magnitude present in the Dunedin-Schenectady broadcast besides the roaring static. Listeners reported that, at times, voices from New Zealand seemed to have an "echo or shadow." This was a phenomenon known as "world echo," caused by the reception of two signals, one that had traveled by the direct route from Dunedin to Schenectady, the other that took the long way around the globe and arrived a fraction of a second later.[71] World echo, like the static that occasionally drowned out Byrd's voice, suggested that radio did not travel through the abstract, frictionless space of Bakhtinian adventure-time but instead had a messier trajectory through wires, towers, radio stations, and the ionosphere. Just as listeners heard oceans of polar ice in radio static, so world echo allowed listeners to hear planetary scale in the time delay between the two signals.[72] As with the pops and hisses of shellac discs that gave voice to a forest ecology (see chapter 1), radio static and world echo from the Dunedin broadcast are examples of how noise can, in Kate Lacey's words, disturb the "structural amnesia" inherent in processes of representation."[73]

Byrd returned to the United States a national hero several times over and even became a film star with the release of Paramount's *With Byrd at the South Pole* (1930). It was not long before he was planning a return voyage to Little America that was poised to be an even grander media event than the first, with the admiral signing a lucrative contract with CBS Radio and General Foods.[74] The eyes and ears of the world were on Byrd and his party as they reestablished a base camp at Little America in 1934. Byrd was a radio presence back in America as he had been six years earlier: he set off fireworks to kick off the Chicago World Fair, rang the Liberty Bell, and received an award from CBS for his "outstanding service to radio broadcasting."[75] Byrd proclaimed that radio had "ended the isolation" of the Antarctic continent, but he had ambivalent feelings about that achievement. Radio was priceless "as a practical thing," he said, but added that he could "see where it is going to destroy all peace of mind, which is half the attraction of the polar regions."[76] It was peace of mind that Byrd was after when he made the unexpected announcement that he would station himself alone for six months at the remote Bolling Advance Weather Base, 123 miles south of Little America.[77] The original plan had been to send two other crew members to the base, but Byrd insisted on taking the assignment alone, despite protests from friends and advisers. Byrd spoke of his desire to be by himself, to "taste peace and quiet and solitude long enough to find out how good they really are." "I wanted something more than just privacy in the geographical sense," he wrote. "I wanted to sink roots into some replenishing philosophy . . . out there on the South Polar barrier, in cold and darkness as complete as that of the Pleistocene."[78]

Byrd hoped that the weather hut on the Ross Ice Shelf would become Thoreau's hut at Walden Pond, and he referred to Thoreau several times in the memoir of his experience, *Alone* (1938). Byrd's early weeks at the Advance Weather Base went well, and he communicated to the outside world that he was experiencing the "pearl" of tranquility.[79] His memoir describes moments of rapturous awareness, when "thoughts of life and the nature of things flow smoothly, so smoothly and so naturally as to create an illusion that one is swimming harmoniously in the broad current of the cosmos." Byrd wrote that he had discovered what Thoreau meant by the phrase, "my body is all sentient" and experienced moments when he felt "more alive than at any other time in my life." "Freed from materialistic distractions, my senses sharpened in new directions, and the random or commonplace affairs of the sky and the earth and the spirit, which ordinarily I would have ignored if I had noticed them at all, became exciting and portentous."[80]

Byrd was not entirely free from "materialistic distractions," however, since the sharpening of his senses was aided by a "battered green Victrola" that he took with him to the Advance Base. He experienced his own version of frozen music when the oil in the phonograph's works froze, and he had to place the machine on his stove. He described how "the record began to turn, very slowly at first, making lugubrious notes, then faster and faster." On another occasion, he was dazzled when the Antarctic aurora seemed to blend with the sounds of the Victrola playing Beethoven's *Fifth Symphony* from the door of his shack. "As the notes swelled, the dull aurora on the horizon pulsed and quickened and draped itself into arches and fanning beams which reached across the sky until at my zenith the display attained its crescendo. The music and the night became one; and I told myself that all beauty was akin and sprang from the same substance."[81] Like the metal detector hobbyists of the previous chapter, Byrd linked portable mediated sounds with the visual experience of the lived environment.[82] Byrd's multisensory knot did not indicate buried treasure but instead was a means to link sound technology with the experience of the natural world, an Antarctic version of Thoreau's habit of listening to the sounds produced by wind on the telegraph lines around Walden Pond.[83]

FIGURE 11.   Byrd listening to his "battered green Victrola" at the Advance Base in Antarctica. Papers of Admiral Richard E. Byrd, Byrd Polar Research Center Archival Program, Ohio State University, Columbus.

Byrd's intimations of cosmic harmony came to an abrupt end, however, when, after experiencing intermittent headaches and dark moods, he blacked out for twenty minutes on May 31. When he regained consciousness, Byrd found himself to be so weak that he could barely move, and he came to the realization that he was suffering from carbon monoxide poisoning caused by the exhaust from the gasoline-powered generator that supplied energy to his radio transmitter.[84] The static and world echo of the Dunedin-Schenectady broadcast of 1930 had revealed radio's infrastructure through sound; Byrd's collapse from the poisonous fumes of his generator was an index of a different sort of media materiality. Here was the dirty, polluting, fossil fuel–dependent underside to the seemingly immaterial modern Mercury, and it is here that Byrd's story descends most fully into darkness.

Byrd described June 1 as a "never-ending day" when "nothing really happened": "I lived a thousand years, and all of them were agonizing." The ensuing month of June became a "long nightmare" and "an eternity of darkness," in which he lived "from minute to minute." It now took enormous effort to complete even the most basic of everyday tasks, which meant that Byrd's perception of space was as distorted as his sense of time. "The bunk was a continent's breadth away," he wrote, "and I had to cross an interminable plateau to reach it."[85] Like Captain DeLong trapped on the icebound *Jeannette*, the globetrotting explorer had become immobilized: the heroic aviator was plunged into the darkness of a cramped, underground bunker; the project of scientific progress was arrested; and the pearl of tranquility darkened to become a black pearl of terror and desperation. In his account of the first Little America expedition, Byrd had written that the Antarctic was "the last stronghold of inertness," a place where "inertia governs a vast empire" with the power to "subjugate those who do not arise to resist it." "Men who are limited and lazy," he continued, "when denied free scope for the play of mind and body, find themselves slipping, as if drawn by centripetal action, into a dull, stupid, dispirited monotony."[86] Six years later he found himself slipping into the empire of inertia that he had described, as his Antarctic idyll became shrouded in a poisonous cloud of gasoline fumes; the momentum of his adventure narrative froze into a dull, dispirited monotony; and the cosmic harmonies he heard were transposed to a bleaker, more lugubrious key. Byrd wrote that during his ordeal at the Advance Base, he experienced "the soul of inertness."[87]

Byrd slowly regained the strength required to operate his radio, but he was reluctant to ask Little America for help, out of both pride and concern for the safety of the men who would be sent to rescue him. The unusual quality of Byrd's radio communications eventually led the officers at Little America to deduce that something was amiss, and they sent a rescue party to his hut. They found Byrd shockingly gaunt and enfeebled and took him back to Little America, where he recovered and completed the second expedition. The press spun the episode as a heroic struggle for survival, but, according to one historian, the collapse at the Advance Base was a blow to Byrd's health and self-esteem that haunted him for the rest of his life.[88] Byrd's long nightmare was not heard over the radio at the time, but it belongs in the history of dark eco-sonic radio nonetheless, in part because Byrd's expeditions served as inspiration for another tale of an "eternity of darkness" at the Antarctic, one that takes us further into the darkness of the abandoned mine.

DARK ADVENTURE

The first sound we hear is radio static, akin to the "surging, rushing sounds" that drowned out Admiral Byrd's New Zealand broadcast. Next comes the shriek of a radio signal changing frequency as the dial is turned, followed by short bursts of broadcasting content as though the listener were scanning the dial. We hear an announcer say, "the following is transcribed"; then, the peppy tune of an advertising jingle; fragments of an on-the-spot news report; and various station identifications. Theme music swells to indicate that we have settled on a station just in time for the opening of a program, and an announcer declares that we are now listening to *Dark Adventure Radio Theater*. Over the sound of a howling wind the host gives a preview of what is to come: "The frozen wastes of the Antarctic continent. Men of science braving an unknown and unforgiving world. An expedition to the ends of the earth resulting in death and madness." After a commercial message from the show's sponsor, the feature presentation begins: a radio adaptation of H. P. Lovecraft's "At the Mountains of Madness" (1936).

The jingle, the single-sponsor format, and the stentorian tones of the announcer's voice all give the impression that this broadcast is contemporary with the Mercury Theater's "Hell on Ice," but it was made in 2006 by Sean Branney and Andrew Leman of the H. P. Lovecraft Historical Society. Branney and Leman formed the organization in 1986, based on their shared background in theater and passion for Lovecraft's work. They combined those interests in their production of a 2005 film adaptation of Lovecraft's "Call of Cthulhu," made in the style of silent cinema of the 1920s. Their next Lovecraft adaptations were a series of audio productions that mimicked the conventions of the radio dramas of the 1930s. Leman stated that they wanted to immerse the audience in Lovecraft's world by using the kinds of storytelling that were popular during the author's day.[89] The first of these audio productions, "At the Mountains of Madness" (2006), was followed by six subsequent shows, making the *Dark Adventure* series the most comprehensive body of media adaptations of Lovecraft's work.[90] It makes sense that Lovecraft's oeuvre would find an outlet on radio, in part because American radio broadcasting was in its golden age during his peak years as a writer, but also because his brand of cosmic horror is perhaps best served by the darkness of the abandoned mine.

Lovecraft's most famous stories, such as "The Call of Cthulhu" (1928), "The Dunwich Horror" (1929), and "The Shadow over Innsmouth" (1936), construct an overarching worldview that has been called the "Cthulhu mythos." According to Lovecraft's biographer and sometime collaborator August Derleth, the Cthulhu stories concern a race of godlike aliens called the Old Ones or Elder Things, who attempt to gain control over humanity and who manifest themselves in "strange, out-of-the-way places" that afford uncanny dislocations of time and space.[91] Lovecraft's tales are horrific not simply because they contain monstrous creatures or acts of violence and madness but because at the "bleak heart" of the Cthulhu mythos lies an understanding that humankind is "not only insignificant, but doomed." According to Lovecraft scholar Charles P. Mitchell, Lovecraft reduces the human race to "a mere bobbing cork in the raging torrent of the cosmos, and there is no way for humanity to defeat the Old Ones. The most they can do is win a temporary stalemate, to postpone the eventual return and triumph of these hostile, powerful, ruthless godlike entities."[92] Lovecraft's grim worldview has dark ecological potential because it decenters humans in planetary history and warns of their potential annihilation.

Despite its interplanetary scope, the Cthulhu mythos is rooted in a very specific sense of local place. For Lovecraft, as for Thoreau, that place is New England. In a passage that sounds like Thoreau's famous account of climbing Mount Katahdin in Maine, Lovecraft wrote that the experience of the natural landscape around Providence, Rhode Island, had "keenly touched" his sense of the fantastic and that the "brooding, primitive landscape" of rural New England held for him "some vast but unknown significance, and certain dark wooded hollows near the Seekonk River took on an aura of strangeness not unmixed with vague horror."[93] Like Thoreau, Lovecraft was a New England writer who drew inspiration from the natural landscape, although that influence was manifested in a different literary genre and in a different emotional register.

The Cthulhu stories are set in places that resemble the region around the author's hometown of Providence, and protagonists are often associated with the fictional Ivy League institution, Miskatonic University. Lovecraft's narratives interpenetrate local places and cosmic horrors in a way that resonates with Morton's notion of a dark ecological aesthetic in which "the essence of the local isn't familiarity but the uncanny, the strangely familiar and familiarly strange."[94] In "The Colour Out of Space" (1927) a meteorite contaminates the land in rural Massachusetts; in "The Shadow over Innsmouth" (1936) a reef off the coast of a small New England town is a gateway to a shadowy world of monstrous sea creatures; and "The Shadow Out of Time" (1935) is one of several stories in which a professor from Miskatonic University confronts mysterious alien presences around the globe. Of the various strange and out-of-the-way places where occult secrets are discovered by Miskatonic professors, the work that Lovecraft considered to be his best, "At the Mountains of Madness," takes place in Antarctica.

The 2006 *Dark Adventure* adaptation of "At the Mountains of Madness" is initially framed as an interview with Miskatonic professor William Dyer, a member of a recent expedition to the Antarctic.[95] Lovecraft scholars have argued that the story is the culmination of the author's "lifelong fascination with the Antarctic" and that the early parts of the novel show the influence of Byrd's 1928–30 expedition.[96] Like Byrd's sojourns in Little America, news of the Miskatonic expedition reaches the American public through radio reports, and the *Dark Adventure* adaptation conveys Dyer's reminiscence through installments of a 1930s-style news show called *Worldwide Wireless News*. Faux news broadcasts report on a geology professor in the crew named Lake, who takes a subexpedition to an unknown region of the continent, where he discovers a titanic mountain range taller than any on the planet (echoes here of Byrd's discovery of the Rockefeller Range). Just as Lovecraft felt an aura of "strangeness" and "vague horror" in the hollows near the Seekonk River, so Lake describes the mountains as "nightmare spires" suggestive of "a vague, ethereal *beyondness* far more than terrestrially spatial."[97]

Lake uses the expedition's powerful drill to dig into the rock near the mountains and strikes a fifty-million-year-old limestone cave system that contains a vast deposit of ancient fossils. The fossils date from Antarctica's ancient equatorial climate and so are a "gateway to secrets of inner earth and vanished aeons."[98] Of this paleontological treasure trove, the most striking items are fourteen remarkably preserved specimens that defy categorization. Partly vegetable and partly animal, they seem adapted to a marine life and yet are equipped with leathery wings. At the end of this momentous day, Lake sends word that he is bringing these astonishing bodies back to the subbase for a more thorough examination. The next morning Dyer leads a party to the subbase and is shocked to discover that Lake and all of his men are dead.

Thus far, plot information about the Miskatonic expedition has been conveyed via the *Worldwide Wireless News* segments. At this point, however, we return to the interview format that began the show and then to a mode of first-person narration from the point of view of Professor Dyer. The show is thus structured in a manner similar to Welles's "War of the Worlds" broadcast, which, according to Neil Verma, combined the two dominant formulas used by radio producers of the 1930s to create a sense of auditory space: a "kaleidosonic style" that depicts a "shifting sonic world" by aurally leaping from place to place and an intimate mode in which the listener is positioned alongside a "carefully selected character for the duration of the drama." Verma notes that act 1 of the Mercury Theater's "War of the Worlds," which features fake news reports of a Martian invasion occurring across the country, is a paradigmatic example of the kaleidosonic style. During act 2, the narration shifts to the first-person journal of the astronomer Richard Pierson (played by Welles) and so is a paradigmatic example of the intimate style.[99] *Dark Adventure*'s "At the Mountains of Madness" makes a similar shift, moving from the kaleidosonic mode of the *Worldwide Wireless News* reports to an intimate alignment with Dyer, and it is from this position that we return to Lake's subbase.

Dyer reveals that Lake's camp had been the scene of a horrific slaughter, with the bodies of men and dogs disassembled by some unknown force. He and a graduate student named Danforth decide to investigate and fly one of the expedition's airplanes over the mountains. There they discover the ruins of a vast "blasphemous city" that bears witness to "an elder and utterly alien earth" that thrived long before the human race "shambled out of apedom."[100] The discovery of the alien city is a classic Lovecraftian moment in which humans are decentered in planetary history, and its depiction in the style of a 1930s radio drama makes it legible as an ironic inversion of the Mercury Theater's "War of the Worlds": Dyer and Danforth become the alien invaders landing their flying machine on the surface of a foreign planet.

The massive scale of the utterly alien city is also quintessentially Lovecraftian in that it illustrates how the author's work is "notoriously challenging" to adapt to visual forms of media. Mitchell writes that Lovecraft's unimaginable alien beings and vast oneiric cities would require enormous budgets to reproduce on the screen with anything like their intended emotional impact.[101] The philosopher Graham Harman claims that Lovecraft's "monstrous perversions of known geometrical law" are "impossible to film or paint," but they still have a powerful effect on readers who "can sense the metaphysical darkness of any place where such perversions are permitted to exist"; he uses the city in "At the Mountains of Madness" as his prime example.[102] The fact that a small, independent production company like *Dark Adventure* can successfully create this scene in a manner that allows listeners to revel in its "metaphysical darkness" is a testament to the ease with which radio theater can depict even the most strange and terrifying of locations at relatively low costs.[103]

Dyer and Danforth land their plane and descend into the ruins of the alien city, where they discover murals carved into the rock walls that tell the history of an ancient civilization of the leather-winged creatures, which Dyer refers to as the "Elder Things." Like John Muir standing before an Alaskan glacier, the two protagonists fall into an abyss of planet-time as they stand before the murals. They learn about how the Elder Things traveled through interstellar ether on their membranous wings to arrive on a primordial, lifeless earth; how they created the first life on earth under the sea for food and then made slaves for themselves in the form of "multicellular protoplasmics masses" called shoggoths; and how they descended into the depths of a subterranean sea beneath their Antarctic city to escape from the changing climate of the earth's ice age.[104]

Lovecraft presents Dyer and Danforth's exploration in the mood of gothic horror and gives the ruined city the kind of historical density that Bakhtin refers to as "castle time."[105] That mood changes, however, as Dyer begins to sympathize with the city's ancient civilization. He is impressed, for example, that they had scientific and mechanical knowledge that far surpassed that of humans and had a society whose intellectual and aesthetic life was "highly evolved." Gripped by curiosity, Dyer and Danforth decide to continue their descent to find the "sunless sea" described in the murals. Entering an ancient causeway leading down into a dark abyss, they are shocked to encounter the recently slain bodies of several Elder Things. It is here that Lovecraft's dark adventure reaches the deep freeze. Standing over the bodies of the Elder Things, Dyer feels that he and Danforth are transformed into "mute, motionless statues." Like Admiral Byrd touching the soul of inertia at the Advance Base, Dyer is cast into a temporal abyss that "seemed aeons" but actually "could not have been more than ten or fifteen seconds." Dyer's feelings of empathy, which were first revealed at the murals, blossom forth in this endless moment, as he muses that the Elder Things "were not evil things of their kind. They were the men of another age and another order of being": "Radiates, vegetables, monstrosities, star-spawn—whatever they had been, they were men!"[106]

I want to linger on this frozen tableau, since it is both an example of planet-time in a dark ecological register and a volatile pressure point in Lovecraft's opus. In essays about his writing, Lovecraft placed great importance on a quality that he called "outsidedness" or "beyondness," which he thought could make fantasy fiction transcend familiar human experience. Lovecraft denigrated as "junk" the kind of pulp fiction in which Earth voyagers fell in love with humanoid Martian heroines with vaguely exotic, non-Western names. By contrast, he argued that his tales were based on the fundamental premise that "common human laws and interests and emotions have no validity or significance in the vast cosmos-at-large." He wrote, "when we cross the line to the boundless and hideous unknown—the shadow-haunted *Outside*—we must remember to leave our humanity—and terrestrialism at the threshold."[107] It is this quality of outsidedness that makes Lovecraft so compatible with Morton's dark ecology, which casts the natural world as "monstrous and mutating, strangely strange all the way down and all the way through."[108] Likewise, Harman claims that Lovecraft's "primary gift" is the manner in which he poises his creatures "forever on the very brink of knowability," and so he criticizes "At the Mountains of Madness" for exactly the moments of empathy I have described. "The story should have ended with Dyer and Danforth witnessing the Cyclopean city from the air and returning to the campsite in a state of horror and hysteria," Harman argues. Dyer's exploration of the alien city brings it "too close," which, he claims, undermines the city's "innate architectural horror."[109]

The exploration of the city in "At the Mountains of Madness" may indeed go against the grain of much of Lovecraft's work, but I submit that it represents something more than what Harman refers to as the author "losing his edge."[110] Lovecraft's aesthetic was motivated by an ethic of outsidedness, but the sad irony is that, in his own life, he was pathologically adverse to social difference and expressed shockingly racist views in his correspondence. Lovecraft's tendency to cast outsidedness as something monstrous or horrific in his literature can be interpreted as an expression of his own narrow-minded aversion to racial, ethnic, and cultural difference. His desire to transcend "terrestrialism" and his investigation of the strangeness at the heart of the local are to be praised, but his close-minded misanthropy in the face of that project is to be rejected.[111]

With this in mind, we return to Dyer's frozen moment in "At the Mountains of Madness," which hovers between outsidedness and empathy. One reading of this passage is that Lovecraft, through the character of Dyer, is working through his aversion to difference, to achieve what Bakhtin calls creative understanding, which begins with a Lovecraftian outsidedness but moves beyond it. "To understand," Bakhtin writes, "it is immensely important for the person who understands to be *located outside* the object of his or her creative understanding—in time, in space, in culture.... It is only in the eyes of *another* culture that foreign culture reveals itself fully and profoundly."[112] By being outside we ask new questions of another culture and, in the process of answering them, defamiliarize our own. Perhaps Dyer's frozen moment is one in which he sees with the eyes of another in an encounter with beyondness that facilitates understanding as much as madness.

Bakhtin is known for his sonic metaphors, but his language here is visual: creative understanding involves *seeing* with the *eyes* of another. How might radio represent such a moment? Lovecraft claimed that his imagination was "almost wholly visual," but the *Dark Adventure* series shows that his stories make for great radio: we hear the haunting cries of the whippoorwills in "Dunwich Horror" and the eponymous "call" in "Call of Cthulhu." Michel Houellebecq argues that Lovecraft had a "particularly fine-tuned ear," and praises the "maniacal precision" with which he organizes his fictional soundtrack: "When a character sitting across from you places his hands on the table and emits a weak sucking noise," Houellebecq writes, "or when in another character's laugh you discern the nuance of a *cackle*, or bizarre insect stridulation, you know you are inside a Lovecraftian story."[113]

One classic Lovecraft tale can even be read as an allegory of phonography. "The Whisperer in Darkness" (1931) concerns a literature instructor at Miskatonic University who receives a chilling phonograph cylinder that seems to contain inhuman voices that resemble "the drone of some loathsome, gigantic insect ponderously shaped into the articulate speech of an alien species." As the narrator is drawn deeper into the mystery, he discovers a race of "Outer Ones" who have remarkable surgical and mechanical skills that allow them to extract human brains, immerse them in fluid-filled metal cylinders, convey them across interstellar space, and then connect them to instruments that provide sight, hearing, and speech to the brain. "It was as simple as carrying a phonograph record about and playing it wherever a phonograph of corresponding make exists," Lovecraft writes.[114]

"The Whisperer in Darkness" reveals that Lovecraft not only had a fine-tuned ear but a phonographic imagination, and the Outer Ones are an intergalactic version of the Polar explorers who took their musical cylinders with them to an alien world. "At the Mountains of Madness" is another example of the importance of sound in Lovecraft's tales, in particular at the moment of Dyer's creative understanding. *Dark Adventure*'s depiction of the scene in the causeway combines Dyer's monologue with swelling melodramatic music that cues the listener's emotional response. More compelling is what happens next, when the spell of Dyer's frozen moment is broken by the sound of an "insidious musical piping over a singularly wide range." We have heard this sound earlier in the broadcast; it is the eerie wind that resonates from the cave-mouths of the mountains, a strange "composite sound" that includes "a bizarre musical whistling or piping."[115]

The wind serves as an ominous keynote for the city-exploration sequence, and its composite quality is depicted by modulating its pitch, a technique that makes it legible as both a sound effect and as music. Standing over the dead Elder Things, Dyer and Danforth realize that this sound is not produced simply by the wind but is made by one of the monstrous shoggoths, which oozes up the causeway toward them. In a striking moment of audio-production technique, the piping of the wind is morphed into the voice of the shoggoth by use of a vocoder or similar device, which forms the sound into the mysterious word, "tekeli-li!"[116]

Dark Adventure's whispering wind demonstrates radio's ability to create what Arnheim calls an "acoustic bridge" between different classes of sound. Arnheim writes that radio's lack of a visual component of representation facilitates new expressive hybrids, as when "the human being in the corporeal world talks with disembodied spirits, music meets speech on equal terms."[117] The piping and speaking of the wind in "At the Mountains of Madness" creates such an acoustic bridge, which might be compared to the sheets of Arctic wind in "Hell on Ice." Recall the scene when wind drowns out the crew's singing during Captain DeLong's final divine service on the ice pack, which I argued had an eco-sonic edge because it diminished human endeavors in the face of planetary forces. By contrast, *Dark Adventure* personifies natural forces and so blurs the lines between the human and nonhuman. Where the wind in "Hell on Ice" obliterates the human voice, the wind in "At the Mountains of Madness" speaks with a human voice.[118] *Dark Adventure* gives a sonic dimension to Dyer's confusion of outsidedness and empathy with the eerie whispering of the wind and demonstrates the potential of the acoustic bridge as an eco-sonic technique that can bring a nonhuman perspective as close as an icy wind at your ear.

The fact that the wind says the word "tekeli-li" shows the presence of an influence on "At the Mountains of Madness" apart from the Byrd expeditions. Edgar Allen Poe's odd novel, *The Narrative of Arthur Gordon Pym of Nantucket* (1838), is an account of a young man who, through a series of remarkable misadventures, finds himself in the far southern seas. At the book's conclusion, Pym approaches the South Pole, where the horizon appears to become a vast waterfall and "gigantic and pallidly white birds" fly overhead calling, "tekeli-li!" The book's depiction of this polar chasm is a version of a long-standing theory that the earth is hollow, with openings at the poles. Athanasius Kircher's *Mundus subterraneus* (1665) postulated an immense whirlpool at the North Pole, down which the waters of the world's oceans proceeded through the body of the earth, to emerge at an open sea at the South Pole.[119] In Poe's day, this theory was associated with John Cleves Symmes, who claimed that the earth was "hollow and habitable within." There is evidence that Poe was familiar with Symmes's theory, and he openly praised J. N. Reynolds, one of Symmes's chief proponents.[120]

Thoreau makes reference to Symmes in *Walden*, in the same passage where he compares Arctic exploration to the quest for one's own higher latitudes. "It is not worth the while to go round the world to count the cats in Zanzibar," Thoreau writes. "Yet do this even till you can do better, and you may perhaps find some 'Symmes' Hole' by which to get at the inside at last."[121] It was not just Thoreau who connected the hollow earth theory to polar exploration. Symmes spoke of making a journey to the Far North, where he hoped to find a "warm country and rich land." One adviser to the *Jeannette* expedition informed Captain DeLong that he would encounter tropical heat issuing from "the hollow center of the earth," and when the ship went missing, editorials in the *Cincinnati Enquirer* wondered whether DeLong had reached a climate of "tropical mildness" inside the planet, where "the mastodon, extinct to us, disporteth in all the glory of his generally assumed antediluvian existence" and where men had the "magnificent physical proportions now only attributable to the prehistoric races."[122]

Lovecraft's "At the Mountains of Madness" is a late entry in a tradition that portrays the Antarctic as a portal to a subterranean city and the earth's ancient past. We should note that cultural fantasies of polar exploration and the hollow earth theory share a similar faith in the earth's boundless supply of natural resources. The hope that the poles might open onto a "final frontier" is akin to the "extraterrestrialist" faith that the exploration of other planets will allow Western imperialism and capitalist expansion to continue unabated in the face of the obvious limits to growth that exist on a finite world populated by seven billion people.[123] In the past several decades, we have come to recognize that the polar regions are neither an untouched antediluvian paradise nor a blasphemous chasm to an alien abyss, but they are something just as monumental: part of an early warning system for the global implications of climate change. My last case study of dark eco-sonic radio leaves the icy poles for another part of that planetary alarm system.

LAST CHANCE TO HEAR

In the mid-1970s an English comedy writer pitched an idea to the BBC for a radio anthology series. The series was called *The Ends of the Earth,* and each episode was to conclude with the destruction of the planet. The BBC did not pick up *The Ends of the Earth,* but the idea became the seed for one of the most successful radio series of all time. The writer was Douglas Adams, and the series was *The Hitchhiker's Guide to the Galaxy* (1978–80).[124] *Hitchhiker's* went on to become a best-selling series of novels, a television series, a video game, and a feature film, but it had its roots in radio, and Adams should be recognized as an important eco-sonic auteur.

Hitchhiker's debt to *The Ends of the Earth* can be heard in the radio series' first episode, when the show's unlikely protagonist Arthur Dent must cope, first, with the prospect of his house being demolished to make way for an automobile bypass, and then with the destruction of the entire planet to make way for a hyperspace bypass.[125] Luckily, Arthur's friend Ford Prefect turns out to be an alien researcher for the eponymous guidebook, and the two hitch a ride with the fleet of starships sent to destroy the earth. Ford, we might note, hails from a planet near Betelgeuse, the same as Lovecraft's Elder Things. This narrative frame allows the series to be heard as another reaccentuation of "War of the Worlds," in which the Martians succeed in destroying human civilization, but Professor Pierson escapes by hitching a ride in one of their invading spaceships.

Hitchhiker's begins under the shadow of planetary destruction and maintains an ecological perspective thereafter. Listeners learn about the evolution of quirky life forms like the "babel fish," for example; that the earth is a living computer akin to James Lovelock's "Gaia" theory; and that humans are only the third most intelligent animals on the planet, behind dolphins and mice. The series also burlesques the glossy technofuture depicted in much science fiction by featuring robots that are clinically depressed, intelligent doors who give off an air of smug self-satisfaction, and sentient elevators who spend their time sulking in basements.

Despite *Hitchhiker's* cynical attitude toward technology, the series brought a new degree of technological sophistication to radio drama. Adams spoke of his desire to bring the multitrack production style of contemporary popular music to radio. "Having grown up with [the Beatles'] *Sgt. Pepper* [1967] and [Pink Floyd's] *The Dark Side of the Moon* [1973] it seemed to me that radio production was lagging behind all the things that could be done with sound," he stated. "I wanted the thing to sound like a rock album, to do everything I could to convey the idea that you actually were on a spaceship or an alien planet—that sense of a huge aural landscape."[126] To create the destruction of the earth in the first episode, the staff of the BBC's Radiophonic Workshop used an eight-track tape recorder to combine an eerie synthesized wind, a clap of thunder, an explosion, a train crash, and an animal moan— the latter to provide an "ecological touch."[127] Just as radio allowed *Dark Adventure* to animate Lovecraft's vast cities and octopus-headed aliens, so Adams and his collaborators mobilized cutting-edge production techniques to create alien soundscapes, impossible (or at least highly improbable) technological contraptions, and a major character named Zaphod Beeblebrox, who has two heads and three arms. Zaphod's unusual anatomy is played as a throwaway joke on the radio series, but it created a major stumbling block when the series was adapted for television and film—a nice indication of radio's relative ease with such fantastic effects.

The Hitchhiker's Guide to the Galaxy radio series should be part of the eco-media curriculum, but its dark eco-sonic qualities are best appreciated when it is heard in relation to another BBC series that Adams created several years later. In 1985 the World Wildlife Fund (WWF) asked Adams to write an article to raise awareness about endangered species. Adams agreed and met Mark Carwardine of the WWF in Madagascar, where the two searched for a rare species of lemur called the aye-aye. As Adams explained it, Carwardine's role was to be "the one who knew what he was talking about," while his own role was to be "an extremely ignorant non-zoologist to whom everything that happened would come as a complete surprise."[128] In other words, Adams was to be a lot like his character Arthur Dent.

The first trip went so well that Adams and Carwardine traveled around the world together in 1988 and 1989 to seek out other endangered species and documented their travels in a radio series titled *Last Chance to See* (1989). Adams stated that it was his deliberate intention from the start to do the series for radio and not television, due in large part to the former's portability. With radio, he said, "you're not encumbered by equipment," and "people's reactions to you are not modified by the fact that you're pointing a bloody great television camera at them."[129] The portability of sound media allowed Adams, Carwardine, and a single sound engineer (either Gaynor Shutte, Chris Muir, or Stephen Faux) to travel to remote areas while doing the least possible damage to the local ecosystem.[130]

Hitchhiker's had been a generic hybrid of comedy and science fiction, and *Last Chance to See* merged the nature documentary with fantasy and science fiction, with the result that the earth was transformed into an unfamiliar planet and nonhuman animals into what Morton calls "strange strangers." In one episode, Madagascar is described as a "tiny, fragile, separate planet," and the aye-aye as "the kind of weird and wonderful creature that a writer of humorous science fiction might concoct on a really good day."[131] Several episodes place the featured animal species in the realm of the fantastic. We are told of the legend that the Yangtze River dolphin is the reincarnation of a drowned princess, for example, and that the giant lizards on the island of Komodo are the source of Chinese myths about dragons. Adding to the slippage between sci-fi, fantasy, and documentary is the fact that *Last Chance to See* and *Hitchhiker's* literally speak in the same voice. Both share Adams's authorial voice to be sure, but also the distinctive voice of the actor Peter Jones, who played the role of the eponymous Guide in the first series and narrates Adams and Carwardine's travels in the second.

Critics tended to understand *Last Chance to See* in terms of genre hybridity. One article in the popular press explained that "the fantastical beings of the sci-fi comedy series have been replaced by equally unbelievable characters, but this time they are of a bestial nature."[132] This generic mixing also served to turn humans into aliens, and Adams told an interviewer that the joke in *Hitchhiker's* was that "the world is destroyed by a hideous alien species," but that in *Last Chance to See* we discover that "it's actually us that's destroying the world rather more slowly but equally effectively."[133]

Last Chance to See may have worked to make the earth strange, but in stark contrast to Lovecraftian outsidedness, Adams and Carwardine were dedicated to fostering cross-species creative understanding. Adams stated that his goal as a writer was "to find different perspectives on everyday things so that we would see them afresh." He was inspired by the realization that animals have "completely different perceptual systems" than humans, and so from another species' point of view the world is a "completely different place." Adams talked about trying to see the world through the perceptual framework of a different animal, seeing a world that's familiar to us but "through a different set of eyes, a different body, with different things it needs to achieve in order to survive, and suddenly the world looks staggeringly different."[134] Radio as a medium is quite well equipped to accomplish that goal, since it can present main characters who are plants or nonhuman animals as easily as galactic presidents with two heads.[135]

In one of the most striking moments of the series, the team lowers a microphone into the Yangtze River, to try to experience how the noise of commerce on the river might interfere with the Yangtze River dolphin's echolocation. Adams describes hearing "everything that was happening in the Yangtze for many, many miles around, jumbled cacophonously together . . . a sustained shrieking blast of pure white noise, in which nothing could be distinguished at all." "As I watched the wind ruffling over the bilious surface of the Yangtze," he wrote, "I realized with the vividness of shock that somewhere beneath or around me there were intelligent animals whose perceptive universe we could scarcely begin to imagine, living in a seething, poisoned, deafening world, and that their lives were probably passed in continual bewilderment, hunger, pain, and fear."[136] As presented on the radio, this is a moment in which Adams prompts listeners to have an experience of creative understanding through the auditory channel, to hear with the ears of another.

Despite their efforts, Adams and Carwardine do not succeed in seeing a Yangtze River dolphin in the wild and must settle on seeing one in captivity. The species was on the brink of extinction when *Last Chance to See* was recorded, and despite the coordinated rescue efforts described in the episode, it was declared functionally extinct in 2006. It is painful to listen to the episode with this knowledge, and the show as a whole makes for an unusual affective cocktail, mixing Adams's scintillating wit with the grim subject matter of habitat destruction and extinction. Perhaps this explains why *Last Chance to See* was far less popular than *The Hitchhiker's Guide to the Galaxy* as a radio series and resulted in Adams's poorest selling book. "Here was a big issue I really wanted to talk about and I was expecting to do the normal round of press, TV and radio. But nobody was interested," Adams said. "I thought it was the most important thing I'd ever done and I could not get anyone to pay any attention."[137]

Given its focus on species extinction, it is not an accident that much of the series takes place on islands. In one episode, Adams states that "to understand how anything very complex works, or even to know that there is something complex at work, man [sic] needs to see little tiny bits of it at a time. And this is why small islands have been so important to our understanding of life." He gives the example of Charles Darwin finding the data he needed to construct a theory of evolution on the Galapagos Islands. "The island of Mauritius," Adams continues, "gave us an equally important but more somber idea—extinction."[138] Mauritius was the home of the dodo bird, which was hunted to extinction in the 1600s, and Adams and Carwardine visit the island to see the Mauritius kestrel. They also visit Rodrigues Island to find the Rodrigues fruit bat, Madagascar in search of the aye-aye, the island of Komodo to see the Komodo dragon, and Robinson Crusoe Island in pursuit of the Juan Fernandez fur seal.

The island settings and theme of extinction on *Last Chance to See* make the series an apt way to conclude my tour of eco-sonic radio at the ends of the earth, which has moved from the representation of vast and impenetrable polar regions to finite and fragile island ecosystems. Radio is perhaps the most appropriate medium for documenting travel to such places because it is a lightweight, portable, and sturdy technology that can give voice to alien others. There is a telling moment in the television remake of *Last Chance to See*, which was produced by the BBC in 2010. Sadly, Douglas Adams passed away in 2001, and so for the TV series the actor Stephen Fry accompanied Carwardine to return to the locations visited in the original radio series. In one episode the crew prepares to visit the remote Codfish Island off the coast of New Zealand in the hopes of seeing a species of flightless parrot called the kakapo. Fry explains to the viewer that access to the nature preserve is tightly controlled and limited, and so they have been forced to sacrifice a member of their television-production crew for this leg of the voyage. The camera follows Fry as he walks out of frame, revealing the sound recordist Don Anderson holding a microphone. Fry unplugs Anderson's recorder, cutting off his voice in mid-sentence. Onscreen subtitles inform us that the director, Ben Southwell, has been enlisted to record sound on Codfish in Anderson's place. Though played for laughs, this scene acknowledges how the television crew is too large and unwieldy to accomplish what the nimble radio crew had done in the original series.

We will return to questions of portable sound technology in the concluding chapter, but first I want to return one last time to Thoreau, who complained about going "round the world to count the cats in Zanzibar."[139] *Last Chance to See* is, of course, a series dedicated to doing exactly that. In fact, each episode of the show ends with Peter Jones reading variations on a recurring tagline: there are two hundred Yangtze River dolphins left " . . . and counting"; there are currently forty-one kakapos " . . . and counting"; in the half hour since this program began, the number of species extinctions in the Amazonian rain forest will have increased by another one " . . . and counting"; and so on. Thoreau thought of counting Zanzibar's cats, the higher polar latitudes, and Symmes's Hole as the antithesis of his hut at Walden Pond. We are learning, however, that we must strike a balance between "cosmos and hearth" to count cats (and kakapo), keep watch on both the higher and lower latitudes, and even fall into the abyss of Symmes's Hole so that we may to come out the other side with a better appreciation of the strangeness and immensity of life on this planet.[140] Radio has a role to play in all those projects, once it is tuned to an eco-sonic frequency.

The Run-Out Groove

The run-out groove is the area on a phonograph disc after the last track on the side has finished, where the needle continues to ride in the groove, but no sound is produced. Like the leader and countdown on a reel of film, the run-out groove is a media liminal zone where featured content gives way to esoteric technical information about the materiality of the format. It is here, for example, where we can find the record's matrix number and cryptic messages etched by the record-cutting engineer. The run-out groove is also a convenient metaphor for the concluding chapter of a book concerned with the materiality of sound media.

Eco-Sonic Media begins with a description of Katie Paterson's artwork *As the World Turns* (2001), which synchronizes a phonograph record with planetary rhythms but, in the process, makes the apparatus fall silent. The fact that Paterson's eco-critical intentions produces no audible output prompted me to ask whether there could be a sound media that was ecologically sound. I have looked for answers to that question in popular forms of media rather than conceptual artworks like Paterson's—hence my interest in the everyday experience of something like the run-out groove, which can prompt critical thinking along the same lines as *As the World Turns*. In the run-out groove, media consumption hovers between content and the raw materiality of playback such that listeners might ponder the energy required to drive the turntable and the materials that constitute the spinning disc. Moments of insight during the run-out groove usually take place in the silence after the final track on the disc. There have been occasions, however, when that silence was broken.

Records can be pressed in such a way that when the needle reaches the end of the run-out groove, it becomes trapped in an endless loop of sound called a "locked groove." The most famous example occurs on UK pressings of the Beatles' *Sgt. Pepper's Lonely Hearts Club Band* (1967), which breaks the silence of the run-out groove with several seconds of sonic chaos known as the "Sgt. Pepper Inner Groove." The final track on the album is, of course, "A Day in the Life," which concludes with an apocalyptic orchestral maelstrom followed by the resolution of a thunderous E-major chord played simultaneously on three pianos. That final epic chord continues for more than forty seconds, and the engineers at Abbey Road captured all of its dying tones by applying heavy doses of audio compression and carefully lifting the volume faders until the microphones were picking up the sound of the studio's air conditioning system rumbling in the background.[1]

The LP seems to have reached its definitive conclusion with this monumental act of closure, but after the needle passes into the run-out groove, it is locked into a never-ending whirlwind of looped sound that includes incomprehensible voices and a high-pitched whistle audible only to dogs.[2] "Sgt. Pepper's Inner Groove" exists within the space of the run-out groove, where the materiality of the medium makes its presence felt, but it breaks the silence of that space with an endlessly recycled fragment of sound that is audible to nonhumans as well as humans. The "Inner Groove" suggests that sound media's liminal zones may provide a space for eco-critical content, but that we will need to foster new ways of listening to fully appreciate it.

The two endings of the *Sgt. Pepper* LP provide a useful point of comparison as I reach the run-out groove of this book. Each enacts a different form of "finalization": M.M. Bakhtin's term for the shaping of the "inner side" of an utterance so as to signal its end and cue the possibility of responding to it.[3] Most academic books strive for a finalization akin to the majestic resolution of the E-major chord at the end of "A Day in the Life," in a conclusion that ties up loose ends and polishes the argument so that it is amenable to scholarly dissemination. Taking such an approach, I would review my argument that eco-sonic media are defined by sustainable infrastructure, communication with nonhuman nature, the experience of place and planet, and the representation of environmental crisis. I would revisit some of the book's recurring themes as well, such as those having to do with the plasticity of sound, minimal media, traditional technological knowledge, and the noise of media infrastructure.

Readers will find such concluding cadences in this chapter, but the needle will keep moving beyond them. In fact, this chapter is less like the resolution of the final chord and more like the quirky, never-finished locked groove. The latter approach is suited to an era when eco-critics claim that the "end of the world" has already happened. It is time to figure out what comes *after* conclusions, and eco-minded writers should shape the inner side of their utterances to prompt not only quiet contemplation but paths to practical action. The project of "greening the media" should extend beyond academic publication to include strategies for engaging with material things besides texts, people besides academics, and beings besides people. I have asserted throughout this book that green-media archaeology can uncover alternative media histories that are models for emergent practices. In what follows, I attempt to make good on that claim by taking my case studies out of the word processor and into the world.

In the previous four chapters, I have taken the advice of Richard Maxwell and Toby Miller and studied the sound media "up, down, and sideways," that is, in terms of their production, circulation, reception, interpretation, and disposal.[4] This chapter brings two additional dimensions to that methodology: an "in" and an "out." The former addresses the subjective, phenomenological, and multisensory experience of sound media, inspired by Donna Haraway's notion of a partial and embodied "situated knowledge" that finds a "larger vision" by being "somewhere in particular."[5] Henry David Thoreau's journal writings and the experiment at Walden Pond are examples of a form of situated knowledge that reaches "a connective truth through the commonplace particulars of daily life in a place exemplary only in its ordinariness."[6] In the field of media studies, phenomenological and multisensory studies of the cinema have moved into similar terrain, as have experiments in making media infrastructures "perceived, sensed, felt, and understood as part of life."[7] The analysis in this chapter moves further "in" to the book's historical case studies through accounts of constructing a no-wattage phonograph, interacting with a roller canary as a biotechnology of ambient sound, and moving through my local environment equipped with a metal detector.

The move to an individual register risks losing sight of the social and so requires a complementary movement "out" toward collaboration, place-based pedagogy, and environmental activism. Anna Lowenhaupt Tsing argues that more attention needs to be paid to the collaborative relationships that form the basis for environmental campaigns, because they draw our attention to cultural and political configurations that can change the arena of conflict.[8] My experiments involve collaboration with antique phonograph enthusiasts, metal-detector hobbyists, missionary organizations, canary breeders in the United States and Germany, and volunteer workers at a campus radio station. In each case, I find areas of common interest where the seeds of green-media initiatives might flourish.

The experiments in this chapter are intended to speak to interested readers as well as to teachers interested in adding sound to the green-media curriculum. I hope that what follows will present new ways to think about eco-sonic media and, at the same time, provide some practical models for classroom activities. My experiments do not exhaust the domain of the eco-sonic, and in each of the following four sections I suggest future research projects that can sustain the dialogue between sound studies and eco-criticism. The finalization of this book, then, is more like the playful "Inner Groove" than the apocalyptic climax of "A Day in the Life," both because it spirals out rather than fades out and because it resonates with my desire for a research strategy that encourages critical engagement without "cutting off the springs of hope." Tsing writes that hope is most important "when things are going badly in the world."[9] The consensus of the international community of scientists and environmental activists is that things are indeed going badly in the world. What follows are four sites where I have found springs of hope in my corner of sound studies.

THE PHONOGRAPH PROJECT

Chapter 1 evaluates early phonography in terms of the sustainability of its infrastructure. There is more research to be done on the ecological dimensions of the sound-media industries, throughout history and around the world. Eco-minded scholars should seek out the ambimodern practices of "first users," people in rural areas, and communal modes of media consumption. The study of sound infrastructure can help to foster interdisciplinary collaboration since it requires the expertise of historians, scholars specializing in the media industries, and social scientists pursuing the life-cycle analysis of media products and services.

For the first of my run-out groove experiments, I decided to add a new dimension to my study of phonographic infrastructure through a mode of scholarly productivity that Ian Bogost calls "carpentry": the construction of artifacts as a "philosophical practice."[10] I was inspired by Thomas Thwaites's account of how he built a toaster from scratch, traveling to Wales to obtain iron ore and smelting it in a makeshift furnace in a London car lot. The "toaster project" took Thwaites nine months, cost him almost two thousand dollars, and resulted in a monstrous approximation of a device that he could have purchased for six dollars. The main objective of the toaster project was not to cut costs or even to warm slices of bread but to explore "the ever-widening gulf between general knowledge and the specialisms that make the modern world possible." Thwaites's particular choice of "specialism" was inspired by a passage in the final installment of Douglas Adams's *Hitchhiker's Guide to the Galaxy* series. In the book *Mostly Harmless* (1992), we read that the protagonist Arthur Dent, stranded on a planet populated by nontechnological humans, was unable to build a toaster. "He could just about make a sandwich and that was it."[11]

Thwaites and Adams chose a toaster to demonstrate that even the most mundane of modern technologies surpassed the technical understanding of the general populace, but they might have chosen a record player instead. In fact, the phonograph and the toaster were technological cousins: the first commercially successful toaster was marketed by Thomas Edison's General Electric Company in 1909, just as Edison's phonograph was becoming a common fixture in American homes.[12] Eager to translate Thwaites's initiative to the realm of media technology, and curious about what might be learned by Bogost's carpentry, I embarked on the "phonograph project." My goal was to discover "minimal phonography": a convivial technology of sound playback that was low tech, no-wattage, and simple enough that that I could build it myself. I was after a level of complexity roughly equivalent to Charles Kellogg's imaginary phonograph consisting of a rose needle and the skin of an onion.

My search for minimal phonography began at the annual Antique Phonograph Show in Union, Illinois, where I sought out the traditional technological knowledge of antique phonograph collectors. The show was a vibrant outpost of residual media culture, featuring a stunning assortment of vintage spring-wound phonograph machines, 78 rpm records, spare parts, repair manuals, and blank recording cylinders. Here were the resources for relearning the protocols of the Green Disc era, but I was overwhelmed by the complexity of the spring motors and the high cost of the antique machines. I felt a bit like Arthur Dent contemplating the construction of a toaster and decided that I needed something cheaper, smaller, and easier to build. I turned to media archaeology as a means to search the archive for alternative designs.

I spoke about my project with media scholar and collector Patrick Feaster at the Union show, and he gave me a valuable suggestion about where to look next. Following Patrick's lead, I traced a line of historical research that led me to an event that took place on November 10, 1955. It was on that day that Brig. Gen. David Sarnoff, chair of the board of the Radio Corporation of America, appeared at the Overseas Press Club of America in New York City to debut a small hand-operated phonograph. The ten-ounce "phonette" was created by RCA technical director Arthur Van Dyck, who demonstrated the device by holding its base with one hand and cranking a metal handle with the other. As Van Dyck turned the handle, the device played a message on "the meaning of American freedom."[13]

The phonette's message was symptomatic of its intended use as a weapon in the Cold War struggle against international communism. In fact, several months before the demonstration in New York, Sarnoff had shown the device

The Run-Out Groove / 147

FIGURE 12. RCA's phonette: a small, hand-operated phonograph. Billy Graham Center Archives, Wheaton, IL.

to President Dwight D. Eisenhower as part of his plan for a "Political Offensive against World Communism." In a memorandum of that title, Sarnoff wrote,

> There are millions of persons in the world who do not have electric power receptacles, electron tubes, batteries or any of the electrical and mechanical marvels which the free world has and takes for granted. A simple, hand-operated phonograph device costing no more than a loaf of bread, could be produced in quantities and supplied gratis to millions of persons living behind the Iron and Bamboo Curtains and in other critical areas. An unbreakable and intelligible record, made of cardboard and costing less than a bottle of Coca-Cola, could carry our messages to these people. Such records could be dropped from the sky like leaflets and the messages they carried could not be jammed.[14]

To achieve that goal, Sarnoff had given the RCA design team the following specifications:

1. Low Cost.
2. Light weight, small parts, adaptable to easy shipment by various means.

3. Simplicity, ruggedness, freedom from service adjustment and repair.
4. High intelligibility on speech in any language.
5. Records which will give dozens of playings before wearing out, and thus permit circulation beyond the first user.
6. Playing time—2 minutes minimum.

This set of requirements had the following design implications:

1. The major material used in the instrument should be plastic.
2. Electronic circuits are inadvisable.
3. Power supplies requiring replacement of any part are inadvisable.
4. Energy sources depending upon an electrical supply of any sort are inadvisable.
5. Energy sources of mechanical nature are inadvisable if they include springs, gears, governors, etc.
6. Frequency range and other audio reproduction characteristics should be such as to maximize intelligibility of speech.[15]

The result was a small, lightweight, hand-powered sound playback instrument that did not require a horn for acoustic amplification.

The design specifications for RCA's phonette are similar to those for the JAN P-49 portable 16 mm film projector manufactured by the American military during World War II. Media historian Haidee Wasson writes that the JAN was intended to be mobile, tough, low in cost, mass produced, and "easy to use, maintain, and fix."[16] The JAN and the phonette demonstrate that institutions and protocols outside of the entertainment industry can be good resources in the search for alternative designs, ones that avoid a logic of frequent upgrades, built-in obsolescence, and mechanisms easier to discard than repair.[17] In fact, the phonette would be at home in E. F. Schumacher's environmental classic, *Small Is Beautiful* (1973); Schumacher, after all, was interested in "intermediate" technologies that were cheap and "accessible to virtually everyone."[18] More than a recipe for an anticommunist propaganda device, the RCA design specifications might be blueprints for a green phonography that has yet to be developed.

The phonette had taken me closer to my goal of minimal phonography, but another organization took that design and made it even more beautifully small. As with Sarnoff's propaganda initiative, this organization was guided by goals far removed from the consumer marketplace. RCA received numerous requests for information about the phonette, one of which came from a Christian missionary organization called Gospel Recordings (now Global Recordings Network). While working as a Christian missionary in Honduras during the mid-1930s, Joy Ridderhof heard a colleague express his desire for phonograph records that conveyed a Gospel message in Spanish.[19] Ridderhof kept thinking about this idea after her return to California, and in 1938 she made a Spanish-language recording of Bible verses. The disc was popular with missionaries, and it was not long before she was being asked to make records in other languages. Ridderhof's operation grew at an impressive rate during the postwar era, to the extent that the company's ambition became the distribution of recordings of the "good news" in every human tongue. As of this writing, Global Recordings Network has a catalog of recordings in more than six thousand languages.

To reach potential converts living in remote areas far from urban centers, Gospel Recordings had to provide playback machines as well as records. In the company's early years, Ridderhof had collected, repaired, and distributed old phonograph players, but in the 1940s she hired engineers to design machines expressly for the company's clientele. The engineers at Gospel Recordings, like those at RCA and the U.S. military, were called on to develop playback devices that had "the utmost ruggedness, stability with temperature, and ability to keep working under adverse climatic conditions."[20] Ridderhof told her engineers that they needed to make a gramophone "without any mechanism that can go wrong . . . something that even a child can use without breaking it. A hand-wind, motorless machine"—hence their interest in RCA's phonette, which Gospel Recordings adapted as the "Turntalk."[21]

An even smaller and lighter device was developed in 1964. The CardTalk consisted of a folded piece of cardboard that had a needle attached to one side.[22] A disc was placed on a metal spindle affixed to the cardboard and spun manually with a stick or a pen. The rest of the cardboard flap was folded over so as to insert the needle into the disc's groove. The folded cardboard served as the resonating medium during playback. Here was a no-wattage, minimal phonography whose operation was far simpler than a spring motor and whose primary materials could be pulled from the recycle bin. After examining documents from the Gospel Recordings archive and following instructions posted online by the composer Chris DeLaurenti, I built several CardTalk players. I have adapted DeLaurenti's easy-to-follow instructions and printed them here. My variation on the device uses cactus needles.

What did I learn from my experiment in media carpentry? First, I learned that shifting my desired outcome from a piece of academic writing to the construction of a media device entailed a change in the research questions I asked, the case studies I examined, the archives I visited, and the collaborators with whom I worked. Furthermore, the phonograph project forced me to think about the essential features of "durative" sound media.[23] What did I consider to be the minimal requirements of phonography? Was minimal functionality the ability to document ephemeral sounds, to initiate a certain kind of social interaction, or to provide a platform for sound art? In short, what did I want from recorded sound? I felt as though I was reexperiencing Thomas Edison's dilemma after he built the first phonograph but wasn't sure how to market it: should it be a business dictation device, a sonic version of the family photo album, or a mechanical music box?

My uncertainty about what I wanted from recorded sound stood in stark contrast to the clarity with which Ridderhof and her missionary clients approached that question. Consider a Gospel Recordings pamphlet titled *Discs on Duty*, which dramatized missionary letters testifying to the importance of the company's recordings:

> Here their minds are so dulled by sin they must hear the same simple truths over and over again. The records are invaluable—they never have to rest, not even become short of breath!

> The old witchdoctor forbade his family to play the records, but when alone he listened to them—playing them over and over until he was won by their message.

> We're so thankful for the records for they travel with the nomadic tribes, and continue to give the gospel to these who are so hard to reach.

> We could not leave our station, and the only one to answer the call to the distant villages was an illiterate, new Christian. But he took them clear gospel messages and songs by means of the records. And so, many heard for the first time.[24]

Records "work longer hours than we can," wrote one missionary. "We can hear them being played at night as we go off to sleep. They stay about when we have to leave and we can depend on them always saying the same thing, and not being put off by hecklers."[25] Missionaries were happy to delegate the difficult task of addressing disinterested or even hostile audiences to portable devices like the CardTalk. Missionaries knew what they wanted from recorded sound—a talking machine that was portable, tireless, and accurate—and perhaps it was this clarity that enabled them to strip the technology down to its bare essentials.

The CardTalk was useful in this particular social milieu, but what function could it possibly have in our contemporary media culture? Let me make clear that my goal is not to try to convince the millennial generation to trade their MacBooks for CardTalks. I do believe, however, that placing those objects side by side can have pedagogical benefits. When we force that comparison, we recognize that the CardTalk is worthy of praise for its low-cost, no-wattage, nontoxic, biodegradable material form, as well as for its lack of dependence on unfair labor practices and the extraction of finite resources. The comparative strengths of the laptop computer are, of course, immediately apparent: it has much higher sound quality, can be easily operated at the push of a button, and has a massive capacity for data storage and access to a seemingly infinite online catalog of sounds. We should note as well that there are energy efficiencies created by the digital distribution of sound when compared to the energy costs of transporting heavy phonograph discs around the planet.

A discussion of the relative merits of the CardTalk and laptop can help us learn how to make ecological assessments of media technology, but rather than forcing a choice between one technology or the other, I found myself wanting to utilize the best features of each. When I imagined CardTalk and laptop as two points on a phonographic continuum, my thoughts turned to the vast spaces between them, which were populated by "intermediate" technologies superior to the former but simpler, cheaper, and more energy efficient than the latter.[26] Acoustic-era phonograph players and the phonette would be found in this intermediate zone, as well as imaginary media technologies such as digital tablets with a hand-crank attachment for energy supply, cardboard speaker systems, or a public-address system that draws its energy from the muscle power of dancers. One of the lessons of the phonograph project, then, was that in the search for convivial media, it is best to begin with all the possible design options on the table.

The time that I spent building and testing my CardTalk was time that I gave my digital devices a much-needed rest. In that regard, the phonograph project convinced me that in addition to intermediate and hybrid technologies, we should also encourage a mixed menu of media consumption. Despite the efficiencies of digital distribution, there is a significant "rebound effect" that arises due to the fact that the "convenience, selection, and quality" of digital streaming can lead to the consumption of considerably more hours of media content.[27] That is, the energy saved by not transporting physical objects (records, DVDs, etc.) can be offset by the fact that people are consuming more media more of the time.[28] Eco-media scholars should strive to offset the rebound effect by fostering those contexts in which small or minimal media can take up the slack.

For example, a CardTalk may not offer much competition to a digital tablet when it comes to sound quality or access to catalog, but the two are more evenly matched in their ability to inspire a sense of wonder at the sheer fact of recorded sound. David Sarnoff claimed that much of the value of the phonette lay in the fact that it was "fun to play with" and that virtually everyone who encountered the machine "delighted in spinning it." That included President Eisenhower, who "played with the thing for quite a while when given one."[29] Media historians have often used a rhetoric whereby early, toy-like media technologies give way to art forms that are understood as being more advanced, developed, or mature. Consider the narrative that contrasts early visual "toys" like the zoetrope, zoopraxiscope, and phenakistoscope with the cinema or the statement that "with Caruso the phonograph ceased to be a toy."[30] The phonograph project made me want to reverse the direction of that rhetorical trajectory and look for media's future in the history of children's devices that are small, lightweight, and durable and often feature short-form content like nursery rhymes. Kid's media devices could be an important resource for green designs and protocols, as well as a fun item on a mixed menu of media consumption.

At one point in his "toaster project," Thomas Thwaites asked himself, "are toasters ridiculous?" A desire for warm bread may be totally reasonable, but Thwaites wrote that, at times, he could feel that "some things make such a marginal contribution to our lives that we could do without them and not even notice."[31] There were certainly moments when, as I strained over my wobbly cardboard contraption trying to coax a bleat out of my cactus needle, I wondered whether there might be something ridiculous about recorded sound. I found those moments of doubt to be productive, not because they made me renounce contemporary culture and become the Unabomber, but because they sharpened my recognition that the media culture we inhabit is not the only, nor even the best, of all possible worlds. Those doubts fostered an attitude toward contemporary media culture akin to what Sherry Turkle calls "realtechnik," which is "skeptical about linear progress" and open to reconsidering decisions, acknowledging costs, and recognizing "the things we hold inviolate."[32] I care about the culture of recorded sound, and that is why I want to think carefully about it and, ultimately, make it accountable to the eco-crisis. Recorded sound makes an important contribution to my life, but that does not make it non-negotiable.

In sum, the phonograph project convinced me that there are new melodies to be heard in old media. At the end of *Walden*, Henry David Thoreau tells the story of a "strong and beautiful bug" that emerged from an old wooden table that had stood in a farmer's kitchen for sixty years. "Who knows what beautiful and winged life," Thoreau asks, "may unexpectedly come forth from amidst society's most trivial and handselled furniture, to enjoy its perfect summer life at last!"[33] This wonderful story strikes me as Thoreau's version of the "toaster project," since it gives a mundane piece of household furniture a new, "winged life." Chapter 1 was my attempt to tell a similar story, one in which a lac insect crawled out of an old phonograph disc. Reconsidering Thoreau's story in light of the phonograph project, I want to ask, what sounds might emerge from a new generation of hand-cranked music players, do-it-yourself radio kits, low-power radio transmitters, or "circuit bent" musical instruments made from discarded electronic devices?[34] What winged life might result from harmonizing those devices with the best aspects of contemporary digital culture? What would a new media culture sound like whose starting point was the CardTalk?

CardTalk Assembly Instructions

You will need:

    Measuring tape

    Box cutter

    Scissors

    Pencil

    Ruler

    Tape

    Small binder clip

    Adhesive furniture pads

    Nylon flange

    Piece of cardboard in good condition

1. Measure and cut out a rectangular piece of cardboard, 8.5 inches wide by 23.5 inches long.
2. Place the cardboard so that one of the 8.5 inch sides is in front of you. With a pencil mark the side of cardboard facing up as "inside" and then flip it over and mark the other as "outside."
3. Place the "outside" facing up. Starting from the bottom edge and measuring up, make marks along the long portion of the cardboard at the following spots: 8.5 inches up, 16 inches up, and 16⅜ inches up.

4. Use the ruler to draw lines across the "outside" of the cardboard at the hash marks you made in step 3.
5. Use the box cutter to slit the outer layer of the cardboard at the three lines you have drawn. Do not cut all the way through the cardboard! These incisions make the cardboard flexible to fold.
6. Turn the cardboard over so the "inside" is facing up. Starting on the left corner of the bottom edge, measure 6 inches to the right and make a hash mark. Measure 3 inches up from the hash mark on the bottom edge and make another hash mark. This is where the spindle will go.
7. Gently poke a hole through the spindle mark with the box cutter or scissors. Carefully put the nylon flange through the hole from the "outside" so that it pokes out of the "inside" hole. Put a piece of tape over the hole on the "outside" to keep the flange in place.
8. Place the "inside" facing up. Fold the board along the incisions made in step 3 to make a triangle.
9. On the top of the flap that hangs down to touch where you have placed the spindle, measure 5.5 inches from the left edge and make a mark on "outside" edge.
10. Take the scissors and cut a 1 inch slit from the edge of the hanging flap.
11. Take the binder clip, squeeze the handles, and slide it into the slit on the hanging flap. The lip of the clip should face left.
12. Place a cactus needle between the lips of the binder clip, just inside the cardboard.
13. Place four adhesive furniture pads on the "inside" bottom flap, about 2¼ inches above, below, and to the left and right of the spindle.
14. Put a 78 rpm record on the spindle. Play a disc by gently rotating the record clockwise. You may have to experiment with situating the cactus needle.[35]

AVIAN AMBIENT

In chapter 2 I argue that sound media are eco-sonic when they foster an appreciation of, or facilitate communication with, nonhuman nature. This line of inquiry can be extended in a number of ways: through the study of the role of sound technology in cultures of pet keeping, farming, hunting, or fishing, or through research on biomedia technologies, the sonic representation of animals in the media, or sonic behaviors that humans share with other species. Eager to bring a phenomenological dimension to my study of canary culture, I decided that what was needed was not Bogost's carpentry but a mode of scholarly activity that I want to call "husbandry": the care of nonhuman beings as a philosophical practice. The model here is Donna Haraway's analysis of her interactions with companion animals, which she describes as "vulnerable, on-the-ground work that cobbles together nonharmonious agencies and ways of living that are accountable both to their disparate inherited histories and to their barely possible but absolutely necessary joint futures."[36] To be accountable to the conjoined history of humans and canaries, I embarked on an experiment in cross-species sociality, zoosemiotic communication, and no-wattage sonic entertainment in the home. The first step was to find a roller canary with whom I could collaborate.

Recall that during the same decades when native birds like the passenger pigeon were disappearing from American skies, huge numbers of canary birds were being imported into American homes. A century later another kind of avian extinction has quietly taken place, as the once-flourishing culture of canary keeping disappears from American cultural life. At midcentury the song of a canary could be heard in one out of four American homes, and Americans could listen to radio shows and phonograph records meant for the simultaneous enjoyment of birds and people. For reasons discussed in chapter 2, canary culture drifted to the peripheries of American life, and even Max Stern's Hartz Company, which had played such a key role in the canary trade during the first half of the century, sold its pet-care interests to become a financial operation called Hartz Capital.[37]

I needed to find the traditional biotechnological knowledge associated with canary culture where it still existed. Linda Hogan, a well-regarded canary breeder and author of *The Complete Canary Handbook*, kindly replied to my e-mail inquiries and told me about a small community of roller-canary enthusiasts who still held competitions in the Midwest. In December 2013 I attended a canary competition at a Comfort Suites Hotel in Oakbrook Terrace, Illinois, and it was there that I heard live roller canaries for the first time. I sat in a cramped hotel room, where four cages were carefully stacked on top of one another in front of a black screen. After a few moments of silence, the birds commenced a chorus of rapturous trills. Roller canaries sing with a closed beak, which produces a muted, miniature sound. Just as human ventriloquists speak with their lips shut to create the illusion of "throwing" their voice, so the rollers created an uncanny illusion of sonic depth. It was as though their song was an aural window onto an idyllic natural space somewhere in the distance, and I felt a better appreciation of the birds' decorative function in the Victorian domestic interior. The continuous rolling sound of the four canaries was mesmerizing and suggested a state of sonic plenitude in which vocal production was unmoored from the economy of breath.

I spoke with a trainer named Robert Wild after the competition, who offered to show me the roller canary–breeding operation at his home in the Chicago suburbs. It was there that I purchased my own roller canary, who we named Bing, after Bing Crosby, a singer known for his whistling talents. I heard Bing's first roller song as I played a recording by the whistler Fred Lowery. So began a three-way conversation between Bing, myself, and media technology. I found Bing's singing to be quite infectious, and, conversely, he would often respond to my whistling or guitar playing. We learned how to prompt each other's sonic outbursts, and in our crosstalk I recognized the similarities in our approaches: we were both constrained by the economy of breath, and we both tended to fall into similar kinds of simple, repeated, rhythmic patterns. I began to imitate his tours, and I fancied that I could hear a few of my stock melodies enter his repertoire. To paraphrase Haraway, Bing and I were training each other in acts of communication that we did not fully understand.[38]

As I became more familiar with Bing's vocabulary, I developed a new appreciation for hobbyist literature that gave human names and meanings to canary vocalizations. I also discovered the practical value of the bird media used by mid-twentieth-century pet owners. Bing seemed to pay close attention to the sound of canary training records and would frequently sing along with them. These records served the important function of reminding Bing of his vocabulary during the molting season, when male birds stop singing for months at a time. As this three-part harmony developed, it became more and more difficult to determine which sounds belonged to me, Bing, or a recording. We were enmeshed together in an aural contact zone, singing with a compound voice.[39]

Several months into my experiment, I added a new component to this bird media console: a canary yellow iPhone 5C.[40] MP3 players were an important part of my domestic soundscape in the pre-Bing era, largely because of my affection for Brian Eno's digital applications "Bloom," "Trope," and "Air," which generate an infinite stream of his signature ambient sounds. As an academic who often works at home, I fulfilled Eno's intention that ambient music was to be used to "induce calm and a space to think."[41] When set on "infinite" mode, Eno's apps enacted another fantasy of sonic plenitude, creating an endless aural "tint" to my domestic space that seemed divorced from any material source.

If the "phonograph project" led me to compare the CardTalk and a laptop, the "avian ambient" experiment prompted a similar comparison between my yellow smartphone and my yellow canary bird. Bloom and Bing both produce ambient sounds for my domestic space, but the latter has his own biological rhythms that need to be accommodated. Bird media is not on demand, and it works according to a temporal architecture shaped by daily and seasonal cycles. Bing produces noisy "chops" in the morning and long, mellifluous songs in the evening. Bing cannot be turned on and off like a smartphone app, nor can his volume be adjusted. Admittedly, this can be quite annoying, and I was reminded of Vicki Hearne's assertion that humans are troubled by parrots not because of their ability to utter human phrases but from their "aggravating refusal to let you choose the topic."[42] It occurred to me that we want devices like our smartphones to be "smart" in the sense of clever, intelligent, and knowledgeable, but not in the sense of forward, impudent, and cheeky. We don't want our devices to be moody or to have their own agendas. By the latter definition, Bing was a lot smarter than my smartphone.

I can take my yellow smartphone with me wherever I go, but Bing is confined to a cage. That confinement is, of course, a high cost to pay for sonic entertainment and zoosemiotic communication in the comfort of my home. I told myself that canaries had grown accustomed to captivity and that Bing lived in a cage that was twice the size of the typical domestic canary dwelling. In fact, when we tried to entice Bing out of his cage to explore a safe area of our apartment, he left only by accident and was visibly frightened by the experience. Despite all of that, I could never shake my feelings of guilt about keeping a bird in a cage. That discomfort was not without a benefit, however, which was that it forced me to face the costs of my desire for soothing, effortless sounds in my home. By comparison, Eno's Bloom app did not prompt me to acknowledge the suffering of the workers who had made my smartphone, which was just as present in the device as the all-too-visible bars of Bing's cage.

Despite his physical confinement, Bing had a degree of agency in the compound sound medium that we were cocreating. He seemed to enjoy singing with me as I listened to music, whistled, or strummed a guitar. I knew that my interpretation of his "enjoyment" was an act of anthropomorphism, but it was what David Haberman calls an intentional act of anthropomorphism, one that is an "intentional strategy for connecting with the nonhuman world."[43] Some of the moments when I felt most connected to Bing were when we seemed to be immersed together in the act of listening:

when I listened to him, or he listened to me, or we both listened to a recording. Kate Lacey refers to "listening out" as an attention to others and otherness in the act of listening that is the prerequisite of citizenship and communicative action.[44] When Bing and I listened together, I felt that we were exploring a form of listening out that was a prerequisite of eco-citizenship and zoosemiotic communicative action.

Bing may have been confined to our apartment, but a surprising side effect of the avian ambient experiment was that I began to hear his rolling song throughout the day wherever I went: in the sound of running water, for example, or the noise of traffic. Bing's song began to function as an "acoustic bridge" between music and noise, voice and sound, nature and culture. One result was that the sound of wild birds began to seem more familiar and familial to me. My experience suggests that pet songbirds can play a role in creating what the animal geographer Jennifer Wolch calls "zoopolis," a renaturalized city that allows for interactions with animals that give urban dwellers "the local, situated, everyday knowledge of animal life required to grasp animal standpoints or ways of being in the world."[45] Interacting with a pet songbird is only one way for students of sound to open their ears to the nonhuman sounds around them. Once we begin to listen to the world of natural sound—what Bernie Krause calls "the great animal orchestra"—we want to hear more, and that desire can fuel the action required to preserve and protect natural habitats.[46]

Listening out to nonhuman sound does not mean confining one's attention to the local sphere. After all, birdsong can allow us to tune in to the global flows of bird migration. In chapter 2, I track the "unnatural" migration of canaries from the Canary Islands to Europe and America. To obtain a different vantage point on the global flow of songbirds, I traveled to the capitol of the nineteenth-century roller-canary trade: St. Andreasberg, high in the Harz Mountains of Germany. St. Andreasberg is no longer a quaint mining village where families raise roller canaries in their cottages, but it pays tribute to that heritage in the form of the Harzer Roller Kanarien Museum. Caretaker and canary breeder Jochen Klähn gave me a tour of the museum and, at one point, brought me to a room full of rollers, which he coaxed into song by playing a worn phonograph disc of canaries made in the 1930s on an antique, spring-wound phonograph player.

The exhibits at the Kanarien Museum depicted the canary trade as a hybrid geography interweaving people, organisms, and machines.[47] The museum's display included photographs depicting St. Andreasberg bird sellers who carried massive loads of wooden birdcages on their backs through the Harz Mountains to port cities like Hamburg. From there steamer ships took the birds to London and New York to satisfy the demand for the signature St. Andreasberg sound. The geographic scope of the canary network is impressive, but it should be understood in relation to the ancient routes of bird migration on the one hand and the cables, satellites, and wireless transmitters of digital audio networks on the other. When the global mobility of migratory cranes is taken into account, for example, some of the excitement about the "space annihilating" properties of digital technologies falls away, and "they are reduced to their more proper position within a planet that has ever been a global mobility."[48] This is not a matter of rejecting or disparaging digital technology but of putting it in its place.[49]

My experiment in sound-media husbandry resulted in new collaborations, conversations, critical comparisons, and eco-ethical commitments. In chapter 2, I listen for the overlaps between nature and culture that might be heard when we consider roller canaries to be biotechnologies. Such a project encourages an attention to the human overtones in canary voices, but there was always something else there; something more than the sum of human desire. If chapter 2 presents canaries as "old media," I want to suggest here that they are something older than old media; they are what I want to call, with reference to H.P. Lovecraft's ancient and mysterious Elder Things, "elder media." John Muir was listening to elder media when he heard the "voice" of Yosemite Falls or an earthquake that sounded like a "living creature."[50] The Kaluli people of Papua New Guinea were tuning in to elder media when they heard birdcalls as "spirit reflections" of the dead.[51] The environmentalist Aldo Leopold was listening to elder media when he described the migratory cranes that visited Wisconsin marshes as beings "out of the remote Eocene" and heard their call as "the symbol of our untamable past, of that incredible sweep of millennia ... not in the constricted present, but in the wider reaches of evolutionary time."[52]

We don't need to go to Yosemite, the rain forest, or the Wisconsin marshes to have contact with elder media. The domestic pets of zoopolis might provide a closer-to-home encounter with the natural world that is a sonic gateway to wild places and so remind us that nonhuman life is all around us if only we have ears to hear it.[53] There are moments when I hear Bing in the register that Leopold describes. In those moments his song is not a quaint "tweet" but something mysterious, majestic, and strange—something that might be best translated as "tekeli-li!"

THE CAMPUS SONOSPHERE

Tracking the various cultural meanings given to the song of a particular species of bird along its migratory route would be one way to extend the investigation of sound, place, and planet in chapter 3. Alternately, ecomedia critique could be directed toward mobile-sound technologies intended to be taken into natural spaces, or that allow users to hear infrastructural systems; sonification projects that operate on a planetary scale; the role played by sound in discourses of the local; or the sonic dimension of global travel and tourism.[54] Ethnographic studies could explore how the experience of transnational sound-media content is localized through networks of distribution or at broadcasting and recording studios.

My analysis of portable divination media in chapter 3 felt incomplete without a phenomenological and embodied perspective. Moreover, I wanted to develop pedagogical exercises that would demonstrate the relationships among sound, place, and planet to students. I decided to explore the Northwestern University campus, where I work, both to experience the multisensory admixture of mobile divination and to discover techniques that would make the campus perceivable "not as a point, but as a membrane; not as a picture, but as a channel through which voices, noises and music travel."[55]

Metallophones would be the primary equipment for this experiment, and I began by making a visit to Windy City Detectors in Chicago. The store is owned by Ron Shore, who began selling metal detectors from his basement in 1986, not long after the first wave of metal detecting had crested. Interest in the practice declined in the 1990s, to such a degree that Shore nearly closed shop. The onset of the financial crisis in 2008 changed the situation dramatically, and as the price of precious metals skyrocketed, so did the metal-detector trade. Shore's business doubled every year for three years, and he told me that the recent cycle of reality television shows like *Diggers* had given sales an additional boost.[56] Shore warned me that the hobby took a lot of patience and was not for everyone. He suggested that I rent a basic detector and digging tool and make my first attempt at treasure hunting at the Lake Michigan beach.

So it was that, early one summer morning, I found myself walking with the "slow and creeping step" of the diviner on an Evanston beach, listening for signals from my metallophone. I have to admit that I felt extremely self-conscious and was painfully aware of receiving suspicious looks from other patrons of the beach. Now I understood hobbyist complaints about unkind stereotypes of treasure hunters that circulated in popular culture. Beachcombers were a particularly maligned group, and Joan Allen's handbook described the stock image of the beachcomer as an "unshaven derelict in grimy rags" who "peers through a gin-haze from beneath his battered straw hat."[57] It is certainly unfair to portray all beachcombers as drunken derelicts, but it is also true that the practice can come across as fairly antisocial. Passages of a popular beachcombing manual by Warren Merkitch take a rather misanthropic view of the simple pleasures of beachgoers. He writes of the "warped antics" of people who like to be buried in the sand, for example, while coldly observing that they mean "money in the pocket," because "one of them is sure to lose something of value." In the parallel universe of Merkitch's book, the best time to visit the beach is during or just after a rainstorm, since that is when bathers leave in a hurry and may forget their valuables.[58] Of all the types of treasure hunters, perhaps beachcombers had the most strained relationship with the other users of the public places to which they were drawn.

Most of the other people that I saw exercising or walking dogs on the beach were wearing headphones like me. Arguably, we were all equally antisocial, encased in "auditory bubbles" of portable sound media that constituted a "denial of the physicality" of our shared space.[59] Despite the dirty looks of my fellow beachgoers, one might argue that my metal detector made me more in tune with our shared place than those listening to music or an audiobook. Metal detecting is a good illustration of what David Beer calls "tuning out," whereby media users distract themselves from the "aural ecology" without fully removing themselves from it. That is, the sounds generated in earphones are not the only sounds that can be heard, and rather than understanding users of mobile sound to be simply isolated, Beer agues that they are instead placed "in a constant web of interactions" with the environment and its inhabitants.[60]

Metal detecting is a vivid example of this kind of "tuning out," because the signals arising from the device are so sporadic. My attention was fixed on the device's output, but most of the time that output was silence, meaning that I spent most of my time listening to the sounds of wind and waves. The headphones even filtered out the frequencies of many human sounds, thereby amplifying the natural soundscape. One lesson of this experiment, then, was that not all portable headphone listening is the same, and we need to think in more nuanced terms about the range of relationships between portable sound signals and the surrounding aural ecology.

My listening experience at the beach might have been a little too contemplative, given that the soothing sounds of wind and waves were interrupted only once or twice by the tones of the device. My first attempt at treasure hunting was a bust: my only discovery was a small, unremarkable metal rod. For my second attempt, I took the advice of treasure-hunting manuals and did historical research to find a spot on the Northwestern campus that promised to be the location of historical artifacts. I wanted to find a public gathering place along the lines of a fairground or park, and after perusing old yearbooks and maps in the university library archives, I settled on Deering Meadow as my best bet, since it had been the site of campus events since the mid-nineteenth century.

On several summer mornings I could be found in Deering Meadow with my rented metal detector in hand. After my fruitless search on the beach, I was excited to hear numerous "mid" or "high" tones in my headphones, which indicated the presence of underground coins or other valuable metals. I began to enjoy the anticipation of hearing the pleasing chime in my ears, which I could then trigger again and again as I pinpointed the precise location of the object. I also liked the tactile process of excavation, getting my hands in the dirt with the roots and worms that were normally hidden beneath the path of my daily campus commute. It seemed to me that this practice should be included in the investigation of the multisensory experience of the media.[61] I was considerably more successful at locating objects here than I had been at the beach. In fact, Deering Meadow was what the hosts of *Diggers* would call a "nectar sector": "an area with a high concentration of artifacts."[62] Most of my discoveries were pennies—the three oldest dating from 1919, 1939, and 1970—but I was surprised at how thrilling it could be to unearth a one-cent coin that in another context I would let fall between the couch cushions without a second thought.

I felt a strong personal connection to the artifacts I had unearthed, and, taking another cue from *Diggers*, I decided to narrate them in the conditional tense of the "could have been." Perhaps the 1919 penny was dropped by a Northwestern student going through compulsory military drills in the Meadow to support the war effort. The 1939 coin could have fallen from the pocket of one of the five hundred students who held a mass meeting that year to protest another looming war in Europe. In 1970 two thousand students buried four coffins to protest the killings at Kent State University. Maybe my penny was buried at the same time. Then again, perhaps it had found its way into the grass during the maypole dancing that accompanied the first Earth Day celebration that year.[63]

What was clear to me was that the combination of research, divination, excavation, discovery, and narration had worked a powerful mojo on these otherwise worthless pennies. In other words, I can testify to rhabdomancy's potential as a form of alternative hedonism. In a poem titled "Wünschelrute"—often translated as "The Divining Rod"—written by Joseph von Eichendorff around the same time that Washington Irving wrote "The Money Diggers," we read that "a song sleeps in all things" and that song begins to sound when touched by the "magic word" of the poet.

Eichendorff uses the rod as a metaphor for the power of poetry, but the poem also describes divination's ability to give voice to objects.[64] My electronic metallophone drew a sleeping song from a handful of old coins to produce a melody seductive enough to compete with the advertising jingles that encourage reckless consumer practices. More can be done to build on the ecological potential of that song, perhaps by harmonizing local practices of recycling, scrapping, or treasure hunting with waste-picking initiatives around the world.

Metal detectors are not the only sound technologies that produce subterranean signals, and other devices can give students access to campus infrastructure. To that extent, they can play a part in a program of what David W. Orr calls "ecological literacy." Orr notes that campus is often where students "learn the lesson of indifference to the ecology of their immediate place." "The typical campus is the place where knowledge of other things is conveyed," he writes, but the campus itself, as "land, buildings, and relationships is thought to have no pedagogic value." Sound technologies can help to reveal the infrastructural systems that supply the campus with food, water, and electricity or that transport its waste to "distant and unknown places."[65] Consider the listening devices used to locate leaks in underground water pipes, for example. Including devices such as these in the study of sound technology creates a contact zone between students, academics, and other kinds of laborers working on campus.

Digital media have a place in this project as well, especially given their ability to facilitate planetary awareness. Digital applications such as iBird, Leafsnap, TreeBook, AllTrails, and RockHound augment natural spaces with information from online databases and so function as technological "edge species" that operate between "the techno-ecosystem of our cities and the natural ecosystem of our countryside and landscapes."[66] These and other applications might be used to foster an appreciation of nonhuman mobility or provide a tangible connection between local and distant practices of eco-activism.

Clearly, a number of sound technologies could be used to expand the campus sonosphere, but in terms of practical classroom activities, the best place to begin might be a practice that requires nothing more than mobile ears. Hildegard Westerkamp defines a soundwalk as "any excursion whose main purpose is listening to the environment. It is exposing our ears to every sound around us no matter where we are," to "rediscover and reactivate our sense of hearing."[67] A related practice involves making a sound recording while walking and then using that recording to create a sonic script for subsequent "audio walks." The Canadian artist Janet Cardiff has gained international recognition for this kind of site-specific, audio-enhanced walk. Cardiff uses binaural microphones to provide listeners with a remarkably accurate aural image of movement through a particular space. She then overdubs music, sound effects, and commentary to guide the listener through a heightened experience of a given space.[68]

Students of sound should be exposed to a continuum of portable sound practices, ranging from the no-wattage sound walk to high-tech digital applications. One benefit of offering students such a mixed menu of options is that it can broaden participation in sound media. Consider the fact that Westerkamp and Cardiff, and indeed many of "the major figures in the field of soundwalking" are women, a notable contrast to many other areas of "electroacoustic sound art and research."[69] In chapter 3, I argue that waste pickers could be collaborators in the creation of a more politically engaged culture of green divination. Soundwalkers are another adjacent community that can bring new users and new signals to the project of portable eco-sonic media.

Westerkamp's sound walks and Cardiff's audio walks are the models for two campus listening walks described later in this section. A third, which I call a "signal walk," involves the use of listening devices such as metal detectors, leak detectors, or related digital applications. Students could be assigned to take all three walks across the same campus terrain on different occasions, or the three walks could be split across different groups who share their experiences with the class. In either case, the exercise can illustrate how attention to sound can function to recalibrate our sense of local place. To paraphrase Ludwig Wittgenstein, after students have taken these three walks, they will have passed through any given place on campus a number of times, from all sorts of directions—each time traversing it as part of a different journey.[70] With any luck, when they are done, they will have a better sense of place and planet, as well as a better sense of the eco-critical possibilities of portable sound media.

Three Campus Listening Walks

1) *Sound Walk:* Take an excursion, alone or in a group, with a guide or self-directed, in which you focus your attention on listening to the campus soundscape. The rules: walk for at least thirty minutes, no talking, and no headphones. What do you hear? It's been said that you can tell a lot about a society by seeing what kind of buildings dominate the landscape. What sounds dominate your campus soundscape? What sounds in the campus environment do you like and dislike? What role do media technologies play in the campus

soundscape? What are the natural or nonhuman sounds that you hear? You might begin the walk by paying attention to the sounds of your body and then direct your ears to sounds nearby.

2) *Signal Walk:* Take a walk on campus during which the emphasis is on receiving signals from a divination device, metal detector, underground leak detector, or some other form of portable sonification. Prepare for your walk by doing historical research to find the areas on campus with the most potential for discovery and insight. Your goal is to encounter previous inhabitants and local lore and/or the institutional resource flows of the campus infrastructure. In either case, the signals of your audio device should be used to give voice to unseen objects and entities. Be sure to narrate and curate any objects you discover, using the past conditional mode of the "could have been."

3) *Audio Walk:* Use sound recordings and/or digital applications to construct a guided audio tour of the campus for your fellow students. This might involve using sound to laminate a sense of campus history onto the visual experience of the present, but try to draw on the technology's ability to make audible global flows and planetary forces. The emphasis should be on linking near and faraway places and times and giving voice to entities that exist beyond human scale.

RE: RADIO

The pops and hisses of bugs in the phonographic system; sonic zooms that play with geographic scale; plasmatic vocal transformations and zoosemiotic whistles; short forms like the locked groove: all of these constitute the fuzzy outlines of an eco-sonic poetics. Sound scholars should expand on this list and bring an auditory dimension to the discussion of eco-criticism and eco-media aesthetics. For example, R. Murray Schafer's call for a "radical radio" consisting of around-the-clock ocean sounds is an aural analogue to an "ecocinema" that operates through a "cinematic stretching of patience."[71] Radio should be added to histories of wildlife documentary, and radio documentary in general should be central to the development of what Nadia Bozak calls a "secondhand media" practice that is portable, local, and works with "leftovers and remains."[72] The fact that radio is good at "creating drama out of situations in which there is literally nothing to see" makes it a powerful tool for conveying the dangers of global warming, which are not "tangible, immediate or visible in the course of day-to-day life."[73] Scholars interested in developing radio's dark ecology should seek out narrative and stylistic models across radio history, in traditions around the world, and in modes of production ranging from low power, to short wave, to national networks, to podcasting.

For my final experiment I wanted to extend the textual analysis of radio drama in chapter 4 outward, toward a form of collaboration that considers the ecology and economy of sound media as a single issue.[74] Andre Gorz argues that "ecology has its full critical and ethical impact only if the devastation of the Earth and the destruction of the natural foundations of life are understood as the consequences of a mode of production." In other words, it is not the human species that is the cause of the "slow violence" of the eco-crisis but a particular Western, patriarchal, colonial, capitalist system. An eco-media critique resists a mode of production that demands the "maximization of output" through recourse to "technologies that violate biological equilibria."[75]

We must question models of economic development that are based on the myth of perpetual growth not only because they violate biological equilibria but also because they exploit workers. Sound-media technology has been complicit in that exploitation to the degree that its history is marked by declining employment opportunities for sound professionals. James Kraft argues that sound technologies radically transformed the experience of being a musician, changing "a diffused, labor-intensive, artisanal structure into a centralized, capital-intensive, highly mechanized one." "For the majority," he writes, "the change meant dislocation, restricted or lost opportunity, and sustained conflict with management."[76] Phonograph records, the film soundtrack, radio broadcasting, jukeboxes: all of these technological developments faced strong resistance from musicians and their labor unions. In our own era, digital sampling and autotune capabilities have put session musicians and backup singers out of work, digital audio workstations threaten the existence of brick and mortar recording studios and their staff of engineers, and the flipside of the consumer cornucopia of online music is that digital downloading has made it extremely difficult to earn a living as a musician. Martin Scherzinger points to the "sad irony" that live performance, "precisely that modality *not* intrinsic to the promise of networked digital technologies," seems to be the only sector that is thriving in the era of Web 2.0.[77]

A mixed menu of media consumption is beneficial because it decreases energy use, but it can also provide opportunities for diverse workers in the sound industries and, in the process, preserve valuable traditional technological knowledge. With that in mind, I wanted to experiment with ways to implement a mode of eco-sonic media production that is both good for the planet and for full employment among sound workers. I was inspired by Tim Jackson's proposal for a new economy based in low-carbon activities that employ people in the delivery of local services such as "food, health, public transport, community education, maintenance and repair." Jackson argues that this "Cinderella economy that sits neglected at the margins of consumer society" represents activities that have the potential to "provide meaningful work with a low-carbon footprint."[78] Environmental activist Bill McKibben places a similar emphasis on community services in his assessment of economic activity, and when he turns this criteria to the domain of cultural production, he champions local radio as the "ideal broad community vehicle."[79]

My final experiment was to embark on an open-ended collaboration with the Northwestern campus radio station. It is a curious fact that academics working in the field of media studies have so rarely written about or worked with the radio stations in their own backyard. I am lucky to have Northwestern's WNUR in my backyard, an award-winning campus station that has been on the air since 1950 and has the power to reach audiences throughout the Chicago area. I saw WNUR as a laboratory for developing modes of media production that would aim to maximize creative collaboration and minimize the material impact on the environment.

The first step was to broaden the culture of radio on campus, and so I organized a Sound Studies Listening Group (SSLG, affectionately known as "Slug"). SSLG took part in the #WOTW75 project put together by Jennifer Stoever and Neil Verma, which invited people to listen to Orson Welles's classic "War of the Worlds" radio play on the seventy-fifth anniversary of its original broadcast and post about it live on Twitter.[80] More than thirty people gathered in our apartment to hear the show, making for an exhilarating group-listening experience that hinted at the possibilities for hybrid media practices that combined old-time radio and new social media.

The next phase of the experiment will involve relaunching a defunct student organization called NURD (Northwestern University Radio Drama), to establish links between student actors, writers, and sound designers interested in working in audio. Eventually, I hope that WNUR will be the testing ground for a model of labor-intensive, low-carbon media production that I call LILC Radio.

Instructions for Labor-Intensive, Low-Carbon (LILC) Radio

1. Create a radio broadcast as a live event at a local station. It should be performed for a copresent studio audience as well as a remote listening public.

2. All the sounds of the broadcast should be produced at the site of performance, and the use of prerecorded sounds should be kept to a minimum.
3. Use as little electricity during the performance as possible, apart from what is needed for the broadcasting infrastructure. Performers and listeners should be encouraged to turn off electric lights.
4. Employ as many collaborators and participants as possible. The goal is full employment, not labor efficiency. For example, if given the choice between hiring a string quartet or a single keyboard player to emulate a string quartet on a keyboard, hire the string quartet.
5. Encourage the audience to listen to the broadcast on low- or no-wattage receivers and in groups.
6. Eco-sonic option: Make your broadcast represent environmental crisis or increase the audience's "ecological awareness," understood as the sense of "the innumerable interrelationships among lifeforms and between life and non-life."[81]

Notice that, apart from the optional sixth point, the instructions for LILC Radio place no limits on content, genre, or setting. Compare that aesthetic latitude to the famous Dogme 95 manifesto written by Danish film directors Lars von Trier and Thomas Vinterberg, which asked filmmakers to take a "Vow of Chastity" by shooting on location with live sound and handheld cameras, using no special lighting, no "superficial action," and narratives that take place in the present.[82] LILC Radio does not enforce artistic chastity but instead celebrates the proliferation of sonic and narrative pleasures, aiming to amplify radio's liberating freedom from the expense and limitations of costume, makeup, and set design. The dark ecological genres described in chapter 4—horror, noir, and science fiction—are a good place to begin the corpus of LILC Radio.

The four experiments described here are only small steps in the direction of greening the media. Though small, they are significant in that they mark an "eco-ethical choice" to make sound media accountable to environmental degradation.[83] In seeking out hybrid technologies and mixed menus, my experiments aim to reduce the harmful effects of media consumption at the same time that they allow sound culture to flourish. Now, as the needle is drifting toward the end of the groove, it is time to move toward the finalization of this concluding chapter, and, in the spirit of chapter 4, I will do so with the help of a classic work of radio science fiction: the adaptation of Ray Bradbury's "There Will Come Soft Rains" broadcast on NBC's *Dimension X* in 1950.

The story is set in the future world of 1985 and concerns a fully automated house equipped with cleaning robots, beds that make themselves, self-warming blankets, a kitchen that prepares meals, a self-building fireplace, and a library equipped with talking books. A family of four inhabit the house until a cataclysmic nuclear war destroys human civilization. "The happy time was over," Bradbury writes. Though all the human occupants are dead, the house lives on: the stove continues to prepare breakfast; the robots clean; the sprinkler turns on and off. Perhaps most disturbing, the house continues to talk, as recorded voices intone mundane daily reminders such as "tick tock seven o'clock, time to rise open your eyes" and "seven-nine, breakfast time." The house's eerie, undead voices make the story perfect for radio adaptation.

At nine o'clock in the evening, a recorded voice above the house's fireplace recites Sara Teasdale's poem, "There Will Come Soft Rains." The poem describes a tranquil natural space filled with swallows, frogs, trees, and robins, none of whom are aware that they inhabit the site of a devastating human war. The final lines of the poem are

> Not one would mind, neither bird nor tree,
> If mankind perished utterly;
> And Spring herself, when she woke at dawn.
> Would scarcely know that we were gone.

The recorded voice finishes reading the poem as empty chairs face one another between the silent walls.

That night, a tree falls on the house and starts a fire. Recorded voices call for help as part of an automatic fire-alarm system, but soon the blaze triggers a cacophony of recorded voices announcing the time and the weather, giving reminders, reading menus, and reciting poetry. Eventually, the fire consumes the film spools, withers the wires, and cracks the circuits, and the house collapses into silence. At dawn the next morning a single wall remains standing, from which emanates a recorded voice that speaks the final lines of the Teasdale poem until the needle becomes stuck in the groove: "would scarcely know that we were gone ... that we were gone ... that we were gone ... that we were gone ... that we were gone."[84]

The apocalyptic needle stick is a dark variation on the locked groove and functions nicely to provide finalization for the broadcast. Bradbury was not the first writer to use the skipping phonograph record as a trope to signal the inauthenticity and insincerity of modern communication. John M. Picker argues that Kurtz's final repeated phrase, "The horror! The horror!" in Joseph Conrad's *Heart of Darkness* (1898), is perhaps the greatest needle stick in modern literature, "voicing not a unified, coherent singularity but a divided, paralyzed vision of self that persists throughout modernist writing."[85] Bradbury's needle stick is certainly meant to register as a modernist critique of postwar consumer culture, but it also enacts media infrastructure becoming audible in a moment of social collapse. The uncanny announcements in the burning house can be heard, then, not just as disembodied sounds but as the voices of circuits, wires, spools, and steel needles.

Our lives have become more immersed in mediated sounds and voices than Bradbury imagined, and there is something fitting in the fact that, for contemporary listeners, the story takes place not in the future, as it was intended to be heard, but in the past. We can hear this apocalyptic tale, then, not as a dire warning about the future but as an allegory of the present. The crisis is upon us, the sixth great extinction is happening, and the catastrophic event of unstoppable global warming has already occurred. We need to move beyond the paralyzing fear of an immanent apocalypse and instead begin to make the best of the situation we actually face.[86]

An eco-sonic ear listens with a sense of hope to the gloomy ending of "There Will Come Soft Rains," since mediated sounds continue even after the end of the world. In that regard, the broadcast ends with "the sound of the end of the world but not an apocalypse, not a predictable conclusion."[87] The needle stick can be heard, then, as the sound of something beginning, as an invitation to a more eco-sonic understanding, and as a means to reassess and reimagine the media culture that we inhabit, by listening to it again and again and again and again.

Notes

INTRODUCTION

1. The ecological crisis is typically understood to include oil spills, rainforest destruction, global warming, pesticides, and mass extinction. Carolyn Merchant, *Radical Ecology,* 2nd ed. (New York: Routledge, 2005), 17. See also John Opie, *Nature's Nation* (Fort Worth, TX: Harcourt Brace, 1998), 5.

2. Nadia Bozak, *The Cinematic Footprint* (New Brunswick, NJ: Rutgers University Press, 2012), 5.

3. Elizabeth Grossman, *High Tech Trash* (Washington, DC: Island Press, 2006), 6. On e-waste, see Heather Rogers, *Gone Tomorrow: The Hidden Life of Garbage* (New York: New Press, 2005), 201–3; and Jonathan Sterne, "Out with the Trash: On the Future of New Media," in *Residual Media,* ed. Charles Acland (Minneapolis: University of Minnesota Press, 2007), 16–31.

4. Allison Carruth, "The Digital Cloud and the Micropolitics of Energy," *Public Culture* 26, no. 2 (2014): 350. Carruth defines "the cloud" as "all Internet-based platforms that store and deliver content from remote servers" (341). See also Teresa Brennan, *Globalization and Its Terrors* (London: Routledge, 2003), 5–6; Bozak, *Cinematic Footprint,* 28; and James Glanz, "Power, Pollution and the Internet," *New York Times,* September 22, 2012, 1.

5. See Noel Sturgeon's discussion of "environmental cultural studies," which emphasizes "historically and culturally specific analyses of the intertwining of political economy, cultural production, and ideological representations." *Environmentalism in Popular Culture* (Tuscan: University of Arizona Press, 2009), 11.

6. Sean Cubitt, "Everybody Knows This Is Nowhere: Data Visualization and Ecocriticism," in *Ecocinema Theory and Practice,* ed. Stephen Rust, Salma Monani, and Sean Cubitt (New York: Routledge, 2013), 280. See also the collection *Ecosee: Image: Rhetoric, Nature,* which confines its project to a consideration of the role of "image-based studies" in "understanding the construction and contestation of space, place, nature, environment, and ecology." Sidney I.

Dobrin and Sean Morey, eds., *Ecosee: Image: Rhetoric, Nature* (Albany: SUNY Press, 2009), 2.

7. National Resources Defense Council, *Televisions: Active Mode Energy Use and Opportunities for Energy Savings*, issue paper, March 2005, www.nrdc.org/air/energy/energyeff/tv.pdf, 2; see also pages 17–18. A 2011 report estimates that the annual electricity consumption of residential consumer electronics was 196 Terawatt-hours (TWh) in 2010, "an amount equal to 13.2% of residential electricity consumption" and 5.1 percent of total US electricity consumption. Televisions accounted for 34 percent of residential CE electricity consumption. See Fraunhofer Center for Sustainable Energy Systems, *Energy Consumption of Consumer Electronics in U.S. Homes in 2010* (Cambridge, MA: Fraunhofer Center for Sustainable Energy Systems, 2011), 11, 13, 17.

8. Fraunhofer Center, *Energy Consumption*, 111. See also Paul W. McRandle, who writes, "Bigger-screen televisions, particularly plasma screens, can devour over four times the power of an older cathode ray tube set. Some plasma TVs eat up more energy annually than a refrigerator (one Panasonic set used 849 kilowatt hours/year, versus 670 kwh/year or less for many fridges)." "Supersized TVs and Electronics," *World Watch* 19, no. 6 (2006): 17.

9. As a general rule, as television screens get bigger, power consumption goes up regardless of the technology used. See McRandle, "Supersized TVs," 17.

10. Fraunhofer Center, *Energy Consumption*, 111.

11. Richard Maxwell and Toby Miller, "Ecological Ethics and Media Technology," *International Journal of Communication* 2 (2008): 334–35.

12. Richard Maxwell and Toby Miller, *Greening the Media* (Oxford: Oxford University Press, 2012), 17–18. See also Jonathan Sterne's and Lisa Parks's essays on media infrastructure: Sterne, "Out with the Trash," and Parks, "Falling Apart: Electronics Salvaging and the Global Media Economy," both in Acland, *Residual Media*, 16–31, 32–47; and Jonathan Sterne, *MP3: The Meaning of a Format* (Durham: Duke University Press, 2012).

13. My ultimate goal might be described in terms of Carolyn Merchant's description of a "radical ecology" that "pushes social and ecological systems toward new patterns of production, reproduction, and consciousness that will improve the quality of human life and the natural environment. It challenges those aspects of the political and economic order that prevent the fulfillment of basic human needs. It offers theories that explain the social causes of environmental problems and alternative ways to resolve them. It supports social movements for removing the causes of environmental deterioration and raising the quality of life for people of every race, class, and sex" (*Radical Ecology*, 8).

14. Jonathan Sterne defines sound studies as "the interdisciplinary ferment in the human sciences that takes sound as its analytical point of departure or arrival. By analyzing both sonic practices and the discourses and institutions that describe them, it redescribes what sound does in the human world, and what humans do to the sonic world" ("Sonic Imaginations," in *The Sound Studies Reader*, ed. Jonathan Sterne (London: Routledge, 2012), 2.

15. R. Murray Schafer, "Radical Radio," in Radiotext(e), ed. Neil Strauss (New York: Semiotext[e], 1993), 293; Hildegard Westerkamp, "Soundwalking," in Autumn Leaves, Sound and the Environment in Artistic Practice, ed. Angus Carlyle (Paris; Double Entendre, 2007), 49–54; Pauline Oliveros, "Auralizing the Sonosphere: A Vocabulary for Inner Sound and Sounding," Journal of Visual Culture 10, no. 2 (2011): 162–68; Douglas Kahn, Earth Sound Earth Signal (Berkeley: University of California Press, 2013); Jonathan Sterne, The Audible Past (Durham: Duke University Press, 2003); and Sterne, "Out with the Trash," in Acland, Residual Media, 16–31. Schafer defines "acoustic ecology" as "the study of sounds in relationship to life and society . . . the effects of the acoustic environment on the creatures living in it." The Soundscape (Rochester, VT: Destiny Books, 1994), 205. See also Emily Thompson, The Soundscape of Modernity (Cambridge: MIT Press, 2002); John M. Picker, Victorian Soundscapes (New York: Oxford University Press, 2003); Karin Bijsterveld, Mechanical Sound (Cambridge, MA: MIT Press, 2008); Barry Blesser and Linda-Ruth Salter, Spaces Speak, Are You Listening? Experiencing Aural Architecture (Cambridge, MA: MIT Press, 2007); Alain Corbin, Village Bells: Sound and Meaning in the Nineteenth-Century French Countryside (New York: Columbia University Press, 1998); Peter A. Coates, "The Strange Stillness of the Past: Toward an Environmental History of Sound and Noise," Environmental History 10, no. 4 (2005): 636–65; Raymond W. Smilor, "Cacophony at 34th and 6th: The Noise Problem in America, 1900–1930," American Studies 18, no. 1 (1977): 23–38; and Douglas Kahn, "Radio of the Sphere," in Radio Territories, ed. Erik Granly Jensen and Brandon LaBelle (London: Errant Bodies, 2006), 219–30. Composer Pauline Oliveros writes of the "sonosphere" as the "sonic envelope of the earth" and its relation to the biosphere ("Auralizing the Sonosphere," 162).

16. Donald Worster states that environmental history aims to "deepen our understanding of how humans have been affected by their natural environment through time, and conversely . . . how they have affected that environment and with what results." "Transformations of the Earth," *Journal of American History* 76, no. 4 (1990): 1089. Whenever "the natural and the cultural confront or interact with one another," Worster writes, "environmental history finds its essential themes" (1090). See also Dipesh Chakraberty, "The Climate of History: Four Theses," *Critical Inquiry* 35, no. 2 (2009): 197–222.

17. Historian Carroll Pursell argues that "the notion that technology develops in a progressive and linear way, and that each improvement drives out its inferior antecedents, has left the general public, and many policy makers as well, with a grossly distorted view of technological change. Historians of technology have the data to give exposure to such fallacious bromides as what can be done will be done, bigger is always better, people rather than guns kill people, and wood and water are simple and easy compared with steam iron and steam, let alone plastic and nuclear power." "The History of Technology as a Source of Appropriate Technology," *Public Historian* 1, no. 2 (1979): 21.

18. Timothy Morton, *The Ecological Thought* (Cambridge, MA: Harvard University Press, 2010), 5. Teresa Brennan argues that the responsible reaction

to planetary destruction is to deliberately reverse course, "not out of nostalgia but out of the desire to keep living" (*Globalization*, 156). Green marketer John Grant writes that "we consumerized our way into this mess," and there are "grounds for doubt that we can entirely consumerize our way out of it." *The Green Marketing Manifesto* (London: Wiley and Sons, 2010), 189.

19. Donald Worster, "Nature and the Disorder of History," *Environmental History Review* 18, no. 2 (1994): 13–14.

20. Robert L. Thayer Jr. asks whether, "with unsentimental reason and respect," we might "learn from first peoples how to share a mutual community of reciprocity between human and nonhuman life?" *LifePlace: Bioregional Thought and Practice* (Berkeley: University of California Press, 2003), 61. Benjamin Kline refers to Native Americans as "prototypical environmentalists." *First along the River*, 2nd ed. (San Francisco: Acada Books, 2000), 14–15. Worster writes that one of the benefits of environmental history is that it "sets before us models of human communities that have been more successful than we in some respects" ("Disorder of History," 13). See also Suneetha M. Subramanian and Balakrishna Pisupati, eds., *Traditional Knowledge in Policy and Practice* (Tokyo: United Nations University Press), 2010.

21. Regis Debray, *Media Manifestos* (London: Verso, 1996), 113. For a discussion of "media ecology" understood as the study of "media as environments," as in the work of Marshall McLuhan, Walter Ong, and others, see Heise, "Unnatural Ecologies," *Configurations* 10, no. 1 (2002): 149–68.

22. Jussi Parikka, *What Is Media Archaeology?* (Cambridge: Polity, 2012), 2, 64. Parikka writes that "the danger lies in being drawn into writing about 'curiosities' for their own sake, instead of asking . . . why is this particular technology important, and what is the argument behind this research into this curiosity of media history?" (65).

23. T. Morton, *Ecological Thought*, 98. See also Frederick Buell, *From Apocalypse to Way of Life* (New York: Routledge, 2004).

24. J. Grant, *Green Marketing Manifesto*, 87.

25. Paterson describes her process: "I recorded the sounds of three glaciers crunching along in Iceland. I brought the water back from each icecap, cast the water into an LP using dental silicone, then I froze the real glacier water inside, which gave me three records made of ice that played the actual sounds of the glacier—the cracking of the ice. . . . The records lasted two hours before they melted." Robert Bound, "Light Bulb Moment," *Monocle* 2, no. 18 (2008): 92–93.

26. T. Morton, *Ecological Thought*, 11. Morton writes, "environmental art must deeply explore materiality." He continues, "Ecological art, and the ecological-ness of all art, isn't just *about* something (trees, mountains, animals, pollution, or so forth). Ecological art *is* something," reminding us that all art is ecological "insofar as it is made from materials and exists in the world" (107). Bozak writes that "because it is as resource-dependent as any other facet of industrial culture, all cinema can be considered 'environmental' insofar as filmmaking technology is constituted by the biophysical world, its residues contribute to atmospheric

health, and how it is represented on the screen has a hand in determining human interaction with that nebulously defined realm called nature" (*Cinematic Footprint*, 88).

27. Maxwell and Miller, *Greening the Media*, 7.

28. T. Morton, *Ecological Thought*, 19.

29. On the recovery of scavenged materials by artisans, see Martin Medina, *The World's Scavengers* (Lanham, MD: AltaMira, 2007), 66.

30. Only a century earlier passenger pigeons had numbered in the billions and had traveled in such large numbers that it could take twelve hours for a single flock to pass overhead. Philip Shabecoff, *A Fierce Green Fire* (New York: Hill and Wang, 1993), 168–69. Approximately 130 species of birds have vanished over the past century and a half. The World Conservation Union currently lists 1,213 birds as threatened, about 12 percent of all avian species. By the end of the century 1,000 species of birds might disappear, which would be a thousand times the background extinction rate. Sarah DeWeerdt, "Bye Bye Birdie," *World Watch* 19, no. 4 (2006): 28–33. On the passenger pigeon, see Kline, *First along the River*, 44; Mark V. Barrow Jr., *Nature's Ghosts: Confronting Extinction from the Age of Jefferson to the Age of Ecology* (Chicago: University of Chicago, 2009), 96–100; and Alan Weisman, *The World without Us* (New York: St. Martin's Press, 2007), 43.

31. Donna J. Haraway, *The Companion Species Manifesto* (Chicago: Prickly Paradigm, 2003), 4.

32. Thomas A. Sebeok, "Zoosemiotic Components of Human Communication," in *How Animals Communicate*, ed. Thomas A. Sebeok (Bloomington: Indiana University Press, 1977), 1055–56.

33. Donella Meadows, Jorgen Randers, and Dennis Meadows write that "of the large animals that are relatively well studied, scientists now estimate that 24 percent of the world's 4,700 mammal species, an estimated 30 percent of the 25,000 fish species, and 12 percent of the world's nearly 10,000 bird species are in danger of extinction." *Limits to Growth: The 30-Year Update* (White River Junction, VT: Chelsea Green), 2004, 85.

34. See interviews with Kubisch here: Christoph Cox and Christina Kubisch, "Invisible Cities: An Interview with Christina Kubisch," *Cabinet*, no. 21 (Spring 2006), accessed December 22, 2014, http://cabinetmagazine.org/issues/21/cox .php; and Matteo Milani, "Walking in the City with Christina Kubisch," *Digicult*, accessed December 22, 2014, www.digicult.it/digimag/issue-045 /walking-in-the-city-with-christina-kubisch/.

35. Ursula K. Heise, *Sense of Place and Sense of Planet* (New York: Oxford University Press, 2008), 62.

36. On the projection of moving images and "the immobility of its spectators," see Anne Friedberg, *The Virtual Window* (Cambridge, MA: MIT Press, 2006), 5, 242. See also Rick Altman, who writes that, "as in Plato's cave, movie theaters hold our bodies in a fixed position in relation to the screen." *Sound Theory, Sound Practice* (New York: Routledge, 1992), 5. Similarly, Lev Manovich points out that while "the cinema screen enabled audiences to take a

journey through different spaces without leaving their seats," it did so at the cost of "a new, institutionalized immobility of the spectator." *The Language of New Media* (Cambridge, MA: MIT Press, 2001), 107.

37. See Michael Bull, *Sound Moves* (London: Routledge, 2007); Tia DeNora, *Music in Everyday Life* (Cambridge: Cambridge University Press, 2000); Iain Chambers, "The Aural Walk," in *Audio Culture*, ed. Christoph Cox and Daniel Warner (New York: Continuum, 2004), 98–101; and Sumanth Gopinath and Jason Stanyek, eds. *The Oxford Handbook of Mobile Music Studies*, 2 vols. (New York: Oxford University Press, 2014).

38. Medina, *World's Scavengers*, 69; Kate Soper, "Alternative Hedonism, Cultural Theory and the Role of Aesthetic Revisioning," *Cultural Studies* 22, no. 5 (2008): 567–87.

39. David Barrett, "Motohiko Odani, Joe Gilmore and Andrea Polli," *Art Monthly*, no. 287 (2005): 29–30. Polli also released a CD titled *Sonic Antarctica* (Gruenrekorder, Gruen 064, 2008), which features recordings of the Antarctic soundscape made during her seven-week National Science Foundation residency in Antarctica.

40. Yvonne Volkart, "The End of the World of White Men," and Andrea Polli, "N.," both in *Ecomedia*, ed. Sabine Himmelsbach and Yvonne Volkart (Oldenburg, Germany: Hatje Cantz Verlag, 2007), 168, 127.

41. T. Morton, *Ecological Thought*, 16–17.

42. Finis Dunaway, "Seeing Global Warming: Contemporary Art and the Fate of the Planet," *Environmental History* 14, no. 1 (2009): 24–25.

43. George H.W. Bush, quoted in Bill McKibben, *The End of Nature* (New York: Random House, 2006), xxiv.

44. Indeed, the Western lifestyle may very well have to change "beyond recognition" (J. Grant, *Green Marketing Manifesto*, 29). Patrick Curry argues that the theme of limits must be central to ecocentric counternarratives and a culture of green citizenship. *Ecological Ethics: An Introduction*, 2nd ed. (Cambridge: Polity, 2011), 162. In regard to technology, Langdon Winner asks, "in an age in which the inexhaustible power of scientific technology makes all things possible, it remains to be seen where we will draw the line, where we will be able to say, here are possibilities that wisdom suggests we avoid." *The Whale and the Reactor* (Chicago: University of Chicago Press, 1986), xi.

CHAPTER 1. GREEN DISCS

1. Otto Wilson, "The 'Hundred Thousand' Insect," *Nature* 12 (November 1928): 292–95.

2. T. Morton, *Ecological Thought*, 107.

3. Sterne, *MP3*, 11.

4. I am riffing here on Brian Larkin's definition of infrastructure as the "totality of both technical and cultural systems that create institutionalized structures whereby goods of all sorts circulate, connecting and binding people into collectivities." *Signal and Noise* (Durham: Duke University Press, 2008), 5–6. Geoffrey

C. Bowker and his colleagues define infrastructure as a broad category that refers to "pervasive enabling resources in network form." See "Toward Information Infrastructure Studies: Ways of Knowing in a Networked Environment," in *International Handbook of Internet Research*, ed. Jeremy Hunsinger, Lisbeth Klastrup, and Matthew Allen (Dordrecht: Springer, 2010), 98. I am also inspired by Lisa Parks's project of *"infrastructure re-socialization*—a technological literacy project that urges publics to notice, document, and ask questions about infrastructure sites and become involved in discussion and deliberations about their funding, design, installation, operation, and use." See "Earth Observation and Signal Territories," *Canadian Journal of Communication* 38, no. 3 (2013): 285–307.

5. Robert B. Gordon, *A Landscape Transformed* (Oxford: Oxford University Press, 2001), 3. See also Richard Heinberg, "What Is Sustainability?," in *The Post Carbon Reader*, ed. Richard Heinberg and Daniel Lerch (Healdsburg, CA: Watershed Media, 2010). For Donella Meadows, Jorgen Randers, and Dennis Meadows, "a sustainable society is one that can persist over generations; one that is farseeing enough, flexible enough, and wise enough not to undermine either its physical or its social systems of support" (*Limits to Growth*, 254).

6. I refer here to Carroll Pursell's argument that the history of technology "might enhance the efficacy of current efforts to promote alternative technologies," with history as "a great museum of the past" and a resource for new designs ("History of Technology," 21).

7. Bruno Latour defines "actant" as "something that acts or to which activity is granted by others.... An actant can literally be anything provided it is granted to be the source of an action." "On Actor-Network Theory: A Few Clarifications," *Soziale Welt* 47, no. 4 (1996): 369, 373. See also Latour, *Reassembling the Social* (Oxford: Oxford University Press, 2005), 54.

8. Jennifer Daryl Slack and J. Macgregor Wise, *Culture and Technology* (New York: Lang, 2007), 113. Latour describes a network as consisting of "exclusively related yet very distant elements with the circulation between nodes being made compulsory through a set of rigorous paths giving a few nodes a strategic character" ("Actor-Network Theory," 369). For Jane Bennett, assemblages are "ad hoc groupings of diverse elements" that function "despite the persistent presence of energies that confound them from within." *Vibrant Matter: A Political Ecology of Things* (Durham: Duke University Press, 2010), 23–24.

9. Slack and Wise, *Culture and Technology*, 130.

10. Latour talks about ants in *Reassembling the Social* (9) and asserts that "the ANT-scholar has to trudge like an ant" (25). Latour also uses an insect metaphor in his description of networks as an "Ariadne's thread" of "interwoven stories" linking nature, politics, discourse. *We Have Never Been Modern* (Cambridge, MA: Harvard University Press, 1993), 3.

11. Jussi Parikka, *Insect Media: An Archaeology of Animals and Technology* (Minneapolis: University of Minnesota Press, 2010), xiv, xx.

12. Latour, *Reassembling the Social*, 176.

13. Curry, *Ecological Ethics*, 173–75. Subramanian and Pisupati define traditional knowledge as "a dynamic knowledge system [that] distinguishes itself from mainstream knowledge in its methods of knowledge generation, transmission and the principles and values related to its use for various purposes. It advocates, in general, a respectful and reciprocal relationship with natural resources, including habitats and plants and animals that humans interact with" (*Traditional Knowledge*, 3).

14. Anna Lowenhaupt Tsing, *Friction: An Ethnography of Global Connection* (Princeton: Princeton University Press, 2005), 160.

15. Bozak, *Cinematic Footprint*, 34. Scott MacDonald argues that the celluloid filmstrip "encapsulates the way in which modern life and the natural world are imbricated: the light-sensitive silver salts that create a visible image when exposed to light are suspended in a thin layer of gelatin, one of the chief ingredients of which is collagen. Collagen is produced by boiling the bones and tissues of animals. Celluloid, the base on which the emulsion is layered, is made from cellulose. That is, the 'life' we see moving on the screen is a kind of re-animation of plant and animal life within the mechanical/chemical apparatus of traditional cinema." "The Ecocinema Experience," in Rust, Monani, and Cubitt, *Ecocinema Theory*, 18.

16. Sterne, "Out with the Trash," in Acland, *Residual Media*, 17.

17. Jennifer Gabrys, *Digital Rubbish: A Natural History of Electronics* (Ann Arbor: University of Michigan Press, 2011), 5. Jonathan Sterne writes that "emphasis on virtuality, the ethereal, ideational, immaterial, and experiential dimensions of new media leads many writers to accept the myriad strategies ... [used] to move computer trash into the backspaces of modern life" ("Out with the Trash," in Acland, *Residual Media*, 16).

18. Ivan Illich, *Tools for Conviviality* (New York: Harper and Row, 1973), xxiv; Gordon, *Landscape Transformed*, 4.

19. Ernest J. Parry, *Shellac: Its Production, Manufacture, Chemistry, Analysis, Commerce and Uses* (London: Pitman and Sons, 1935), 1. See also G. Clarke Nuttall, "Shellac and the Lac Industry," supplement, *Scientific American* 69 (June 1910): 371–72; Angelo Brothers, *Shellac* (Calcutta: Angelo Brothers, 1956), 9; Elizabeth Brownell Crandall, *Shellac: A Story of Yesterday, Today and Tomorrow* (Chicago: Day, 1924), 23; and H.A.F. Lindsay and C.M. Harlow, *The Indian Forest Records: Report on Lac and Shellac*, vol. 8 (Allahabad, India: Pioneer, 1921), 17–21.

20. Lindsay and Harlow, *Indian Forest Records*, 2; Angelo Brothers, *Shellac* (1956), 10.

21. J.L. Cloudsley-Thompson, *Insects and History* (New York: St. Martin's Press, 1976), 212; "Shellac Substitute," *Time* 42, no. 23 (1943): 68. On insects as swarms, see Parikka, *Insect Media*, xxxiv.

22. Lindsay and Harlow, *Indian Forest Records*, 1–2. The author of an article in the *Scientific American* writes that the insect was "nothing more or less than an animated miniature syphon" and describes the resin as a "small, red, dome-shaped excrescence. Owing to the myriads of these excrescences they tend to

run into one another and form a regular incrustation on the branches" (Nuttall, "Lac Industry," 371–72).

23. Wilson, "Hundred Thousand," 292–95; Cloudsley-Thompson, *Insects and History*, 213.

24. Parry, *Shellac*, 8; P.K. Bose, Y. Sankaranarayanan, S.C. Sen Gupta, *Chemistry of Lac* (Namkum, India: Indian Lac Research Institute, 1963), 4, 5.

25. See Latour's discussion of translation in Slack and Wise, *Culture and Technology*, 118–19.

26. Frank A. Montgomery, "From Bugs Comes Out Shellac," *Baltimore Sun*, October 10, 1937, SM9.

27. Lindsay and Harlow, *Indian Forest Records*, 8.

28. "Little Bugs and Big Business," *Popular Mechanics* 67, no. 5 (1937): 692–93, 146A–48A.

29. Parikka, *Insect Media*, 6–7, 33.

30. Ernest Callenbach, *Ecology* (Berkeley: University of California Press, 2008), 61–63; Richard Heinberg, *The Party's Over* (Gabriola Island, Canada: New Society, 2005), 10; Callenbach, *Ecology*, 41–42. Carolyn Merchant argues that an ecological perspective "unites the laws of nature with the processes of production through exchanges of energy. All animals, plants, and minerals are energy niches involved in the actual exchange of energy, materials, and information." "The Theoretical Structure of Ecological Revolutions," *Environmental Review* 11, no. 4 (1987): 269.

31. Latour, "Actor-Network Theory," 378.

32. Wilson, "Hundred Thousand," 292–95. The move from the industry of the lac to the industry of the lac worker is the move from an ecosystem, which Donald Worster defines as "a subset of the global economy of nature—a local or regional system of plants and animals working together to create the means of survival," to an "agroecosystem": "an ecosystem reorganized for agricultural purposes—a domesticated ecosystem," "a restructuring of the trophic processes in nature, that is, the processes of food and energy flow in the economy of living organisms" ("Transformations," 1092–93).

33. Angelo Brothers, *Shellac*, 2nd ed. (Calcutta: Angelo Brothers, 1965), 43.

34. Rai Bahadur Misra, *The Cultivation of Lac in the Plains of India* (Calcutta: Government of India Central Publication Branch, 1929), 6. After 1874 "dye export trade registered a sharp and steady fall, being unable to withstand the competition from the synthetic aniline dyes which had been discovered by this time." By 1902 the dye had ceased to be an article of export. S. Krishnaswami, "Lac through the Ages," in *A Monograph on Lac*, ed. B. Mukhopadhyay and M.S. Muthana (Ranchi, India: Indian Lac Research Institute, 1962), 8. See also Angelo Brothers, *Shellac* (1965), 11.

35. A 1934 report estimated that the industry provided income for up to one million people, while in 1971 the number was placed at four million. See "Supersession of Indian Shellac," *Times of India*, May 11, 1934, 3. The 1971 report stated that lac was cultivated largely by *adivasi* people or "tribals," who "live mainly in the forests and come to the village markets to sell forest

produce." Kirloskar Consultants, *Survey of India's Export Potential of Shellac* (Poona: Kirloskar Consultants, 1971), 2:2. See also B.M. Ghatge, "Marketing of Lac," in Mukhopadhyay and Muthana, *Monograph on Lac*, 272.

36. Parry, *Shellac*, 157. In one system the tenants paid rent for the right to cultivate lac, which then became the property of the lessee. In another the landlord provided the brood and took a percentage of the profits (Lindsay and Harlow, *Indian Forest Records*, 49).

37. Parry, *Shellac*, 22, 36.

38. Lindsay and Harlow, *Indian Forest Records*, 13; Paul W. Kearney, "It's All Done with Shellac," *Natural History* 66 (May 1957): 243; Bose, Sankaranarayanan, and Gupta, *Chemistry of Lac*, 5; Parry, *Shellac*, 16. A 1962 monograph states that since the lac insect is "dependent entirely upon the host-plant on which it lives and feeds, it will be realized that successful cultivation of lac depends upon proper use of the lac insect as also of the host-plants." Lac required free circulation of air and so was best located on the outskirts of the deep jungle, where it was possible for wind or other insects to transport the larvae to new trees (M.S. Roonwal, "Lac Hosts," in Mukhopadhyay and Muthana, *Monograph on Lac*, 54.

39. Joshua Farely, "Ecological Economics," in Heinberg and Lerch, *Post Carbon Reader*, 265. In *Limits to Growth* Meadows, Randers, and Meadows write, "A standing forest is a resource in itself, performing vital functions beyond economic measure. Forests moderate climate, control floods, and store water against drought. They cushion the erosive effects of rainfall, build and hold soil on slopes, and keep rivers and seacoasts, irrigation canals and dam reservoirs, free from silt. They harbor and support many species of life" (74). On ecosystem services, see pages 83–84. A comparison can be made with the production of rubber. See Jeyamalar Kathirithamby-Wells, "The Implications of Plantation Agriculture for Biodiversity in Peninsular Malaysia," and Michael R. Dove, "Rubber Kills the Land and Saves the Community: An Undisciplined Commodity," both in *Beyond the Sacred Forest: Complicating Conservation in Southeast Asia*, ed. Michael R. Dove, Percy E. Sajise, and Amity A. Doolittle (Durham: Duke University Press, 2011), 62–90, 91–122.

40. Parry, *Shellac*, 158–59. See also Wilson, "Hundred Thousand," 293–94.

41. A 1943 report states that there were numerous small manufacturers and two factories with modern machinery in Calcutta. The largest percentage of lac production came from small factories with three to twenty-five *bhattas*. See India, Central Agricultural Marketing Department, *Report on the Marketing of Lac in India* (Delhi: Government of India Press, 1943), 26.

42. Parry, *Shellac*, 56, 65, 69. The report on page 69 is cited in the text as "Report on Manufacture of Shellac," Statistical Reporter, Vol. II, 1876, p. 406.

43. Jan-Christopher Horak, "A Neglected Genre: James Sibley Watson's Avant-Garde Industrial Films," *Film History* 20, no. 1 (2008), 38; Tom Gunning, "Before Documentary: Early Nonfiction Films and the 'View' Aesthetic," in *Uncharted Territory*, ed. Daan Hiertogs and Nico De Klerk (Amsterdam: Stichting Nederlands Filmmuseum, 1997), 15–17; Frank Kessler and Eef Masson, "Layers of Cheese," and Vinzenz Hediger and Patrick Vonderau, "Record,

Rhetoric, Rationalization," both in *Films That Work*, ed. Vinzenz Hediger and Patrick Vonderau (Amsterdam: Amsterdam University Press, 2009), 80, 38. For an example of press accounts of shellac, see "Insects Make Shellac," *Rome (NY) Semi-Weekly Citizen*, October 12, 1892, 6.

44. Elizabeth Wiatr argues that industrial films shared formal and structural qualities with discourses of tourism and development and often inscribed industry into "evolutionary notions of historical time." "Between Word, Image, and the Machine: Visual Education and Films of Industrial Process," *Historical Journal of Film, Radio and Television* 22, no. 3 (2002): 337–38. On "non-modern systems of knowledge," see Tariq Banuri and Frederique Apffel Marglin, eds., *Who Will Save the Forests?* (London: Zed Books, 1993), 1.

45. "The Shellac Market—Conditions Affecting Supply," *Talking Machine World* 16, no. 4 (1920): 69.

46. Max Weber, *The Protestant Ethic and the Spirit of Capitalism* (1930; repr., London: Routledge, 1996), 59–60.

47. Ben Singer, "The Ambimodernity of Early Cinema," in *Film 1900: Technology, Perception, Culture*, ed. Annemone Ligensa and Klaus Kreimeier (New Barnet, UK: Libbey, 2009), 38.

48. T. Morton, *Ecological Thought*, 26–27. On bioplastics, see Eugene S. Stevens, *Green Plastics* (Princeton: Princeton University Press, 2002), 105; and Rogers, *Gone Tomorrow*, 213.

49. Roland Barthes, *Mythologies* (New York: Hill and Wang, 1995), 97.

50. On bioplastics, "biodegradable plastics whose components are derived entirely or almost entirely from renewable raw materials," see Stevens, *Green Plastics*, 104. On the Great Pacific Garbage Patch, see Weisman, *World without Us*, 152.

51. Angelo Brothers, *Shellac* (1965), 44.

52. In India, lac was used by artisans and carpenters to smooth and varnish woodwork, to add color, and to make tools. Jewelers used it to hold ornaments, as well as in toys and boxes. See Sir George Watt, *The Commercial Products of India* (London: Murray, 1908).

53. In the late 1880s Edison used carnauba, a wax made from leaves of Brazilian palm trees, and the mineral wax ozocerite for his wax cylinder masters. Leah S. Burt, "Record Materials: Chemical Technology in the Edison Recording Industry," pt. 1, *Journal of the Audio Engineering Society* 25, nos. 10–11 (1977): 713.

54. Raymond R. Wile, "The Launching of the Gramophone in America 1890–1896," *ARSC Journal* 24, no. 2 (1977): 186; H. Courtney Bryson, *The Gramophone Record* (London: Benn, 1935), 12–13. See also Thi-Phoung Nguyen et al., "Determining the Composition of 78-rpm Records," *ARSC Journal* 42, no. 1 (2011): 27; "Shellac Is Held to Have Some Unique Values," *Washington Post*, April 25, 1937, R9; Warren Rex Ison, "Record Materials: Evolution of the Disc Talking Machine," pt. 2, *Journal of the Audio Engineering Society* 25, nos. 10–11 (1977): 719.

55. Angelo Brothers, *Shellac* (1956), 93–94; see also "Unique Values," R9; and Ison, "Record Materials," 718. According to Lloyd MacFarlane, the shellac

mixture had the following advantages: "extreme pliancy under the influence of heat and extreme hardness (although brittle), when cool, and a minimum of contraction and expansion." *The Phonograph Book* (New York: Rider-Long, 1917), 54. On the characteristics of shellac, see M. Venugopalan, "Uses of Lac," in Mukhopadhyay and Muthana, *Monograph on Lac,* 221; and Bryson, *Gramophone Record,* 151). In 1917 *Talking Machine World* reported that shellac represented approximately five-eighths of the material used to make the "better class of records." "The Increase of Shellac Prices," *Talking Machine World* 13, no. 5 (1917): 64.

56. William Kennedy Laurie and Antonia Dickson write that at the Edison Phonograph Works in Orange, New Jersey, the "component properties of the wax" were "locked in the bosom of one trusty familiar," and the entire cylinder department was noted by an "inquisitorial secrecy." *The Life and Inventions of Thomas A. Edison* (New York: Crowell, 1894), 146. As an illustration of that secrecy, one account describes how Edison hid the crucial chemical ingredient in his wax mixture: "When the vat of wax reaches a certain stage in the operation Mr. Edison is notified, where-upon he emerges from a sanctum sanctorum with a small paper bag in one hand. The contents he personally dumps into the vat and waits until he has seen it thoroughly amalgamated with the other ingredients. Every effort to discover the identity of that mysterious and potent chemical by analysis has met with dismal failure. The secret still remains a personal property of the 'Wizard of Menlo Park'" (MacFarlane, *Phonograph Book,* 9). Secrecy was rampant in acoustic-era recordings as well: "A partition runs across one corner. A recording horn projects through a curtained opening in this partition. The artists see only this horn into which they sing. The Phonograph attached to the horn stands back of the partition. How it is equipped and how it does its work are department secrets that even the artists are not permitted to know." "Our New York Recording Plant," *Edison Phonograph Monthly* 4, no. 9 (1906): 8. Ogilvie Mitchell writes that "to get behind the scenes of the recording room ... is a very difficult matter, for the secrets there are most jealously guarded." *The Talking Machine Industry* (London: Pitman and Sons, 1922), 66. On Edison and secret ingredients for Amberol cylinders, see Marsha Siefert, "Aesthetics, Technology, and the Capitalization of Culture: How the Talking Machine Became a Musical Instrument," *Science in Context* 8, no. 2 (1995): 441. On the composition of shellac records, see Andre Millard, *America on Record,* 2nd. ed. (Cambridge: Cambridge University Press, 2005), 202–3; and "Lac Bug vs. Jitterbug," *Newsweek,* April 27, 1942, 59–60. Ison claims a standard recipe was 13.5 percent shellac and 75 percent fillers such as limestone and red slate flour ("Record Materials," 720).

57. "Shellac for Talking Machine," *Talking Machine World* 2, no. 12 (1906): 60. A 1929 report states that the "largest quantity" of Indian shellac is exported to the United States of America, "where it is mostly used for the manufacture of gramophone records and in electrical works. About 42 per cent of the total quantity exported finds its way to the United States" (Misra, *Cultivation of Lac,* 13). See also Nuttall, "Lac Industry," 371–72. In 1935 it was estimated that

about half of the shellac produced was for the manufacture of records (Parry, *Shellac*, 170). In 1939 a report held that "the gramophone record industry provides the largest single outlet for the consumption of shellac . . . 30–35% of the total shellac exported." H.K. Sen and S. Ranganathan, *Uses of Lac* (Namkum, India: Indian Lac Research Institute, 1939), 2. On shellac for telephone components, see "Shellac High in Price," *New York Times*, November 1, 1903, 26.

58. "Technical Notes on the Use of the Gramophone Recording Apparatus," booklet, July 1890, Emile Berliner Papers, Library of Congress, Washington, DC, 5. Translation by Patrick Feaster. Thanks to Patrick Feaster for sharing this source.

59. Henry Seymour, *The Reproduction of Sound* (London: Tattersall, 1918), 109–11. See also O. Mitchell, *Talking Machine Industry*, 43; and MacFarlane, *Phonograph Book*, 34. In 1935 Bryson wrote that "a gravity motor, activated by a heavy weight, is the usual source of motive power for the rotation of the turntable. Fluctuations in angular velocity must be reduced to the absolute minimum—a difficult matter—and the gravity motor provides at once the simplest, most reliable, and steadiest source of energy possible" (*Gramophone Record*, 66).

60. Rick Kennedy, *Jelly Roll, Bix, and Hoagy* (Bloomington: Indiana University Press, 1994), 30. Susan Schmidt Horning discusses gravity weights in Columbia's London studio circa 1911 and in Decca recording studios in 1939: "Electrical current was subject to line loss and current variations, so the mechanical governor driven by weight provided a constant rate of speed more precise than spring or electric motors; it also eliminated vibrations and smoothed out the cogging effect of the rotating motor." *Chasing Sound: Technology, Culture and the Art of the Studio Recording* (Baltimore: Johns Hopkins University Press, 2013), 15, 83, 84.

61. Mark Katz, *Capturing Sound* (Berkeley: University of California Press, 2005), 37, 39.

62. Susan Schmidt Horning, "Chasing Sound: The Culture and Technology of Recoding Studios in America, 1877–1977" (PhD diss., Case Western Reserve University, 2002), 17–18. On batch production, see Horning, *Chasing Sound*, 13.

63. Marsha Siefert writes that "master voices" of statesmen and opera singers "possessed the type of *technical* ability for voice production that meshed with the available recording technology": "with its limited frequency range and need for bright and directed tones, acoustic recording required the sonic extremes—speed, dramatic contrast, and ringing tones—that were also cultivated by vocal training and enhanced by operatic composition and performance practice" ("Aesthetics," 430–31).

64. Sterne, *Audible Past*, 247, 251. Bryson writes that "the normal vocal power of the human voice is only about ten millionths of a watt, and one of the most difficult problems of the early recorders was how to capture a sufficient part of this infinitesimally small amount of energy great enough directly to energize the diaphragm and cutting stylus" (*Gramophone Record*, 18). See also the discussion in Joseph P. Maxfield and Henry C. Harrison, "Methods of High

Quality Recording," *Transactions of the American Institute of Electrical Engineers* 45 (February 1926): 336.

65. Sterne, *Audible Past*, 22, 62.

66. Sergei Eisenstein, *Eisenstein on Disney*, ed. Jay Leyda (Calcutta: Seagull Books, 1986), 21, 27. On Eisenstein and plasmaticness, see Esther Leslie, *Hollywood Flatlands* (London: Verso, 2002), 231–35; and Nicholas Sammond, "Who Dat Say Who Dat? Racial Masquerade, Humor, and the Rise of American Animation," in *Funny Pictures: Animation and Comedy in Studio-Era Hollywood*, ed. Daniel Goldmark and Charlie Keil (Berkeley: University of California Press, 2011), 134.

67. Michel Chion, *Film, a Sound Art* (New York: Columbia University Press, 2009), 337–38. Thomas Elsaesser and Malte Hagener argue that sound is "more malleable than the image because it has always (long before digital technology enabled visual morphs) been endowed with the power of metamorphosis, i.e. it can alter its form at all times." *Film Theory: An Introduction through the Senses* (New York: Routledge, 2010), 137. Feminist scholars interested in the potential for nonvisual representation to elude or critique dominant conventions of visual spectacle have made similar observations. Britta Sjogren for example, describes the asynchronous female voice in cinema as being "abstract, amorphous, contradictory," and in constant flux. *Into the Vortex: Female Voice and Paradox in Film* (Urbana: University of Illinois Press, 2006), 8–9.

68. "Mr. Gilbert Girard, Mimic," *Talking Machine News* 5, no. 61 (1907): 280; Ulysses (Jim) Walsh, "Gilbert Girard," *Hobbies* 52, no. 12 (1948): 33.

69. On Girard, see "Why the Animals Understand Me," *Popular Science* 105, no. 4 (1924): 50.

70. Girard's mimicry was an extramodern performance form imported to the phonograph from the variety stage. It that regard, it is significant that Girard's vocal skills were often paired with other modes of entertainment that had predated the modern media: note how the examples feature auctions, circuses, parades, and nursery rhymes. *Scene at a Dog Fight* (1901) gives the howls, snarls, and yelps of a Bowery dog fight. Girard had counterparts in other national phonograph industries of this era. Amanda Weidman describes recordings made in India between 1904 and 1907 by mimicry artists like "Professor Naidu." On the record *Street Life in Madras*, Professor Naidu uses his voice alone to depict marketplace sellers, an old woman, a Muslim boy, a horse, and a young girl. "Sound and the City: Mimicry and Media in South India," *Journal of Linguistic Anthropology* 20, no. 2 (2010): 294–96, 299.

71. Erika Brady, *A Spiral Way* (Jackson: University Press of Mississippi, 1999), 21; Dickson and Dickson, *Life and Inventions*, 151.

72. Berliner's hand-propelled gramophone was demonstrated in May 1888. Edgar Hutto Jr., "Emile Berliner, Eldridge Johnson, and the Victor Talking Machine Company," *Journal of the Audio Engineering Society* 25, nos. 10–11 (1977): 666.

73. Wile, "Launching," 177, 185.

74. Michael W. Sherman, *The Collector's Guide to Victor Records*, 2nd ed. (Tustin, CA: Monarch Record Enterprises, 2010), 19; Hutto, "Emile Berliner," 667. On Johnson, see William Howland Kenney, *Recorded Music in American Life* (New York: Oxford University Press, 1999), 46.

75. Advertisement for Bagshaw Needle Company, *Talking Machine World* 16, no. 6 (1920): 84. Sterne writes that his "emphasis on the very early moments of technologies and practices at times leads me to concentrate on a relatively small, elite (white, male, European or American, middle-class, able-bodied, etc.) group of people" (*Audible Past*, 28). Sterne discusses Victor's system of interchangeable needles in his discussion of media technologies as musical instruments; see his "Media or Instruments? Yes," *Offscreen* 11, nos. 8–9 (2007): 11.

76. "Builders of Lowell," *Lowell (MA) Sun*, February 16, 1926, 10. On the manufacture of needles in the United Kingdom, see O. Mitchell, *Talking Machine Industry*, 55; "Evolution of the Talking Machine Needle Industry," *Talking Machine World* 18, no. 1 (1922): 59; and "Made in Lowell," *Lowell (MA) Sun*, June 8, 1911, 1.

77. "The Process of Making Talking Machine Needles," *Talking Machine World* 12, no. 9 (1916): 4. One guide stresses that "it is unadvisable to use any needle twice." B. Clements-Henry, *Gramophones and Phonographs* (1913; repr., London: Cassell, 1927), 32.

78. Bagshaw Needle Company, advertisement, *Talking Machine World* 16, no. 5 (1920): 84.

79. Giles Slade, *Made to Break: Technology and Obsolescence in America* (Cambridge, MA: Harvard University Press, 2006), 16; Rogers, *Gone Tomorrow*, 115.

80. "Uses for Records and Needles," *Talking Machine World* 14, no. 5 (1918): 67; "What Becomes of the Needles?," *Talking Machine World* 1, no. 6 (1905): 22; "The Great Used Needle Problem," *Talking Machine World* 12, no. 3 (1916): 23. See also MacFarlane, *Phonograph Book*, 67. A 1921 cartoon in the *Brooklyn Daily Eagle* shows a woman disposing of a box full of used needles by pouring them out her back window. Next we see a group of chickens pecking at the discarded needles. In the last panel, the woman gasps in shock to discover that all the birds are dead. Don Herold, "Old Phonograph Needles Aren't as Good to Eat as They Look," *Brooklyn Daily Eagle*, August 2, 1921, 1.

81. "Talker Needles in Grenades," *Talking Machine World* 14, no. 4 (1918): 1.

82. "Selecting Needles That Will Give Best Results," *Talking Machine World* 9, no. 10 (1913): 18C. Lloyd MacFarlane explains in his 1917 *Phonograph Book* that "the stouter or thicker the steel needle, the louder the volume it will produce, and, conversely, the thinner the needle the less intense are the vibrations and the smaller the volume sent up to the diaphragm by the needle through the stylus bar. The heavier needle flexes the diaphragm more violently than does its weaker brother" (65).

83. Dorchester Mapes, "The Needle Question," *Talking Machine World* 15, no. 8 (1919): 114; Millard, *America on Record*, 203. A trade journal article

describes how the ideal needle had to "shape itself to the groove" or else it could "injure the record and give forth rasping, grating sounds": "A needle point which is soft, improperly pointed, or badly polished, wears down quickly, does not fit the sound groove perfectly, and is sure to injure the record by spreading the groove or otherwise destroying some of the finer sound waves." "Importance of the Needle," *Talking Machine World* 1, no. 6 (1905): 15.

84. Paolo Cherchi Usai, *The Death of Cinema* (London: British Film Institute, 2001), 6, 13, 17. The passage I adapt here is "cinema is the art of moving image destruction." Given "scratches or tears on the print caused by the projecting machine or its operator," "the viewer is an unconscious . . . witness to the extinction of moving images that nobody cares to preserve" (ibid.).

85. "The Jeweled Phonograph Needle," *Talking Machine World* 13, no. 2 (1917): 11.

86. "The Biggest Thing Any Phonograph Can Claim," *Talking Machine World* 13, no. 4 (1917): 28; Clements-Henry, *Gramophones*, 33.

87. Mapes, "Needle Question," 114.

88. "Evolution of the Fibre Needle," *Talking Machine World* 4, no. 10 (1908): 43–44. A 1922 handbook on the phonograph industry claimed that "for the last nine or ten years a miniature war has been waged between the supporters of the old-fashioned steel needle and the followers of the new cult. There can be no doubt that the army of the latter is increasing. Recruits are coming in every day and the fibre has gained a firm footing in the gramophone world" (O. Mitchell, *Talking Machine Industry*, 58). Hall is the kind of modern listener described by Emily Thompson, one who consumed sound quality as much as particular sounds. Thompson depicts a modern listener that derives pleasure "from knowing that he had obtained the clearest and best-sounding reproduction possible, and his consummate taste enabled him to avoid the noises that characterized the inferior records that he had rejected" (*Soundscape of Modernity*, 237).

89. "Success of the Fibre Needle," *Talking Machine World* 4, no. 7 (1908): 22; "Care Necessary in Production of Fibre Needles," *Talking Machine World* 12, no. 11 (1916): 102.

90. Victor bought B&H Fibre needles in 1910, known as "Victor Fibre Needles"; see "The Victor Fibre Needles," *Voice of Victor* 5, no. 5 (1910): 6.

91. On the use of hedgehog spines, see O. Mitchell, *Talking Machine Industry*, 59–60.

92. "Tusks from Ariz. Cacti Valued Commercially," *Arizona Republican*, February 4, 1914, A2; "Phonograph Should Be Used with Care," *Arizona Republican*, March 1, 1919, 10. On Permo, see "Cactus Needle Meets with Favor," *Talking Machine World* 17, no. 7 (1921): 154; "Uses Thorns for Talker Needles," *Talking Machine World* 16, no. 7 (1920): 80; "Venus Needles," *Talking Machine World* 15, no. 12 (1919): 187; "Thorn Needle," *Talking Machine World* 6, no. 2 (1910): 19; and "No Barks from Dogfish Needles," *Talking Machine World* 11, no. 8 (1915): 5. A 1923 article in the *New York Times* credits the novelist Harold Bell Wright with being the first to try needles made from biznaga

cacti: "Wright was gathering material for a novel when he discovered this new kind of phonograph needle. He found growing on the large round stems that make up the body of the plant, spikes hanging from one-half an inch to five inches, and in size and contour much like the familiar phonograph needle. Removing the spikes with steel shears such as are employed in clipping barbed wire, he tested them on his own phonograph and discovered that they were exceedingly hard, resisting breakage to an extraordinary degree. Each needle can be used a half dozen times before it shows, either in appearance or in the tones it produces, any signs of wear." "Cactus for Jazz Records," *New York Times*, September 2, 1923, 16. An ad from 1918 claims that a variety of scrub cactus from Oregon provided needles that were "admirably fitted" for record players and gave "pleasing sweetness and softness to the tone." "Making Needles from Cactus," *Talking Machine World* 14, no. 4 (1918): 51.

93. On Hall's factory in Chicago, see "Evolution," 43–44; "Glimpses of the B. & H. Fibre Needles in the Making," *Talking Machine World* 12, no. 11 (1916): 60; and "Interesting Story of the Fibre Needle," *Talking Machine World* 15, no. 10 (1919): 134–36. Chicago Victrola distributors created a display in large windows on Wabash Avenue, featuring "needles in various processes of manufacture from the crude bamboo pole to the finished product.... The display attracted a large crowd who evinced a keen interest in the evolution of the fibre needle." "Make an Effective Display of Fibre Needles," *Talking Machine World* 12, no. 12 (1916): 83.

94. Johnson Electric Motor Company, advertisement, *Talking Machine World* 16, no. 1 (1920): 71.

95. Pekka Gronow and Ilpo Saunio. *An International History of the Recording Industry* (London: Cassell, 1999), 37, 55.

96. Shelton Electric Motors, advertisement, *Talking Machine World* 12, no. 3 (1916): 33.

97. Roberts Electric Phonograph Motor Company, advertisement, "The Electric Age Comes to the Phonograph Industry," *Talking Machine World* 16, no. 4 (1920): 204.

98. Kline, *First along the River*, 61. Rogers writes that "in 1910 only 10 percent of American dwellings had electricity, but by the end of the 1920s the majority of urban homes were wired" (*Gone Tomorrow*, 65).

99. Sherman, *Collector's Guide*, 85; E. Thompson, *Soundscape of Modernity*, 240. See also Hutto, "Emile Berliner," 672.

100. Katz, *Capturing Sound*, 40. See also Paddy Scannell, *Radio, Television, and Modern Life* (Cambridge, MA: Blackwell, 1996), 62–63; Jason Loviglio, *Radio's Intimate Public* (Minneapolis: University of Minnesota Press, 2005); and Jacob Smith, *Vocal Tracks* (Berkeley: University of California Press, 2008).

101. As the author of a 1954 study of musical style put it, radio technologies like the microphone and loudspeaker "obviated the necessity of vitality in singing" and even made vitality unpopular by stimulating a demand for "the languid, caressing vocals facilitated by the microphone" Hughson F. Mooney, "Songs, Singers and Society, 1890–1954," *American Quarterly* 6 (Fall 1954):

228, cited in Horning, "Chasing Sound," 45. Fidelity was the goal, judging by the comments of the two Bell Labs researchers who designed electrical recording, Maxfield and Harrison: "Phonographic reproduction may be termed perfect when the components of the reproduced sound reaching the ears of the actual listener have the same relative intensity and phase relation as the sound reaching the ears of an imaginary listener to the original performance would have had" ("High Quality Recording," 334).

102. In 1920 *Talking Machine World* noted that the supply of shellac had become a problem of "vital interest" to the industry and warned of the "grave danger" of a general shortage ("Shellac Market," 69). See also O. Mitchell, *Talking Machine Industry*, 70.

103. An article in *Billboard* explains the significance of order M-106 for recording companies: "this means that by stretching their shellac, using substitutes, reclaiming old disks, etc., they may turn out as many records as they wish, as long as they do not exceed the shellac quota." "Diskers Ready New Plans," *Billboard*, April 25, 1942, 68. See also Lizabeth Cohen, *A Consumers' Republic* (New York: Knopf, 2003), 64–65; and Susan Strasser, *Waste and Want* (New York: Holt, 2000), 237–38. An article appeared in many papers in May 1942, titled "Why You Must Do with Less to Help Win This War." Its section "Shellac for Hitler" describes how "there's enough shellac in six records to waterproof the primer cups on 100,000 rounds of .30-caliber cartridges, so make the old tunes last." "Why You Must Do with Less," *Coshocton Tribune*, May 15, 1942, 3. See also "U.S. Orders Output of Phonograph Records Cut 70%," *Washington Post*, April 15, 1942, 3; and "Substitute for Phonograph Records Shellac Discovered," *Los Angeles Times*, August 17, 1942, 24. On shellac rationing, see Kenney, *Recorded Music*, 194–95; and David L. Morton Jr., *Sound Recording: The Life Story of a Technology* (Baltimore: Johns Hopkins University Press, 2004), 100–101.

104. Cohen, *Consumers' Republic*, 67. See also Gary Cross, *An All-Consuming Century* (New York: Columbia University Press, 2000), 84; and Strasser, *Waste and Want*, 230–31. Rogers writes, "World War II brought what would be the last great surge of reuse for decades" (*Gone Tomorrow*, 100).

105. RCA-Victor, Decca, and Columbia, advertisement, *Evening Capital (Annapolis, MD)* April 24, 1942, 1; Jackson's Furniture Store, advertisement, *Oakland Tribune*, April 24, 1942, 17C. The Boyd R. Felty Music Store of Lebanon, Pennsylvania, placed an ad in the *Lebanon Daily News*, urging readers to trade in old records for new (May 9, 1942, 3). The *Boston Globe* encouraged readers to return old records to dealers and declared that there was a "great reservoir of shellac" in the nation's cabinets, attics, and cellars. "Big Scrap Shellac Drive Starts," *Boston Globe*, June 4, 1942, 7.

106. "Victor Out with a One-for-Three Salvage Plan," *Billboard*, May 2, 1942, 21; "Diskers to Keep Cheap Labels In; Decca Used Plan," *Billboard*, May 9, 1942, 22; "Victor Inaugurates Campaign to Avert Possible Shellac Shortage," *Billboard*, January 24, 1942, 58; "Columbia Stars Dansant Disk Nights," *Billboard*, May 23, 1942, 19; "Patriotic Disk Salvage," *Billboard*, June 13, 1942,

20; "Victor Joins Columbia in RFOFMI Disk Salvage Plan," *Billboard*, July 18, 1942, 23; Gladys Chasins, "Recordings: Scrap Fights Two Ways," *Billboard*, September 25, 1943, 83.

107. "Record Hunt," *Time* 40, no. 6 (1942): 62.

108. According to the organization Upstream, "Product Stewardship" is "the act of minimizing health, safety, environmental and social impacts, and maximizing economic benefits of a product and its packaging throughout all lifecycle stages, and "Extended Producer Responsibility" is "a mandatory type of product stewardship that includes, at a minimum, the requirement that the producer's responsibility for their product extends to post-consumer management of that product and its packaging." See "EPR Definitions and Principles," *Upstream*, accessed December 22, 2014, http://upstreampolicy.org/solutions/product-stewardship-extended-producer-responsibility/epr-definitions-and-principles/. See also Sterne, "Out with the Trash," in Acland, *Residual Media*, 26–27; and J. Grant, *Green Marketing Manifesto*, 125. On EPR legislation intended to make manufacturers generate less waste, see Rogers, *Gone Tomorrow*, 281. On voluntary simplicity, see Curry, *Ecological Ethics*, 246–47; and Strasser, *Waste and Want*, 259–60.

109. "Broken Phonograph Records Returned for New Purchases," *Baltimore Sun*, April 26, 1942, 18.

110. Edison's 1912 Blue Amberol cylinders were made from celluloid, "the first synthetically-produced plastic" (L. Burt, "Record Materials," 714–15). See also Walter L. Welch, "Edison and His Contributions to the Record Industry," *Journal of the Audio Engineering Society* 25, nos. 10–11 (1977): 663; D. Morton, *Sound Recording*, 28; Stevens, *Green Plastics*, 109–10; "Lac Bug vs. Jitterbug," 59–60; J. Harry DuBois and Frederick W. John, *Plastics*, 5th ed. (New York: Van Nostrand Reinhold, 1974), 18; Strasser, *Waste and Want*, 103; Kearney, "Done with Shellac," 243; John Kimberly Mumford, *The Story of Bakelite* (New York: Stillson, 1924), 32; DuBois and John, *Plastics*, 21; and Gronow and Saunio, *International History*, 36. Jeffrey L. Meikle refers to Bakelite as the first synthetic plastic. "Material Doubts: The Consequences of Plastic," *Environmental History* 2, no. 3 (1997): 278.

111. "Shellac Market," 69; Seymour, *Reproduction of Sound*, 192.

112. "Records without Shellac," *Newsweek*, August 17, 1942, 73–74. On Capitol, see "Non-Shellac Disk on Market," *Billboard*, August 22, 1942, 20. See also "Shellac Substitutes Said to Be Cooking in Maxwork Vats," *Billboard*, December 5, 1942, 20.

113. "Plastic Music," *Time* 46, no. 17 (1945): 86; "RCA-Victor Beats Field with Plastic Disk," *Billboard*, September 8, 1945, 14; "Better and Brighter," *Time* 46, no. 10 (1945): 52. In 1946 RCA announced a Red Seal De Luxe series, pressed in "Vinylite"; see Sherman, *Collector's Guide*, 110; and Edward Hicks, *Shellac: Its Origin and Applications* (New York: Chemical, 1961), 113. On transparent vinylite "picture discs," see "First Vogue Glamour Disks Reach Press," *Billboard*, March 30, 1946, 26. On the rapid growth for plastics after World War II, see Rogers, *Gone Tomorrow*, 118, 121.

114. DuBois and John, *Plastics*, 68; Ison, "Record Materials," 722.

115. Peter C. Goldmark, *Maverick Inventor* (New York: Dutton, 1973), 131.

116. Ison, "Record Materials," 722. On V-Discs, made of "unbreakable plastic compound requiring no shellac," see "Palitz Handling Recording for Army 'V Discs,'" *Billboard*, October 30, 1943, 14; "RCA-Victor," 14; Goldmark, *Maverick Inventor*, 127; and Millard, *America on Record*, 203–4.

117. Ison, "Record Materials," 723. Ison writes that "the largest element of uncertainty in the process was the condition of the shellac itself. Often it was loaded with impurities such as grass, weeds, gravel, plain dirt, and it seemed, anything else that would add weight to the shipment" (719).

118. "Better Things for Better Living ... through Chemistry" was the slogan for the DuPont Company beginning in 1935 and served as a "widely imitated" example of a new postwar vocabulary for American business. See William L. Bird Jr., *Better Living: Advertising, Media, and the New Vocabulary of Business Leadership, 1935–1955* (Evanston: Northwestern University Press, 1999), 22–23.

119. On renewable resources, see Robert B. Gordon and Patrick M. Malone, *The Texture of Industry* (New York: Oxford University Press, 1994), 43. Farely writes that a "sustainable economy cannot extract renewable resources faster than they can regenerate, use up critical nonrenewable resources faster than renewable substitutes are developed, or emit wastes faster than they can be absorbed." "Ecological Economics," in Heinberg and Lerch, *Post Carbon Reader*, 262. When we use nonrenewable materials, "we draw down stocks created in the distant past. Once mined, these non-renewable resources are gone forever" (Gordon, *Landscape Transformed*, 4). S.K. Khanna, "Record Materials: Vinyl Compound for the Phonographic Industry," pt. 3, *Journal of the Audio Engineering Society* 25, nos. 10–11 (1977): 724.

120. Stevens, *Green Plastics*, 15; Maxwell and Miller, *Greening the Media*, 59. On PVC and cancer in workers, see Meikle, "Material Doubts," 292.

121. "The Poison Plastic," *Greenpeace*, June 2, 2003, www.greenpeace.org/international/en/campaigns/toxics/polyvinyl-chloride/the-poison-plastic/. See also "PVC Free Solutions," *Greenpeace*, June 2, 2003, www.greenpeace.org/international/en/campaigns/toxics/polyvinyl-chloride/pvc-free-solutions/; and "Polyvinyl Chloride," *Greenpeace*, accessed December 1, 2014, www.greenpeace.org/international/en/campaigns/toxics/polyvinyl-chloride/.

122. Ison notes that "the working formula normally included 25% scrap.... Boxes labeled 'scrap' [lay] around the presses, in the warehouses.... It was not uncommon for the scrap to include soft drink bottles, litter, pieces of masonry, or other unwanted material, all of which were ground up together and mixed in with the next batch of compound" ("Record Materials," 719–20).

123. Strasser, *Waste and Want*, 267. Heinberg and Lerch write that "as petroleum production expanded in the twentieth century to power a growing fleet of motor vehicles, cheap petroleum by-products became the building blocks for whole new classes of products and packaging. Plastics were novelties in the 1930s but their use virtually exploded after World War II and has

experienced continued growth ever since" (Heinberg and Lerch, *Post Carbon Reader*, 367).

124. Stevens, *Green Plastics*, 17.

125. "RCA-Victor," 84.

126. "One Record Holds Entire Symphony," *Life*, July 26, 1948, 39.

127. Gabrys, *Digital Rubbish*, 5. On the LP and extended time for the production of jazz records, see Michael Jarrett, *Soundtracks* (Philadelphia: Temple University Press, 1998), 56–57.

128. Maxwell and Miller, *Greening the Media*, 39; Juliet Schor, *Plenitude* (New York: Penguin, 2010), 38; Strasser, *Waste and Want*, 281. Maxwell and Miller write that "the goal of LCA is to educate manufacturers and businesses about a product's connection to the environment at all stages of its existence in order to improve 'environmental performance'.... LCA combines scientific research and studies of industry practices to assess a company's performance and indicate ways to replace old processes and components with new ones that are more ecologically sound" (*Greening the Media*, 174n66).

129. Bozak, *Cinematic Footprint*, 62, 122, 57. See also Schor, *Plenitude*, 135–36; and Susan Sontag's comments on an "ecology of the image," in *On Photography* (New York: Anchor Books, 1990), 180.

130. See, for example, Sterne on the "dream of verisimilitude," in *MP3*, 4.

131. Christopher Manes, "Nature and Silence," in *The Ecocriticism Reader*, ed. Cheryll Glotfelty and Harold Fromm (Athens: University of Georgia Press, 1996), 15–16.

132. Kate Lacey argues that noise "*disturbs* the 'structural amnesia' inherent in processes of representation. Noise, then, far from being just an irritating side-effect of modernity, actually offers a different perspective on modern life and the sound of media within it. Putting noise back into the history of media offers a way to put the history of the media back into social history, back into the history of the senses and of aesthetics." *Listening Publics* (Cambridge: Polity, 2013), 91. On noise as "a methodological exercise ... to demonstrate how media archaeology can be used to find the neglected," see Parikka, *What Is Media Archaeology?*, 91.

133. Illich, *Tools for Conviviality*, 6–7. See also Carroll Pursell, "The Rise and Fall of the Appropriate Technology Movement in the United States, 1965–1985," *Technology and Culture* 34, no. 3 (1993): 629–37.

134. Illich, *Tools for Conviviality*, 11. At one point, Illich compares television and phonograph records: "Limited resources can be used to provide millions of viewers with the color image of one performer or to provide many people with free access to the records of their choice" (34).

135. Compare this reorientation to E. F. Schumacher's goal of achieving "the maximum of well-being with the minimum of consumption." *Small Is Beautiful* (1973; repr., New York: Harper Perennial, 2010), 61. See also Merchant on Herman Daly's "steady state economy" (*Radical Ecology*, 36).

136. William McDonough and Michael Braungart, *Cradle to Cradle: Remaking the Way We Make Things* (New York: North Point, 2002), 16.

137. Merchant, *Radical Ecology*, 36–37.

138. Dr. Mohammad Monobrullah, Senior Scientist, Lac Production Division, Indian Institute of Natural Resins and Gums, personal correspondence, April 25, 2013. On the influence of climatic factors on lac insects, see Lindsay and Harlow, *Indian Forest Records*, 5.

139. "Threat to Indian Shellac Industry," *Times of India*, April 29, 1947, 4. An article in the *New York Times* reported that the discovery of "new synthetic resins in the United States" had "brought the Indian shellac industry face-to-face with a severe crisis" and was "threatening the incomes of more than three million Indian families." "Shellac Crisis in India," May 30, 1947, 31.

140. "Indian Lac Cess Committee," *Times of India*, April 24, 1937, 6. See also "Development of Lac Industry," *Times of India*, October 30, 1936, 4; "Recommendation of Lac Committee," *Times of India*, October 28, 1948, 4; "Outlook for Shellac," *Times of India*, December 2, 1952, 4; "Slump in Shellac Industry," *Times of India*, October 30, 1952, 4; "Lac's Part in Plastics," *Times of India*, December 25, 1941, 10. A 1971 survey of the industry reports, "the last two decades lac export earnings have fallen from $25 million to $6 million," and the "decline has been due mainly to the competition from synthetic substitutes" (*Export Potential*, 1:4, 6). While addressing manufacturers, Dr. H.K. Sen, director of the Indian Lac Research Institute in Ranchi, discussed "the importance of maintaining a high standard for shellac and shellac products in order to be able to compete with the uniform qualities of synthetic resins now being put in the market in increasing quantities." "Shellac Industry in India," *Times of India*, October 24, 1936, 15.

141. Kim Fortun, *Advocacy after Bhopal* (Chicago: University of Chicago Press, 2001), xiii. Christopher Key Chapple argues that "modern environmentalism in India ... began with the disaster in Bhopal." "Toward an Indigenous Indian Environmentalism," in *Purifying the Earthly Body: Religion and Ecology in Hindu India*, ed. Lance E. Nelson (Albany: SUNY Press, 1998).

142. John Michael Greer, *The Long Descent* (Gabriola Island, Canada: New Society, 2008), 59, 155. The Crap-o-phone is an example of what Ravi Sundaram calls "pirate modernity," whereby "technological gadgets are never thrown away, but reused, sold, repaired and used again." *Pirate Modernity* (London: Routledge, 2010), 3.

CHAPTER 2. BIRDLAND MELODIES

1. Scholars have interpreted "His Master's Voice" in a number of ways: as an illustration of the Western tendency to project the wonder inspired by new media onto supposedly less rational others (like animals); as an allegory of the phonograph's ability to preserve the voices of the dead; and as a sign of the emerging power dynamics in the market for mechanically reproduced sounds. On the Nipper logo, see Kenney, *Recorded Music*, 54–55; Siefert, "Aesthetics," 417–18; Brady, *Spiral Way*, 47–48; Sterne, *Audible Past*, 301–7; and Lisa Gitelman, *Scripts, Grooves, and Writing Machines* (Stanford: Stanford

University Press, 1999), 123. Siefert argues that "His Master's Voice" aligns the dog and the phonograph as paradigms of "fidelity," thereby allowing them into the middle-class American parlor ("Aesthetics," 417–18). Erica Fudge discusses the Nipper image in terms of a tension between the dog's similarity and difference to humans: Nipper has the capacity to listen to virtual sounds like humans do, but he is depicted as listening to his human master's voice, such that "human superiority is reinscribed." *Animal* (London: Reaktion Books, 2002), 69.

2. Akira Mizuta Lippit, *Electric Animal* (Minneapolis: University of Minnesota Press, 2000), 21. Lippit writes that "cinema perhaps best embodied the transfer of animals from nature to technology" (23). Jonathan Burt makes a thoughtful critique of Lippit's argument, stating that "the disengagement from the animal, its reduction to pure sign, reinforces at a conceptual level the effacement of the animal that is perceived to have taken place in reality even whilst criticizing that process." *Animals on Film* (London: Reaktion Books, 2002), 29.

3. Edmund Russell, "The Garden in the Machine: Toward an Evolutionary History of Technology," in *Industrializing Organisms*, ed. Susan R. Schrepfer and Philip Scranton (New York: Routledge, 2004), 2, 6. On animals as tools, see Arnold Arluke and Clinton R. Sanders, *Regarding Animals* (Philadelphia: Temple University Press, 1996), 173.

4. Donna J. Haraway, *When Species Meet* (Minneapolis: University of Minnesota Press, 2008), 250.

5. Haraway, *Companion Species Manifesto*, 4.

6. Fudge, *Animal*, 127–28. Annabelle Sabloff argues that a "post-humanistic, biocentred position" requires a move "from dependence on the linguistic to define our humanity to a more serious investigation of additional forms of human knowing, such as haptic, olfactory, pheromonal, and aural." She continues, "We need to move away from the notion that verbal language completely sets us apart and somehow elevates humanity. In the scheme of things, verbal language is just one evolutionarily newer way to communicate, but do we know whether it is necessarily a better way? ... To my mind, any theoretical perspective that ... strives to capture purposeful, cognitively implicated activity not easily articulated in language ... has great potential in the investigation of human relations with the rest of the natural world." *Reordering the Natural World* (Toronto: University of Toronto Press, 2001), 182–83. See also Arluke and Sanders, who write, "we strongly believe that mind is a social accomplishment ... although animals cannot speak to us in our own terms, we must not throw up our hands and conclude that crossing species barriers and understanding animals' experience is impossible" (*Regarding Animals*, 49–50).

7. Zoosemiotics is "the scientific study of signaling behavior in and across animal species," as opposed to anthroposemiotics, that is, a species-specific system. Sebeok, "Zoosemiotic Components," in Sebeok, *How Animals Communicate*, 1055–56.

8. Johnson, quoted in Hutto, "Emile Berliner," 667. See also Kenney, *Recorded Music*, 47.

9. The phonograph historian Patrick Feaster has discussed a similar confusion that can arise from the multiple meanings of the word "reproduction"; he offers the terms "induction" and "eduction" to describe, respectively, the "drawing-in" process of inscription and the "drawing-out" process by which signals are converted into sound. "The Following Record": Making Sense of Phonographic Performance, 1877–1908" (PhD diss., Indiana University, 2007), 30–31.

10. The *OED* defines one usage as "to practise or sing (a tune) in an undertone; to go over (a song or tune) quietly or silently; to produce subsong." *OED Online*, s.v. "record," Oxford University Press, accessed December 23, 2014, www.oed.com.turing.library.northwestern.edu/view/Entry/159868. According to an 1856 handbook, "the practicing, which goes by the name of learning, or *recording*, is only a kind of exercise of the organs, in order that they may again easily produce the accustomed tones." J.M. Bechstein, *Cage and Chamber-Birds* (London: Bohn, 1856), 4–5.

11. Adding human interventions in birdsong to the category of recording builds on Douglas Kahn's expansive definition of phonography as "all mechanical, optical, electrical, digital, genetic, psychotechnic, mnemonic, and conceptual means of sound recording as both technological means, empirical fact, and metaphorical incorporation, including nineteenth-century machines prior to the invention of the phonograph." *Noise, Water, Meat* (Cambridge, MA: MIT Press, 2001), 16.

12. Peter Marler, "The Evolution of Communication," in Sebeok, *How Animals Communicate*, 62. Eugene S. Morton and Jake Page argue that, due to the huge energy requirements of flight, birds have placed a premium on a "sonic system of communication that demarcates territory, minimizes altercations, and communicates over long distances and in forested areas, where visual contact is unlikely." *Animal Talk* (New York: Random House, 1992), 52–53.

13. W. John Smith, "Communication in Birds," in Sebeok, *How Animals Communicate*, 567.

14. Lesley J. Rogers and Gisela Kaplan, *Songs, Roars, and Rituals: Communication in Birds, Mammals, and Other Animals* (Cambridge, MA: Harvard University Press, 2000), 131; Georges-Louis Lecler [Comte de Buffon], "The Natural History of the Canary Bird," *New York* 3, no. 10 (1792): 620.

15. Most birds are "close-end learners who lose the ability to learn new songs once they reach adulthood. A smaller number of birds are open-ended learners, such as mockingbirds, starlings, and canaries." David Rothenberg, *Why Birds Sing* (New York: Basic Books, 2005), 17. Canaries "are able to change their songs from season to season when they are adults. It appears that they go on learning throughout their lives" (Rogers and Kaplan, *Songs, Roars, and Rituals*, 132). See also Marler, "Evolution of Communication," in Sebeok, *How Animals Communicate*, 62; and Gordon M. Burghardt, "Ontogeny of Communication," and Smith, "Communication in Birds," both in Sebeok, *How Animals Communicate*, 77; 566.

16. H.G. Adams, ed., *Bechstein's Handbook of Chamber and Cage Birds* (London: Ward and Lock, 1857), 54.

17. J.-C. Hervieux de Chanteloup, *A New Treatise of Canary-Birds* (London: Lintot, 1718), 50; John Walsh, ed., *The Bird Fancyer's Delight* (London: Walsh, n.d., ca. 1715). See also Rothenberg, *Why Birds Sing*, 19; and James J. Parsons, "The Origin and Dispersal of the Domesticated Canary," *Journal of Cultural Geography* 7, no. 2 (1987): 24.

18. "Canary Birds: Points about a Strange Industry," *San Francisco Chronicle*, May 4, 1890, 2; Hartz Mountain Products, *Canary Care* (New York: Hartz Mountain Products, 1936), 3; Charles N. Page, *Feathered Pets*, 12th ed. (Des Moines, IA: printed by author, 1898), 52–53; Bechstein, *Cage and Chamber-Birds*, 277; H. G. Adams, *Cage and Singing Birds* (London: Routledge, 1854), 83–84; George H. Holden, *Canaries and Cage-Birds*, 2nd ed. (Boston: Holden, 1888), 9–10; Adams, *Bechstein's Handbook*, 33–34; Charles Reiche, *The Bird Fancier's Companion*, 10th ed. (New York: Reiche and Brother, 1871), 14; C. F. and G. H. Golden, *Holden's New Book on Birds* (Boston: Holden, 1892), 11. An account from 1870 claims that the story comes "by well-authenticated tradition." "The Canaries We Have Among Us," *Brooklyn Daily Eagle*, December 29, 1870, 2. See also Tim Birkhead, *A Brand-New Bird* (New York: Basic Books, 2003), 81. Parsons writes that canaries on the Canary Islands were "an adaptable forager feeding largely on seeds," living in small flocks "through open fields and forests except in the driest parts of the islands. [They are] found from sea level to at least 5,500 feet on Tenerife, half way to the summit of its snow-capped peak" ("Origin and Dispersal," 20).

19. Barthes, *Mythologies*, 142–43.

20. Alfred W. Crosby, *Ecological Imperialism*, 2nd ed. (Cambridge: Cambridge University Press, 2004), 71, 80. The indigenous Canary Islanders were "the first people to be conquered and colonized by Europeans." Felipe Fernandez-Armesto, *The Canary Islands after the Conquest* (Oxford: Clarendon, 1982), 2. See also John Mercer, *The Canary Islanders* (London: Collings, 1980), 156–57. See Bernd Herrmann and William Woods on the passenger pigeon: "the population of passenger pigeons was formerly kept down due to human-wildlife competition for tree nuts. This competitive network was disrupted when disease, warfare, and other consequences of European colonization decimated Indian populations and lifeways. The consequent enrichment of food and space led to the mushrooming populations of pigeons that so greatly impressed European visitors and Euro-American settlers.... In short, the superabundance of passenger pigeons, before they were wiped out, was an anthropogenic incident." "Neither Biblical Plague nor Pristine Myth: A Lesson from Central European Sparrows," *Geographical Review* 100, no. 2 (2010): 177. Page writes that "in the days of Queen Elizabeth a cage bird was a luxury to be enjoyed only by persons who were very wealthy, but now every family in the land can easily afford one of these charming songsters to brighten their home" (*Feathered Pets*, 54). See also Julia Breittruck, "Pet Birds: Cages and Practices of Domestication in Eighteenth-Century Paris," *InterDisciplines* 3, no. 1 (2012): 7; and Louise E. Robbins, *Elephant Slaves and Pampered Parrots* (Baltimore: Johns Hopkins University Press, 2002), 113.

21. Mercer, *Canary Islanders*, 160. On native Canarians as slaves in the 1300s, see Crosby, *Ecological Imperialism*, 79–80, 87. Crosby calls the 1402 invasion "the birth year of modern European imperialism" (*Ecological Imperialism*, 81). See also Lawrence R. Walker and Peter Bellingham, *Island Environments in a Changing World* (Cambridge: Cambridge University Press, 2011), 162–63, 202–3.

22. Birkhead, *Brand-New Bird*, 85, 18. Parsons argues that "European sailors who stopped off on these islands were much attracted to the congenial canary birds they encountered and carried them off in some numbers. In certain cases, it has been suggested, they may have obtained the birds from natives and so [they were] already habituated to captivity" ("Origin and Dispersal," 21). See also James J. Parsons, "A Detailed History of the Domesticated Canary Bird," *American Cage-Bird Magazine*, March 1989, 17. Wild canaries, "nested in low bushes and filled the forests with melody whose sweetness was equaled only by that of the nightingales. The early inhabitants, so far as is known, never tried to capture or domesticate them.... Spanish soldiers [began] the conquest of these enchanting little birds. Their gentleness and lack of hostility to man made them easy victims. Moreover, they did not seem to resent captivity." Madge Macbeth, "Canaries in the Canary Islands," *All-Pets Magazine* 27, no. 10 (1956): 68. In an 1870 account of London, an author wrote that "sailors, who have returned from long voyages, will stop in the street when they see a bird-seller's stand, look at it for a moment with open mouth, and taking out a handful of silver, will give the bird-fancier any price he chooses to ask for a sweet singing bird. The bird will serve as a gift to some female relative, a wife, or as, in many cases, some woman of the town will receive the cage and its occupant as a gift from the drunken Jack-Tar." Daniel Joseph Kirwan, *Palace and Hovel* (Hartford, CT: Belknap and Bliss, 1870), 397–98.

23. Crosby, *Ecological Imperialism*, 100.

24. Fernandez-Armesto, *Canary Islands*, 170, 160; Mercer, *Canary Islanders*, 195. According to the historian John Mercer, the indigenous people and their culture were exterminated to a degree "beyond anything effected by the Spaniards in the Americas: general enslavement, official large-scale deportations, total annexation of the land, destruction of the way of life, [and] enforced acceptance of the Spanish beliefs and values" (213).

25. Joseph Roach, *Cities of the Dead* (New York: Columbia University Press, 1996), 4–5. Anson D. F. Randolph's book *Autobiography of a Canary* makes explicit connections between canaries and slavery (New York: Randolph, 1866).

26. Ida Shaper Hoxie, "The Singing Village of Germany," *Ladies Home Journal* 18, no. 9 (1901): 2.

27. An 1854 handbook claimed that the Germans were the world's "most extensive and systematic bird trainers" (Adams, *Cage and Singing Birds*, 26). An author claimed in 1932 that, for hundreds of years, the Hartz Mountains and the town of St. Andreasberg in Germany had been famous as "the home of the most highly trained rollers in the world." Idella Grider Manisera, "What Weighs Half an Ounce—and Sings?," *Los Angeles Times*, October 30, 1932, I5).

28. William Wells, "The Sweet Singers of the Father-Land," *Ladies' Repository* 33 (November 1873): 371. See also "The Roller Canary," *Bird News* 1, no. 5 (1909): 4.

29. Page, *Feathered Pets*, 61–62; Golden, *Holden's New Book*, 32.

30. Hoxie, "Singing Village," 2. See also Wells, "Sweet Singers," 371. According to an account from 1893, "Canary-bird breeding in Germany has, from the start, been chiefly a house industry of poor and needy people.... Almost every family then had in the sitting-room, in the bedroom, or in the garret a breeding place for the birds." George H. Murphy, "Canary Breeding in Germany," *Current Literature* 12, no. 1 (1893): 66. See also Page, *Feathered Pets*, 56. Birkhead writes that St. Andreasberg was built around a silver mine that opened in 1521 and that by 1882 "three-quarters of the eight hundred families in St. Andreasberg were rearing canaries, and in some years the town exported as many as 12,000 male birds" (*Brand-New Bird*, 37).

31. Holden, *Canaries and Cage-Birds*, 10.

32. Wells, "Sweet Singers," 371; Page, *Feathered Pets*, 84. At the cruelest extreme of these practices of sensory isolation, we find accounts of trainers who "put out the eyes of their birds with a hot needle, so that they would sing as well at night as during the daytime" (75). See also Golden, *Holden's New Book*, 23; Adams, *Cage and Singing Birds*, 102; and Manisera, "Half an Ounce," 15. "If you wish to teach the Birds airs, or artificial notes of any kind, they must hear nothing that can in any way distract their attention. Every time you enter the room, the oftener the better, and especially when you feed them, whistle, or play on a flute or flageolet, the tune you wish them to learn. Whistle or play that, and no other. Repeat, and repeat, and repeat, until they can pipe it correctly." John Timbs, ed., *Manual of Cage-Birds, British and Foreign* (London: Bogue, 1847), 23. See also Henry B. Hirst, *The Book of Cage Birds* (Philadelphia: Duke, 1843), 64; E.A. Maling, *Song Birds, and How to Keep Them* (London: Smith, Elder, 1862), 91; Holden, *Canaries and Cage-Birds*, 11; and Adams, *Bechstein's Handbook*, 55.

33. Sterne, *Audible Past*, 23–24, 159.

34. G.E.W. "A Seminary for Teaching Birds How to Sing," *Scientific American* 79, no. 2 (1898): 23.

35. Hugo Leichtentritt, "Mechanical Music in Olden Times," *Musical Quarterly* 20, no. 1 (1934): 18; Adams, *Bechstein's Handbook*, 54; Hirst, *Book of Cage Birds*, 25, 61.

36. On sixteenth- and seventeenth-century pet keeping, see Keith Thomas, *Man and the Natural World* (New York: Pantheon, 1983), 110–11; and Mary D. Sheriff, "Reflecting on Chardin," *Eighteenth Century* 29, no. 1 (1988): 20. On the serinette, see Birkhead, *Brand-New Bird*, 65. Other paintings that feature canaries include Joseph Caraud's *The Pet Canaries* (ca. 1875) and Seymour Guy's *Girl with Canary* (1860s).

37. Wells, "Sweet Singers," 371; Maling, *Song Birds*, 91; F.H. Stauffer, "The Bullfinch Academy," *Oliver Optic's Magazine* 59, no. 3 (1868): 104.

38. Olive F. Gunby, "A Canary Bird College," *Atlanta Constitution*, April 15, 1900, B6. According to one newspaper article, the bird organ inspires the

birds to "sing well" and "prompts them to make the best of their powers" (Gunby, "Canary Bird College," B6). See also "Bird Professors," *Youth's Companion* 75, no. 15 (1901): 196; and "Canary-Bird Culture in Milwaukee," *Current Literature* 23, no. 4 (1898): 364. One description had the "bird organ" consisting of "two sheet-iron cylinders, one inside the other. The lower one contained water. Certain pulleys and weights caused the upper half to settle down slowly and steadily, so that air was expelled through a whistle and gave numerous variations of tone.... [It was used] in the breeding room, so that the birds got their first impressions of music before and during their first hours outside the nest." Mara Evans, "Rollers and Choppers," *Saturday Evening Post*, January 7, 1928, 22. See also "Roller Canary," 4. By one account it made "three distinct sounds, a whistle, a rapid staccato bass note and a call like that of a cuckoo." Paul Paddock, "When Canaries Go to School," *Popular Mechanics*, August 1927, 258. See also Page, *Feathered Pets*, 62; and "Training Canary Birds to Sing King Edward's Latest Fad," *Chicago Daily Tribune*, October 11, 1903, 13. A 1901 account of German training technology described "a machine driven by air and water which sings all day long with perfectly attuned notes in imitation of a first class canary." "Singing Schools for Birds," *Brooklyn Daily Eagle*, March 8, 1901, 6. A 1953 article describes how "the Germans had many quaint methods in fixing song passages in their birds' repertoire—for instance, ingenious instruments were invented which were operated by air or water, some were metal organolas blown with the lips, or bellows which produced sounds like the soughing wind rising and falling, or the effect of deep mellow cadences of chuckling laughter; other contraptions made from wood, metal pipes or bottles were operated by water running through them which gave bubbling and rippling-water effects." Andrew F. Demaine, "The Roller Canary," *All-Pets Magazine* 24, no. 6 (1953): 22.

39. John Smith, *The Roller and German Country Canary* (London: Feathered World, n.d., ca. 1900s), 9. A. F. Demaine writes that St. Andreasberg originated the "invention and use of ingenious contraptions operated by hand, water and air, producing rolling, bell-like and watery sounds which the birds quickly mimicked and gradually absorbed into their repertoire." *The Roller Canary*, 7th ed. (London: Cage Birds, 1955), 10–11.

40. The phrase "phonography by other means" is a riff on Pavle Levi's suggestive book, *Cinema by Other Means* (New York: Oxford University Press), 2012. See also Stauffer, "Bullfinch Academy," 104.

41. Michel Chion, *Audio-Vision* (New York: Columbia University Press, 1994), 98–99, cited in Sterne, *MP3*, 5.

42. Holden, *Canaries and Cage-Birds*, 12; Golden, *Holden's New Book*, 32. In 1904 a writer held that the goal was "a gentle, undulating motion up and down the scale" and that a single "unmusical note" spoiled the roller. "Canary Opera," *Cincinnati Enquirer*, January 3, 1904, A3. Trainers were to avoid faults such as sharp tones, rasping sounds, and nasal notes. Birds that produced such "impure" sounds were to be taken away from the rest of the cohort, "for this kind of loud flute is so penetrating in tone that it stands out conspicuously, ugly

and persistent, while the other are singing, and absolutely spoils the effect of the whole orchestra." H.W. Gutierrez, *The Roller Canary*, 5th ed. (London: Poultry World Limited, n.d., ca. 1920), 38. See also Manisera, "Half an Ounce," I5.

43. Holden, *Canaries and Cage-Birds*, 12; Manisera, "Half an Ounce," I5. One handbook explained that "what constitutes beauty" in a canary song was "the order or sequence of the tours, the manner in which they pass one over the other, the bridging over, as it were, the modulation, and the general connectivity" (Gutierrez, *Roller Canary*, 62).

44. Golden, *Holden's New Book*, 32; Page, *Feathered Pets*, 62; Holden, *Canaries and Cage-Birds*, 12.

45. Gutierrez, *Roller Canary*, 78, 82, 88.

46. Holden, *Canaries and Cage-Birds*, 13. On bedridden friends, see Page, *Feathered Pets*, 63. For one author, the best canary song was "soft and sweet, every tone being true, mellow, and musical" (Golden, *Holden's New Book*, 32).

47. Holden, *Canaries and Cage-Birds*, 14.

48. Bijsterveld, *Mechanical Sound*, 94; Picker, *Victorian Soundscapes*, 44. See also Smilor, "Cacophony," 24.

49. Henry Oldys, *Cage-Bird Traffic of the United States* (repr., Washington, DC: Government Printing Office, 1907), 168. The importation of foreign birds was encouraged by a decline in the trade of native songbirds, which in turn was due to the rise of a bird-protection movement and "the interest in bird life awakened by the efforts of [the American Ornithologists' Union] and the various State Audubon societies" (Oldys, *Cage-Bird Traffic*, 167). On steam power and ocean travel in relation to the "deluge" of European migration between 1820 and 1930, see Crosby, *Ecological Imperialism*, 5.

50. An 1870 report claimed that 40,000 canaries were imported annually into the United States and that "the importers all do business in New York City, and are located in Chatham and William streets" ("Canaries We Have," 2). Imports stayed strong through the 1920s: in 1922 America imported 192,000 canaries, and by 1928 it was estimated that there were 4 million canaries in American homes. The export of German canaries "greatly increased since the fleet steamer has learned to plow the waves over the ocean to the shores of the New World" (Wells, "Sweet Singers," 371). See also Reiche, *Bird Fancier's Companion*, 16. One importer estimated that 80,000 canaries were brought into the United States in 1873 and that every steamer from Germany brought about 2,500 birds. "Among the Birds and Beasts," *Forest and Stream: A Journal of Outdoor Life* 1, no. 10 (1873): 148. See also Murphy, "Canary Breeding," 66; and "The Canary," *Boston Daily Globe*, November 18, 1917, SM15. In 1909 a bird-fancier magazine estimated that nearly half a million were imported annually. "The Canary," *Bird News* 1, no. 1 (1909): 7. See also Evans, "Rollers and Choppers," 94; and Paddock, "Canaries Go to School," 259. In 1907 it was estimated that 300,000 cage birds, largely canaries, were annually imported into the United States (Oldys, *Cage-Bird Traffic*, 165). Parsons writes that between 1905 and 1915, some 3,250,000 birds were imported to the United States, almost all of them from Germany ("Origin and Dispersal," 30).

51. Wells, "Sweet Singers," 371. Parsons writes that "by 1850 Harz Mountain Roller Canaries were being exported to England and the United States, the birds having a special reputation for the excellence of their song. The development was at its peak from the 1870s to at least the turn of the century" ("Detailed History," 26–27). In 1884 there were between fifty and sixty bird stores in New York City: "the increase of the bird trade in the city has progressed with the growth of the town.... There are only eight or nine large stores here that engage in the business, but outside of these there are several houses that do an irregular exchange in birds, particularly canaries, houses such as liquor saloons, cigar places and the stores occupied by barbers." "Nature's Tiny Warblers," *Brooklyn Daily Eagle*, February 3, 1884, 8. An 1886 article claimed that in Brooklyn there were "few households which contain no bird of some sort or kind." "Household Birds," *Brooklyn Daily Eagle*, July 25, 1886, 11. German training techniques were imported along with the birds: a 1904 article describes how a Chicago bird dealer named Eugene Frank was raising 5,000 canaries a year, which he taught to sing through the use of a water cylinder bird organ. "Teaching 5000 Canaries to Sing," *Chicago Daily Tribune*, November 20, 1904, F1.

52. Kenney, *Recorded Music*, 74. Kenney writes that between 1865 and 1917 more than twenty-five million immigrants, mostly eastern and southern Europeans, entered the United States (67).

53. See Lawrence W. Levine, *Highbrow, Lowbrow* (Cambridge, MA: Harvard University Press, 1988), 102, 146.

54. Enrico Caruso, Campanini's successor as premier operatic tenor, achieved a remarkable degree of celebrity due in large part to his career as a recording artist, starting with the release of his first records in 1903 (Kenney, *Recorded Music*, 50).

55. Golden, *Holden's New Book*, 11. Note how another author compares canaries to human musicians: "If the Nightingale is the chantress of the woods, the Canary bird is the musician of the chamber: the first owes all to nature; the second derives something from our arts." Lecler, "Natural History," 619.

56. "Noted Composer Dead," *Philadelphia Record*, November 23, 1902, cited in Michael Remson, *Septimus Winner: Two Lives in Music* (Lanham, MD: Scarecrow, 2002), 64; Remson, *The Songs of Septimus Winner* (Lanham, MD: Scarecrow, 2003), 17. Winner published many songs under the name Alice Hawthorne, such as "Der Deutscher's Dog" ("O Where, O Where Has My Little Dog Gone?") and "Ten Little Indians." On the huge popularity of "Listen to the Mockingbird," see Remson, *Septimus Winner*, 62–63. He notes that King Edward VII of England whistled it as a child, and Abraham Lincoln is reputed to have said, "It is a real song. It is as sincere and sweet as the laughter of a little girl."

57. Arthur A. Schomburg, "Listen to the Mocking Bird," *New York Amsterdam News*, January 29, 1930, 8; Eric Lott, *Love and Theft* (New York: Oxford University Press, 1995), 55–56.

58. Schomburg, "Mocking Bird," 8; Remson, *Septimus Winner*, 62–63; Rothenberg, *Why Birds Sing*, 171. A press account from 1879 states, "There was

then in Philadelphia an original character commonly called 'Whistling Dick,' a colored individual, Richard Milburn by name, well known through all the streets of the city. His visible, or rather, audible, means of support was whistling, an accomplishment in which he excelled, really making some beautiful music, while he strummed an indifferent accompaniment on a guitar. He was principally famous for his imitations of the mockingbird, and this fact first suggested to Mr. Winner the happy thought of perfecting a ballad of that nature. This he accomplished, and the ever-popular 'Listen to the Mockingbird' was the result. It was written to suit the small compass of Whistling Dick's voice, to whom he taught it, and who did very much towards starting it on its way to success. On this account Mr. Winner placed Mr. Milburn's name on the first editions, which pleased that colored gentleman hugely." George Birdseye, "America's Song Composers, VI: Septimus Winner," *Potter's American Monthly* 90, no. 12 (1879): 433. By some accounts, Milburn was a barber; see Gerald B. Jordan, *Philadelphia Inquirer*, February 12, 1985, D1.

59. Alexander Weheliye argues that black subjects in America have not had "the same access to alphabetic writing as white subjects and therefore were also barred, both discursively and materially, from writing's attendant qualities of reason, disembodiment, and full humanity by a variety of repressive and at times violent mechanisms." *Phonographies* (Durham: Duke University Press, 2005), 36.

60. For one author, the whistle "needs no inglorious lubrication of joints and greasing of keys like its dearest relative the flute. It is not subject to the vocalist's eternal cold. It knows no inferno of tuning and snapping strings, nor does it need resin for its stomach's sake and its often infirmities. Its only approach to the baseness of mechanism is in a drainage system akin to that of the French horn, but far less brazen in its publicity." Robert Haven Schauffler, "A Defense of Whistling," *Atlantic Monthly* 106 (September 1910): 416. Raymond Williams distinguishes between "modes of communication which depend on immediate human physical resources and those other modes which depend on the transformation, by labour, of non-human material. The former, of course, can not be abstracted as 'natural'. Spoken languages and the rich area of physical communicative acts now commonly generalized as 'non-verbal communication' are themselves, inevitably, forms of social production. " *Problems of Materialism and Culture* (London: Verso, 1980), 55; see also *Culture* (Glasgow: Fontana, 1981), 88. Gary Tomlinson writes that "singing and its musical offshoots arguably form one of three fundamental modes of human cultural expression, alongside speaking and writing (that is, plastic inscription broadly conceived)." *The Singing of the New World* (Cambridge: Cambridge University Press, 2007), 5–6.

61. Michael Denning, *Culture in the Age of Three Worlds* (London: Verso, 2004), 118.

62. Tim Brooks, *Lost Sounds: Blacks and the Birth of the Recording Industry, 1890–1919* (Urbana: University of Illinois Press, 2005), 25–31. See also my discussion in *Vocal Tracks*, 18–19.

63. Lindon Barrett, *Blackness and Value: Seeing Double* (New York: Cambridge University Press, 1999), 57–58, cited in Weheliye, *Phonographies*, 37. See also Weheliye, *Phonographies*, 37. See also my discussion in *Vocal Tracks*, 149.

64. Siefert, "Aesthetics," 430–31.

65. Clements-Henry, *Gramophones*, 116.

66. John Yorke Atlee recorded a whistled version of "Mocking Bird" even earlier, circa 1890 to 1896.

67. M.M. Bakhtin, *Problems of Dostoevsky's Poetics* (Minneapolis: University of Minnesota Press, 1984), 6. Bakhtin describes Dostoevsky's novels as featuring "a plurality of consciousnesses, with equal rights and each with its own world," which "combine but are not merged in the unity of the event" (6). On "reported speech," Valentin N. Volosinov writes, "speech within speech, message within message, and at the same time also speech about speech, message about message." "Reported Speech," in *Readings in Russian Poetics*, ed. Ladislav Matejka and Krystyna Pomorska (Ann Arbor: University of Michigan Press, 1978), 149.

68. See Brandon LaBelle, who describes the whistle as "a conduit of exchange between human and animal, where the small yet no less dramatic sonorities of the nightingale or the robin may inspire corresponding vocalities." *Lexicon of the Mouth* (New York: Bloomsbury, 2014), 175–76.

69. Ulysses (Jim) Walsh, "Joe Belmont, 'The Human Bird,'" in *Hobbies* 53, no. 1 (1948): 35.

70. Ama Barker, "The Man Who Comes Nearest to Dr. Dolittle," *New York Tribune*, September 2, 1923, SM10.

71. An 1873 account of the sounds of a bird store in New York reads, "if your ear is fine and you can separate the noises of Chatham street—muffle, as it were, the rumble of the street car, the din and rattle of the carts and wagons, you will distinguish no end of twitter coming from the establishment in question. Sometimes this chorus, if a streak of sunshine slide into the store, rises in volume of chirps until it sounds like a band of tiny piccolos" ("Birds and Beasts," 148).

72. Film theorists have tended to discuss superimposition in terms of its ability to depict the interaction of real and supernatural characters or the coexistence of mental states and the physical world. See Andre Bazin, "The Life and Death of Superimposition," *Film-Philosophy* 6, no. 1 (2002), www.film-philosophy.com/index.php/f-p/article/view/665/578; and Daniel Morgan, "The Afterlife of Superimposition," in *Opening Bazin*, ed. Dudley Andrew and Herve Joubert-Laurencin (New York: Oxford University Press, 2011), 127–41. Sound has been praised for its particular ability to convey a sense of resonance, overlap, or harmony: Rudolf Arnheim writes of radio's aesthetics of "overlay," for example, and Don Ihde describes the dynamics of the "auditory field." On overlay, see Arnheim, *Radio: An Art of Sound* (1936; repr., New York: Da Capo, 1972), 121. On the auditory field, see Ihde, *Listening and Voice* (Albany: SUNY Press, 2007), 73–83; Edmund Carpenter and Marshall McLuhan, "Acoustic Space," in *Explorations in Communication*, ed. Edmund Carpenter and

Marshall McLuhan (Boston: Beacon, 1960), 67; and Steven Connor, "The Modern Auditory I," in *Rewriting the Self*, ed. Roy Porter (London: Routledge, 1996), 206–7.

73. Jan Radway writes, "the notion of inherent resources rests on a naturalism or biologism with respect to the human species about which feminism has taught me to be highly suspicious. If humans have the inherent capacity to move physically and to sing, do they not also have an inherent capacity to represent and to organize representations, to narrative and to tell stories? . . . Would such a privileging of the body work to exclude important cultural activities of women whose bodies have traditionally been more rigorously worked over, policed, and contained than men's? Why are song, dance, theater, and sport somehow more fundamental, more popular than narrative, pictorial representation, or decoration?" "Maps and the Construction of Boundaries," *International Labor and Working-Class History*, no. 37 (Spring 1990): 23.

74. "A School Where Whistling Is Encouraged," *New York Herald*, November 9, 1924, SMA9; "Flight of the Mockers," *Los Angeles Times*, August 18, 1914, I16. On female whistlers, see John Lucas and Allan Chartburn, *A Brief History of Whistling* (Nottingham: Five Leaves Publications, 2013), 15.

75. An 1888 newspaper wrote that "just now the craze in wealthy circles is for lady whistlers. No reception or private concert, whether for social or charitable purposes, is considered complete unless the program contains one lady whistler." "Chirrup, Trill, Whew!," *Boston Daily Globe*, February 26, 1888, 12.

76. Charles Dudley Warner, "Whistling Women," *Harper's New Monthly Magazine* 84 (January 1892): 323.

77. "She Whistled for Royalty," *Chicago Daily Tribune*, September 16, 1888, 26. See also "Puckers Faultlessly," *Boston Daily Globe*, October 31, 1888, 5. Shaw's promotional materials stated that when she was "little Allie Horton she was a good deal of a tom-boy, and something of a whistler; but she was 'shut up' so often that she eventually dropped the habit." Mrs. Alice J. Shaw, *America's Phenomenon: La Belle Siffleuse* (Aberdeen, Scotland: Middleton, 1891), 2. Her parents discouraged her whistling, and she had given up the habit by the time she was married in 1873 to W. H. Shaw, a widower with three sons by a previous marriage. The Shaws moved to Detroit, where the couple had two daughters. Mr. Shaw's business failed in 1878, and they moved to Cincinnati, where Alice attempted to support the family through dressmaking. When W. H. deserted the family in 1885, Alice was forced to return to her father's home in New York with all the children. "Mrs. Shaw Gets a Divorce," *Washington Post*, November 15, 1888, 7; "Mrs. Shaw, the Whistler," *Cincinnati Enquirer*, November 18, 1888, 9.

78. Tracy C. Davis writes that one common reason for nineteenth-century women's attraction to the footlights was the "sudden total financial self-dependence following the death of a presumed lifelong provider." *Actresses as Working Women* (London: Routledge, 1991), 13, 53. See also "Chirrup, Trill, Whew!," 12; Daniel H. Resneck, "Whistling Women," *American Heritage* 33, no. 5 (1982): x; and *Alice J. Shaw*, 44.

79. "Whistling Women," *Cincinnati Enquirer*, December 18, 1888, 4.

80. "Hit and Miss," *Detroit Free Press*, January 6, 1888, 8; "Chirrup, Trill, Whew!," 12.

81. *Times* (London), July 5, 1888, cited in *Alice J. Shaw*, 22–23. Shaw seems to have been an early adopter of the phonograph's practical applications: we read that "it is the intention of Mrs. Shaw to practice, for the future, into the phonograph, and thus to preserve permanent traces of effects which would otherwise be wasted. Such traces will be preserved in 'phonographic cabinets' and may be brought out and rendered audible at pleasure by every possessor of the instrument" ("She Whistled for Royalty," 26).

82. "Hit and Miss," 8.

83. See Ben Singer, *Melodrama and Modernity* (New York: Columbia University Press, 2001). On Sybil Sanderson Fagan, see Resneck, "Whistling Women." Not only did Shaw have to negotiate cultural anxieties about female performers on the stage, but her act required her to make the provocative gesture of puckering her lips. The press discussion surrounding Shaw and her emulators reveals the erotic charge that such a gesture could evoke ("Hit and Miss," 8). See also "The Financial Whistle," *New York Times*, November 15, 1888, 5. Shaw's appearances clearly titillated male audiences, and whistling even came to function as a metonym for the modern woman. A poem published in the *Brooklyn Daily Eagle* the year of Shaw's first English tour breathlessly declared, "For piquancy and moral spice / And many other things as nice / Give me, I pray, oh, ancient churl / The racy, modern, whistling girl" ("The Whistling Girl," April 10, 1887, 10). Shaw's success was due in part to her ability to strike a balance between "moral spice" and public decorum, and she was praised for the way in which she controlled her body onstage. "In expressing the different emotions of that which she sings Mrs. Shaw never once distorts her face or even alters an expression," wrote one reviewer. "She is always calm, self-possessed and dignified" ("Whistling Women," *Cincinnati Enquirer*, 4).

84. A *Philadelphia Inquirer* reviewer noted that while she had a particularly good staccato note that resembled "the 'bird calls' of the street fakirs," hers was "far sweeter." The reviewer added that Shaw was "liable to set all the girls in town whistling. It is no longer simply mannish to whistle" (October 18, 1888, cited in *Alice J. Shaw*, 16). Publicity materials emphasized the fact that Shaw whistled "entirely from note, and exactly as the music is written," reinforcing the impression that she was part of the tradition of trained classical performances in which the written score was paramount (*Alice J. Shaw*, 2).

85. *Boston Journal*, November 1, 1888, and *Pall Mall Gazette* (London), July 19, 1888, both cited in *Alice J. Shaw*, 10, 29.

86. Estella M. Place, "Teaching Humans to Be Songbirds," *American Magazine* 109 (1930): 69; "Whistling Is Encouraged," SMA9; "Flight of the Mockers," I16; Hector Alliot, "Whistling Art at Auditorium," *Los Angeles Times*, March 4, 1914, I18; Agnes Woodward, *Whistling as an Art* (New York: Fischer, 1923), ix.

87. Place, "Teaching Humans," 69; "Whistlers Trained in Western School," *New York Tribune*, October 20, 1918, F18.

88. Woodward's techniques had names like the Hewie Chirp, Reverse Chirp, the Trill, the Whit-Cha, the E-Chew, the Cudalee, and the Lup-Ee. For more on notating birdcalls, see Jeremy Mynott, *Birdscapes* (Princeton: Princeton University Press, 2009).

89. In 1913 the *Los Angeles Times* could refer to her as "our little queen of whistlers." Hector Alliot, "Young Artist to Make First Bow," August 22, 1913, sec. 3, p. 4.

90. "Whistled in Church,' *Washington Post*, October 9, 1927, F4. McKee told a reporter, "I just imagine what kind of song I would like to make if I were a bird, and then I whistle it." "Songs of the Birds Inspire These Girls," *Los Angeles Times*, January 21, 1912, sec. 2, p. 9.

91. "Margaret McKee: Whistling Concert," brochure, 1919, *Traveling Culture: Circuit Chautauqua in the Twentieth Century*, Redpath Chautauqua Collection, University of Iowa Libraries (hereafter cited as RCC, UIL), accessed January 12, 2015, http://digital.lib.uiowa.edu/cdm/compoundobject/collection/tc/id/53702/rec/6.

92. In the 1927 Vitaphone short, Margaret McKee was billed as "The California Mocking Bird." She also appeared on the radio show *Roxy's Gang*, toured on the vaudeville circuit in the early 1920s, and recorded for Victor. Grace Kingsley, "Margaret McKee Again to Have Whistling Act," *Los Angeles Times*, August 7, 1920, sec. 2, p. 5.

93. Carolyn Merchant, "Women of the Progressive Conservation Movement: 1900–1916," *Environmental Review* 8, no. 1 (1984): 57.

94. Leslie Kemp Poole, "The Women of the Early Florida Audubon Society: Agents of History in the Fight to Save State Birds," *Florida Historical Quarterly* 85, no. 3 (2007): 300. See also Robin W. Doughty, *Feather Fashions and Bird Preservation* (Berkeley: University of California, 1975), 1; Mary Joy Breton, *Women Pioneers for the Environment* (Boston: Northeastern University Press, 1998), 256; and Amelia Birdsall, "A Woman's Nature: Attitudes and Identities of the Bird Hat Debate at the Turn of the 20th Century" (senior thesis, Haverford College, 2002), 29.

95. "An Appeal to the Women of the Country in Behalf of the Birds," *Science* 7, no. 160 (1886): 205. Another essay in the same volume declared that "the initiative in the movement for the protection of birds must be with the 'wives, sweethearts, and mothers,' and not alone with the laws and lawmakers." William Dutcher, "Destruction of Bird-Life in the Vicinity of New York," *Science* 7, no. 160 (1886): 199. An editorial in the Audubon Society publication *Bird-Lore* appealed to women as mothers: "Oh, human mother! will you again wear for personal adornment a plume taken from the dead body of a bird-mother, the plume that is the emblem of her married life as the golden circlet is of your own, the plume that was taken from her bleeding body because her motherhood was so strong that she was willing to give up life itself rather than abandon her helpless infants! Whenever you are tempted in the future to wear a Heron's plume, think for a moment of your own motherhood, and spare the bird-mother and her little ones." William Dutcher, "The Snowy Heron," *Bird-Lore* 6, no. 1 (1904): 40.

96. Mark V. Barrow Jr., *A Passion for Birds* (Princeton: Princeton University Press, 1998), 118–19.

97. A. Birdsall, "Woman's Nature," 31–33; Carolyn Merchant, "George Bird Grinnell's Audubon Society: Bridging the Gender Divide in Conservation," *Environmental History* 15, no. 1 (2010): 7; Derek Bouse, *Wildlife Films* (Philadelphia: University of Pennsylvania Press, 2000), 99; Barrow, *Passion for Birds*, 127–28; Barrow, *Nature's Ghosts*, 103–4; Breton, *Women Pioneers*, 255–56.

98. Daniel J. Philippon, *Conserving Words* (Athens: University of Georgia Press, 2004), 85.

99. Merchant, "Women," 70. The movement culminated in the 1913 Tariff Act, which outlawed the import of wild bird feathers into the United States; see Merchant, "Grinnell's Audubon Society," 14.

100. "The Slaughter of the Innocents," *Harper's Bazaar*, May 22, 1875, 338. The article was later attributed to Mary Thatcher (Higginson); see A. Birdsall, "Woman's Nature," 6–7.

101. J.A. Allen, "The Present Wholesale Destruction of Bird-Life in the United States," *Science* 7, no. 160 (1886): 195. Amelia Birdsall writes that "the women of the Audubon Societies met. And they discussed birds. And they held lectures, and slideshows, and spoke to children, and wrote pamphlets. They supported the founding of 'Bird Day' in schools, and an annual Christmas Day bird count. They even designed a series of hats that featured the latest styles, but were completely bird-free, naming them 'Audubonnets'" ("Woman's Nature," 57).

102. "To Save the Passenger Pigeon," *Forest and Stream* 74 (January 1910): 172.

103. "Reproduces Bird Songs and Calls," *North Adams (MA) Evening Transcript*, April 12, 1929, 11; "Bird Life," *Bath (ME) Independent and Enterprise*, April 13, 1907, 5. In 1912 Avis's bird imitations were called "the most wonderful accomplishment of the human voice to which we have ever listened." Rev. Edwin Whittier Caswell, "The Harbingers of Spring," *New York Observer and Chronicle*, April 4, 1912, 425. By one account, Avis "threw upon the screen the musical notes of many of the bird songs which he sang or whistled, so that the audience might join in the liquid flow of bird melody." "Bird Calls," *Lewiston Daily Sun*, January 25, 1908, 2.

104. "The Bird Man Is Coming," *Kingston (NY) Daily Freeman*, January 22, 1916, 1.

105. "Charles Crawford Gorst, the Bird Man," brochure, 1920/1929, *Traveling Culture*, RCC, UIL, accessed January 12, 2015, http://digital.lib.uiowa.edu/cdm/compoundobject/collection/tc/id/40463/rec/1. Gorst is listed as a member of the American Ornithologists' Union here: John Hall Sage, "Thirty-Fourth Stated Meeting of the American Ornithologists' Union," *Auk* 34, no. 1 (1917), 80. Founded in 1883 by professional male ornithologists, the union was one of the earliest organizations to recognize the human threat to bird life; see A. Birdsall, "Woman's Nature," 30.

106. "Charles Crawford Gorst: Whistling and Bird Songs," brochure, 1920/1929, *Traveling Culture*, RCC, UIL, accessed January 12, 2015, http://digital.lib.uiowa.edu/cdm/compoundobject/collection/tc/id/49114/rec/4.

107. Caswell, "Harbingers of Spring," 425; "Bird Man Is Coming," 1. Evidence suggests that some of Avis's talks were illustrated by motion pictures. A 1915 press account describes "motion pictures showing birds in their natural haunts. There were pictures of little birds being fed by their mothers, pictures of birds preparing their nests and going about their other activities. Some of the pictures were taken while the camera was within three feet of the subjects." "Takes Hearers to Wood Nooks," *Rochester Democrat and Chronicle*, March 23, 1915, 17. On the role of photography in bird-watching, see Barrow, *Passion for Birds*, 160–61.

108. "Bird Calls," 2; "Bird Life," 5. For an example of the "art of spatial illusion" used by voice performers since the eighteenth century, see Steven Connor, *Dumbstruck: A Cultural History of Ventriloquism* (Oxford: Oxford University Press, 2000), 254–55.

109. "Bird Life," 5; "Burton Holmes on South America," *Daily Standard Union* (Brooklyn), February 8, 1912, 9; "Wood Nooks," 17. See also "Bird Calls," 2; "Whistles Songs of Birds," *Boston Daily Globe*, February 12, 1906, 4; and Advertisement, *Boston Daily Globe*, September 11, 1925, A15. We might compare these sonic performances to Jonathan Burt's assertion that nature photography offered "one form of modern technology" that could be used to "escape from other effects of modernity" (*Animals on Film*, 97).

110. "Bird Life," 5; "Bird Man Is Coming," 1.

111. Avis's act relied on audiences that were familiar with the calls of native birds and could associate them with specific places, seasons, and times of the day. The pleasure of recognition was part of the act, and Avis sometimes concluded with a memory test, during which he repeated some of his earlier imitations and asked the audience to identify the birds on cards ("Wood Nooks," 17). Avis's performances suggest that bird species were aural personalities that served as a source of shared knowledge and provided Avis with a quick and effective way to establish common ground with large audiences. We might compare this dynamic to Steven Feld's influential description of the Kaluli people of New Guinea, for whom bird sounds provided a day-to-day means to reckon "time, space, season, and weather." *Sound and Sentiment*, 3rd ed. (Durham: Duke University Press, 2012), 84. The nature writer John Burroughs certainly reckoned time, space, and season through reference to birds, as is made clear in this passage, which links particular birds to certain months of the year: "the birds that come in March, as the bluebird, the robin, the song sparrow, the starling . . . the April birds, such as the brown thrasher, the barn swallow, the chewink, the water-thrush . . . the May birds, the kingbird, the wood thrush, the oriole." *The Birds of John Burroughs* (Woodstock, NY: Overlook, 1988), 150. The sounds of birds can be a resonant component of the "auditory environment" and can work to structure what Alain Corbin refers to as the "temporal architecture" of a community (*Village Bells*, 110).

112. Charles Kellogg, *Charles Kellogg the Nature Singer, His Book* (Morgan Hill, CA: Pacific Science Press, 1930), 12; Lee Shippey, "The Lee Side o' L.A.," *Los Angeles Times*, January 11, 1934, A4. A 1903 press account described how, as a boy, Kellogg would "lie down in the woods and listen to the birds instead of going to school or playing with other lads." "Bird Talk," *Courier-Journal*, June 14, 1903, 8.

113. Kellogg, *Nature Singer*, 12; "Knows 15 Animal Languages," *Cincinnati Enquirer*, October 14, 1911, 13; "Reproduces Song of Birds Perfectly," *Nashville Tennessean*, September 24, 1916, B20.

114. "B.F. Keith's Vaudeville," *Boston Daily Globe*, October 10, 1911, 11; Kellogg, *Nature Singer*, 146–47.

115. Kellogg's *New York Times* obituary stated that he was "born with the throat of a bird; that is, with a syrinx, or the half-rings of a songbird, in addition to the normal larynx." "Charles Kellogg, Imitator of Birds," *New York Times*, September 5, 1949, 17. Another reporter claimed that he had "a peculiarly constructed palate, no tonsils, and the cord connecting the teeth with the lower lip is entirely missing." "Knows 15 Animal Languages," 13. See also "Bird Man," *Sun*, December 17, 1916, IF14; "Reproduces Song," B20; and "Get the Pitch and Vibrate," *Detroit Free Press*, January 11, 1914, D8. On the avian syrinx, see Rogers and Kaplan, *Songs, Roars, and Rituals*, 81–83; and Morton and Page, *Animal Talk*, 65.

116. "Kellogg, the Bird Man," brochure, 1904/1932, Traveling Culture, RCC, UIL, accessed January 12, 2015, http://digital.lib.uiowa.edu/cdm/compoundobject/collection/tc/id/54690/rec/1.

117. "An Interview with Kellogg," *Voice of Victor* 12, no. 1 (1917): 4–5.

118. Kellogg and Burroughs traveled to Jamaica together in 1902; see Burroughs, *The Writings of John Burroughs* (Boston: Houghton, Mifflin, 1905), 13:240–41. See Kellogg's account of spending time with Muir, in Kellogg, *Nature Singer*, 243–44.

119. "Kellogg Brings Nature onto Stage of Orpheum," *Minneapolis Morning Tribune*, February 9, 1913, D8.

120. Kellogg, *Nature Singer*, 239–40.

121. Ibid., 283, 299. "Travel-Log Is Made of Trunk of Huge Tree," *Arizona Republican*, December 30, 1917, A2.

122. "Interview with Kellogg," 4–5. On imaginary media, see Parikka, *What Is Media Archaeology?*, 58.

123. Kellogg, *Nature Singer*, 138.

124. David L. Haberman, "Faces in the Trees," *Journal for the Study of Religion, Nature and Culture* 4, no. 2 (2010): 184–85, 176. Bennett writes that "a touch of anthropomorphism . . . can catalyze a sensibility that finds a world filled not with ontologically distinct categories of beings . . . but with variously composed materialities that form confederations. In revealing similarities across categorical divides and lighting up structural parallels between material forms in 'nature' and those in 'culture,' anthropomorphism can reveal isomorphisms" (*Vibrant Matter*, 99). See also Fudge, *Animal*, 76.

125. On verbal captions for photographs, see Roland Barthes, *The Responsibility of Forms* (Berkeley: University of California Press, 1991), 14–15. For Barthes, "the text constitutes a parasitical message intended to connote the image.... The text burdens the image, loads it with a culture, a morality, an imagination" (ibid.). See also W.J.T. Mitchell, *Iconology* (Chicago: University of Chicago Press, 1986), 43–44.

126. Also note that record companies such as Par-o-ket (1916), Grey Gull (1919), Oriole (1921), and Black Swan (1921) even named themselves after birds. Lynn Bilton, "The Phonographic Menagerie," *Intertique*, September 1994, www.intertique.com/The%20phonographic%20menagerie.htm. See also Resneck, "Whistling Women," 58.

127. "Birds Give 'Opera' at Flower Show," *New York Times*, February 27, 1935, 21; "Belmont Canary Opera at Jordan's This Week," *Boston Daily Globe*, April 27, 1931, 3; Walsh, "Joe Belmont," 36. At the personal request of John D. Rockefeller Jr., the Belmont Bird Symphony opened Roof Gardens in Rockefeller Center in 1935. "Canaries' Ways," *Time* 25, no. 10 (1935): 43.

128. Birkhead, *Brand-New Bird*, 44. Karl Reich first recorded birds in 1910 and trained them "for recording work by using a dummy recording-machine." Birds were allowed to fly around the room, and "food was placed actually in the mouth of the horn; the bird was trained to ignore the clockwork mechanism, and even to sing inside the horn." Peter Copeland, Jeffery Boswall, and Leonard Petts, *Birdsong on Old Records* (London: British Library of Wildlife Sounds, 1988), 9, 12.

129. Joeri Bruyninckx, "Sound Sterile: Making Scientific Field Recordings in Ornithology," in *The Oxford Handbook of Sound Studies*, ed. Trevor Pinch and Karin Bijsterveld (Oxford: Oxford University Press, 2012), 139.

130. The acoustic phonograph had been used as a tool of bird training: in 1903 the proprietor of a bird store in Washington installed a phonograph among his birds and made it repeat tunes "over and over again." In 1925 a California woman used phonograph records to train her canaries to sing tunes like "Yankee Doodle." "New Use of Phonograph," *Washington Post*, October 25, 1903, E3; "Canary Cage with Thick Wall Helps Birds Learn Tunes," *Popular Mechanics*, June 1925, 905; "Yankee Doodle Only Tune in Canary's Repertoire," *Los Angeles Times*, March 10, 1937, 10; "Canaries Echo Phonograph Records," *Washington Post*, February 13, 1938, TS8; "Phonograph Inspires Bird," *Washington Post*, February 18, 1912, M3; "Death Chair a Bird Cage," *New York Times*, February 19, 1912, 3; Evans, "Rollers and Choppers," 22. The use of the phonograph in training could lead to a modern variation on the problem of birds imitating the serinette too closely: a careless trainer who forgot to turn off his phonograph when the record was finished found that one of his birds had learned to imitate exactly "the scratchy sound of the record running on and on!" (Manisera, "Half an Ounce," I5). See also Cyrilla P. Lindner, "Trains Birds to Become Vocalists," *Brooklyn Daily Eagle*, 1927; "Training Canaries in a Death Chamber," *Popular Mechanics*, February 1913, 198–99; "German Bird Expert Makes Canaries Sing Like Nightingales," *Chicago Daily Tribune*, August 22, 1924, 4.

131. "The Hartz Group History," Hartz Mountain Industries, accessed December 3, 2014, www.hartzmountain.com/history/index.htm; Arnold Nicholson, "Songbird Assembly Line," *Saturday Evening Post*, December 5, 1947, 134; "Guaranteed to Sing," *New Yorker*, September 17, 1938, 15.

132. Nicholson, "Songbird Assembly Line," 36, 132.

133. "Guaranteed to Sing," 16; "Hartz Group History"; Nicholson, "Songbird Assembly Line," 134.

134. "Canary Foods Returning to Radio," *Variety*, September 17, 1941, 31.

135. "American Radio Warblers," *Variety*, October 22, 1941, 34.

136. Advertisement, *Mason City Globe-Gazette*, April 8, 1935, 6; "Radio Warblers Live Birds, Not Impersonators," *Chicago Daily Tribune*, February 16, 1936, SW6. Detroit News station WWJ received a letter from G. E. Deuble of Cleveland, Ohio, who wrote, "We have a canary bird, whose cage is in the room with our radio receiving set. This bird was a Christmas gift to my wife. We didn't know it could sing until the canaries at Station WWJ began. Our bird looked into the loud-speaking horn, twisted his head from side to side, and then started to sing himself." "Broadcast by Birds," *Radio Age* 2, no. 2 (1925): 29.

137. "Canaries May Be Latest to Get Mechanical Kick," *Billboard*, March 9, 1940, 8.

138. "Free Singing Lessons Await Your Canary on WGN Program," *Chicago Daily Tribune*, February 21, 1937, W9.

139. One author explained that canaries were "now in the hands of the scientific planners": "The singing lesson is given with a phonograph record on which the American Radio Warblers sing along with an organ that plays Johann Strauss' 'Voice of Spring' and the 'Skaters Waltz'.... You simply get him a little phonograph and, after he's had his song food, you play 'Voices of Spring' for him. This will put a song in his throat even if there's none in his heart." Renwicke Cary, "Around the Plaza," *San Antonio Light*, April 14, 1948, C1.

140. Evans, "Rollers and Choppers," 88. The designation "chopper" was previously a derisive term for an "imperfectly educated bird" that "cannot sing a song without a concluding bar or two of 'chop, chop, chop'" ("Singing Schools," 6).

141. "Canaries Turn to Jazz Songs; Radio Is Cause," *Chicago Daily Tribune*, December 8, 1934, 12.

142. Samuel Lubell and Walter Everett, "Nine Old Canarymen," *Collier's* 104, no. 24 (1939): 21. In 1949 a writer for *All-Pets Magazine* noted that new breeds had "the rollicking loud song that to a roller breeder would be anathema, but you know we are not all fanciers of the grand opera, and if we would judge by our radio programs grand opera would appear to be in big minority, so it is evident there are a lot like me that can appreciate the unaffected hop skip and jump, so to speak, of the chopper.... Dealers prefer the chopper over the roller ... as they find more people want a chopper than want rollers." Armistead Carter, "Type Canaries," *All-Pets Magazine* 20, no. 8 (1949): 7.

143. Nicholson, "Songbird Assembly Line," 134.

144. Haraway, *Companion Species Manifesto*, 20–21.

145. Kenney, *Recorded Music*, 78.

146. *Canaries: Their Care and Management,* Farmers' Bulletin 1327 (Washington, DC: U.S. Department of Agriculture, 1923), 1. During the shortage of supply from Germany, dealers looked to Asia, which helped to spur postwar interest in the mynah bird. An Arizona newspaper wrote in 1920 that "if you have a little canary in your home, and you adopted him before the war, he is very likely a German bird; if he is a war baby, he is doubtless an American product. For since the war began we have for the first time been raising our own canaries." Frederic Haskin, "Our Infant Canary," *Arizona Republican,* April 10, 1920, 3. See also "Guaranteed to Sing," 15).

147. "Hartz Mountain Products," 3.

148. Advertisement, *All-Pets Magazine* 16, no. 13 (1945): 6.

149. Gustav Stern, quoted in Nicholson, "Songbird Assembly Line," 137. During 1955 most of the 533,550 canaries imported into the United States came from the Netherlands, Japan, Belgium, and West Germany. Carl L. Shipley, "Capitol Counsel," *All-Pets Magazine* 27, no. 12 (1956): 8.

150. Robin W. Doughty, *The Mockingbird* (Austin: University of Texas Press, 1988), 57. Birkhead points to the role of the Royal Society for the Protection of Birds in the "slow but sure decline in British bird keeping" (*Brand-New Bird,* 5). Cage birds had long been associated with human slavery, as in the African American poet Paul Laurence Dunbar's poem "Sympathy" (1899), which famously declared that the caged bird's song was not a "carol of joy or glee" but a prayer for freedom, its wings bruised and bloodied from beating them against the bars. Paul Laurence Dunbar, *The Collected Poetry of Paul Laurence Dunbar,* ed. Joanne M. Braxton (Charlottesville: University of Virginia Press, 1993), 102. The troubling associations between bird keeping and America's racist history became more difficult to ignore during the decades of the postwar civil rights movement, and we might note that Dunbar's poem provided the title to Maya Angelou's autobiography, *I Know Why The Caged Bird Sings* (1969). Henry David Thoreau expressed a similar sentiment in *Walden,* when he declared himself to be "neighbor to the birds; not by having imprisoned one, but having caged myself near them." *Walden* (1854; repr., New York: Signet Classics, 1980), 62.

151. Brian Eno, "Ambient Music," in Cox and Warner, *Audio Culture,* 95–96.

152. Bijsterveld, *Mechanical Sound,* 46, 48.

153. See Keir Keightley, "Turn It Down! She Shrieked: Gender, Domestic Space and High Fidelity, 1948–59," *Popular Music* 15, no. 2 (1996): 149–77; and Jacob Smith, *Spoken Word* (Berkeley: University of California Press, 2011).

154. Merchant, "Grinnell's Audubon Society," 6.

155. R.G. Busnel and A. Classe, *Whistled Languages* (Berlin: Springer-Verlag, 1976), 23; Thomas A. Sebeok and Donna Jean Umiker-Sebeok, introd. to *Speech Surrogates: Drum and Whistle Systems,* ed. Thomas A. Sebeok and Donna Jean Umiker-Sebeok (The Hague: Mouton, 1976), xiii.

156. Mercer, *Canary Islanders,* 66. On the Gomera whistle language, see Mercer, *Canary Islanders,* 172, 254. On Silbo Gomera, see Lucas and Chartburn, *Brief History,* 96–97.

157. "Whistlers," *Boston Daily Globe*, June 5, 1904, 2A51.

158. Busnel and Classe, *Whistled Languages*, 11. One study claimed that "technical progress and the use of radio receivers, time-pieces, tinned food, telegraphy and telephony ... have all contributed to reduce the usefulness of whistled communication" (15–16). Sebeok and Umiker-Sebeok write that drum-and-whistle languages frequently filled the functions that are performed in Western society by devices like the telegraph, radio, and telephone (introd. to *Speech Surrogates*, xxi). A 1922 article describes the Gomeran "system of whistling signals" that conveyed "bits of news and information over considerable distances with great rapidity" and consequently made radio telephony "practically unknown." "Canary Islanders' Whistling Makes Radio Unnecessary," *New York Times*, July 23, 1922, 31.

159. See R. E. Ritzenthaler and F. A. Peterson, "Courtship Whistling of the Mexican Kickapoo Indians"; William M. Hurley, "The Kickapoo Whistle System: A Speech Surrogate"; George M. Cowan, "Mazateco Whistle Speech"; and "Whistled Tepehua"; all in Sebeok and Umiker-Sebeok, *Speech Surrogates*, 1410–11, 1426–33, 1385–93, 1400–1409.

160. Kellogg, *Nature Singer*, 147–49.

161. "Whistling Language Used by Indian Tribe," *Washington Post*, January 6, 1924, EA2.

162. Ibid.

163. Busnel and Classe, *Whistled Languages*, 38, 103.

164. "Charles Crawford Gorst."

165. Erving Goffman, "The Interaction Order," in *The Goffman Reader*, ed. Charles Lemert and Ann Branaman (Oxford: Blackwell, 1997), 237.

166. See "State of the World's Birds 2013," *BirdLife International*, accessed January 10, 2015, www.birdlife.org/datazone/sowb.

167. Paul Shepard, *The Others: How Animals Made Us Human* (Washington DC: Island Press, 1996), 141.

CHAPTER 3. SUBTERRANEAN SIGNALS

1. John Walker Harrington, "The Canary Birds of War," *Popular Science*, August 1918, 258; "Canaries in Warfare," *Literary Digest* 54 (June 1917) 1958.

2. The town of St. Andreasberg was built around a silver mine that opened in 1521, and "generations of miners protected themselves from bad air underground by taking small birds with them." In the Harz Mountains, "birds were the miners' saviors; for centuries locally caught chaffinches had been carried underground to warn of poisonous gas. Once canaries arrived in the Harz region around 1800, they took over this role" (Birkhead, *Brand-New Bird*, 13, 37).

3. "Canaries Act as Mine-Gas Detectors," *Popular Mechanics*, March 1911, 315; "Birds to Aid Mine Rescue," *Literary Digest* 48 (January 1914): 60. See also "Oxygen-Equipped Cage Used for Mine-Rescue Birds," *Popular Mechanics*, September 1922, 383.

4. On instrument-mediated perception, see Vivian Sobchack, *The Address of the Eye* (Princeton: Princeton University Press, 1992), 173. On remote sensing, see Lisa Parks, *Cultures in Orbit* (Durham: Duke University Press, 2005), 4. On the divining rod as an "autoscope," see "The Divining Rod," *Nature* 65 (October 1897): 568. Also consider Mark B. N. Hansen's discussion of media as devices that mediate between "a living being and the environment." "Media Theory," in *Theory, Culture, Society* 23, nos. 2–3 (2006): 299–300.

5. Heise, *Sense of Place*, 30, 55–56, 62. On Google Earth as "post-environmental media," see Denis Cosgrove, "Images and Imagination in 20th-Century Environmentalism," *Environmental and Planning A* 40, no. 8 (2008): 1878.

6. Merchant, *Radical Ecology*, 240.

7. Heise, *Sense of Place*, 64.

8. Doreen Massey, *Space, Place, and Gender* (Minneapolis: University of Minnesota Press, 1994), 5, 154, 168–69.

9. Doreen Massey, *For Space* (London: Sage, 2005), 151.

10. Medina, *World's Scavengers*, 69, ix. Medina writes that "about fifteen million people worldwide depend for their livelihoods on scavenging—the equivalent of the total population of Chile" (vii). See also Rogers, *Gone Tomorrow*, 210.

11. Soper, "Alternative Hedonism," 571. On alternative hedonism as "sources of satisfaction that lie outside the conventional market," see Tim Jackson, *Prosperity without Growth* (London: Earthscan, 2009), 148. On salvage, see John Michael Greer, *The Ecotechnic Future* (Gabriola Island, Canada: New Society, 2009), 70–71.

12. Bull, *Sound Moves*, 3, 9, 18; Bull, "To Each Their Own Bubble," in *MediaSpace*, ed Nick Couldry and Anna McCarthy (London: Routledge, 2004), 288. David Morley, "Domesticating Dislocation in a World of 'New' Technology," in *Electronic Elsewheres*, ed. Chris Berry, Soyoung Kim, and Lynn Spigel (Minneapolis: University of Minnesota Press, 2010), 10–11, 13. Elsaesser and Hagener write that, in the era of iPods and cell phones, sound becomes "a mobile cloud or an invisible cloak that we can wrap ourselves into, in order to protect us from the (acoustic) demands of a noisy environment" (*Film Theory*, 132). On the iPhone as "existential bubble," see Francesco Casetti and Sara Sampietro, "With Eyes, with Hands," in *Moving Data: The iPhone and the Future of Media*, ed. Pelle Snickars and Patrick Vonderau (New York: Columbia University Press, 2012), 21. On portable media, see Haidee Wasson, "Suitcase Cinema," *Cinema Journal* 51, no. 2 (2012): 148–52; Wasson, "The Other Small Screen: Moving Images at New York's World Fair, 1939," *Canadian Journal of Film Studies* 21, no. 1 (2012): 81–103; and Charles R. Acland, "Curtains, Carts and the Mobile Screen," *Screen* 50, no. 1 (2009): 148–66. See also Shuhei Hosokawa, "The Walkman Effect" (1984) in Sterne, *Sound Studies Reader*, 105.

13. See Chambers, "Aural Walk," in Cox and Warner, *Audio Culture*, 98–101. For a different take, see David Beer, "Tune Out: Music, Soundscapes and the Urban Mise-en-Scene," *Information, Communication and Society* 10, no. 6 (2007): 846–66.

14. William J. Mitchell, *Placing Words* (Cambridge: MIT Press, 2005), 9.

15. Manovich, "Poetics of Augmented Space," in Everett and Caldwell, *New Media*, 76, 78. Manovich writes that the power of Cardiff's walks "lies in the interactions between the two spaces—between vision and hearing ... and between present and past" (81). Adriana de Souza e Silva builds on Manovich's work in her discussion of the "hybrid space" created when mobile, networked devices embed the Internet in "outdoor, everyday activities," thereby connecting physical and digital spaces. "From Cyber to Hybrid: Mobile Technologies as Interfaces of Hybrid Spaces," *Space and Culture* 9, no. 3 (2006): 262. Recent work on the "mediaspaces" and "electronic elsewheres" of radio and television broadcasting indicate that a historical perspective can illuminate the intersections of cultural data, media technology, and physical space. See Berry, Kim, and Spigel, *Electronic Elsewheres;* and Couldry and McCarthy, *MediaSpace*.

16. On media archaeology and the "amnesia of the digital," see Parikka, *What Is Media Archaeology?*, 13.

17. Lisa Gitelman, *Always Already New* (Cambridge, MA: MIT Press, 2006), 7.

18. Jeffrey Sconce, *Haunted Media* (Durham: Duke University Press, 2000); Leigh Eric Schmidt, *Hearing Things* (Cambridge, MA: Harvard University Press, 2000). See also the discussion of imaginary media in Parikka, *What Is Media Archaeology?*

19. Sterne, *Audible Past*, 95, 99. See also Sconce on "electronic presence" (*Haunted Media*, 6).

20. Sir William Barrett and Theodore Besterman find the earliest reference to the divining rod in a 1430 document written by a mine surveyor. *The Divining-Rod: An Experimental and Psychological Investigation* (London: Methuen, 1926), 7.

21. Warren Alexander Dym, *Divining Science: Treasure Hunting and Earth Science in Early Modern Germany* (Boston: Brill, 2011), 9; Rosalind Williams, *Notes on the Underground: An Essay on Technology, Society, and the Imagination* (Cambridge, MA: MIT Press, 1990), 55; Lewis Mumford, *Technics and Civilization* (New York: Harcourt, Brace, 1934), 74. Duane A. Smith argues that "mining contributed mightily to accelerating American growth, to underwriting American industrialization, to shaping the American economy, and to creating modern America, a twentieth-century world power." *Mining America: The Industry and the Environment, 1800–1980* (Lawrence: University Press of Kansas, 1987), 25.

22. Lewis Mumford, *The City in History* (New York: Harcourt, Brace and World, 1961), 450–51. Mumford continues, "Few of us correctly evaluate the destructive imagery that the mine carried into every department of activity, sanctioning the anti-vital and the anti-organic. Before the nineteenth century the mine had, quantitatively speaking, only a subordinate part in man's industrial life. By the middle of the century it had come to underlie every part of it. And the spread of mining was accompanied by a general loss of form throughout society: a degradation of the landscape and a no less brutal disordering of

the communal environment" (*City in History*, 450). Betsy Taylor and Dave Tilford write, "mining precious minerals is one of the most environmentally destructive activities in which humans participate. Mountains are moved in search of increasingly low-grade ore, creating permanent scars on the landscape. Separating the metal from the ore often involves toxic chemical processes. . . . Much of this process goes solely to support the production of luxury goods." "Why Consumption Matters," in *The Consumer Society Reader*, ed. Juliet B. Schor and Douglas B. Holt (New York: New Press, 2000), 472. See also Merchant, *Radical Ecology*, 42, 44.

23. Carolyn Merchant, *The Death of Nature* (New York: HarperCollins, 1989), 24–25, 30. Merchant describes a Renaissance worldview that saw the cosmos as a living organism, and the earth as a "beneficent, receptive, nurturing female. . . . A commonly used analogy was that of the female's reproductive and nurturing capacity and of mother earth's ability to give birth to stones and metals with 'her' womb through marriage with the sun. For most traditional cultures, minerals and metals ripened in the uterus of the earth mother, mines were compared to her vagina, and metallurgy as the human hastening of the birth of the living metal in the artificial womb of the furnace—an abortion of the metal's natural growth cycle before its time. Miners offered propitiation to the deities of the soil and subterranean world, performed ceremonial sacrifices, and observed strict cleanliness, sexual abstinence, and fasting before violating the sacredness of the living earth by sinking a mine" (*Radical Ecology*, 42).

24. Georgius Agricola, *De re metallica* (1556 repr., New York: Dover, 1950), 38–39. Agricola argues that the divining rod "passed to the mines from its impure origin with the magicians. Then when good men shrank with horror from the incantations and rejected them, the twig was retained by the unsophisticated common miners, and in searching for new veins some traces of these ancient usages remain." In the end, he concluded that "a miner, since we think he ought to be a good and serious man, should not make use of an enchanted twig, because if he is prudent and skilled in the natural signs, he understands that a forked stick is of no use to him" (41).

25. See Merchant, *Death of Nature*, 140–41. Seventeenth-century German treasure hunters had also been primarily male, and one study refers to divination for treasure as "a kind of magic specifically attributed to men." Johannes Dillinger and Petra Feld, "Treasure-Hunting: A Magical Motif in Law, Folklore, and Mentality, Wurttemberg, 1606–1700," *German History* 20, no. 2 (2002): 175. In 1820, one author wrote that "if any female has ever exercised the gift of divining by the witch hazel, it has not come to the knowledge of the writer" ("The Divining Rod," *American Journal of Science and Arts* 11, no. 2 (1826): 204.

26. Thomas Welton, trans., *Jacob's Rod* (1693; repr., London: printed by author, 1875), 22.

27. Charles Musser, *The Emergence of Cinema* (Berkeley: University of California Press, 1990), 17–19. See also Jeffrey Sconce, "The Talking Weasel of Doarlish Cashen," in Berry, Kim, and Spigel, *Electronic Elsewheres*, 35. For

more on Kircher, see Siegfried Zielinski, *Deep Time of the Media* (Cambridge: MIT Press, 2006), 101–75; and Friedrich Kittler, *Optical Media* (Cambridge, UK: Polity, 2010), 73–74.

28. Barrett and Besterman, *Divining-Rod*, 12–13. Kircher concluded that "the effect comes from the hands of the operator" and that his experiments indicated that a rod of elm responded to underground water: "the reason appeared to be that trees take in metallic vapours through their roots, and these are left in the wood. When a stick imbued with such vapours is pointed at the ground, the vapours flow out of it and are greedily swallowed by the earth." He also proposed that hazel rods moved over metal: "he accepts the possibility on the grounds that all metals continually put out exhalations, which affect different plants in different ways." Joscelyn Godwin, *Athanasius Kircher's Theatre of the World* (Rochester, VT: Inner Traditions, 2009), 155–56. On negotiation of premodern magic and modern demystification, see Schmidt, *Hearing Things*, 109. On Kircher, see Zielinski, *Deep Time*, 125.

29. Geological Survey, U.S. Department of the Interior, *Water Dowsing* (Washington, DC: U.S. Government Printing Office, 1988), 5. Barrett and Besterman refer to a 1638 reference to the use of the rod by Germans in Welsh silver mines (*Divining-Rod*, 11). Keith Thomas describes seventeenth- and eighteenth-century treasure seeking in England, where the prevalent assumption was that "the country was riddled with caches of treasure," a belief that made sense "in the absence of an alternative system of deposit banking," which meant that "it was still common for rich men to keep their valuables in a box under the bed or to bury them in the ground." *Religion and the Decline of Magic* (London: Weidenfeld and Nicolson, 1971), 234–35.

30. "Divining Rod," *American Journal*, 202. "Jacques Aymar; or, The Divining Rod," *Monthly Reader, a Magazine*, July 1, 1813, 234.

31. Heidi Rae Cooley, "It's All about the Fit: The Hand, the Mobile Screenic Device, and Tactile Vision," *Journal of Visual Culture* 3, no. 2 (2004): 137, 141.

32. "The Divining Rod," *American Journal*, 202–3. See also "Divining Rod," *Nature*, 568. Commentators had offered a variety of theories to account for the movements of the forked twig. One example was a "theory of corpusculary emanations," which held that a form of sympathy was established between the wand and currents of "subtle matter" that flowed from hidden water, metals, or the bodies of criminals. "Jacques Aymar," 234. See also "Wands, and the Divining Rod," *American Phrenological Journal* 18, no. 6 (1853): 127. A text from 1693 explains that "there emanates or exhales generally from all bodies some subtle particles," and this was the reason that "our hair stands on end, and that we have a horror when we pass through a place where a man has been killed, or where a corpse has been buried" (Welton, *Jacob's Rod*, 59). On the "corpuscular theory" that corpuscles rise from minerals into porous wood, see Barrett and Besterman, *Divining-Rod*, 249; and Welton, *Jacob's Rod*, 57–58. Another idea was that "differences in temperature" caused involuntary muscular movements in diviners. "Dr. Raymond on the Divining Rod," *Scientific American* 51, no. 17 (1884): 264.

33. "A History of the Divining Rod; with the Adventures of an Old Rodsman," *United States Magazine and Democratic Review* 26, no. 131 (1850): 218.

34. Alan Taylor, "The Early Republic's Supernatural Economy: Treasure Seeking in the American Northeast, 1780–1830," *American Quarterly* 38, no. 1 (1986): 9–10. See also Gerard T. Hurley, "Buried Treasure Tales in America," *Western Folklore* 10, no. 3 (1951): 198. In addition to divining rods, early nineteenth-century treasure seekers also used "seer-stones" to obtain visions of hidden treasure. A "glass-looker" placed a seer-stone in a hat and "stuck his face in so as to exclude all light, sometimes staring for hours at a stretch" (Taylor, "Supernatural Economy," 10). See also John L. Brooke, *The Refiner's Fire: The Making of Mormon Cosmology, 1644–1844* (Cambridge: Cambridge University Press, 1996), 30–31.

35. Taylor, "Supernatural Economy," 11–12. Hurley writes that guardian spirits were often "negroes," animals, or slaves killed to protect the treasure ("Buried Treasure Tales," 200). One account of the treasure-seeking procedure described drawing a circle around the spot, dropping nine new nails, walking around the circle with the course of the sun, and reading from the Bible. In other instances, elaborate rods were constructed, using, for example, the tip of a "young heifer's horn" "filled with quicksilver, oil of amber, and dragon's blood," to which two "slender branches of whalebone" were fastened ("History," 225). See also Thomas, *Decline of Magic*, 236. On mining spirits, see Dym, *Divining Science*, 11.

36. Washington Irving, *Tales of a Traveller* (1824; repr., Boston: Twayne, 1987), 215, 227, 234.

37. Ibid., 246.

38. Ibid., 251–52.

39. Ibid., 255, 259.

40. Dym, *Divining Science*, 4. On the inhalation and exhalation of metals, see page 73. Seventeenth-century German lore described treasure "as if it was alive and able to move independently within certain limits" (Dillinger and Feld, "Treasure-Hunting," 164). On metallic exhalations, the connection between metals and plants, and the metaphor of gold as an underground tree, see Merchant, *Death of Nature*, 26, 28–29. Medieval alchemists adapted theories such as these, claiming, for example, that the movement of the planets influenced the earth's exhalation of minerals (Herbert C. Hoover, quoted in Agricola, *De re metallica*, 44). See also Mircea Eliade, *The Forge and the Crucible* (New York: Harper and Row, 1962), 8, 41, 45. Williams describes how minerals were regarded as "living organisms that grew inside the earth as an embryo develops in the uterus" and discusses the wide assumption that "minerals could grow and propagate" (*Notes on the Underground*, 24). See Godwin on Athanasius Kircher's belief that "trees take in metallic vapours through their roots, and these are left in the wood" (*Athanasius Kircher's Theatre*, 155–56). Thoreau tells an anecdote of an old potter who lived on Walden Pond "before the Revolution," who claimed that "there was an iron chest at the bottom, and that

he had seen it. Sometimes it would come floating up to the shore; but when you went toward it, it would go back into deep water and disappear" (*Walden*, 131).

41. Joscelyn Godwin, *Athanasius Kircher* (London: Thames and Hudson, 1979), 88–89.

42. Brooke, *Refiner's Fire*, 30–31.

43. Hoover, quoted in Agricola, *De re metallica*, 217. Mumford writes that the mine was a profoundly alienating and modern environment: "the first completely inorganic environment to be created and lived in by man . . . it is a dark, a colorless, a tasteless, a perfumeless, as well as a shapeless world: the leaden atmosphere of a perpetual winter" (*Technics and Civilization*, 69–70). For Dym, mining spirits were "born of the waving shadows, eerie sounds, and grotesque forms that confounded the underground worker" (*Divining Science*, 51). On mine spirits, gnomes, kobolds and "Tommy Knockers," see Walter Kafton-Minkel, *Subterranean Worlds* (Port Townsend, WA: Loompanics Unlimited, 1989), 36–39.

44. Taylor, "Supernatural Economy," 12–14.

45. Latour, *Reassembling the Social*, 195. Notice how the image of divination occurs to Thoreau: "My instinct tells me that my head is an organ for burrowing, as some creatures use their snout and fore paws, and with it I would mine and burrow my way through these hills. I think that the richest vein is somewhere hereabouts; so by the divining-rod and thin rising vapors I judge; and here I will begin to mine" (*Walden*, 71).

46. Massey, *Space, Place, and Gender*, 154, 5, 168–69. Some of those social relations, she writes, "will be wider than and go beyond the area being referred to in any particular context as a place'" (169).

47. Michel de Certeau, *The Practice of Everyday Life* (Berkeley: University of California Press, 1988), 107–8.

48. Taylor, "Supernatural Economy," 8, 19. Taylor writes that the rural poor were "beginning to feel capitalism's imperatives but still thought that sudden wealth could only be had from outside the natural economy" (19). Thomas writes, "whole families were rumoured to owe their rise to lucky finds with the ploughshare or spade. These stories served to account for otherwise puzzling instances of social mobility; they are common in many static societies where it is assumed that only luck can change a man's fortunes" (*Decline of Magic*, 235). Mumford makes a similar point with regard to mining: "In contrast to the forethought and sober plodding of the peasant, the work of the miner is the realm of random effort. . . . Neither the peasant nor the herdsman can get rich quickly: the first clears a field or plants a row of trees this year from which perhaps only his grandchildren will get the full benefits. . . . But the rewards of mining may be sudden, and they bear little relation . . . either to the technical ability of the miner or the amount of labor he has expended" (*Technics and Civilization*, 67).

49. George M. Foster, "Peasant Society and the Image of Limited Good," *American Anthropologist* 67, no. 2 (1965): 296–97, 306. Dillinger and Feld define peasant society as "self-sufficient rural communities that engage

predominantly in agriculture ... marked by the closeness and social control of village life," in which "the gain of one individual was the loss of all others" and "newly acquired wealth [was viewed] as a gift from the devil or as a treasure" ("Treasure-Hunting," 179).

50. Dillinger and Feld, "Treasure-Hunting," 181. For Dym, "mining was an area in which the transition from agrarian to market economies was striking, and early prospectors were frequently also farmers" (*Divining Science*, 14).

51. Irving, *Tales of a Traveller*, 264.

52. The story thus dramatizes what Worster describes as the compression of what we call "nature"—"the complex forces and interactions, beings and processes"—into the "simplified abstraction" of "land" ("Transformations, 1100–1101).

53. See the discussion in Heise, *Sense of Place*, 51.

54. Anthony Giddens, *The Consequences of Modernity* (Oxford: Polity, 1990, 18–19). Giddens distinguishes between place as "the physical settings of social activity as situated geographically" and space, which "lacks reference to a privileged locale which forms a distinct vantage-point." "In pre-modern societies," he writes, "space and place largely coincide, since the spatial dimensions of social life are, for most of the population, and in most respects, dominated by 'presence'—by localized activities" (18–19, 20). Irving's story dramatizes the occult connotations in Giddens's use of the term "phantasmagoric," suggesting that places are penetrated by "ghostly presences" in time as well as space. See John Tomlinson, *Globalization and Culture* (Chicago: University of Chicago Press, 1999), 58. Irving's tale serves as another indication that the divining rod was both part of the network of modernity and potentially a form of resistance to it: it was ambimodern in Ben Singer's sense of a cultural expression at once modern and countermodern (Singer, "Ambimodernity," in Ligensa and Kreimeier, *Film 1900*, 39, 49).

55. Some of the primary causes of this disembedding were the emergence of modern organizations and the circulation of "symbolic tokens" like money that lacked any regard for the specific individuals or groups that handled them (Giddens, *Consequences of Modernity*, 21–22).

56. Massey, *For Space*, 64–68.

57. Tomlinson writes that "the paradigmatic experience of global modernity for most people ... is that of staying in one place but experiencing the 'displacement' that global modernity *brings to them*." *Globalization and Culture*, 9, 59.

58. "What is special about place," Massey writes, "is not some romance of a pre-given collective identity or of the eternity of the hills" but rather the negotiated "throwntogetherness" of its various social relations, including both human and nonhuman inhabitants. She continues, "the throwntogetherness of place demands negotiation ... [and] implicate us ... in the lives of human others, and in our relations with nonhumans they ask how we shall respond to our temporary meeting-up with these particular rocks and stones and trees" (*For Space*, 140–41).

59. "Divining Rod," *American Journal*, 212. See also Schmidt's discussion of Enlightenment debunking of previous beliefs about oracle voices: *Hearing Things*, 98. As scholars such as Schmidt and Charles Hirschkind have shown, modern sound technologies were often "driven by an interest in the illusionist effects of natural magic, such as talking statues, speaking trumpets, and the arts of ventriloquism." "Cassette Sermons, Aural Modernities and the Islamic Revival in Cairo," in Sterne, *Sound Studies Reader*, 64.

60. Henri Mager, *Water Diviners and Their Methods*, trans. A. H. Bell (London: Bell and Sons, 1931), 4–5. See also Barrett and Besterman, *Divining-Rod*, 233; and Adolf Schmid, device for detecting subterranean waters, U.S. Patent US841188 A, January 15, 1907.

61. One author writes that "the metal or fluid, with the muscles of the arms, forms a circle analogous to the connection of wires or artificial machines, and that the twigs are strongly attracted towards the line of communication." "Arts and Sciences: The Divining Rod," *Worcester Magazine and Historical Journal*, October 1, 1825, 28. Another essay, from 1850, holds that since water is negatively charged and the atmosphere is positively charged, "the body of the diviner or rodsman, then, makes a good conductor between the electricity of the atmosphere and the earth" ("History," 220). See also Hugh Robert Mill, "Belief and Evidence in Water Divining," *Nature* 120 (December 1927): 883; Mager, *Water Diviners*, 7–8; and Barrett and Besterman, *Divining-Rod*, 250–52. In his 1899 book, *The Theory of Water Finding by Divining Rod*, W. F. Tompkins wrote that the Water-Finder was the "receiving instrument" for electric currents, such that the rod became a "part of the Diviner" in a manner similar to the indications given by "the hands of a clock," a steam-gauge, or an "automatic weighing engine and scale." C. V. Boys, "Water, Water, Everywhere," *Nature* 61 (November 1899): 2. For comparisons to radio, see Hugh Robert Mill, "Behind the Divining Rod," *Nature* 119 (February 1927): 311–12; and Mill, "Belief and Evidence," 883. Dym writes that "the pre-modern dowser spoke of mineral fumes and a God-given talent to zero-in on subterranean treasures, but his successor spoke of receptivity to galvanic or electrical impulses from below" (*Divining Science*, 6, 138).

62. Robert V. Bruce, *Bell: Alexander Graham Bell and the Conquest of Solitude* (Boston: Little, Brown, 1973), 344–45. See also "Professor D. E. Hughes, F. R. S," *Nature* 61 (February 1900): 325–26.

63. Bell requested that all metal be removed from the bed but later discovered that under the mattress of horsehair was another mattress composed of steel wires that may have affected the results. "Prof. Bell: His Machine," *Chicago Daily Tribune*, July 30, 1881, 2; George M. Hopkins, "A New Use for the Induction Balance," *Scientific American* 45, no. 5 (1881): 66; Alexander Graham Bell, "Upon the Electrical Experiments to Determine the Location of the Bullet in the Body of the Late President Garfield," *American Journal of Science* 25, nos. 145–50 (1883): 22; Iver E. Sullivan, "Garfield's Wire Bedspring Thwarted Effort to Save Him," *Washington Post*, July 28, 1935, B5; Bruce, *Bell*, 346–47. See also Richard Menke, "Media in America, 1881: Garfield, Guiteau, Bell, Whitman," *Critical Inquiry* 31, no. 3 (2005): 638–64.

64. "Prospecting Metal Veins by the Induction Balance," *Scientific American* 42, no. 10 (1880): 154.

65. This image can be found in lab notes, June 27, 1882–March 23, 1883, box 384, Laboratory Notebooks, vols. 19 and 20, 1882–86, Bell Family Papers, Library of Congress, 59.

66. William J. Mitchell, *Me++* (Cambridge: MIT Press, 2003), 58.

67. In 1892 George M. Hopkins, who had worked with Bell, published an article in which he described an induction balance of his own design that also used a telephone receiver to provide audio feedback; Alfred Williams and Leo Daft demonstrated a similar apparatus in 1903 (Hopkins, "New Use," 114). See also the account of F. H. Browne, who placed wires in the earth and listened to feedback with a telephone and then used the device to hunt for buried treasure: "He Finds Buried Metal," *Chicago Daily Tribune*, July 30, 1899, 12; "Locating Metals," *Electrical World* 41, no. 14 (1903): 950; Mager, *Water Diviners*, 40.

68. "The Gold Finder," *Los Angeles Times*, July 10, 1904, B8. On the phonendoscope, an "improved and very sensitive stethoscope, for locating underground streams of water . . . intensifying the murmurs of subterranean streams as to render them audible," see "A Scientific Divining-Rod," *Literary Digest*, July 6, 1912, 17.

69. I am borrowing Oliveros's phrase for sonosphere; see "Auralizing the Sonosphere," 162. See also Kahn's argument that the experience of "natural radio" foreshadows Blue Planet images from space (*Earth Sound Earth Signal*).

70. "Electric Aid for Gold-Seekers," *Chicago Daily Tribune*, September 13, 1881, 12; M. Hopkins, "Unscientific and Scientific Divining Rods," *Scientific American* 67, no. 8 (1892): 114; "A Modern Divining-Rod," *Current Literature* 31, no. 6 (1902): 677; "Gold Finder," B8; "Telephone Workers Use Divining Rod to Locate Cables," *Hempstead (NY) Sentinel*, February 9, 1922, 6. Hopkins wrote that the rod's movements were not due to the action of water or minerals but to "the voluntary or involuntary movement of the muscles of the hands and arms" ("New Use," 114).

71. "History's Greatest Metal Hunt," *Life* 38, no. 21 (1955): 25; "Good Prospecting for Uranium Seen," *New York Times*, April 13, 1954, 52.

72. "The Study of the Divining Rod," *Literary Digest*, February 15, 1913, 341.

73. "WEAF to Broadcast Noise of Electron," *New York Times*, August 9, 1929, 25.

74. "Scientists to Hear Cosmic Ray's 'Ticks,' Like Those of Clock," *New York Times*, December 28, 1931, 1.

75. "Broadcasts Sound of Deadly Radium," *New York Times*, May 1, 1932, 10; "Device Detects Radium," *New York Times*, March 14, 1929, 18; Collie Small, "For 'Gold' in the Atomic Age, the Forty-Niners Listen in the Hills," *Collier's*, September 10, 1949, 16; Bill Stapleton, "Uranium Rush," *Collier's*, October 2, 1953, 36.

76. See U.S. Atomic Energy Commission and U.S. Geological Survey, *Prospecting for Uranium* (Washington, DC: U.S. Government Printing Office,

1951); "Reading Taste of Public Goes West," *Washington Post*, August 3, 1955, 13; "Official Handbook Tells '49-ers' How to Go after Scarce Uranium," *New York Times*, July 2, 1949, 1; Alden P. Armagnac, "Black Box Points Way to Oil and Gold," *Popular Science*, February 1956, 117; and Otto Fried, "The Prospector's Partner: A Combination Geiger Counter–Portable Radio," *Popular Mechanics*, March 1957, 161. See also "'49 Uranium Rush," *Popular Mechanics* 91, no. 2 (1949): 89; "Want to Hunt Your Fortune in the Hills? Uranium Rush Is On," *Wall Street Journal*, August 31, 1950, 1; "Hunt Your Fortune," 1; and "Prospecting with a Geiger Counter," *Popular Science*, April 1955, 231. On the uranium boom, see D. Smith, *Mining America*, 125.

77. Divining rods were also employed in the search for oil in the West, and in that capacity were known as "wiggle-sticks" or "doodle-bugs." On divination in the West, see "Divining Rod," *American Journal*, 204. On rods and oil, see Schram et al. v. Pearl Oil Corporation, et al., No. 8088, Court of Civil Appeals of Texas, Austin, 90 S.W.2d 846 (Tex. App. 1936), LEXIS 446, January 22, 1936. Geiger counters were used to search for western oil as well, and some articles explained how subterranean oil formations revealed "a peculiar and characteristic pattern of radioactivity" that could be identified with Geiger counters. Armagnac, "Black Box," 256; Michael Day, "Now They're Hunting Oil with Atomic 'Guns,'" *Popular Mechanics*, June 1953, 88.

78. "Geiger Counter Sales Booming," *Los Angeles Times*, September 1, 1950, 16; Charles N. Stabler, "Uranium Search," *Wall Street Journal*, August 28, 1953, 1.

79. "In One Evening You Can Assemble a Vacation Geiger Counter," *Popular Mechanics* 104, no. 2 (1955): 145; J.P. McEvoy, "Uranium's New Horatio Alger," *American Mercury*, November 1953, 15; "She Strikes Uranium Riches; Hustles Off to Beauty Shop," *Chicago Daily Tribune*, July 9, 1955, B11.

80. Fried, "Prospector's Partner," 161; Gus Wesenfeld, "Treasure Finder's Pal," *Popular Mechanics*, August 1961, 190. Another device was intended for "emergency applications in wartime" and converted a radio set into a portable radiation detector. Alden P. Armagnac, "Your New Eyes and Ears," *Popular Science* 154, no. 5 (1949): 186.

81. "History's Greatest Metal Hunt," 27.

82. Hearing and mishearing are also themes in "The Big Uranium Strike" (March 20, 1956), an episode of *The Phil Silvers Show*; and "The Uranium Mine" (January 26, 1955) of *Amos 'n Andy*.

83. At the height of the uranium boom, a reporter for the *Chicago Daily Tribune* complained that uranium occurred in country that was "cleft by canyons sometimes almost a mile deep ... capped by eroded peaks, weird arches, fantastic bridges" and was seldom "close to a motor highway, almost never near to a road." The writer concluded that uranium "seems to shun the places where men live." Robert Casey, "Uranium Hunt Saps Gifts of Vitality, Hope," *Chicago Daily Tribune*, September 26, 1955, A4. See also Cal Bernstein, "Uranium Opens a New Scenic Wonderland," *Washington Post*, November 13, 1955, AW20.

84. Uranium mining became big business: "from the shovel and Geiger counter of the lonely prospector, uranium mining has grown in less than four years to an industry that ranks with the major metal mining industries of the country." Jack R. Ryan, "Uranium Amateur Yields to Expert," *New York Times*, January 3, 1954, F1. See also Floyd B. Odlum, "Uranium Mining Stages Fast Growth in 4 Years," *Los Angeles Times*, April 19, 1958, A8.

85. Armagnac, "Eyes and Ears," 166. See also J.D. Ratcliff, "The Amazing Geiger Counter," *Los Angeles Times*, December 15, 1946, E8; Thomas E. Mullaney, "U.S. Now Ranks Second in Uranium Mining as Government Lends Aid to Prospectors," *New York Times*, February 24, 1952, F1; and Small, "Atomic Age," 56.

86. Blesser and Salter, *Spaces Speak*, 82. See also Carolyn Birdsall, "Earwitnessing: Sound Memories of the Nazi Period," in *Sound Souvenirs*, ed. Karin Bijsterveld and Jose van Dijck (Amsterdam: Amsterdam University Press, 2009), 169–70, 176–77. See also Connor, "Modern Auditory I," in Porter, *Rewriting the Self*, 210.

87. Timothy Morton, *Hyperobjects* (Minneapolis: University of Minnesota Press, 2013), 7.

88. "Buried Shells Found by Induction Balance," *Popular Mechanics*, February 1916, 205; "An Electric Divining-Rod," *Popular Science*, February 1920, 54; "Detecting Buried Shells," *Boston Daily Globe*, November 21, 1915, 40; "Detecting Buried Shells with Induction Balance," *Scientific American* 113 (November 1915): 425.

89. See "Company History: Fisher Research Labs," Fisher Research Labs, accessed December 29, 2014, www.fisherlab.com/about.htm; and E.C. Hanson and W.L. Carlson, apparatus for detecting minute values of energy, U.S. Patent 1,437,240, November 28, 1922.

90. Frank H. Schubert, "The Portable SCR-625 Mine Detector," in *Builders and Fighters: U.S. Army Engineers in World War II*, ed. Barry W. Fowle (Fort Belvoir, VA: Office of History, U.S. Army Corps of Engineers, 1992), 168, 166.

91. Hanson W. Baldwin, "Ten Vital Weapons," *New York Times*, June 11, 1944, SM8.

92. "Huge Radio Surpluses to Be Sold by Makers," *New York Times*, August 24, 1945, 22; Eric Jensen, "Treasure Finders: Do They Really Work?," *Popular Mechanics*, August 1967, 113.

93. See "Garrett History," *Garrett Metal Detectors*, accessed December 29, 2014, www.garrett.com/mediasite/history.aspx.

94. Norman Carlisle and David Michelsohn, *The Complete Guide to Treasure Hunting* (Chicago: Regnery, 1973), 23–24; Tom Zito, "His Fortune Is Where He Finds It," *Washington Post*, December 27, 1970, G20.

95. Art Lassagne, Metal Detector Handbook (Alamo, CA: Gold Bug Books, 1967), 35–37; Karl Von Mueller, Treasure Hunter's Manual, no. 7 (Dallas, TX: Ram Books, 1974), 127. A recent guidebook describes the need for hobbyists to learn how to distinguish between the "solid and repeatable signal" made by a coin and the "clipped sound" made by junk: "a chopping, broken 'dip-bidda-dip'

sound occurs more often on junk targets," whereas "the coin sound will generally start and stop suddenly . . . like a 'pow, pow, pow' sound with each sweep of the coil." Vince Migliore, Metal Detecting for the Beginner, 2nd ed. (Folsom, CA: Blossom Hill Books, 2010), 130–31. Hobbyists learned to locate and analyze what Jean-Paul Thibaud refers to as a "visiophonic knot," a "convergence point between the audible and the visible." "The Sonic Composition of the City," in The Auditory Culture Reader, ed. Michael Bull and Les Back (New York: Berg, 2003), 337.

96. Holly Grossl, "Modern Gold Diggers Go Shooting for Coins," *European Stars and Stripes* (Darmstadt, Germany), August 27, 1975, 9.

97. I am building on Thibaud's discussion of a "visiophonic knot"; see "Sonic Composition," in Bull and Back, *Auditory Culture Reader*, 337.

98. Dorothy Townsend, "Beachcombing Business Buzzing," *Los Angeles Times*, August 21, 1966, B1.

99. Len Buckwalter, "Treasure Hunting: A Regal Reward," *New York Times*, February 4, 1973, 451; Gerald T. Ahnert, "Probing for Treasure with Electronic Detectors," *New York Times*, June 22, 1975, 139. See also Dee Wedemeyer, "Thousands Seek a Pot of Gold, Not at the End of a Rainbow, but Underfoot," *New York Times*, October 18, 1976, 50. Joan Allen estimates that thirty thousand hobbyists were active in 1973 in the United Kingdom. *Glittering Prospects: All You Need to Know about Treasure Hunting* (London: Elm Tree Books, 1977), 1.

100. Kristen Haring, *Ham Radio's Technical Culture* (Cambridge, MA: MIT Press, 2008), 2. Haring observes that technical hobbies are "largely practiced by men," although metal-detector enthusiasts went out of their way to describe the participation of female family members (4). One claimed that while men usually operated the detector, women made particularly good "diggers." On female radio hobbyists, see pages 44–46. See also Grossl, "Modern Gold Diggers," 9. Warren Merkitch asserts that his teenage daughters shared his enthusiasm for beachcombing: "Each beachcombing excursion is an exciting, competitive trip that . . . thousands of families would find beneficial." *Beachcomber's Handbook* (Segundo, CO: Examino, 1976), 7. One writer refers to metal detecting as "the greatest thing for family togetherness" since the weekend vacation, while another claims that "roaming over open fields or deserted beaches with a portable metal detector is a pleasant outdoor activity that the whole family can enjoy." Skip Ferderber, "Metal Detector Takes Humdrum Out of Life for Glendale Family," *Los Angeles Times*, August 28, 1970, J6. See also Ahnert, "Probing for Treasure," 139; and Gordon Grant, "Beachcoming: Key to Health," *Los Angeles Times*, September 1, 1971, B1.

101. See Stephen Webbe, "Treasure Awaits Those Who Search," *Daily Herald*, September 6, 1979, sec. 2, p. 1. On "rockhounds," see Beatrice Johnson, "The Family Hobby," *True Treasure* 7, no. 12 (1973): 34.

102. "Remnants of Past Hunted," *News Journal* (Mansfield, OH), April 19, 1977, 11; Wedemeyer, "Thousands," 50.

103. Advertisement, *True Treasure* 7, no. 12 (1973): 67. A 1973 treasure handbook described such events as a "sort of rodeo for treasure hunters," where

hobbyists got to practice with their detectors, learn some valuable pointers, meet fellow enthusiasts, and engage in "free-for-all searches for buried treasure" (Carlisle and Michelsohn, *Complete Guide*, 32–33). During competitive treasure hunts, participants had a limited amount of time to locate coins and tokens that had been buried in a fenced-off search area (33–34). See also Wedemeyer, "Thousands," 50; and advertisements, in *True Treasure* 8, no. 2 (1974): 9; and *True Treasure* 4, no. 10 (1970): 52.

104. Frank L. Fish, *Buried Treasure and Lost Mines* (Chino, CA: Amador, 1966), 6; V. Lee Oertie, "Metal Detectors . . . Can They Really Spot Buried Treasure?," *Popular Science*, April 1963, 202; Ahnert, "Probing for Treasure," 139. See also Webbe, "Treasure Awaits," sec. 2, p. 1. A 1973 guidebook urged treasure seekers to consult books, newspapers, courthouse records, maps, public libraries, and even aerial photographs from university archaeology departments or the U.S. Forest Service (Carlisle and Michelsohn, *Complete Guide*, 6–15). Allen recommended "talking with elderly people. . . . Many of their stories will be handed-down gossip" (*Glittering Prospects*, 59). A recent guidebook encourages hobbyists to develop an eye "for sites that were busy in the past and make for good hunting in the present. . . . Look for abandoned sites, dead industries, forgotten trails, and long-lost locations of group gatherings" (Migliore, *Metal Detecting*, 101).

105. Western iconography is an index of the postwar historical moment. Robert B. Ray describes how Hollywood films from this time "returned again and again, explicitly or implicitly, to the frontier's continuing significance in American life." *A Certain Tendency of the Hollywood Cinema, 1930–1980* (Princeton: Princeton University Press, 1985), 301, 251.

106. Fish, *Buried Treasure*, 20–21, 43–44, 63–64. As they had been a century earlier, Fish's guardian spirits are often workers killed at the site of their labor: like an African American who died without revealing his secret cache of gold, for example; or a Chinese gold miner killed by bandits.

107. Allen, *Glittering Prospects*, 36.

108. Gerry Fleming, "Space-Age Prospectin'," *Outdoor Outlook*, November 4, 1973, 5; E.S. LeGaye, *The Electronic Metal Detector Handbook* (Houston: Western Heritage, 1969), 148. See also Allen, *Glittering Prospects*, 36. We might say that hobbyists developed a form of vernacular topoanalytic research, which Gaston Bachelard defines as "the systematic psychological study of the sites of our intimate lives." *The Poetics of Space* (Boston: Beacon, 1969), 8.

109. Hoping to fend off such criticisms, Allen wrote a code of conduct for hobbyists whose first rule was, "Don't interfere with archaeological sites or ancient monuments" (*Glittering Prospects*, 134–35, 20). For a discussion of mediated remote sensing and televisual archaeology, see Parks, *Cultures in Orbit*, 110.

110. Ben A. Franklin, "An Army of Relic Hunters Is Despoiling Civil War Battlegrounds," *New York Times*, August 12, 1975, 31. To "combat these invaders," the Park Service resorted to "psychological warfare" by placing thousands of quarter-size iron and steel slugs around the area in an attempt to discourage

the hobbyists. A decade later an article in the journal *Antiquity* claimed that the very mention of the words "metal detector" was "guaranteed to raise the hackles of many archaeologists." T. Gregory and J. G. Rogerson, "Metal-Detecting in Archaeological Excavation," *Antiquity* 58, no. 224 (1984): 179.

111. David Lowenthal, *The Past Is a Foreign Country* (Cambridge: Cambridge University Press, 1985), 245. An advertisement for White's metal detectors is titled "Treasure Americana." A photograph shows an antique chest in an attic filled with a stereoscope, old phonograph horn, pistol, and kerosene lamp. Copy recounts stories of a customer who found a high school class ring from 1953 and a family who uncovered a jar filled with silver dollars and war bonds.

112. See the description of the *Diggers* DVD at the National Geographic online store, accessed January 12, 2015, http://shop.nationalgeographic.com/ngs/product/dvds/adventure-and-exploration/diggers-season-two-dvd-r.

113. The occult is never far from away on National Geographic's *Diggers*, and several episodes involve supposedly haunted spaces, as when they visit the Trans-Allegheny Lunatic Asylum.

114. Concerned Archaeologists and Their Supporters, "Stop Airing Their 'Digger' Programs," petition to the National Geographic Channel, the Travel Channel, and Spike TV, accessed January 10, 2015, www.change.org/petitions/the-national-geographic-channel-the-travel-channel-spike-tv-stop-airing-their-digger-programs-3. See also Keith Kloor, "Archaeologists Protest 'Glamorization' of Looting on TV," *Science* and *American Association for the Advancement of Science*, March 1, 2012, http://news.sciencemag.org/2012/03/archaeologists-protest-glamorization-looting-tv; and Brett French, "'Diggers' TV Show Strikes Nerve," *Billings (MT) Gazette*, March 15, 2012, http://billingsgazette.com/news/state-and-regional/montana/diggers-tv-show-strikes-nerve/article_78af2cef-5c13-5ea1-b3d0-ba81b47df92e.html.

115. Charles Ewen, "National Geographic's Diggers Redux," Society for Historical Archaeology, July 19, 2012, www.sha.org/blog/index.php/2012/07/national-geographics-diggers-redux/; Ewen, "Boom, Baby!," Society for Historical Archaeology, May 21, 2012, www.sha.org/blog/index.php/2012/05/boom-baby/. See also Ewen, "National Geographic's Diggers: Is It Better?," Society for Historical Archaeology, February 1, 2013: www.sha.org/blog/index.php/2013/02/national-geographics-diggers-is-it-better/; and Ewen, "Diggers: Making Progress," Society for Historical Archaeology, May 21, 2014, www.sha.org/blog/index.php/2014/05/diggers-making-progress/.

116. Walter Benjamin, "The Storyteller," in *Illuminations*, ed. Hannah Arendt (New York: Schocken Books, 1968), 89–90.

117. Lassagne, *Metal Detector Handbook*, 3; Robert Galbreath, "Explaining Modern Occultism," in *The Occult in America: New Historical Perspectives*, ed. Howard Kerr and Charles L. Crow (Urbana: University of Illinois Press, 1983), 18–19. See also Sean McCloud, *Making the American Religious Fringe* (Chapel Hill: University of North Carolina Press, 2004), 101. Manuals often began with the disclaimer that older practitioners might resent the revelation of secret techniques. See, for example, Merkitch, *Beachcomber's Handbook*, 7.

118. In 1977 one could find ads for two-day classes put on by the Institute of Dowsing in Wilmington, North Carolina, or Treasure Dowsing Seminars for Treasure Hunters and Prospectors, put on by the Georgia-based Geo-Mental Technics; see the advertisement in *Lost Treasure* 2, no. 6 (1977): 33, 39; and H. R. Whitaker, "Can a Man Really Find Happiness (and Water) with a Forked Twig?," *Chicago Tribune*, October 20, 1968, 87. Reports stated that U.S. Marines in Vietnam were using the divining rod to locate enemy tunnels, and their apparent success made rhabdomancy "almost a respectable subject." John Randolph, "Divining Rods Used in Defense of Khe Sanh," *Los Angeles Times*, March 24, 1968, J4.

119. Robert L. Thayer Jr. defines a bioregion as a "unique region definable by natural (rather than political) boundaries with a geographic, climatic, hydrological, and ecological character capable of supporting unique human and non-human living communities. . . . [A bioregion is] variously defined by the geography of watersheds, similar plant and animal ecosystems, and related, identifiable landforms . . . and by the unique human cultures that grow from natural limits and potentials of the region." *LifePlace: Bioregional Thought and Practice* (Berkeley: University of California Press, 2003), 3. For Kirkpatrick Sale, bioregion is "a life-territory, a place defined by its life forms, its topography and its biota, rather than by human dictates; a region governed by nature, not legislature." *Dwellers in the Land* (Athens: University of Georgia Press, 1991), 43.

120. LeGaye, *Electronic Metal Detector*, ii, 198.

121. Von Mueller, *Treasure Hunter's Manual*, 25. Mueller wrote in his popular manual that he had known men and women who had blossomed into "entirely new individuals" after a few months of treasure hunting. The hobby produced "an entirely new spiritual outlook" and made "old rundown bodies begin to respond with a new vigor" (ibid.).

122. For a range of scholarly approaches to sonic mobility, see the two volumes of Gopinath and Stanyek, *Oxford Handbook.*

123. Dunaway, "Seeing Global Warming," 24–25. See William Cronon on "wildness in our own backyards": "The Trouble with Wilderness," in *Uncommon Ground*, ed. William Cronon (New York: Norton, 1995), 86. See also Frauke Behrendt, "The Sound of Locative Media," in *Convergence* 18, no. 3 (2012): 288; Behrendt, "Auditory Edges and Media Ecotones: Framing the Mobile Listening Experiences of GPS Sound Walks," in *The Global Composition*, ed. Sabine Breitsameter and Claudia Soller-Eckert, proceedings of the Global Composition Conference on Sound, Media and the Environment, Hochschule Darmstadt, Media Campus Dieburg, Germany, July 25–28, 158.

124. I take that phrase from Giles Slade's book, *Made to Break*, on the history of planned obsolescence.

125. On the "bottle bonanza" or "bottle boom," see Carlisle and Michelsohn, *Complete Guide*, 91–92.

126. J. Grant, *Green Marketing Manifesto*, 261.

127. Ewen, "National Geographic's Diggers: Is It Better?"

128. Soper, "Alternative Hedonism," 571. On alternative hedonism as "sources of satisfaction that lie outside the conventional market," see Jackson, *Prosperity without Growth*, 148. On salvage, see Greer, *Ecotechnic Future*, 70–71.

129. Medina, *World's Scavengers*, 69, ix.

130. Medina, *World's Scavengers*, 262. For more information on international waste pickers' associations, see Women in Informal Employment: Globalizing and Organizing (WIEGO), http://wiego.org; and Global Alliance of Waste Pickers, http://globalrec.org.

131. Manovich, "Poetics of Augmented Space," in Everett and Caldwell, *New Media*, 76.

132. Postwar treasure seekers provide an example of what Jean and John L. Comaroff might describe as an "occult economy." Comaroff and Comaroff define occult economies as the pursuit of wealth through an appeal to "techniques that defy explanation in the conventional terms of practical reason" and suggest that they are a response to "a world in which the only way to create wealth seems to lie in forms of power/knowledge that transgress the conventional, the rational, the moral" ("Millennial Capitalism: First Thoughts on a Second Coming," in *Millennial Capitalism and the Culture of Neoliberalism*, ed. Jean Comaroff and John L. Comaroff (Durham and London: Duke University Press, 2001), 2, 19, 26).

133. Kline, *First along the River*, 92–93. See also Sam Binkley, *Getting Loose* (Durham: Duke University Press, 2007), 137.

134. David Hesmondhalgh writes that "in the early 1970s, after decades of these relatively favorable conditions, the advanced capitalist economies hit the beginning of the Long Downturn that continued into the 1990s." *The Cultural Industries* (Los Angeles: Sage, 2007), 84–85. See also David Harvey, *The Condition of Postmodernity* (Cambridge: Blackwell, 1990), 129.

135. Binkley, *Getting Loose*, 37, 47.

136. Heinberg, *Party's Over*, 75.

137. Harvey, *Condition of Postmodernity*, 145.

138. Rogers, *Gone Tomorrow*, 139.

139. Von Mueller, *Treasure Hunter's Manual*, 25; LeGaye, *Electronic Metal Detector*, 148; Carlisle and Michelsohn, *Complete Guide*, 3.

140. Lassagne, *Metal Detector Handbook*, 2. Some metal-detecting guidebooks make explicit reference to the crisis in value and the shift away from currency connected to gold. See, for example, LeGaye, *Electronic Metal Detector*, 150–51.

141. Webbe, "Treasure Awaits," sec. 2, p. 1.

142. Lowenthal, *Foreign Country*, 11, xv.

143. "Facts and Figures on E-Waste and Recycling," Electronics Take Back Coalition, February 21, 2012, www.electronictakeback.com, 7.

144. Jack Nicas, "Metal Detectors Hit the Jackpot," *Wall Street Journal (Online)*, July 30, 2011, www.wsj.com/articles/SB10001424053111904233404576462161651031814.

CHAPTER 4. RADIO'S DARK ECOLOGY

1. Orson Welles and Peter Bogdanovich, *This Is Orson Welles*, ed. Jonathan Rosenbaum (New York: HarperCollins, 1992), 9–10.

2. Lucas Bessire and Daniel Fisher, eds. *Radio Fields* (New York: New York University Press, 2012), 1. Vinod Pavarala and Kanchan K. Malik write that "radio broadcasting leaps the barriers of isolation and illiteracy and it is the most economic electronic medium to broadcast and receive.... Radio reaches communities at the very end of the development road—people who live in areas with no phones and no electricity. Radio reaches people who can't read or write. Radio is a relatively economical medium, and even in very poor communities, radio penetration is vast." *Other Voices: The Struggle for Community Radio in India* (London: Sage, 2007), 153. See also Jason Loviglio's comments on the importance of radio in moments of crisis, "to bear witness to something that is happening, to make an event in the most literal terms a public one: in the case of Hurricanes Katrina and Rita in New Orleans in 2005, and Hurricane Sandy in the northeast in 2012, local community stations were sometimes the only source of information in communities devastated by floods." "Public Radio in Crisis," in *Radio's New Wave*, ed. Jason Loviglio and Michele Hilmes (New York: Routledge, 2013), 40. See also Nina Huntemann, "A Promise Diminished: The Politics of Low-Power Radio," in *Communities of the Air*, ed. Susan Merrill Squier (Durham: Duke University Press, 2003), 78.

3. See Martin Shingler and Cindy Wieringa, *On Air* (London: Arnold, 1998), 87. According to Erik Barnouw, radio dramatists learned that "about five per cent of the theater's 'business' may be very valuable.... The remaining ninety-five percent became impracticable and useless.... We find radio discarding the superfluous for its own characteristic, severe concentration on essential plot matters." *Handbook of Radio Writing* (1939; repr., Boston: D.C. Heath, 1949), 16–18. Barnouw sums up that radio's central characteristics relate to qualities of economy and compression (15). On radio station KTAO in New Mexico, see Keya Lea, "KTAO: The Solar Powered Radio Station," *Green Passive Solar Magazine*, April 7, 2011, http://greenpassivesolar.com/2011/04/ktao-solar-powered-radio-station-taos/.

4. I follow Neil Verma's definition of radio drama or the "radio play" to denote "a radio broadcast that has a scene in which a character performs an action.... A drama is a story but it also must conjure a place." *Theater of the Mind* (Chicago: University of Chicago Press, 2013), 5.

5. Bozak, *Cinematic Footprint*, 41–42; Richard J. Hand, *Terror on the Air* (Jefferson, NC: McFarland, 2006), 14; Andrew Crisell, *Understanding Radio*, 2nd ed. (London: Routledge, 1994), 157. See also Shingler and Wieringa, who write that radio "can allow its audience to see in the dark, to see the invisible, to see the unseeable" (*On Air*, 74). Note that Lovecraft's Old Ones lose their vision from living in the darkness and develop "obscure special senses . . . partly independent of light." H. P. Lovecraft, *At the Mountains of Madness and Other Novels* (Sauk City, WI: Akham House, 1964), 63, 75.

6. Richard J. Hand, *Terror on the Air*, 14; Lacey, *Listening Publics*, 94. Hadley Cantril and Gordon W. Allport write that radio "skeletonizes the personality of the speaker or performer." *The Psychology of Radio* (New York: Harper and Brothers, 1935), 14. See also Verma's fascinating suggestion that we think of radio dramas as "fossilized invertebrates in the contemporary media ecology, caught between objecthood and thingliness, between oil and geology." "A Paleontology of Quiet," *Journal of Sonic Studies* 7, accessed July 2, 2014, www.researchcatalogue.net/view/87824/87825.

7. T. Morton, *Ecological Thought*, 16–17, 54.

8. Bill McKibben, Eaarth: Making a Life on a Tough New Planet (New York: St. Martin's Press, 2010), 45. See also T. Morton, Hyperobjects, 7; and F. Buell, Apocalypse, 76–78.

9. Michael J. McDowell writes that "for Bakhtin as for Darwin, every creature defines itself . . . by its interaction with other beings and things." "The Bakhtinian Road to Ecological Insight," in Glotfelty and Fromm, *Ecocriticism Reader*, 374–75. Robert Stam suggests that Bakhtin's sonic metaphors argue for "an overall shift in priority from the visually predominant logical space of modernity . . . to a 'postmodern' space of the vocal." *Subversive Pleasures* (Baltimore: Johns Hopkins Press, 1989), 19.

10. M.M. Bakhtin, *The Dialogic Imagination* (Austin: University of Texas Press, 1981), 420.

11. I draw on Stam's essay on adaptation: "Beyond Fidelity: The Dialogics of Adaptation," in *Film Adaptation*, ed. James Naremore (New Brunswick, NJ: Rutgers University Press, 2000), 64, 68. On contextualization, see Richard Bauman and Charles L. Briggs, "Poetics and Performance as Critical Perspectives on Language and Social Life," *Annual Review of Anthropology* 19 (1990): 68.

12. Verma, *Theater of the Mind*, 5.

13. Heise, "Unnatural Ecologies," 165, 167. Lawrence Buell suggests that a key ingredient in an environmentally oriented work is that the "nonhuman environment is present not merely as a framing device but as a presence that begins to suggest that human history is implicated in natural history." *The Environmental Imagination* (Cambridge, MA: Harvard University Press, 1995), 7.

14. Bakhtin, *Dialogic Imagination*, 84, 250, 243. Chronotopes, for Stam, are "concrete spatiotemporal structures" in literature that "limit narrative possibility, shape characterization, and mold a discursive simulacrum of life and the world" (*Subversive Pleasures*, 11).

15. For example, Rob Nixon writes that the Maldive Islands have become "the canary in the mine shaft of the climate crisis." *Slow Violence and the Environmentalism of the Poor* (Cambridge, MA: Harvard University Press, 2011), 265. See also Elizabeth DeLoughrey's discussion of "visualizing the planetary environment" through reference to spaces such as "the high seas, Antarctica, and outer space. "Satellite Planetarity and the Ends of the Earth," *Public Culture* 26, no. 2 (2014): 260. On Antarctica as a "proxy for outer space," see page 263.

16. Jeffrey Sconce argues that "War of the Worlds" portrays catastrophe at the level of the social body, military technology, and the media, a point underlined by Neil Verma (Sconce, *Haunted Media*, 114; Verma, *Theater of the Mind*, 71–72). Paul Heyer writes that with "Hell on Ice," "we can hear an anticipation of the apocalyptic tone that would make ... War of the Worlds so chilling." *The Medium and the Magician* (Lanham, MD: Rowman and Littlefield, 2005), 68.

17. Emma DeLong, ed., *The Voyage of the Jeannette: The Ship and Ice Journals of George W. Delong* (Boston: Houghton, Mifflin, 1883), 1:45, 48–49. The ship *Pandora* was renamed the *Jeannette* for the expedition, after Bennett's sister. "Preparing for Arctic Search," *New York Tribune*, March 17, 1879, 2. George W. Melville writes that the object of the *Jeannette* expedition was "to reach the North Pole by following up the Kuro-Shiwo," the "black current of Japan" that runs around the Japanese Islands northward to the Bering Strait. *In the Lena Delta* (Boston: Houghton, Mifflin, 1885), 1–2. See also Aaron Sachs, *The Humboldt Current Avant-Garde Exploration and Environmental Thought in 19th-Century America* (New York: Penguin Books, 2006), 274; and Leonard F. Guttridge, *Icebound* (Annapolis, MD: Naval Institute Press, 1986), 36–37.

18. Editorial, *Washington Post*, July 10, 1879, 2; Guttridge cites one press report that announced that, should the *Jeannette's* voyage be a success, "it will be one of the most brilliant geographical adventures ever won by man. The solution of the Northern mystery would be the event of the nineteenth century" (*Icebound*, 3).

19. James Naremore, *The Magic World of Orson Welles* (Dallas: Southern Methodist University Press, 1989), 86.

20. Edward Ellsberg, *Hell on Ice: The Saga of the "Jeannette"* (1938; repr., New York: Dodd, Mead, 1938), 110, 161. Ellsberg also writes that "sounds on the ice traveled unusual distances and boomed and reverberated as if from an overhead dome or the roof of a mammoth cave" (149). John Muir wrote of the sounds in the region: "the deep bass of the gale, sounding on through the rugged, ice-sculptured peaks and gorges, is delightful music to our ears." *The Cruise of the Corwin* (1917; repr., Boston: Houghton Mifflin, 2000), 3, 5.

21. Schafer, *Soundscape*, 43.

22. Ellsberg, *Hell on Ice*, 112.

23. Rick Altman, "Deep Focus Sound: Citizen Kane and the Radio Aesthetic," in *Perspectives on Citizen Kane*, ed. Ronald Gottesman (New York: Simon and Schuster, 1996), 98.

24. Heyer, *Medium and the Magician*, 46–47.

25. Frank Beacham, "Theatre of the Imagination: The Mercury Company Remembers," *Orson Welles and the Mercury Theatre on the Air*, Voyager V1012L, 1988, laserdisc.

26. DeLong, *Voyage of the Jeannette*, 1:382–83.

27. Barnouw states, "Music, like a lighting effect, can drench a scene almost instantly in its proper atmosphere. In a matter of seconds, it can wipe out one mood and set another" (*Handbook of Radio Writing*, 45).

28. Barnouw writes that radio is a "trio for three singers": sound effects, music, and speech (*Handbook of Radio Writing*, 29). See also Arnheim, *Radio*, 15.

29. Naremore, *Magic World*, 89, 90–91. Naremore makes reference, for example, to how Welles's film *The Magnificent Ambersons* charts a transition from "midland streets" to "grimy highways" (89).

30. Robert B. Ray, *Walden x 40* (Bloomington: Indiana University Press, 2012), 11.

31. Bakhtin, *Dialogic Imagination*, 89–91, 100, 225, 103.

32. DeLong, *Voyage of the Jeannette*, 1:409–10.

33. Thoreau, *Walden*, 213–14, cited in Ray, *Walden x 40*, 9–10.

34. DeLong, *Voyage of the Jeannette*, 1:213. Sachs suggests that Melville was more successful at shifting to the idyllic mode, arguing that he saw "northern landscapes not as potential commodities, nor as desolate wastelands, but as sublime signifiers of the harsh limits imposed by ecological forces" (*Humboldt*, 27).

35. DeLong's journals may have done something similar in their original form, but published versions were said to have been carefully edited to excise accounts of conflict among the crew. Those conflicts came to light in public hearings concerning the voyage and in subsequent publications by Melville and John W. Danenhower. See Melville, *In the Lena Delta*; and Danenhower, *Lieutenant Danenhower's Narrative of the "Jeannette"* (Boston: Osgood, 1882).

36. Guttridge, *Icebound*, 162.

37. Bill McKibben, introd. to Muir, *Cruise of the Corwin*, xv. Sachs describes Muir's Corwin writings as "perhaps the bleakest and most complicated of all his adventures in the Arctic regions" and marked by rich engagement not only with natural landscapes but with the native people of the Arctic regions (*Humboldt*, 311).

38. John Muir, *Travels in Alaska* (Boston: Houghton Mifflin, 1915), 67–68. Elsewhere, Muir wrote that he wanted to read the "records" that Nature had "carved on the rocks" to reconstruct the landscapes of the preglacial age, but in the process he contemplated how the current landscape was "withering and vanishing to be succeeded by others yet unborn." Muir, *The Wilderness World of John Muir* (Boston: Houghton Mifflin, 1982), 247–48. Anna Lowenhaupt Tsing describes Muir as a priest of nature who "worked back and forth between evoking global Nature and its local instances ... in a scale-making project in which the local and the global are wrapped together and charged by the principles of the universal" (*Friction*, 97–98).

39. See Walter Ong's well-known claim that "there is no way to stop sound and have sound." *Orality and Literacy* (London: Routledge, 1996), 32. Jonathan Sterne makes a trenchant critique, as part of his discussion of "audiovisual litany": "strictly speaking, Ong's claim is true for any event—any *process* that you can possibly experience—and so it is not a quality special or unique to sound" (*Audible Past*, 18).

40. Heise, *Sense of Place*, 62. Timothy Morton writes that one kind of ecological art uses technical innovations such as "zooming, stop motion, [and] time-lapse" to "open up the mesh" of ecological interconnection for inspection (*Ecological Thought*, 105).

41. Melville describes DeLong's burial ground overlooking the "frozen Polar Sea": "The lone mountain-top, where, in the awful silence and solitude of that vast waste of Arctic snow, with no requiem but the howling of the remorseless storm ... where the everlasting snows would be their winding sheet and the fierce polar blasts which pierced their poor unclad bodies in life would wail their wild dirge through all time" (*In the Lena Delta*, 340, 344).

42. Climate change is occurring more rapidly in the Arctic than anywhere else. Giddens writes, "the Arctic ice-cap is less than half the size it was 50 years ago. Over that time, average temperatures in the Arctic region have increased by about seven degrees." This is a result of a feedback cycle involving the melting of white, reflective ice into dark, heat-absorbing water. See *The Politics of Climate Change*, 2nd ed. (Cambridge: Polity, 2011), 13–14.

43. As I write this, news accounts tell of record high temperatures in Siberia and a melted lake at the North Pole: "Siberian Heat: Did the Arctic Region Break a Heat Record?," *Huffington Post*, July 7, 2013, www.huffingtonpost.com/2013/07/26/siberia-heat_n_3660212.html?utm_hp_ref = green&ir = Green; Andrew Freedman, "The Lake at the North Pole: How Bad Is It?," *Climate Central*, July 26, 2013, www.climatecentral.org/news/melting-at-north-pole-how-bad-is-it-16294; "Records for Arctic Ice Melt, Greenhouse Gas Emissions in 2012 as World Warms: Report," *Huffington Post*, August 6, 2013, www.huffingtonpost.com/2013/08/06/record-arctic-ice-melt_n_3715226.html.

44. DeLong, *Voyage of the Jeannette*, 1:116. Ellsberg prints the line as "a grand country for any man to learn patience in" (*Hell on Ice*, 72). Notably, Richard E. Byrd wrote that "if the polar regions have taught me anything, it is patience." *Alone* (New York: Putnam's Sons, 1938), 76. We might see a connection here to claims that eco-cinematic imagery asks viewers to slow down in a "cinematic stretching of patience" (MacDonald, "Ecocinema Experience," in Rust, Monani, and Cubitt, *Ecocinema Theory*, 39.) We might read *patience* in these cases as a means to use human frames of reference to describe an encounter with nonhuman temporal scales.

45. Sachs, *Humboldt*, 276.

46. Lisa Bloom, *Gender on Ice* (Minneapolis: University of Minnesota Press, 1993), 6, 3. Bloom writes that "the absence of land, peoples, or wildlife to conquer gave polar exploration an aesthetic dimension that allowed the discovery of the North Pole to appear above political and commercial concerns" (2). On the American conservation movement and turn-of-the-century masculinity, see Susan R. Schrepfer, *Nature's Alters* (Lawrence: University Press of Kansas, 2005), 4–5.

47. On Edison's generator and arc lamps, see Sachs, *Humboldt*, 275.

48. George DeLong to Thomas Edison, April 21, 1879, document series 1879 (D-79–19), Thomas Edison Papers, Rutgers University, NJ, http://edison

.rutgers.edu/index.htm. The telephone was also used in the ship's observatory: "if a man was in the observatory, and he wanted a relief, he would ring for it, or he would ring if anything happened." U.S. House of Representatives, *Jeannette Inquiry* (Washington, DC: Government Printing Office, 1884), 824, 827. In his October 30 journal entry, DeLong wrote that the telephone's wires were broken and "not worth a damn" (*Voyage of the Jeannette*, 1:163). On the Bell telephone, Edison arc light, and Baxter steam engine, see Guttridge, *Icebound*, 59–60. On the failure of the Edison electric generator, see pages 106–7.

49. On Peary, see "Trade in the Quaker City," *Talking Machine World* 6, no. 3 (1910): 29. Scott writes that the two gramophones "brought a touch of home." Quoted in Leonard Huxley, ed., *Scott's Last Expedition* (New York: Dodd, Mead, 1913), 2:340. The records to which I refer are Cdr. Robert E. Peary's *The Discovery of the North Pole* (Victor, 1909), Ernest Shackleton's *My South Polar Expedition* (Edison, 1909), and *The Dash for the South Pole* (Victor, 1909).

50. Bloom, *Gender on Ice*, 78.

51. Press accounts even described Byrd's interaction with amateur radio operators in America. "Bronx Amateur Picks Up Byrd's Arctic Message," *New York Herald Tribune*, May 24, 1926, 13; Everett M. Walker, "Radio Was Byrd's Only Contact with the Outside World," *New York Herald Tribune*, July 4, 1926, SM3A; "Byrd's Radio Worked Always on Pole Flight," *New York Herald Tribune*, June 27, 1926, 18; Raimund E. Goerler, ed., *To the Pole: The Diary and Notebook of Richard E. Byrd* (Columbus: Ohio State University Press, 1998), 24.

52. Robert N. Matuozzi, "Richard Byrd, Polar Exploration, and the Media," *Virginia Magazine of History and Biography* 110, no. 2 (2002): 209–36.

53. "2 Mountain Ranges Discovered by Byrd," *Washington Post*, June 29, 1929, 1.

54. Byrd wrote that they dwelt a "troglodytic existence." Richard Evelyn Byrd, *Little America* (New York: Putnam's Sons, 1930), 177, 158.

55. "Radio Destined to Play Role in Byrd Antarctic Expedition," *New York Herald Tribune*, September 2, 1928, G1. See also Stephen D. Perry, "CBS's Long Distance Radio Experiment: Broadcasting the Byrd Expedition from Little America," *Journal of Radio and Audio Media* 21, no. 1 (2014): 80–95.

56. "Radio Has Lead Role in Byrd's Expedition," *New York Times*, August 5, 1928, 124.

57. See the advertisements in *Radio Broadcast* 15, no. 5 (1929): 348; *Radio Broadcast* 14, no. 3 (1929): 205; *Radio Broadcast* 10, no. 3 (1927): 304; and *Radio Broadcast* 9, no. 4 (1926): 348.

58. "Hour's Amusement Broadcast to Byrd," *New York Times*, May 19, 1929, 16; "Radio Carries Cheer to Byrd in Antarctic," *New York Times*, October 6, 1929, 1; "Byrd's Mother Talks to Son in Antarctic," *Atlanta Constitution*, November 17, 1929, 4; "Stations Will Send Messages to Byrd Crew," *New York Herald Tribune*, October 7, 1928, G1. "It was good to hear the voices of our friends speaking," Byrd wrote, "but there were moments when we stirred uneasily. The last place in the world to which one should send a mushy message is the Antarctic; whatever note it may strike in the heart of the intrepid explorer

to which it is addressed, it brings only pain—severe pain—to his fellows" (*Little America*, 220).

59. "Byrd to Open Radio Show," *Los Angeles Times*, September 2, 1929, A1; "Radio Miracle Launches Show," *Los Angeles Times*, September 3, 1929, A1; "Byrd by Radio Lights 'Poor Richard' Lamp," *New York Times*, January 17, 1930, 3.

60. "Radio to Play Stellar Role in Byrd's South Pole Conquest," *New York Times*, March 18, 1928, 161. See also Orrin E. Dunlap Jr., "Radio Made New Magic in Byrd Polar Flights," *New York Times*, February 9, 1930, sec. 20, p. 5; and Richard E. Byrd, "Radio Invaluable to Byrd at the Bottom of the World," *Boston Globe*, September 22, 1929, B11.

61. Arnheim, *Radio*, 14.

62. "World Hears Byrd's Fame," *Los Angeles Times*, March 12, 1930, 1. See also "Byrd's Voice Leaps over 10,000 Miles from New Zealand," *New York Times*, March 12, 1930, 1; Russell Owen, "Byrd Party Heard Well in Dunedin," *New York Times*, March 12, 1930, 22.

63. C.E. Butterfield, "Byrd, More Than 10,000 Miles Away, Talks with Adolph Ochs in America over Radio Chain," *Olean (NY) Herald*, March 11, 1930, 1.

64. H.I. Phillips, "The Once Over: The Byrd Expedition Broadcast," *Washington Post*, March 14, 1930, 6.

65. Thoreau, *Walden*, 40.

66. "America Hears Byrd and Owen Speak at Dunedin," *Boston Globe*, March 12, 1930, 5; "St. Louis Hears Broadcast," *New York Times*, March 12, 1930, 22; "Capital Listens to Byrd," *New York Times*, March 12, 1930, 22. See also Orrin Dunlap Jr., "Byrd's Voice Flies Back to America on Radio's Wings," *New York Times*, March 16, 1930, sec. 10, p. 16.

67. "Nation Will Hear Byrd from Dunedin," *New York Times*, March 11, 1930, 17. Another writer worried that the connection between Wellington and Sydney would be exposed to "static disturbances and the electrical uncertainties which have led to the abandonment of long waves for long distance service.... This was the only doubtful link in the system" ("Byrd's Voice Leaps," 1).

68. Kahn, *Earth Sound Earth Signal*, 6.

69. DeLong, *Voyage of the Jeannette*, 1:494. On the crewmember Charles W. Chipp's study of auroras, see Raymond Lee Newcomb, *Our Lost Explorers* (Hartford, CT: American, 1883), 183–84.

70. Kahn, *Earth Sound Earth Signal*, 14–16.

71. "World Echo Heard in Byrd Broadcast," *New York Times*, March 12, 1930, 22. See also "Byrd Men Study the Radio 'Roof,'" *New York Times*, November 10, 1929, sec. 20, p. 9; and Dunlap, "Byrd's Voice," sec. 10, p. 16.

72. See also the discussion of Clyde D. Wagoner's voice in the round-the-world broadcast a few months after the Byrd Dunedin communication. "Talking to Oneself around the World," *Literary*, September 20, 1930, 24; "Voice Rounds World in Eighth of Second," *New York Times*, July 1, 1930, 36.

73. Lacey, *Listening Publics*, 91.

74. Goerler, *To the Pole*, 123.

75. "Radio Plays Big Part in Opening New World Fair," *Chicago Daily Tribune*, May 27, 1934, 6; Byrd, *Alone*, 158–59; "Byrd to Address Opening Day Fair Crowds by Radio," *Chicago Daily Tribune*, April 21, 1934, 10; "Chicago Is Ready for Fair Reopening," *New York Times*, May 26, 1934, 13; "Byrd Rings Liberty Bell by Electrical Impulse," *New York Times*, July 5, 1934, 10; "Medal Awarded to Byrd over Radio," *New York Times*, April 1, 1934, 30.

76. Byrd, *Little America*, 91.

77. Richard E. Byrd, *Discovery* (New York: Putnam's Sons, 1935), 167; Goerler, *To the Pole*, 11; Matuozzi, "Richard Byrd," 231.

78. Byrd, *Alone*, 3–4, 7 (reference to *Walden* on page 32).

79. "Byrd Minimizes Perils," *New York Times*, April 16, 1934, 5.

80. Byrd, *Alone*, 103, 120. The reference is to a passage in Thoreau's journals: "My body is all sentient. As I go here or there, I am tickled by this or that I come in contact with, as if I touched the wires of a battery.... The age of miracles is each moment thus returned." *The Journal, 1837–1861* (New York: New York Review of Books, 2009), 349.

81. Byrd, *Alone*, 105, 138–39.

82. Thibaud, "Sonic Composition," in Bull and Back, *Auditory Culture Reader*, 337. Rudolf Arnheim observed, for example, that radio broadcasting tended to become "the auditory foil of daily occupations" since sound follows listeners wherever they turn (*Radio*, 8–9). Elsaesser and Hagener write about the "velcro" quality of sound, which allows it to "cling to any material substance, but also to any semantic substance." They continue, "sound is always poised on the brink of referentiality, but being transient, fleeting and multidirectional, it is also volatile and fickle in the way it attaches itself, or indeed detaches itself from, an image as well as a meaning" (*Film Theory, 148*).

83. See Kahn, *Earth Sound Earth Signal*, 45–46.

84. Byrd, *Alone*, 65. On carbon monoxide, see Goerler, *To the Pole*, 126; and Lisle A. Rose, "Exploring a Secret Land," *Virginia Magazine of History and Biography* 110, no. 2 (2002): 196.

85. Byrd, *Alone*, 175, 181; "Epic of Solitude Related by Byrd," *New York Times*, October 28, 1934, N1. Byrd writes, "I feel as if I had to sink roots into a foreign soil and re-order not only my own life but my philosophy as well. It's like being tossed on a different planet."

86. Byrd, *Little America*, 198.

87. Byrd, *Alone*, 146.

88. Warren R. Hofstra, "Richard E. Byrd and the Legacy of Polar Exploration," *Virginia Magazine of History and Biography* 110, no. 2 (2002): 148.

89. Andrew Leman, e-mail interview, August 30, 2013.

90. The six other shows from the *Dark Adventure* series are "The Dunwich Horror" (2008), "The Shadow Out of Time" (2008), "The Shadow over Innsmouth" (2008), "The Call of Cthulhu" (2012), "The Case of Charles Dexter Ward" (2013), and "The Colour Out of Space" (2013).

91. August Derleth, *HPL: A Memoir* (New York: Abramson, 1945), 73. Lovecraft writes, "All my stories, unconnected as they may be, are based on the

fundamental lore or legend that this world was inhabited at one time by another race who, in practicing black magic, lost their foothold and were expelled, yet live on outside ever ready to take possession of this earth again" (quoted in Derleth, *HPL*, 69–70).

92. Charles P. Mitchell, *The Complete H.P. Lovecraft Filmography* (Westport, CT: Greenwood, 2001), 7–8. Mitchell makes a parallel with the dark pessimism of film noir.

93. S.T. Joshi and David E. Schultz, eds., *H.P. Lovecraft: Lord of a Visible World, an Autobiography in Letters* (Athens: Ohio University Press, 2000), 346.

94. T. Morton, *Ecological Thought*, 50.

95. Lovecraft, *Mountains of Madness*, 3.

96. S.T. Joshi and David E. Schultz, *An H.P. Lovecraft Encyclopedia* (Westport, CT: Greenwood, 2001), 10. Lovecraft describes his "weird fascination" with "pathless realms of remote wonder" and, in particular, the Antarctic continent (347). Michel Houellebecq points out how, in "At the Mountains of Madness," Lovecraft "insists on conveying the latitude and longitude at each point in the drama" but at the same time "brings to life entities well beyond our space-time continuum. He wants to create a sense of precarious balance; the characters move between precise coordinates, but they are oscillating at the edge of an abyss." *H.P. Lovecraft: Against the World, against Life* (San Francisco: Believer Books, 2005), 79.

97. Lovecraft, *Mountains of Madness*, 14, 29. We might compare Lovecraft's prose to Thoreau's famous account of climbing Mount Katahdin in Maine: a "vast, Titanic" place where humans were not intended to be, and that caused reason to be "dispersed and shadowy.... There was there felt the presence of a force not bound to be kind to man. It was a place for heathenism and superstitious rites" *The Maine Woods* (1864; repr., Princeton: Princeton University Press, 2004), 64–65, 70–71. Schrepfer writes that Thoreau's experience on Katahdin was one of "sublime horror" (*Nature's Alters*, 44). John Muir described glaciers as cathedrals but also as "monster glittering serpents ... crawling through gorge and valley"; by forming the landscape, they had a Cthulhu-like influence over human beings (*Travels in Alaska*, 94, 3).

98. Lovecraft, *Mountains of Madness*, 17–19.

99. Verma, *Theater of the Mind*, 63, 68, 72. For other discussions of radio and an intimate address, see Loviglio, *Radio's Intimate Public*; and Allison McCracken, "Real Men Don't Sing Ballads," in *Soundtrack Available: Essays on Film and Popular Music*, ed. Pamela Robertson Wojcik and Arthur Knight (Durham: Duke University Press, 2001), 105–33. Verma defines audioposition as "the place for the listener that is created by coding foregrounds and backgrounds" (*Theater of the Mind*, 35).

100. Lovecraft, *Mountains of Madness*, 43–44, 47.

101. Mitchell, *Lovecraft Filmography*, 7–8. Furthermore, Lovecraft's narratives often stretch over many years or generations, lack central female characters and romantic interest, and feature professors, librarians, and anthropologists as

protagonists: social types that do not lend themselves to easy identification for a broad audience.

102. Graham Harman, *Weird Realism: Lovecraft and Philosophy* (Winchester, UK: Zero Books, 2012), 26. Harman writes, "how difficult it would be to do justice to Lovecraft in cinematic form.... Any film would be forced to commit itself to some distinct appearance of Cthulhu, even though Lovecraft's prose lets us know how impossible this is.... Even in the best case, the most we could do would be to applaud in amusement at the director's jolly good effort. In the strict sense, any filmed version of Lovecraft would fall short of capturing his allusiveness" (80).

103. Hand, *Terror on the Air*, 15.

104. Lovecraft, *Mountains of Madness*, 62.

105. Bakhtin writes that "the castle is saturated through and through with ... the time of the historical past" (*Dialogic Imagination*, 245–46). In "Some Notes on a Nonentity" (1930), Lovecraft writes that, as a child, he was obsessed with literature of the eighteenth century: "one effect of it was to make me feel subtly out of place in the modern period, and consequently to think of *time* as a mystical, portentous thing in which all sorts of unexpected wonders might be discovered" (quoted in Joshi and Schultz, *H. P. Lovecraft*, 346). This temporal dislocation was connected to his interest in natural spaces: "I tend to live more and more in the past—since Providence, though populous, has preserved a phenomenal number of rural and semi-rural oases which link it to its picturesque beginnings" (quoted in Derleth, *HPL*, 32).

106. Lovecraft, *Mountains of Madness*, 61–62, 64, 96–97, 95–96.

107. Lovecraft, quoted in Joshi and Schultz, *H. P. Lovecraft*, 209. Elsewhere, Lovecraft defined "outsideness" as "the aesthetic crystallization of that burning and inextinguishable feeling of mixed wonder and oppression which the sensitive imagination experiences upon scaling itself and its restrictions against the vast and provocative abyss of the unknown." He found that quality embodied by scientists such as Copernicus, Newton, and Einstein, as well as polar explorers like Amundsen, Scott, Shackleton, and Byrd (quoted in Joshi and Schultz, *H. P. Lovecraft*, 258–59).

108. T. Morton, *Ecological Thought*, 61.

109. Harman, *Weird Realism*, 148. Harman also complains that, in "The Shadow Out of Time," when Lovecraft gives a name to one of the star-headed creatures of Antarctica, "all needed distance from the Elder Things is now lost. They are depicted not only as inhabitants of a history filled with rises and declines too much like our own, but even as potential conversation partners who can be addressed by name.... Lovecraft is clearly losing his edge" (228).

110. Ibid., 228.

111. Houellebecq argues that race hatred fueled Lovecraft's work, stemming in particular from his unhappy experiences in New York City, where he referred to "Italo-Semitico-Mongoloid" inhabitants. "No longer the WASP's well-bred racism; it is the brutal hatred of a trapped animal who is forced to share his cage with other different and frightening creatures" (*H. P. Lovecraft*, 107).

112. M.M. Bakhtin, *Speech Genres and Other Late Essays* (Austin: University of Texas Press, 1986), 6–7. See also Dwight Conquergood's concept of "dialogic performance," which imagines a way to bring "self and other together even while it holds them apart," affirming "cross-cultural accessibility without glossing very real differences." "Performing as a Moral Act: Ethical Dimensions of the Ethnography of Performance," *Literature in Performance* 5, no. 2 (1985): 9.

113. Houellebecq, *H.P. Lovecraft*, 70. On "Whisperer in Darkness" and the phonograph, see Joshi and Schultz, *H.P. Lovecraft*, 208.

114. H.P. Lovecraft, "The Whisperer in Darkness," in *The Best of H.P. Lovecraft* (New York: Random House, 1982), 153, 180. On the phonographic allegory of "Whisperer in Darkness," see Derleth, *HPL*, 35–36.

115. Lovecraft, *Mountains of Madness*, 101, 96–97, 43.

116. Ibid., 96–97. Leman of *Dark Adventure* stated that the "tekeli-li" sounds of the shoggoths were some of their best work: "Coming up with a sound that was non-human and non-verbal but still conveyed something like syllables was an achievement" (Leman, interview).

117. Arnheim, *Radio*, 195.

118. We might say that the wind makes audible Lovecraft's uneasy position between the genres of science fiction and horror, given Vivian Sobchack's argument that while the "monster" in horror films tends to be personalized, the "creature" in science fiction films is less personalized and lacks a psyche. Screening Space (New Brunswick, NJ: Rutgers University Press, 2004), 30–32.

119. Joscelyn Godwin, *Arktos: The Polar Myth in Science, Symbolism, and Nazi Survival* (London: Thames and Hudson, 1993), 106–7. See also Godwin, *Athanasius Kircher*, 88; and Edgar Allan Poe, *The Narrative of Arthur Gordon Pym of Nantucket* (1838; repr., New York: Modern Library, 2002), 179.

120. Kafton-Minkel, *Subterranean Worlds*, 250. On Symmes, see Sachs, *Humboldt*, 121–22, 283.

121. Thoreau, *Walden*, 213–14.

122. "Symmes' Hole: The Theory of a Hollow World," *Cincinnati Enquirer*, July 25, 1881, 8; DeLong, *Voyage of the Jeannette*, 1:69; "Symmes' Hole," *Cincinnati Enquirer*, November 12, 1875, 5; "Captain John Cleve Symmes," *Ladies' Repository* 31 (August 1871): 133; "Symmes' Hole," *Cincinnati Enquirer*, September 11, 1878, 4. John Cleves Symmes's son Americus revived the theory in the 1870s. The *New York Times* reported in 1878 that "there has been a very marked revival of interest in Symmes' Hole, and there are not a few persons who openly express their belief in it." Planetary Holes," *New York Times*, June 14, 1878, 4. On Symmes's theory having a "respite in the last few years," tied to the activities of his son, see "Search for the Pole," *New York Tribune*, September 2, 1909, 2. One account imagined the inner world as a place where "the mastodon, extinct to us, disporteth in all the glory of his generally assumed antediluvian existence, where man assumes those magnificent physical proportions now only attributable to the prehistoric races." "A New Polar Expedition," *Cincinnati Enquirer*, January 13, 1884, 12.

123. On extraterrestrialism as a "safety valve" that "enables avoidance of environmental and social problems," see Sturgeon, *Environmentalism*, 81.

124. M.J. Simpson, *Hitchhiker* (Boston: Charles, 2003), 90.

125. Ursula Heise understands this episode as a metaphor for our own cultural moment, in which the "entire planet becomes graspable as one's own local backyard" (*Sense of Place*, 3–4). On the 1970s as the "Doomsday Decade," see Kirkpatrick Sale, *The Green Revolution* (New York: Hill and Wang, 1993), 29.

126. Adams, quoted in Simpson, *Hitchhiker*, 109.

127. Debbie Barham, "Douglas Adams's Guide to the Hitchhiker's Guide to the Galaxy," *BBC Radio 4*, March 5, 1998.

128. Douglas Adams and Mark Carwardine, *Last Chance to See* (New York: Ballantine, 1990), 1–2. *Last Chance to See* was produced in the late 1980s, when concern about the destruction of the rainforests in Amazonia starting to shift to that of greenhouse gases, global warming, and the destruction of forests as carbon sinks. "The idea of global climate change articulated the new realization that places far apart from each other were still connected for their basic survival, especially through the circulation of air and water" (Tsing, *Friction*, 102).

129. Adams, quoted in Simpson, *Hitchhiker*, 246. He added, "If you take a film crew, basically you have to organize it like a military operation, and that would have fundamentally changed the nature of what we were doing."

130. The irony is that, despite this lightweight travel, the team often discovered that "remote areas" no longer exist, that there is no outside, no beyond. After a long and arduous trip to reach Komodo Island, for example, they were surprised to discover a helipad for bringing in European tourists, and on Robinson Crusoe Island off the coast of Chile, they found teenagers who watch American cop shows on satellite television and listen to pop music on portable tape players.

131. Adams and Carwardine, *Last Chance to See*, 2; Simpson, *Hitchhiker*, 245.

132. Martin Cropper, "Bush Brownie Points," *Times* (London), October 7, 1989; Megan Turner, "Galaxy Man Looks Earthwards," *Sunday Mail*, December 2, 1990; Simon Evans, "The Hitchhiker's Guide to Strange Animals," *Advertiser*, December 1, 1990. See also Bryan Rogers, "Discoveries in an Alien World," *Times* (London), November 3, 1990. All accessed December 29, 2014, and available at www.lexisnexis.com/hottopics/lnacademic.

133. Adams, quoted in Turner, "Galaxy Man," x.

134. Adams, quoted in Simpson, *Hitchhiker*, 251; Barham, "Douglas Adams's Guide"; J. Romney, "Hitchhiker Lands Back on Earth," *Herald Sun*, January 11, 1992, 54. Adams said that one of his main goals was to encourage people to overcome "species prejudice": "Just as white, Western Anglo Saxon males have gradually had to learn that we have to treat different races equally and the different sexes equally and so on, the same applies to different species" (quoted in Romney, "Hitchhiker Lands," 54).

135. See Crisell's arguments about how radio can convey objectified fantasy, his example being characters that are plants (*Understanding Radio*, 158–59).

136. Adams and Carwardine, *Last Chance to See*, 166, 174.

137. Adams, quoted in Simpson, *Hitchhiker*, 250.

138. Adams and Carwardine, *Last Chance to See*, 203. See also David Quammen, *The Song of the Dodo* (New York: Scribner, 1996), 606–7. During the voyage of the Corwin, John Muir's understanding of glaciation was aided by his experience on Herald Island. Muir called the island "one of the most interesting and significant of the monuments of geographical change effected by general glaciation" (*Cruise of the Corwin*, 153, 250). On Wrangel Island a species of dwarf woolly mammoth lasted seven thousand years longer than anywhere else and was still alive four thousand years ago (Weisman, *World without Us*, 77). On islands in Western consciousness, see John Gillis, *Islands of the Mind* (New York: Palgrave, 2004). On islands and finiteness, see Walker and Bellingham, *Island Environments*, 3, 5; and Adams and Carwardine, *Last Chance to See*, 203. On the Maldive Islands as an "endangered nation," see McKibben, *End of Nature*, 95–96. On oceanic islands as an "allegory of a whole world," see Richard H. Grove, *Green Imperialism* (Cambridge: Cambridge University Press, 1995), 8–9.

139. Thoreau, *Walden*, 213–14, quoted in Ray, *Walden x 40*, 156–57.

140. Sachs writes of a need for balance between "cosmos and hearth. It is clearly important to cultivate connections to particular pieces of land and to particular heritages and traditions. But it is also important to get lost in the world" (*Humboldt*, 351).

CONCLUSION. THE RUN-OUT GROOVE

1. Mark Lewisohn, *The Complete Beatles Recording Sessions* (New York: Sterling, 1988), 99.

2. *Abbey Road* engineer Geoff Emerick remembered that the group was recorded twice on two tracks of multitrack tape making noises and saying random, nonsense statements. "We chopped up the tape, put it back together, played it backwards and threw it in." It was John Lennon who suggested that they "insert a high-pitch whistle especially for dogs" (Lewisohn, *Beatles Recording Sessions*, 109).

3. Bakhtin, *Speech Genres*, 76.

4. Maxwell and Miller, *Greening the Media*, 9, 17–18.

5. Donna J. Haraway, *Simians, Cyborgs, and Women* (New York: Routledge, 1991), 190, 196.

6. Laura Dassow Walls, *Seeing New Worlds* (Madison: University of Wisconsin Press, 1995), 11.

7. Parks, "Earth Observation," 304.

8. Tsing, *Friction*, 161. Rob Nixon writes of "the value of multiple publics as we strive, among other things, to foster imaginative coalitions that may help redress environmental injustice" (*Slow Violence*, 260).

9. Tsing, *Friction*, 267. David W. Orr writes, "the study of environmental problems is an exercise in despair unless it is regarded as only a preface to the

study, design, and implementation of solutions." *Ecological Literacy* (Albany: State University of New York Press, 1992), 94.

10. Ian Bogost, *Alien Phenomenology; or, What It's Like to Be a Thing* (Minneapolis: University of Minnesota Press, 2012), 92–93. See also Vicki Mayer on "below the line" labor as creative practice in *Below the Line* (Durham: Duke University Press, 2011).

11. Thomas Thwaites, *The Toaster Project* (New York: Princeton Architectural Press, 2011), 13, 15, 35.

12. Ibid., 33.

13. James S. Barstow Jr., "Sarnoff Shows 50-Cent Phonograph to Carry Messages Past Iron Curtain," *New York Herald Tribune*, November 11, 1955, A1. See also "50-Cent Phonograph to Fight Reds Unveiled," *Los Angeles Times*, November 11, 1955, 6.

14. David Sarnoff, "Program for a Political Offensive against World Communism," memo, Radio Corporation of America, April 5, 1955, 31, in the author's collection; Radio Corporation of America, "Hand-Operated Phonograph," November 1955, folder 7, box 33, "Records of Gospel Recordings, Inc.—Collection 36," Billy Graham Center Archives, Wheaton, IL (hereafter cited as BGC). See also "A Cold War Weapon for 50 Cents," *Radio Age*, January 1956, 18.

15. Radio Corporation of America, "Hand-Operated Phonograph."

16. Haidee Wasson, "Protocols of Portability," in *Film History* 25, nos. 1–2 (2013): 240.

17. Parikka, *What Is Media Archaeology?*, 13–14.

18. Schumacher, *Small Is Beautiful*, 35.

19. Ridderhof recalled the missionary saying, "if only they could hear this in their own language, what an impact it would make." Phyllis Thompson, *Capturing Voices* (London: Hodder and Stoughton, 1978), 47.

20. "Record Players for Gospel Recordings," memo, June 4, 1965, folder 46, box 34, "Records of Gospel Recordings, Inc.—Collection 36," BGC.

21. P. Thompson, *Capturing Voices*, 119, 138.

22. See "The 'CardTalk' Cardboard Record Player," Global Recordings Network, accessed January 12, 2015, http://globalrecordings.net/en/cardtalk. See also Nicolas Collins, *Handmade Electronic Music* (New York: Routledge, 2009), 288; and the PBS documentary about the Global Recordings Network, *The Tailenders*, directed by Adele Horne (Blooming Grove, NY: New Day Films, 2005). On July 25, 2006, the film aired on PBS *POV*.

23. Raymond Williams, *Problems*, 55.

24. "Discs on Duty," Gospel Recordings promotional materials, ca. 1946–55, folder 22, box 34, "Records of Gospel Recordings, Inc.—Collection 36," BGC.

25. P. Thompson, *Capturing Voices*, 52.

26. On intermediate technologies, see Schumacher, *Small Is Beautiful*, 163.

27. Arman Shehabi, Ben Walker, and Eric Masanet, "The Energy and Greenhouse-Gas Implications of Internet Video Streaming in the United States," *Environmental Research Letters*, no. 9 (2014): 9.

28. Eco-media scholarship can help us to think through "the inextricable ties between the growth in network infrastructure and the individual's desire to access huge amounts of data from any device, at any time." See Carruth, "Digital Cloud," 358. For Sontag's conservationist approach to images, see *On Photography*, 180. On "voluntary simplicity" as "a partial restraint in some directions in order to secure greater abundance of life in other directions," see Richard B. Gregg, "The Value of Voluntary Simplicity," Pendle Hill Essays 3 (Wallingford, PA: Pendle Hill, 1936), available at www.soilandhealth.org/03sov/0304spiritpsych/030409simplicity/SimplicityFrame.html. Juliet Schor's notion of plenitude "puts ecological and social functioning at its core, but it is not a paradigm of sacrifice. To the contrary, it involves a way of life that will yield more well-being than sticking to business as usual, which has led both the natural and economic environments into decline" (*Plenitude*, 2). See also Dunaway, "Seeing Global Warming," 24–25.

29. "Tiny 50c Hand Phonograph Can Take U.S. Voice to Reds," in BGC; "Tiny, Cheap Phonograph Enlists in War of Words," in BGC.

30. Evan Eisenberg, *The Recording Angel* (New York: Penguin Books, 1988), 147.

31. Thwaites, *Toaster Project*, 34–35.

32. Sherry Turkle, *Alone Together* (New York: Basic Books, 2011), 294.

33. Thoreau, *Walden*, 221.

34. See Collins, *Handmade Electronic Music*.

35. My instructions are based on those provided by Christopher DeLaurenti as "Flap-o-Phone Construction and Assembly Instructions," Canadian Electroacoustic Community, accessed January 10, 2015, http://cec.sonus.ca/econtact/14_3/delaurenti_buildaflapophone.html. See also DeLaurenti's website: http://delaurenti.net/flap/; and DeLaurenti, "The Flap-o-Phone, a Site-Specific Turntable," Canadian Electroacoustic Community, accessed January 10, 2015, http://cec.sonus.ca/econtact/14_3/delaurenti_flapophone.html

36. Haraway, *Companion Species Manifesto*, 7.

37. See "The Hartz Group History."

38. Haraway, *Companion Species Manifesto*, 2; Vicki Hearne, *Animal Happiness* (New York: HarperCollins, 1994), 171. See also Sabloff, *Natural World*, 182–83; Italo Calvino, *Mr. Palomar* (Orlando: Harcourt, 1985), 27; and LaBelle, *Lexicon of the Mouth*, 179.

39. Haraway, *When Species Meet*, 262–63.

40. For Haraway, compound technologies are composed of "human beings or parts of human beings, other organisms in part or whole, machines of many kinds, or other sorts of entrained things made to work in the technological compound of conjoined forces" (*When Species Meet*, 250).

41. Eno, "Ambient Music," in Cox and Warner, *Audio Culture*, 97.

42. Hearne, *Animal Happiness*, 4.

43. Haberman, "Faces in the Trees," 184. See also Bennett, *Vibrant Matter*, 99; and Fudge, *Animal*, 76.

44. Lacey, *Listening Publics*, 165.

45. Jennifer Wolch, "Zoopolis," in *Animal Geographies*, ed. Jennifer Wolch and Jody Emel (London: Verso, 1998), 124.

46. Bernie Krause, *The Great Animal Orchestra* (London: Profile Books, 2012), 97. Think, for example, of the rhetorical importance of whale song in the Save the Whales movement.

47. See Sarah Whatmore, "Hybrid Geographies: Rethinking the 'Human' in Human Geography," in *Human Geography Today*, ed. Doreen Massey, John Allen, and Philip Sarre (Cambridge: Polity, 1999), 33.

48. Massey, *For Space*, 98. On animal geography, see Chris Philo and Chris Wilbert, eds. *Animal Spaces, Beastly Places* (London: Routledge, 2000), 5; and Heidi J. Nast, "Critical Pet Studies?" in *Antipode* 38, no. 5 (2006): 897. On the "unnatural histories" of animals within the human environment, see Nigel Rothfels, *Savages and Beasts* (Baltimore: Johns Hopkins University Press, 2002), 6. On cranes, see the International Crane Foundation website, www.savingcranes.org.

49. My language here echoes Turkle, in *Alone Together*, 294–95.

50. Muir, *Wilderness World*, 144–45, 167, 185–86.

51. Steven Feld writes, "bird sounds are simultaneously heard as indicators of the avifauna and as 'talk' from the dead" (*Sound and Sentiment*, 30).

52. Aldo Leopold, *A Sand County Almanac* (New York: Ballantine Books, 1966), 102–3.

53. Cronon, "Trouble with Wilderness," in Cronon, *Uncommon Ground*, 88, 86.

54. See Frauke Behrendt, "Creative Sonification of Mobility and Sonic Interaction with Urban Space," in Gopinath and Stanyek, *Oxford Handbook*, 2:189.

55. I am adapting Connor, who writes, "The self defined in terms of hearing rather than sight is a self imagined not as a point, but as a membrane; not as a picture, but as a channel through which voices, noises and music travel" ("Modern Auditory I," in Porter, *Rewriting the Self*, 206–7).

56. Nicas, "Metal Detectors."

57. Allen, *Glittering Prospects*, 87. Allen might have been thinking about the 1954 film *The Beachcomber*, in which Charles Laughton plays the eponymous protagonist, who is an unemployed, lascivious drunk. Merkitch writes that most people imagined the beachcomber to be a "lone person in short, tattered pants ... and shaggy windblown hair" (*Beachcomber's Handbook*, 11).

58. Ibid., 13, 15–16.

59. Bull, *Sound Moves*, 3, 9, 18. David Morley asserts that the Walkman is "intrinsically solipsistic" since it is used for "switching off unwanted interaction with others" and for insulating users from geographic place, functioning as a "psychic cocoon" and protective "carapace" of privacy in the public realm. "Domesticating Dislocation," in Berry, Kim, and Spigel, *Electronic Elsewheres*, 10–11, 13.

60. Beer, "Tune Out," 858.

61. Sobchack, *Address of the Eye*; Laura U. Marks, *The Skin of the Film* (Durham: Duke University Press, 2000), 200; Jennifer M. Barker, *The Tactile Eye: Touch and the Cinematic Experience* (Berkeley: University of California Press, 2009); Vivian Sobchack, *Carnal Thoughts: Embodiment and Moving Image Culture* (Berkeley: University of California Press, 2004).

62. See "Diggers Dictionary: A Glossary of Terms," *Diggers*, National Geographic Channel, accessed January 10, 2015, http://channel.nationalgeographic.com/channel/diggers/articles/diggers-dictionary/.

63. "Pres. Holgate Urges Obedience to Drill," *Daily Northwestern*, February 20, 1919, 1; "ROTC Replaced SATC Drill Begins on Monday," *Daily Northwestern*, February 6, 1919, 1; Phyllis Murphy, "Nye, Mass Meeting Climax Peace Week," *Daily Northwestern*, April 21, 1939, 1; "Mass Rally to Celebrate Peace Day," *Daily Northwestern*, April 20, 1939, 1; Harold F. Williamson and Payson S. Wild, *Northwestern University: A History* (Evanston: Northwestern University Press, 1976), 339, 328, 342; Phil Lentz, "Northwestern Strikes," *Daily Northwestern*, May 6, 1970, 1; "Today Is Earth Day," *Daily Northwestern*, April 22, 1970, 1; Greg Hinz, "Festival to Activate Environmental Concern," *Daily Northwestern*, May 1, 1970, 1.

64. Wünschelrute (1835), by Joseph von Eichendorff, can be found in Martin Geck, *Robert Schumann: The Life and Work of a Romantic Composer* (Chicago: University of Chicago Press, 2013), 62. Thanks to Brigitte Weingart for bringing this poem to my attention.

65. Orr, *Ecological Literacy*, 103.

66. Behrendt, "Sound of Locative Media," 288. See also Behrendt, "Auditory Edges," in Breitsameter and Soller-Eckert, *Global Composition*, 158. McKibben argues that, in an era of peak oil, when we need alternatives to expensive, high-carbon emission international travel, "the kind of trip you can take with the click of a mouse" will be called on more and more to substitute for jet travel, making the Internet "the window left ajar in our communities so new ideas can blow in and old prejudices blow out" (*Eaarth*, 205).

67. Westerkamp, "Soundwalking," in Carlyle, *Autumn Leaves*, 49. For Andra McCartney, soundwalking is a "creative and research practice" that involves listening while moving through a place at a walking pace; it is "concerned with the relationship between soundwalkers and their surrounding sonic environment." "Soundwalking: Creating Moving Environmental Sound Narratives," in Gopinath and Stanyek, *Oxford Handbook*, 2:212. See also Schafer, *Soundscape*, 212–13.

68. See Janet Cardiff and Mirjam Schaub, *The Walk Book* (Vienna: Thyssen-Bornemisza Art Contemporary, 2005); and Tina Rigyb Hanssen, "The Whispering Voice," in *Music Sound and the Moving Image* 4, no. 1 (2010): 39–54.

69. McCartney, "Soundwalking," in Gopinath and Stanyek, *Oxford Handbook*, 2:214.

70. Wittgenstein wrote that "the only way to do philosophy is to do everything twice. . . . I'm like a guide showing you how to find your way round

London.... After I have taken you many journeys through the city, in all sorts of directions, we shall have passed through any given street a number of times—each time traversing the street as part of a different journey." Quoted in Ray, *Walden x 40*, 8.

71. R. Murray Schafer, "Radical Radio," in Strauss, *Radiotext(e)*, 297; MacDonald, "Ecocinema Experience," and David Ingram, "The Aesthetics and Ethics of Eco-Film Criticism," both in Rust, Monani, and Cubitt, *Ecocinema Theory*, 19–20, 39, 47.

72. Bozak, *Cinematic Footprint*, 165–67.

73. Crisell, *Understanding Radio*, 155; Giddens, *Climate Change*, 2.

74. Raymond Williams writes that it would be a sign that we were "beginning to think in some necessary ways" when economics and ecology were considered a "single discipline" (*Problems*, 84).

75. Andre Gorz, *Ecologica* (London: Seagull Books, 2010), 27. Dipesh Chakraberty writes, "the crisis of climate change has been necessitated by the high-energy-consuming models of society that capitalist industrialization has created and promoted" ("Climate of History," 216–17). Tsing asks, why should one include the poor of the world—whose carbon footprint is small anyway—by use of such all-inclusive terms as *species* or *mankind* when the blame for the current crisis should be squarely laid at the door of the rich nations in the first place and of the richer classes in the poorer ones?" (*Friction*, 105). By "slow violence" I refer to Nixon's discussion of the "violence that occurs gradually and out of sight, violence of delayed destruction that is dispersed across time and space, an attritional violence that is typically not viewed as violence at all" (*Slow Violence*, 2).

76. James P. Kraft, *Stage to Studio: Musicians and the Sound Revolution, 1890–1950* (Baltimore: Johns Hopkins University Press, 1996), 2. Rick Altman notes that between 1880 and 1910 musicians constituted "one of the fastest-growing professions in the United States" (*Silent Film Sound*, 28).

77. Martin Scherzinger, "Divisible Mobility: Music in an Age of Cloud Computing," in Gopinath and Stanyek, *Oxford Handbook*, 1:96.

78. Jackson, *Prosperity without Growth*, 63, 128–30, 196. On "growing the caring economy," see Naomi Klein, *This Changes Everything* (New York: Simon and Schuster, 2014), 93.

79. Bill McKibben, *Deep Economy* (New York: St. Martin's Griffin, 2007), 2, 137. Huntemann writes that "radio is the most local of the mass media. Geographically bound by the physical properties of electromagnetic waves, radio has traditionally been defined by its broadcast range." "Promise Diminished," in Squier, *Communities of the Air*, 78.

80. Neil Verma, "#WOTW75," *Velvet Light Trap*, no. 74 (Fall 2014), 81.

81. T. Morton, *Hyperobjects*, 128.

82. Lars von Trier and Thomas Vinterberg, "The Dogma 95 Manifesto and Vow of Chastity," *p.o.v., a Danish Journal of Film Studies*, no. 10 (December 2000), http://pov.imv.au.dk/Issue_10/section_1/artc1A.html.

83. Maxwell and Miller, "Ecological Ethics," 334–35.

84. Ray Bradbury, "There Will Come Soft Rains," Collier's Weekly, May 6, 1950, 34; Bradbury, "There Will Come Soft Rains/Zero Hour," adapted for radio by George Lefferts, Dimension X, NBC, June 17, 1950.

85. Picker, *Victorian Soundscapes*, 140. On the needle stick at the end of the film version of Graham Greene's *Brighton Rock* (1947), see the discussion in James Naremore, *More Than Night* (Berkeley: University of California Press, 1998), 70–76. See also Ivan Kreilkamp, "A Voice without a Body: The Phonographic Logic of Heart of Darkness," in *Victorian Studies* 40, no. 2 (1997): 211–44.

86. Frederick Buell writes that the "environmental crisis is no longer an apocalypse rushing toward a herd of sheep that a few prophets are trying to rouse. It is not a matter of the immanent future but a feature of the present. Environmental crisis is, in short, a process within which individual and society today dwell; it has become part of the repertoire of normalities in reference to which people construct their daily lives" (*Apocalypse*, 76).

87. T. Morton, *Hyperobjects*, 108.

Index

"A Day in the Life," 143, 145
acoustic bridge, 135, 158
acoustic era of phonography, 24, 25; and whistling, 54, 59; and birdsong, 67–68; and bird training, 68–69; and portability, 120
actor network, 14–15, 19, 177n7, 177n8
Adams, Douglas, 12, 136, 138–140, 145
Agricola, Georgius, 85, 87, 90
Allen, Joan, 103, 160
ambient music, 74, 156–7
American Radio Warblers, 9, 69–70
Angelo, Martin Kenneth and Elliott, 20
animals: media representation of, 43–44; and language, 44
Antarctica, 11, 120, 127, 129–30, 136
Apple iPod, 10, 83
archaeology, 10, 103, 104–5
Arctic, 11, 114, 119
Arnheim, Rudolf, 122, 135, 236n82
"At the Mountains of Madness," 11, 128, 129–32, 134–5, 136
Audubon Society, the, 61, 62
Austin, Gene, 73
Avis, Edward, 9, 62–64, 66

Baekeland, Leo, 34
Bagshaw, Walter H., 27–28
Bakhtin, M.M., 11, 55, 112, 113, 116–7, 132, 133, 143

Ball, Lucille, 98
Barrett, Lindon, 53
Barthes, Roland, 23, 46, 47, 67
beachcombers, 160–1
Beatles, the, 143, 241n2
Beeblebrox, Zaphod, 137
Beer, David, 161
Behrendt, Frauke, 106
Bell, Alexander Graham, 94–5, 99 107, 120, 123
Belmont, Joseph, 9, 55–6, 59, 63, 66, 67–8
Benjamin, Walter, 105
Bennett, James Gordon, 114
Benny, Jack, 98
Berliner, Emile, 23, 27, 28
Bernhardt, Sarah, 61
Bhopal, India, 40
Bijsterveld, Karin, 74
bioregionalism, 82, 227n119
biotechnology, 8, 9, 43, 44, 73, 80
bird organ, 49, 70, 197–8n38
bird-protection movement, 61–2; and decline of cage birds, 73
birdsong, 45–46; open-ended learner birds, 46, 49, 55; and bird-protection movement, 62; and the phonograph, 67
Birkhead, Tim, 68
Bloom, Lisa, 119
Bogost, Ian, 145, 146, 155
Bozak, Nadia, 1, 16, 36, 111, 165

Bradbury, Ray, 169–70
Branney, Sean, 128
Braungart, Michael, 39
Brooke, John L., 89, 90
Burroughs, Edgar Rice, 64
Burroughs, John, 65, 207n111
Bush, George H.W., 12
Byrd, Richard E. 11, 120–2, 124–7, 126*fig.*, 130, 132

cactus needles, 30, 149, 152
cage birds, 157; as biotechnology, 8, 9, 43, 44, 73; training of, 46; and bird-protection movement, 73; and mining, 80
Campanini, Italo, 51
canary birds, 9, 46–47; roller canaries, 47–51; training methods, 48–49, 69, 70; trade in, 50–51; choppers, 71–72; females, 80; use in mining, 80; Midwestern enthusiast community, 155–6; "Bing," 156–9
Canary Islands, the, 46–47, 75–76, 158, 195n20
Capitol Records, 34
Cardiff, Janet, 83, 163–4
CardTalk, 149–54
Carruth, Allison, 2
Carson, Rachel, 35
Caruso, Enrico, 13, 38, 51, 72, 200n54
Carwardine, Mark, 12, 138–40
Chardin, Jean-Baptiste, 48
Chion, Michel, 26, 49
Collins, Ray, 116
Columbia Records, 34, 35
Columbus, Christopher, 47
conservation movement, the, 44, 61–62, 74
consumer culture, 82, 107
Cook, Frederick, 119
Cooley, Heidi Rae, 87
Corwin, Norman, 118
crap-o-phones, 40–41
Crisell, Andrew, 111
crooning, 31–32
Crosby, Alfred W., 46
Crosby, Bing, 73, 156

Cubitt, Sean, 2
Curry, Patrick, 15, 16

dark ecology, 11, 12, 112, 129, 132
Darwin, Charles, 140
de Bethencourt, Jean, 47
De Certeau, Michel, 91
Debray, Regis, 4
Deitch, Gene, 30
DeLaurenti, Chris, 149
DeLong, George Washington, 114, 116, 117, 123, 127, 135, 136
Derleth, August, 128
Devere, Sam, 53
Diggers, 103–5, 107–8, 160, 162
digital technology: as "cloud," 2, 6, 36; and morphing, 26; and augmented space, 83, 214n15; iPhone, 156–7; and ecological awareness, 159, 163
Dillinger, Johannes, 91
divining rods, 10, 80, 85–87, 89, 96
Dogme 95 manifesto, 168
Doughty, Robin, 73
Dunbar, Paul Lawrence, 211n150

Earth Summit (1992), 12
ecotone, 106, 163
Edison, Thomas, 23, 27, 29, 34, 59, 119, 146, 150, 182n56
Eichendorff, Joseph von, 162
Eisenhower, Dwight D., 147, 152
Eisenstein, Sergei, 25
electric era phonography, 30–31, 67; and birdsong, 68, 72; and polar exploration, 120
Ellsberg, Edward, 114, 115, 116
Eno, Brian, 73–74, 156–7
environmental history, 4, 173n16
extended product responsibility (EPR), 33
extinction, 7, 8, 9, 78, 140–1, 175n30

Feaster, Patrick, 146, 194n9
Feld, Petra, 91
Fish, Frank L., 101, 102
Fisher, Gerhard R., 99

Foster, George M., 91
Fudge, Erica, 44

Gaisberg, Fred, 23
Garfield, James, 94, 95
Garis, Howard R., 64
Garrett, Charles, 100
Geiger, Hans, 96
Geiger counters, 10, 80, 96–98
Gennett Records, 24
Germany, 47–51, 69, 72, 80, 87
Giddens, Anthony, 92
Gillette, King, 28
Gilmore, Joe, 11
Girard, Gilbert, 26, 38, 56–57, 57fig.
Gitelman, Lisa, 83
Global Recordings Network (formerly Gospel Recordings), 149, 150
global warming, 11, 113, 119, 136
Goffman, Erving, 78
Goldmark, Peter, 34, 36, 37fig.
Goodman, Benny, 71, 72
Google, 2, 81–82
Gordon, Robert B., 14, 17
Gorz, Andre, 166
Gouraud, George, 59
Gorst, Charles, 9, 62–64, 66, 78
Grant, John, 107
"Green Disc" era, 7, 14, 29, 39; and portability, 106
Greer, John Michael, 40–41
Grinnell, George Bird, 61
Gruar, Aimee, 7–8
Guanches, 47, 75, 195n20

H.P. Lovecraft Historical Society, the, 128
Haberman, David, 157
Hall, Frederick Durize, 29, 30
Hand, Richard J., 111
Haraway, Donna, 9, 44, 72, 144, 155, 156
Haring, Kristen, 101
Harman, Graham, 131, 133
Hartz Mountain Company, 69, 155
Hartz Radio Canaries, 9, 69–70

Harz Mountain Region, Germany, 47–48, 80, 84, 89
Harvey, David, 108
Hearne, Vicki, 157
Heise, Ursula, 81, 82, 113
"Hell on Ice," 11, 114–9, 135
Hemenway, Harriet, 62
Herrmann, Bernard, 115–6, 118
Hervieux de Chanteloup, J.-C., 46
Hesmondhalgh, David, 108
Hitchhiker's Guide to the Galaxy, the, 12, 136–8, 145–6
Hogan, Linda, 155
Hogarth, William, 48, 74
Hoover, Herbert C., 90
Horning, Susan Schmidt, 25, 183n60
Houellebecq, Michel, 133–4
Houseman, John, 115
Hughes, David, 94–95, 96
hyperobjects, 7, 35

Illich, Ivan, 17, 38–39
induction balance, 94–95, 96, 107
industrial ecology, 14, 17
industrial films, 21
infrastructure, 13, 14, 44, 110, 144, 145, 163, 176–7n4
Irving, Washington, 88–93, 102, 162
islands, 140

Jackson, Tim, 167
JAN P-49 film projector, 148
Johnson, Eldridge R., 27, 44, 55
Johnson, George Washington, 53–54, 55, 59, 66
Jolson, Al, 73

Kahn, Douglas, 3, 123, 124, 194n11
Katz, Mark, 31
Kellogg, Charles, 9, 64–67, 76, 146
Kennedy, Rick, 24
Kenney, William Howland, 51
Kidd, Captain, 88, 96
Kircher, Athanasius, 85, 86, 90, 95, 135
Klahn, Jochen, 158
Kline, Benjamin, 31

Koch, Howard, 114
Kraft, James, 166
Kraus, Bernie, 158
Kubisch, Christina, 9–10

lac insect, 6, 7, 13, 17–19, 20; in shellac records, 38; as emblem of convivial phonography, 39; vulnerability to global warming, 40
Lacey, Kate, 124, 158, 191n132
Last Chance to See, 12, 138–40
Latour, Bruno, 14–15, 19, 23, 91
Leman, Andrew, 128
Leopold, Aldo, 159
life-cycle analysis (LCA), 36
Lippit, Akira Mizuta, 43, 44
"Listen to the Mockingbird," 52–53, 54–55, 61, 66, 68
locked groove, 142–3, 169
long-playing records (LPs), 1, 14, 34, 35, 36
Lovecraft, H.P., 11, 128–9, 131, 132–3, 159
Lovelock, James, 137
Lowenthal, David, 103
Lowery, Fred, 73, 156

MacGimsey, Robert, 73
Manes, Christopher, 38
Manovich, Lev, 83
Massey, Doreen, 82, 91, 92
Maxwell, Richard, 3, 6, 41, 144
McDonough, William, 39
McDowell, Michael J., 112
McKee, Margaret, 9, 60–61, 62
McKibben, Bill, 112, 118, 167
media archaeology, 4–5
Melville, George, 115
Merchant, Carolyn, 82, 85
Merkitch, Warren, 161
metal detectors, 10, 80, 82, 99, 100; hobbyist culture, 100–1; and scavenging, 108–9; and economic crisis, 108–9; Windy City Detectors, 160
Milburn, Richard, 52–53, 55, 200–1n58

Miller, Mitch, 35
Miller, Toby, 3, 6, 41, 144
mine detectors, 99
minimal media, 83, 146, 149
mining, 80, 84–85, 89, 110
Mitchell, Charles P., 129, 131
Mitchell, William J., 94
"Money Diggers, the," 88–93
Morton, Timothy, 4, 7, 11, 12, 22, 112, 129, 132, 138
Muir, John, 61, 65, 118, 131, 159
Mumford, Lewis, 84
Musser, Charles, 85

natural radio, 3, 123–4
Nipper ("His Master's Voice" logo), 42, 55, 77
no-wattage technology, 6, 24, 53, 73, 106, 146, 149, 155
Nylon, Judy, 73–74

obsolescence, 1, 10, 28, 107
Odenwald Bird Company, 69, 70
Oliveros, Pauline, 3
Orr, David W., 163

Painter, William, 28
Parikka, Jussi, 15
passenger pigeon, 8, 175n30
Paterson, Katie, 1, 6, 142
Peary, Robert, 119, 120
phonette, 146–8, 147*fig.*, 152
phonograph needles, 27–30; fiber needles, 29
Picker, John M., 170
plastic, 7, 22–23; bioplastic, 22; the "plasmatic," 25–26
Poe, Edgar Allen, 135
Polli, Andrea, 11
portability, 10, 80, 82, 83, 94–95, 101, 106, 120, 138, 140

Quidor, John, 89

RCA-Victor, 34; "His Master's Voice" logo, 42

radio, 11, 69–70, 76, 97, 110–1, 120–3, 124, 128, 131, 137, 139, 140; "radical radio," 165; local radio, 167
Radway, Janice, 58
Ray, Robert B., 116, 225n105
recorder (or flageolet), 46, 48
recording (of sound), 45–46, 49, 150
Reich, Karl, 68
rhabdomancy, 83, 85, 86–87, 89, 91, 92, 96, 101, 103, 162
Ridderhof, Joy, 149, 150
roller canaries, 49–51; training methods, 48–49, 70; qualities of roller song, 49–50
Roosevelt, Theodore, 61
run-out groove, 142
Rutherford, Ernest W., 96

Sachs, Aaron, 119
Sarnoff, David, 146–7, 148, 152
Saylor, Tim "The Ringmaster," 103
scavenging, 10, 82, 107–9
Schafer, R. Murray, 3, 115, 165
Scherzinger, Martin, 166
Schumacher, E.F., 148
Sconce, Jeffrey, 84, 114
Scott, Robert, 120
sense of place and planet, 10, 80–82, 91, 93, 98, 105, 106–7, 160
serinette, 48–49, 68, 70
Sgt. Pepper's Lonely Hearts Club Band, 143
Shaw, Alice, 9, 58–60
shellac, 6, 7, 13; as bioplastic, 22; Indian industry, 20–23, 40; as ecological economy, 21; as ambimodern, 21–22; in phonograph records, 23–24; and scrap drives, 32–33; compared to vinyl, 35–38; noise of, 38
Shepard, Paul, 79
Shore, Ron, 160
Silbo Gomero, 75–76, 78
Singer, Ben, 22
Slack, Jennifer Daryl, 15
Smith, W. John, 45

sonic captioning, 56–57, 66, 67
sonic superimposition, 56–57, 63, 68, 70
Sony Walkman, 10, 83, 101
Soper, Kate, 82
soundscapes, 50, 63, 72
soundwalks, 162–4
Spencer, Len, 26
St. Andreasberg, Germany, 47–48, 50, 158–9
Stern, Gustav, 69, 72
Stern, Max, 69, 155
Sterne, Jonathan, 4, 14, 16, 25, 27, 48, 84
Stoever, Jennifer, 167
Strasser, Susan, 35
Strauss, Johann, 70
sustainability, 14
Sylvania television sets, 42–43, 55, 75
Symmes, John Cleves, 135, 136

Tanner, Elmo, 73
Taylor, Alan, 90, 91, 103
Teasdale, Sara, 169
Thoreau, Henry David, 116–7, 123, 125, 129, 135, 141, 144, 152–3, 217–8n40, 218n45, 237n97
Thwaites, Thomas, 145, 146, 152
traditional technological knowledge (TTK), 16, 24, 40, 78, 146, 155, 166
transduction, 25, 27
treasure lore, 87–88, 89–90, 91, 102
Tsing, Anna Lowenhaupt, 15–16, 144, 145, 246n75
Turkle, Sherry, 152
Tweety Bird, 74

uranium, 97–98
Usai, Paolo Cherchi, 29

Van Dyck, Arthur, 146
Verma, Neil, 112, 130–1, 167
Victor Talking Machine Company, 27, 31, 42, 44
vinyl, 6, 7, 34–38
Vivaldi, Antonio, 1

"War of the Worlds," 11, 113–4, 130–1, 137, 167
Wasson, Haidee, 148
Watson, Thomas, 123
Weber, Max, 22
Welles, Orson, 11, 110, 111, 113, 115, 167
Westerkamp, Hildegard, 3, 163, 164
whistling, 9, 44, 53; and acoustic phonography, 54, 59; as zoosemiotic communication, 55; female whistlers, 58; in popular music, 73; whistle languages, 75–77
Wild, Robert, 156

Winner, Septimus, 52–53, 55
Williams, Raymond, 53, 58, 201n60
Wise, J. Macgregor, 15
Wittgenstein, Ludwig, 164
Wolch, Jennifer, 158
Woodward, Agnes, 60–61, 62
World Wildlife Fund (WWF), 12, 138
Worster, Donald, 4
Wright, Mabel Osgood, 62
Wyant, George, 103

Zonophone Records, 28
zoosemiotic communication, 9, 44, 55, 155, 157, 158

www.ingramcontent.com/pod-product-compliance
Lightning Source LLC
Chambersburg PA
CBHW030535230426
43665CB00010B/908